THE PRESS UWI BIOGRAPHY SERIES

Douglas Hall, *Editor*

The Press University of the West Indies invites the submission of work to be considered for publication in this biography series. We recognize the need to record the lives and achievements of people of the Caribbean, but we would not exclude biographical account of expatriates who have lived and worked long and hard with us to our mutual advantage.

The series will not be limited to accounts of those who, by whatever means, have achieved wide acclaim or notoriety. Far more numerous than the famous are the many individuals who by stern and skillful performance in the fields, the workshops, the market-places, and in the service of their compatriots have contributed much but remain unrecognized. This series is also for accounts of them, and is dedicated to the solid contributions of the unsung.

1 A Man Divided: Michael Garfield Smith
Jamaican Poet and Anthropologist 1921–1993
DOUGLAS HALL

2 Law, Justice and Empire
The Colonial Career of John Gorrie 1829–1892
BRIDGET M. BRERETON

Forthcoming

3 White Rebel
The Story of T. T. Lewis through the Eyes of Contemporaries
GARY LEWIS

4 Demerara Doctor
Confessions and Reminiscences of a Self-taught Physician
GEORGE GIGLIOLI

Sir John Gorrie, *c.*1889
(Family photograph)

LAW JUSTICE AND EMPIRE

The Colonial Career of John Gorrie 1829-1892

Bridget Brereton

THE PRESS UNIVERSITY OF THE WEST INDIES
● Barbados ● Jamaica ● Trinidad and Tobago

The Press University of the West Indies
1A Aqueduct Flats Mona
Kingston 7 Jamaica W I

 Published 1997
Printed in Canada
ISBN 976-640-035-0
ISSN 0799-057X

01 00 99 98 97 5 4 3 2 1

Cataloguing in Publication Data

Brereton, Bridget M.
Law, justice and empire : the colonial career of John Gorrie, 1829-1892 / Bridget M. Brereton.
p. cm.
Includes bibliographical references and index.
ISBN 976-640-035-0
ISSN 0799-057X
1. Gorrie, John, 1829-1892.
2. Colonial administrators – Biography.
I. Title.
DA565.G6B73 1997
325.309

Set in 11/15pt Adobe Garamond x 27 picas
Book and cover design by Prodesign Ltd., Red Gal Ring, Kingston

Cover illustration: Rex Dixon, "Lesson", March-June 1993
Acrylic, enamel and chalk on canvas – 65" x 45" (157 x 114cm)
Collection – the artist

Map of Jamaica on p33 reproduced from G. Heuman, '*The Killing Time*': *The Morant Bay Rebellion in Jamaica* (1994, ix) by kind permission of Macmillan Publishers Ltd.

Source of maps of Mauritius, the Fiji Islands, The Western Pacific (pp 68, 106, 160): Directorate of Colonial Surveys
Source of map of the Caribbean Islands (p 194): P. Ashdown, *Caribbean History in Maps* (Longman Caribbean 1979), p. 2

To Judy Allen and Jean Ayler
(descendants of John Gorrie)
and in memory of
Patrick Cruttwell (1911-1990)

CONTENTS

ACKNOWLEDGEMENTS

I first became interested in John Gorrie in the early 1970s when I was doing research for my doctoral thesis (subsequently published as *Race Relations in Colonial Trinidad 1870-1900*). In reading the Trinidad newspapers for the years 1886 to 1892, I was astonished at the amount of space devoted to the words and deeds of the colony's chief justice, John Gorrie, and at the intense reactions (both hostile and admiring) he clearly elicited. I soon recognized both that he was a most unusual colonial judge and that he played a significant role in the history of Trinidad and Tobago in the late nineteenth century. When I learned that his posting in Trinidad was the last in a career which included service in Mauritius and the Pacific as well as in the Caribbean, I thought that he might be worth a full-length book, both as a biography of an interesting man, and as a case study of a maverick official with radical views in the late nineteenth century tropical empire.

My primary debt incurred in the researching and writing of this book is to two descendants of John Gorrie, Judy Allen (his great-great-granddaughter) and Jean Ayler (a descendant of his brother). They contacted me in 1987, and have been most encouraging and helpful ever since (and tolerant during long periods when I put Gorrie on the back burner). They made available to me many family papers, including family correspondence, the manuscript of

Gorrie's novel about Mauritius and several of his poems, family documents and pictures. Jean Ayler did much more; she became fully involved in the research effort, travelling all over Britain to read relevant sources, and sending me meticulously typed transcripts of letters and other documents, along with stacks of xeroxes from newspapers. She was, in fact, co-researcher with me for this book, and an unfailing source of information on the Gorrie tribe.

I am also grateful to colleagues who read, and commented on, the various drafts of the book, some the whole thing, some selected chapters: Richard Blackett, the late Patrick Cruttwell, Gad Heuman, Keith Laurence, Richard Lobdell, Woodville Marshall.

I have been greatly helped by the staff of the following libraries and archives: the Libraries of the University of the West Indies at St Augustine and Mona; the Public Record Office, Kew; the British Library (the manuscripts collection and the newspaper collection at Colindale, London); the Rhodes House Library of the University of Oxford; the John Rylands Library of the University of Manchester; the Advocates Library, Edinburgh; the Cambridge University Library; the Edinburgh City Library; the National Archives of Trinidad and Tobago; the Queensland Archives, Brisbane; the Mitchell Library, Sydney.

Finally, I am grateful to the staff of The Press University of the West Indies for their hard work in producing this book.

INTRODUCTION

This is a biographical study of John Gorrie, a Scottish lawyer born in 1829 who, in the second half of the nineteenth century, served as a judge and as chief justice in several multiracial colonies of the British empire including Mauritius, Fiji, and several Caribbean islands. He held radical political and social views, especially a conviction that persons of all ethnic and class backgrounds should enjoy equal justice under the British crown, and was a controversial jurist who inspired both bitter opposition from colonial elites and intense admiration from the 'subject races' in each place where he served. Moreover, Gorrie's beliefs and personality led him to intervene in political issues and debates in a way which ensured that he would often be the focus of public comment and criticism.

Though Gorrie's views were uncommon for a colonial judge of his period, they were not unique. Nineteenth and early twentieth century colonial officials included men of very diverse attitudes and opinions. British imperialism threw up from time to time men like Gorrie, maverick officials who tried to serve the interests of the 'subject peoples' and to make a reality of the trusteeship doctrine. Gorrie was certainly unusual, but his story is not that of a unique eccentric; he belonged to a well established school of 'liberal imperialists' and he was not alone in his belief in the British empire as potentially a force for progress and justice all over the world. This work, therefore, is a case study of a maverick colonial official, a 'socialist judge' who tried to use his judicial office to secure effective justice for ex-slaves, indentured labourers, indigenous peasants and other nonwhite groups in the empire.

When Gorrie took up his first colonial appointment in 1869, he was already forty. His social and political views were fully developed, shaped by a cluster of ideas and influences generated in the middle decades of the nineteenth century. The first chapter attempts to trace Gorrie's formative years in Scotland and London and to show how his radical views were shaped. The traditions of Scottish Dissent must have been among the strongest of these influences, tolerant, broadminded, free of the narrow bigotry which is often associated with Calvinism in Scotland. His father's Relief Church, and the United Presbyterian Church in which it was absorbed, stood for a liberal brand of Presbyterianism, willing to work with other creeds, and open to contemporary scientific and rationalist trends.

As a young man, Gorrie was deeply influenced by the ideas of Richard Cobden and John Bright and remained faithful all his life to their belief in free trade, international cooperation, peace among nations and individual liberty. But he went further than Bright, his mentor and patron, in his sympathy for the aspirations of workingmen and his support for the trades union movement with which he worked in Edinburgh.

Before he met Bright, his main political mentor was Duncan McLaren of Edinburgh, and he followed McLaren into the radical wing of the British Liberal Party. In common with others in this grouping, he disapproved of established churches everywhere, advocated complete free trade, was hostile to the political influence of the aristocracy and the landowners and wanted the reduction of civil and military establishments. He thought that the franchise should be extended, and was in sympathy with Bright's demand for household suffrage (the vote for all male heads of households). In his social views, he was to the left of W.E. Gladstone and Bright, but his ideas were broadly representative of the radical wing of the Liberals, and (unlike Bright) he supported Gladstone on Home Rule for Ireland.

Gorrie was profoundly influenced by the British antislavery movement, which had been in its heyday during the 1830s and 1840s and enjoyed a brief revival in the 1860s as a result of the American Civil War. His enemies were right, in a sense, to brand him a product of Exeter Hall, an antislavery man first and last.[1] He absorbed from this movement a strong belief that slaves and ex-slaves, and by extension all nonwhite people under British control, should be protected from those who did, or might, oppress them. Like others sympathetic to antislavery, Gorrie rejected the Social Darwinist thought of the second half of the nineteenth century and retained the more generous ideas about the 'coloured races' which had been widespread in the 1830s and 1840s. It is hard to know if Gorrie accepted blacks and Indians in Mauritius and the Caribbean, or the indigenous Fijians, as unequivocally his equals morally, intellectually and socially. Perhaps not; and it is not likely that he would have wished his daughters to marry out of their race. But he did believe, passionately, that all nonwhites under British jurisdiction should enjoy absolute equality before the law, as well as special protection from the authorities when that seemed necessary. He wanted them to enjoy opportunities for social, economic and intellectual advancement, and he maintained cordial relations with educated black and mixed-race men in the Caribbean. If he did not regard the poor, uneducated black as an equal, he did see him as "a man and a brother" with a right to protection and assistance from the government and equal standing before the law.

In general, Gorrie's views on race were similar to those of the abolitionists of the 1830s and 1840s, although he went further than them in his unequivocal conviction that persons of all ethnic backgrounds should enjoy legal and civic equality in the British empire. Gorrie believed that ex-slaves, indentured Indians, indigenous Fijians and Polynesian labourers were, indeed, 'inferior' to whites, not innately and genetically inferior, as the Social Darwinists insisted, but unable to deal with whites on equal terms because of disadvantages of education, culture and class position. This 'inferiority' meant that such people needed special protection from powerful local whites through the agency of the colonial governments and the courts of the empire. Gorrie's views on race were profoundly paternalist, but this was a paternalism rooted in the colonial realities and premised on the legal equality of the 'subject races'. He would have agreed with the Lord Chief Justice, who stated in his summing-up in the Anderson suit against him that "in view of the general inferiority at present of the coloured races it was only right that judges should lean to their side when they felt they were being oppressed by the white people, and should endeavor to hold the balance fairly between the two races".[2]

Like the abolitionists, Gorrie was no believer in the *cultural* equality of mankind. There is little evidence to suggest that he especially appreciated the non-Western cultures or religions which he encountered, though he did express admiration for the Fijian chiefly class. True to his age, he seems to have taken for granted the superiority of Christianity and Western culture, and to have believed that their diffusion all over the globe was not only inevitable but – in the long run though often not over the short term – beneficial for the peoples of the world.

These beliefs, derived partly from antislavery influences and greatly strengthened by his involvement in the Jamaican controversy of 1865-68, which is described in chapter two, helped to shape Gorrie's ideas about imperialism. Cobden and Bright had been hostile to colonial adventures in the 1840s and 1850s, and in general the Liberals were not aggressive imperialists. But Gorrie belonged to the wing of the Liberals which advocated a great British empire based on free trade, an empire which would be beneficial to all – British investors, consumers at home, and the 'coloured races' working under benevolent British management. Imperialism would protect the 'native people', develop their capacities and make them prosperous.This was a British empire which would be governed by justice, benevolence and a high sense of moral purpose; "under Providence, the greatest instrument for good that the world has ever seen".[3]

Gorrie believed in the potential of the British empire as a force for progress. He supported new territorial acquisitions, for instance in the Pacific, if this course seemed the only way to avoid anarchy or unrestricted exploitation by lawless whites. If properly managed, British power could protect weaker peoples – ex-slaves, immigrant labourers, indigenous populations just coming into contact with Europeans – and gradually bring them to prosperity and higher civilization (Christianity, science, law and order). This is not very different from the doctrine of trusteeship which was the official orthodoxy of the nineteenth century empire. But Gorrie's social views were more radical than those of most advocates of the trusteeship doctrine, especially his uncompromising belief in the equality of all before the law and his willingness to intervene on behalf of the disadvantaged even if it meant straining or bending normal procedures. And he was unusual in his utter indifference to popularity with the entrenched colonial elites and his lack of interest in enjoying a quiet life.

Gorrie saw his colonial appointments as opportunities to strengthen the British empire by helping the weak and oppressed, thus cementing their bonds to Britain and making an explosion like that at Morant Bay in 1865 unlikely. He believed that white expansion in the Pacific was inevitable and that it was impossible to isolate the indigenous peoples from the developments which would follow. He did not oppose white settlement in places like Fiji nor plantation development in the new Pacific colonies or the old ones in the Caribbean and the Indian Ocean; but he believed that the 'subject races' needed to be protected from the settlers and the planters by the crown and its servants. In this sense, W.G. Donovan of Grenada was correct to call him a "servant of the Empire" and to argue that those who schemed to bring him down were traitors to the Raj: "To ruin a true philanthropist they have sought to undermine an Empire." For Donovan, Gorrie represented Britain as the 'mother of justice', a man who lived (and died) to vindicate British honour and to lay the foundations for strong bonds of confidence between Britain and her West Indian subjects.[4] Believing in British imperialism as potentially an agent for progressive change throughout the world, as a form of expansion based on moral as well as economic motives, Gorrie tried to put into practice the trusteeship ideals which formed the official justification for crown colony government in the nineteenth century tropical empire. He wanted to protect colonial labourers and peasants from unfair treatment and to ensure that they benefitted from British laws and justice. He accepted colonialism and plantation development as a given; his duty was to mitigate their effects and check undue exploitation, so that the positive aspects of European rule would gradually outweigh the negative. These positive aspects included Christianity, law and order (for instance, the elimination of communal or clan warfare in Fiji), the abolition of repellant customs such as ritual cannibalism or infanticide, Western medicine and science, equal justice, higher standards of living. These were the 'goods' which imperialism could bring to the 'subject races', thereby giving the whole colonial enterprise an implicit moral basis for a servant of the crown like Gorrie.

This was the cluster of beliefs and hopes which Gorrie subscribed to when he took up his first colonial appointment in 1869 in Mauritius (chapter three). He served here for over six years, and it was in Mauritius that he developed the judicial style which was to characterize his performance as a judge for the rest of his life: combative, interventionist and 'political', always on the look out for abuses to denounce and correct. It was here, too, that he established a leading trend of his career: his active involvement in a wider, extra-judicial public life. As a close friend and colleague of A.H. Gordon, the reforming governor of Mauritius in the early 1870s, Gorrie played a leading part in important reforms in the treatment of indentured and ex-indentured Indian labourers in the island.

In 1876 Gorrie followed Gordon to Fiji, where he spent seven years as chief justice of the new British colony (chapter four). He was one of a small group of men around Gordon who helped to create the new crown colony and to shape its fundamental political and legal institutions. In effect, Gorrie was a member of Gordon's inner cabinet as well as the colony's sole judge. For Fiji was a frontier society; here, Gorrie had a chance to mould a new society and to help determine future relationships between the indigenous Fijians, the white settlers and the immigrant labourers from the other Pacific islands and (after 1879) from India. His years in the Pacific offered abundant scope for his immense energies and his political and legislative skills. In many ways this was the most creative period of his career.

While he was chief justice of Fiji, he also served as Judicial Commissioner for the Western Pacific (chapter five). Under an 1878 Order in Council, the Western Pacific High Commission was created to enable the crown to bring under its jurisdiction British subjects in the Western Pacific who did not reside in a European colony. Such persons who committed crimes could be brought to Fiji and tried in the High Commissioner's court, which included the chief justice of Fiji with the title of Judicial Commissioner. This appointment greatly extended the scope of Gorrie's work, and involved him (along with Gordon as High Commissioner) in numerous important controversies related to British and Australasian expansion in the vast region. Moreover, for over a year Gorrie acted as High Commissioner during Gordon's absence on home leave, giving him a brief taste of executive power.

In 1883, Gorrie exchanged the Pacific for the Caribbean, where (in a sense) his colonial career had begun when he visited Jamaica in 1866 in connection with the Morant Bay controversy. He served as chief justice of the Leeward Islands, and in a short but energetic term of office (described in chapter six), he helped to effect important reforms in the islands' land laws, and to upgrade the judicial administration of these impoverished little islands.

The last six years of Gorrie's life (1886-92) were spent in Trinidad and Tobago, two islands in the southern Caribbean which were linked administratively in 1889. All the trends of his colonial career seemed to culminate during his service as chief justice of Trinidad and Tobago, the subject of chapters seven, eight and nine. He encouraged poor and uneducated people – black and Indian labourers and peasants, indentured Indians, sharecroppers in Tobago and cocoa 'contractors' in Trinidad – to use the courts to assert their rights and secure justice on an equal footing with the respectable and the propertied. And as had been the case in all his previous postings, he involved himself in many public and political issues far beyond the scope of his judicial duties.

These activities, along with his judicial practices in general and his decisions in specific cases, earned him the bitter enmity of Trinidad and Tobago's small but powerful white elites. They concluded that Gorrie was a serious threat, in both islands, to their control over land, labour and the colonial institutions in general. Trinidad's influential and able politicians, with allies in Tobago and Britain, organized an increasingly serious campaign for his removal from office. This campaign began as early as 1887, only a year after his arrival, but it accelerated in 1891-92. Despite impressive evidence of popular support for Gorrie's administration of justice in Trinidad and in Tobago, the Colonial Office finally decided early in 1892 that it could no longer defend him against his many critics. A commission to investigate the administration of justice in the colony was authorized, and, almost inevitably, its findings were sufficient to allow the governor to suspend Gorrie from office. Already very ill, Gorrie applied for leave to fight his case personally in London; he died soon after arriving in Britain in August 1892. The Trinidad and Tobago elite had succeeded in engineering his removal; the ordinary people of both islands mourned a man whom they recognized as a champion and protector and had elevated to the status of a popular hero.

This biography concentrates on Gorrie the public man, on his career as a crusading colonial judge with radical views. Almost inevitably, it is based mainly on governmental and public records, especially Colonial Office documents and colonial newspapers, which focus on his official actions. But even in the official records, and often in the newspapers, glimpses of his personality shine through. His private correspondence (such as has survived), unpublished writings and family papers also help us to see the man behind the public career.

Gorrie was a man of strong personality and deeply held views. There was something of the bully in him, and he acquired a well deserved reputation for browbeating all kinds of persons who came before him in court. He was impatient, easily irritated, often intemperate in language, and clearly deficient in control over his temper and his tongue – traits which became especially salient in the last years of his life and which caused him endless difficulties. Because of his outspoken views and his actions, he made enemies easily, and no doubt his lack of tact and finesse worsened this situation; but he loved a good fight all his life.

Yet in his personal life Gorrie was immensely social, gregarious and apparently popular even with people who loathed his political views. He threw himself into the social and civic life of each colony in which he served, getting involved in an extraordinary array of groups and activities. Many newspaper reports attest to his thorough enjoyment of social events as varied as balls, picnics, hunting expeditions, archery matches and rifle competitions, sports meetings, church teas, debating society events, and so on. A natural leader, Gorrie tended to dominate every activity he was involved in, but his geniality and evident interest in people softened this trait. So far as the sources allow us to judge, he was an affectionate husband and father; the death of his wife in 1884 and of his youngest child in 1889 darkened the last years of his life.

Though he left Scotland in 1862, he spoke with a broad Scottish accent to the day he died thirty years later; he was a fluent, forceful speaker, capable of brusqueness to the point of rudeness. Gorrie was a large man, physically robust until his last illness; indeed, his strong physique and immense energy, after over twenty years of service in the tropics, amazed contemporaries. In the 1870s, he was described as a "fine-looking man, with short whiskers and moustache". In the early 1880s, in his fifties, he astonished West Indians by walking all over Dominica's forested interior from coast to coast and also exploring Virgin Gorda, in the remote Virgin Islands group, on foot. He contracted malaria while in Mauritius – notoriously unhealthy in the 1870s – but he rarely complained of illness until a few months before his death. Contemporaries used phrases like "powerful frame and robust constitution", "robust health" and "untiring energy" to describe him. His powerful physique was allied to a formidable personality and a strong sense of mission, formed first in Scotland and London, and developed in the several colonies of the British empire where he served the crown and tried to serve the interests of the 'subject peoples' at the same time.

CHAPTER ONE

The Young Scot on the Make: From Kettle to London, 1829-69

Early Life

John Gorrie's father Daniel was born in 1797 in Perthshire, Scotland, the son of a tenant farmer. Educated in Perth and at the University of Edinburgh, he intended to prepare for the ministry of the established Church of Scotland to which his parents belonged. But the young man found that he could not support the principle of state control; he left the established Church and joined the Relief Church, a dissident Presbyterian sect which had originated in Fifeshire with a 1751 dispute over the induction of a minister in Inverkeithing. In 1761 the Presbytery of Relief was formally constituted "for Christians oppressed in their Church privileges"; it was later known as the Relief Church. It was "broadly evangelical, laxer in discipline and doctrine, and prided itself in being nonsectarian and noncovenanting". It was this Church, liberal and independent in character and by tradition, which Daniel served all his life and which must have had a strong impact on John as a child and adolescent. Daniel accepted a 'call' to the congregation at Kingskettle, a small farming village in Fife, at the age of 23, soon after his ordination, and remained there for the rest of his life. In 1847 the small Relief Church merged with the larger United Secession Church, yet another sect that had broken with the established Church of Scotland, to form the United Presbyterian Church.[1]

Daniel Gorrie seems to have been unambitious and perhaps retiring, for although he became widely known as a fine preacher and a superb minister, he never received a city charge, remaining in his country village ministering to the farming people "scattered over a considerable tract of country" until his death in 1852. He was described as "the *beau idéal* of an earnest, Christian-hearted minister, when passing from cottage to cottage, and going in and out among his people". His sermons became famous, and he was an influential member of his church, serving on several committees of the United Presbyterian Church and taking a prominent part in synodical business. He must also have been a man of wide reading, for he was a popular lecturer on science in Fife. True to the traditions of the Relief Church, he was never sectarian or narrow, but "was ever ready to cooperate in every good work with Christian men of every denomination". His daughter Isobel, remembering him fifty years after his death, described him as "one of the best of men, good in every sense of the word, both as a Christian, good in disposition, most unselfish, affectionate and kind". She recalled that he was "tall, 5 feet 11 ½, very fine looking; at the Synods they would always have him on the platform as he adorned it, they said, but giving him his will he would rather have taken a back seat".[2]

Soon after accepting the call to Kingskettle, Daniel married Jane Moffat (1792/93–1863) of Edinburgh. She was the daughter of a surgeon in the Royal Navy. Her mother, Agnes Moffat, lived her last years in Kingskettle with her daughter and son-in-law. From a charming portrait of her in old age, written by her grandson, John's younger brother Daniel, we gather that she was a lively old lady who enjoyed telling risqué stories ("old ladies being more rough-and-ready then than now" as Daniel felt obliged to remind his Victorian readers) and exchanging banter with an eccentric old "humorist of a lawyer of the old school" who used to visit Kingskettle and indulge in horseplay with the minister's mother-in-law. The children of the Manse saw a great deal of their grandmother, and perhaps something of her geniality, fondness for company and lack of prudishness rubbed off on John, who was fifteen when she died in 1844.[3]

Jane Moffat Gorrie seems to have been a strongminded woman, less retiring and gentle than her husband. Her daughter wrote: "My mother was different a good deal in character, she was active and very bustling, more outspoken than my father, did not take long to make up her mind." Clearly ambitious for her sons (presumably she had given up on her unworldly husband), she is said to have taken heroic measures to ensure that young John attended grammar school in St Andrews. In her daughter's words: "When he was sent first to the Madras College he set off in two days after home again, Father would have allowed him to remain at home, Mother said 'no, *he shall go back'*, dressed herself, and walked back all the way to St Andrews with him herself, fainted with the fatigue and John only got time to get his dinner, and tramp back, as there was neither railway nor conveyance of any kind." No wonder that Isobel Gorrie told John's son: "If it had not been for her, your Father would never have been a Chief Justice."[4]

Jane and Daniel had six children, three daughters (one died young) and three sons; John was the fourth child and second son, born in March 1829. Presumably their early education was at the parish school at Kingskettle. The Manse must have been a pleasant home; Isobel remembered it as "a good one, three stories, slated roof, within a large garden which surrounded it, plenty of fruit and flowers". There was little spare cash around when John and his siblings were children; in 1852, when Daniel died, his entire estate was valued at £377, most of which comprised the value of his insurance policy. All the household goods were valued at £50, but the inventory shows that the Manse was comfortably furnished and equipped, and that Daniel owned about 300 books (valued at £6). There was always at least one servant, and John's brother wrote another of his engaging short stories about 'Nanny Walsh', the maid-of-all-work "in the old home-manse of Keppel, where I first saw light of day", who helped to bring up the Manse youngsters. The village was set in lovely country, and most of the people were solid farming folk, with quite a few more prosperous families who constituted the local gentry to which the Manse residents belonged almost *ex officio.* Though the Sabbath was strictly kept, this was a sociable neighbourhood with a round of tea parties and supper gatherings; teetotalism was unknown in the district when John was growing up. Even making allowances for nostalgia, the descriptions of Kingskettle written by John's brother and sister suggest an almost idyllic setting for a secure childhood.[5]

School and University

John went to Madras College, St Andrews, for his secondary education, probably between 1838 (or 1839) and 1843. Madras College was founded by Andrew Bell, a St Andrews native who pioneered the monitorial system of education, known at the time as the 'Madras system' because he inaugurated it at an institution for the orphans of British soldiers in that city. It opened in 1833, and consisted of both a free elementary school for the local poor and a fee-paying grammar (secondary) school which absorbed the old town grammar school. St Andrews was a small, isolated town during John's schooldays, and indeed until 1852 when the railway came. Cows were kept in byres behind the houses; sanitation was primitive and typhoid, cholera and tuberculosis were endemic. Journeys to the town were by public coach, private carriage, or, for the majority who could afford neither, including John, by foot. Boys who did not live in the town had to board. John lodged with a family which advertised in the local papers for "young gentlemen either attending the Madras College or the University". In 1841, he was one of seven student boarders whose ages ranged from 12 to 15; one was a girl, for the College was coeducational from the outset. Madras College had no rector (Scottish for headmaster) at this time, and the senior masters enjoyed great independence; each was called a 'headmaster' and was wholly responsible for his classes with the help of monitors whom he paid himself. The College very soon established a solid reputation, attracting pupils from all over Scotland and from Scottish families overseas.[6]

At this period, Madras College was a distinctively Scottish school, very different from the English type of 'public' boarding school. Not only was there no rector; there was virtually no central administration, no set curriculum, no minimum attendance requirements, no external examinations. Parents were free to choose the subjects they wanted their children to take, the levels of study, and the number of sessions. The core of the grammar school curriculum was English, Latin and mathematics, with some Greek by the 1840s, rounded out by history, geography, painting and French. Rote learning was the norm, with pupils learning long passages of poetry, the Bible, Latin prose and verse, and mathematical propositions. At the end of each quarter, oral 'examinations' open to the public were conducted in each subject and prizes were awarded on the results. These examinations were extensively reported in the local press, for the College was the source of considerable regional pride. Though the College's academic standing even in its first decade was high, discipline was a problem because of overcrowding in the classrooms and the large numbers of adolescents boarding away from parental care in many different houses. Punishment ranged from strokes with the Scottish 'tawse' (strap) to solitary detention to class isolation or 'degradation' to suspension. Swearing and profanity were said to be rife in 1844, as well as bullying and uncouth behaviour by the bigger boys which led some parents to withdraw their daughters.[7]

We do not know if John settled down happily at the College after his strongminded mother had dragged him back. He did win at least two school prizes, in 1841, for grammar and geography. He must have acquired a solid grounding for advanced studies at the University of Edinburgh, especially in Latin and in English literature; like most Scottish university students at this period, he had probably acquired only a smattering of Greek, but may well have started French, a language which he later mastered. In 1843, at the age of 14, he moved to the Scottish capital and entered the University as a student in the Faculty of Arts. He was a student at Edinburgh between 1843 and 1854 or 1855, taking courses in literature, Scottish law, and conveyancing, and he must have been profoundly influenced by the distinctive spirit and traditions of Scotland's premier seat of learning.[8]

Nearly a century and a half after the Act of Union, the Scots continued to cherish a sense of apartness, a conviction of spiritual and intellectual superiority, in relation to their southern neighbours. By common consent, this distinctive Scottish identity was held to rest on three great national institutions: the Kirk, the legal system, and the schools and universities. Scotland had an educational system "which, combining the democracy of the Kirk-elders with the intellectualism of the advocates [lawyers], made expertise in metaphysics the condition of the open door of social advancement".[9]

Above all, Scottish universities were far more democratic and egalitarian in their ethos than their English counterparts at this time. Traditionally, the four universities opened their doors to bright and determined boys from very humble backgrounds, and this gave them a special place in the national life as institutions 'of the people, never of a class', in marked contrast to Oxford and Cambridge. Many Scottish students were desperately poor; as a consequence, it was easy to deride the student body as a 'slovenly and dirty mass'. Several features of university organization made this democratic character possible. First, matriculation at age 14 or 15, or even earlier, made it possible for bright boys with inadequate secondary education to enter university and 'catch up' by attending junior classes in which the professors taught the basics of classical literature, mathematics and science. Thus the lack of a solid sixth form training, especially in the classics, was no bar to entry to a university, and many Scottish boys matriculated without any formal secondary education. There were no matriculation examinations until 1858. Second, undergraduates all underwent a general programme of arts and sciences lasting four years before going on (in some cases) to specialized or professional training in law, medicine, theology or other subjects. Third, the universities were nonresidential; students who could not live at home had to make their own arrangements, allowing poor students to crowd together in cheap lodgings. Finally, the long vacation in the Faculty of Arts ran from mid April to early November, ample time to earn the money necessary to finance the coming session.[10]

Moreover, the curriculum content and the teaching methods in the Faculty of Arts reinforced these democratic tendencies. The four-year programme provided a rigorous course of general education culminating in compulsory philosophy, without which the student could not proceed to professional training. The bias towards philosophy permeated the whole of Scottish university education, imparting a distinctive spirit to the teaching of classics, science, medicine, mathematics and law, and inculcating a tradition of inflexibly strict reasoning from first principles. Teaching was by lectures and tutorial instruction; in the professors' tutorial sessions, undergraduates were free to argue and to question, however famous a scholar their teacher was. The chief mode of assessment was by student essays, which were often publicly discussed and evaluated by students and professor together in the tutorial sessions. The award of prizes and academic honours was often determined democratically by the students' own assessments of each other's performance in these sessions. Vigorous and disciplined writing, forceful argument and keen interest in first principles were all encouraged by these traditions.[11]

When Gorrie was an undergraduate, there was no evaluation of students by marks gained in written examinations. Instead, university life was marked by "informality and boisterous democracy", according to the opponents of the Scottish system (or lack of system). What mattered was the 'class ticket', signed by the professor, stating that the student had attended so many classes in a given course and had written a stated minimum of essays which had received a satisfactory assessment; and performance in the tutorials as evaluated by professor and fellow students. Before 1858, it was commonplace for students not to 'graduate', though they had read all the necessary courses and obtained their class tickets. Degrees were not given much importance; what mattered was that one had gone through the Arts programme. Entry into a course of professional study, such as law, depended not so much on possession of the M.A. degree as on demonstrating one's *ability* to gain it by following the required courses to the professors' satisfaction as attested by class tickets. Gorric himself received neither the M.A. nor the LL.B. degree but followed all the required courses at the University.[12]

During his years as a university student Gorrie supported himself partly by working in legal offices, partly by journalism. For some years he was 'apprenticed' to the office of W.A. Taylor, a 'writer' of Cupar in Fife, and was listed in the 1851 Census as a 'Procurator's Managing Clerk' ('procurator' and 'writer' are Scottish terms for solicitor). Taylor handled the disposal of Daniel's property when he died intestate in 1852. Gorrie also spent some time 'training' with Horne and Lyell in Edinburgh.[13]

These attachments to legal offices were probably more for the sake of training and experience than for income. Journalism was more important here. He recalled in Fiji in 1882 that he had been "the editor of a county newspaper in Scotland". This may have been the *Stirling Observer.* He was also apparently associated with two Edinburgh papers, *The Age,* which folded in 1860, and the *Caledonia Mercury.* When Gorrie died, *The Scotsman* (edited by his lifelong friend, Charles Cooper) stated that he had started an unnamed paper to promote the views of Duncan McLaren, the leading radical in Edinburgh, and had sunk "almost all his means" in the venture, which failed. This may have been either *The Age* or the *Caledonia Mercury*, perhaps the same as the *Weekly Herald and Mercury.* At any rate, it was as a young student in the Scottish capital that he first practised his gift for writing clear, vigorous prose, and acquired a love for the world of journalism which stayed with him all his life.[14]

Between his studies, his legal work in Cupar and Edinburgh, and his journalism, life must have been strenuous for the young man, and cash always short. But he had time for social life. Early in 1851 (he was 22) he persuaded his older sister Isabella to accompany him to a 'Curling Ball' at Cupar. This would be "a grand chance" for her since "ladies are in demand" and at 25 she was still unmarried; for his part, "as it is expected that I bring a lady or two with me, I am anxious to do the thing stylishly".[15]

The New Advocate

Gorrie was admitted to the Faculty of Advocates – that is, called to the Scottish Bar – in June 1856, at the age of 27. This was the end of a protracted and complex process involving both academic and professional training in the law. After following the Arts courses, Gorrie spent several years studying law and conveyancing at the University. Legal education in Scotland, as we might expect, was grounded in philosophy to a far greater extent than in England. After the academic side of legal education was completed (whether or not the student actually took the LL.B. degree), the Faculty of Advocates required a year to intervene between giving up any commercial employment, and admission to the Bar. This period might be spent in preparatory studies; or an aspirant might be allowed to attach himself to an advocate willing to let him see his papers and watch him in court.[16]

The final step was an elaborate oral examination, conducted entirely in Latin, before the Faculty of Advocates, following which the Lords of Council and Session (the Scottish bench) formally admitted the new advocate. This completed the ritual of entry to the Bar; the required fees came to about £350, a large sum, in Gorrie's time. The Edinburgh advocate did not take chambers, but worked either out of Parliament House (where the High Courts sat and the Advocates Library was located) or at home, where he kept his law books, held consultations and read papers; a brass plate on his door or wall announced his calling.[17]

Scottish law, in the mid nineteenth century, was very different from that of England. It was classified as a 'mixed' system, combining principles, rules and concepts modelled on Romano-German and on English law. The Romano-German system – civil law – derives mainly from treatises by jurists, is based essentially on legal principles from which rules are deduced, and tends to be rational, coherent and systematic. English or common law derives mainly from judges' decisions or case precedents. Scottish law derives from judges' decisions, legal treatises and legislation; like all Romano-German systems, it is unitary, that is, there is no separation as in England between Common Law and Equity. When Gorrie was called to the Edinburgh Bar, Scottish civil law was distinct and separate; far more than English law, it rested on generalized rights and principles, and tended to argue from principles to cases, not from particular cases to abstract principles. And it was much closer to continental law systems, a fact that was to be a great advantage to Gorrie when he served in Mauritius where French civil law was still largely in force. The disadvantage was that the professional mobility of the Scots advocate might be more limited. Gorrie explained, many years later, that:

> Scotch law does not carry anywhere else but in Scotland. The consequence is that a Scotch Advocate, as soon as he is called, looks forward to pass his life in Edinburgh, walking up the Mound at nine o'clock, even on a winter morning, with his white tie, either to plead the cases that he has or to make people believe that he is going to plead cases that he has not . . . An English Barrister never thinks of going to Court

> unless he has a case, but we in Scotland must go every day to the Parliament House to make our appearance there, or the Solicitors think we are bidding out of business and have got above our profession, so that we . . . necessarily see a great deal of each other and talk during the whole day – not about legal matters, but when there is no interest in politics going on, about all the gossip of the place. In this way the Scotch Advocate looks forward to pass his time in his own country.[18]

When Gorrie joined the Edinburgh Bar, it enjoyed a solid reputation for vigorous intellectual and political life. Traditionally, the Scottish Bar pursued scholarship and literature, especially local history and 'humane letters', including satirical verse (Gorrie was to try his hand at this). As Gorrie later recalled, the Edinburgh advocates formed a kind of elite clique; his radical mentor, Duncan McLaren, told a House of Commons Committee in 1851 that "in Edinburgh, the aristocracy are the lawyers". Of course, Parliament House was also the scene of much political activity, and advocates generally aligned themselves with one of the three major parties of the day, the Tories, the Whigs and the Liberals/Radicals. Up to 1885, the single most powerful man in the Scottish legal profession was the Lord Advocate, roughly the equivalent of the English Attorney-General, who exercised effective ministerial authority over Scotland on behalf of the British Cabinet. He was invariably a party man and a Government MP. In Gorrie's time, the Lord Advocate wielded enormous powers of patronage in Scotland, usually exercised on a party basis, and he was the centre of a spider's web of committees, sinecures and jobs known to its detractors as 'the old Parliament House system'.[19] When Gorrie was an Edinburgh advocate, the Lord Advocate was a Whig while he was aligned with the Radicals; the conviction that his advancement in the system was blocked as a result may have contributed to his later decision to settle in London.

Nevertheless, he picked up at least one modest crumb from the Whig Lord Advocate; in 1859 or 1860 he was appointed an Advocate-Depute. The actual work of prosecution in the courts was delegated to several Advocates-Depute who appeared as 'crown counsel' and who, during their appointment, were not allowed to engage in criminal defence work (though free to engage in other private practice). No doubt this appointment, which Gorrie held until he left Edinburgh in 1862, helped to boost his income somewhat as well as gave him a chance to practise outside the capital.[20]

Edinburgh Politics

Characteristically, the young advocate plunged into municipal politics almost as soon as he was admitted to the Faculty; Charles Cooper of *The Scotsman* said he had "unwisely neglected his profession to dabble in municipal and imperial politics". He became a member of the group led by Duncan McLaren, the acknowledged leader of Scottish radicalism for some fifty years. "The soul of Liberalism is Dissent", thought Richard Cobden, and in Scotland, the forces of religious nonconformity gave political Liberalism the great strength it enjoyed for much of the century. It was McLaren, more than any other man, who "organized Scottish Dissent as a political force". His base was in the United Presbyterian Church to which he, like Gorrie, adhered, but he forged alliances with other sects to create a formidable coalition which fought for the cause of 'Voluntarism' – the abolition of all compulsory rates or taxes to support a state church – and disestablishment everywhere, England, Scotland, Ireland and the colonies, 'a free Church in a free State'. For McLaren, "Voluntarism and Disestablishment were the very foundations of Radicalism".[21]

In the wider sphere of British politics, McLaren and his Scottish colleagues forged close links with the Cobden/Bright wing of the Liberal Party. He was a lifelong advocate of Free Trade, one of the founders of the 'Manchester School', and the single most influential campaigner in Scotland for the repeal of the Corn Laws. He had known Cobden since 1840, and in 1848 he married Priscilla, John Bright's sister. McLaren lined up the whole of Scottish Dissent behind the anti-Corn Law agitation. He followed Cobden and Bright in their extremely unpopular opposition to the Crimean War, and organized as Lord Provost (mayor) of Edinburgh a successful Peace Conference in 1853 which attracted Cobden, Bright, and several other leading English Liberals and Radicals. It was through McLaren that Gorrie formed a relationship with Bright that was to be very important to his career.[22]

In the arena of Edinburgh politics, McLaren broke away from the 'Whig' mainstream of Liberalism and organized an 'Independent Liberal' party, combining Dissenters, Free Traders, Social Reformers and Radicals, which came to be as much opposed to the Whigs as to the Tories. In the middle decades of the century the Whigs were generally in the ascendant, and McLaren and his followers were determined enemies of 'the old Parliament House system' and its network of patronage. He was the unchallenged leader of Edinburgh radicalism; *The Scotsman* grumbled in 1858 that the old Whig party had been called 'the Family Party' but in fact "the Bright-McLaren party . . . is more sectional, self-seeking, and arrogant than any family party that ever was either truly or falsely alleged to exist", consisting as it did of "the godfather, and two or three exceedingly subordinate subalterns".[23] As the son of a Dissenting clergyman, from a modest home, no doubt developing liberal political views, it was hardly surprising that when Gorrie made his first foray into city politics, it would be as one of the 'subordinate subalterns' of Duncan McLaren.

In 1856 he was elected to the Town Council for the third or St Andrews ward. He was introduced to the election meeting as "a young gentleman of liberal education and who had been well trained to public business". Gorrie and his two fellow McLarenites were all returned, with Gorrie coming third with 334 votes. As a Town Councillor, he served on several committees and as a director of the Original Ragged School. The following year, however, Gorrie declined re-election. *The Edinburgh Courant* reported his explanation to a ward meeting:

> It was no change in his public sentiments that induced him to retire but he found the demands on his time were greater than could be spared from other avocations. The past year however had been both pleasant and profitable to him – profitable because it had enabled him to take a better knowledge of the City's interests; and pleasant because the most cordial feelings had subsisted among all the members of the Town Council.[24]

He returned to the Council in 1860 for a different ward. A newspaper report of his speech at an election meeting suggests that he had already become a competent public speaker. He told the electors that "it seemed to be believed by certain parties, in the city of Edinburgh at least, that a member of the College of Justice [*ie* an advocate] had no right to hold any opinions but those of his seniors and superiors. He would as lief not be, as live to be any one but such as he himself". He went on to denounce local opponents of his political group and hit out at the use of city taxes to support the Church of Scotland, an issue dear to the heart of a son of a United Presbyterian minister. Although Gorrie was unopposed for St Leonard's ward, he received 260 votes, a strong show of support for the Radicals in their opposition to the established Church and for the candidate himself.[25]

Edinburgh politics at this time was dominated by the issue of the 'Annuity Tax'. This was a personal tax levied on occupiers of houses and buildings in Edinburgh to pay for the stipends of clergy of the established Church of Scotland. Objectionable in principle to Dissenters, as well as to Roman Catholics and Episcopalians, it was made more odious by numerous exemptions. The struggle to abolish the tax began in the 1830s, and was accelerated by the secession of the Free Church in 1843, which left many city churches without congregations and highlighted the injustice of the tax. Several bills, all intended to reduce but not to abolish the tax, failed to get through Parliament in the 1850s. In 1860 Lord Advocate Moncrieff introduced a compromise scheme which outraged the Dissenters. Although it reduced the tax to 3d in the pound, it increased the numbers liable to pay; it transferred the administration of church money from the Town Council to Ecclesiastical Commissioners; it combined the annuity tax with the police rates; and it placed the whole body of citizens under a mortgage in security of the clerical annuities to the amount of £4200. The linking of the special tax with the police rates meant that if one objected on conscientious grounds to the clerical charge one would also necessarily refuse to pay the police rates. The Dissenters, the McLaren party and all the Edinburgh Radicals mounted a determined protest against Moncrieff's 'Clerico-Police Tax', but the bill passed through Parliament and became law in 1860.[26]

Gorrie was one of the main speakers at a public meeting held in October 1860 to protest the Act. Quoting a Scottish peer who had told the House of Lords that the Act would relieve the conscience of Dissenters, he went on:

> Relieve the consciences of Dissenters by extending an ecclesiastical tax over a wider area of rental, and a wider sweep of taxpayers, thus nominally reducing the percentage to each, but leaving the Church richer than before, and burdening the city as a whole more heavily than ever! Relieve the consciences of Dissenters by the transparent lie of mixing up the tax with the police rate of the city! Relieve the consciences of Dissenters by taking public property out of the control of the popularly elected representatives, and placing it for the use of one sect under an irresponsible Commission elected by sections and classes of the citizens! Sir, they must have but a mean idea of the consciences of Dissenters . . . I regard this Act as . . . an insulting defiance of ourselves and our principles, which must be resented at all hazards.

Like previous speakers, he advised the citizens not to pay the levy:

> He knew perfectly well how much would be said against the nonpayment of the police tax, and against the impropriety of anyone making statements at a public meeting which could be represented as advising a breach of the law. They were prepared for all such arguments . . . The time has come when we must teach Lord Advocates, and officials generally, that the day has gone by for coercive measures being thrust down the throats of a reluctant community.[27]

At another public meeting, Gorrie returned to the attack: "Those who expected that Dissenters would forego their principles and pay the tax", he warned, "would be disappointed – and the police rates would suffer as well as the other tax." He went on to insist that the Town Council, which had already agreed to elect the Ecclesiastical Commissioners under the Act, should refuse to sign the bonds which, again under the Act, made over the pew-rents of the city churches to the established clergy. This alarmed one of the platform speakers:

> *Mr Miller*: I am very much astonished and grieved at hearing such language from a barrister – a member of the College of Justice, whose duty it is to instill into the minds of the people the duty of obeying the law.
>
> *Mr Gorrie*: I beg to say that is no part of my duty. You will never find me asking people to obey an unjust law.

> *Mr Miller*: I say the whole tenor of Mr Gorrie's speech was that the Council and the members of the Ward should disobey the law. That was its effect on my mind.[28]

The campaign against the annuity tax continued all through the 1860s. The Treasurer of the Town Council signed the bonds in favour of the Ecclesiastical Commissioners under protest, and a deputation of ratepayers presented a memorial asking the Council to "use all lawful and constitutional means to obtain the entire repeal of the Act". Ex-Bailie Fyfe, then McLaren's great ally on the Council, raised an action challenging the legality of the assessment under the Act, and the Lord Advocate had to get a supplementary Act through Parliament to overcome the legal issues. Many citizens and Dissenting clerics refused to pay the police rates, and sales of goods for arrears became quite frequent. When McLaren was elected to Parliament in 1865 he took the issue to the House, and it was largely due to his efforts that the question was finally settled in 1870; a grant was made as compensation for the life interests of the city clergy and the tax was abolished.[29]

McLaren supported the extension of the Parliamentary vote all through his political career, and the Edinburgh Liberals whom he led campaigned for the Reform goals of the Cobden/Bright wing of the national Liberal Party. In 1858, Bright began to organize a highly publicized campaign for parliamentary reform. Though he did not advocate manhood suffrage, he called for the vote for all 40 shilling freeholders and £10 rental occupiers in the counties and for all who paid the poor rates in the boroughs; he also advocated the secret ballot and redistribution of seats. Bright undertook a tour of northern England and Scotland, holding massive Reform meetings at Birmingham, Manchester, Bradford, Glasgow and Edinburgh, addressing vast crowds; his speeches were reported verbatim in the papers and then sold as pamphlets. McLaren organized his public meeting in Edinburgh in December 1858. A massive crowd attempted to hear Bright, but 'hundreds' were unable to get in to the Music Hall; there was much confusion and 'uproar' as people milled around trying to push in. Gorrie was among the persons seated with Bright on the platform, and after the main speech, he spoke as "one of the secretaries of the local [reform] committee" to introduce the delegates present from several Scottish towns and from Darlington,

London and Manchester. After the meeting had passed a resolution calling for the Bright voting proposals, "Mr Gorrie then proposed a petition to Parliament, founded on the resolution already adopted, which was agreed to". Almost certainly, Gorrie met Bright for the first time during this triumphant visit to Edinburgh, and he must have impressed the Radical statesman. According to the London journal *Truth*, Bright personally offered him a post on the *Morning Star* when he came to London.[30]

Civic Activities

Though presumably struggling to establish himself as an advocate, and active in city and Reform politics, Gorrie also became involved in other civic affairs. In particular, he threw himself with typical energy into the new Volunteer movement. In 1859 a national panic about the antics of Napoleon III created the Volunteers, a home defence force armed with rifles by Palmerston's government in a demonstration of confidence in the loyalty and good behaviour of the skilled workers and the lower middle classes who dominated the force. Both Victoria and Albert took a keen personal interest in the movement. Gorrie was active in the initial formation of companies in Edinburgh, and was among the first to be commissioned (as Captain of the First Artisan Company). In fact, he played the leading role in raising two companies of artisans, the "first genuine artisan companies in the Kingdom", according to the historian of the city's Volunteers. He spoke at a meeting convened by the Lord Provost (Mayor) in July 1859 to organize the first companies of the 'Edinburgh Volunteer Rifle Regiment'; he proudly told the meeting that he believed that his Artisan Companies "would prove an example to other towns and an honour to the Country". The rank and file members, skilled workmen, themselves insisted on the designation 'Artisan Company'. As the 'originator' of the First Artisan Company, and its senior officer, Captain Gorrie personally raised funds, held recruiting meetings, and drilled the men. He led his company in regular 'excursions in full marching order' into the countryside; in a visit to the Channel Fleet at Queensferry; and in several days of mock campaigning in the Pentland Hills outside the city. Captain Gorrie also took part in a reception hosted by the Queen for

Edinburgh Volunteer officers in August 1860, and remained active with his company until he resigned his commission in February 1862 because he was about to settle in London.

These companies were organized on the basis of professions or occupations, and there was an Advocates' Company. It seems clear that Gorrie decided to organize and lead an artisan company at least in part because of his egalitarian social ideas. In a long article published in a Scottish paper in 1889, when he was being considered as a candidate for the St Andrews parliamentary seat – an article which was probably inspired if not actually written by Gorrie himself – it is stated that "it was because of Sir John having raised several artisan companies in Edinburgh that the movement took its national proportions, instead of being confined, as at first, to a few companies of professional men". This assertion is at least partially corroborated by the historian of the Edinburgh Volunteers. His involvement in the artisan companies, at a time when he was trying to build up a practice and was active in city politics, indicates his genuine interest (and confidence) in the workingman, as well as his abundant energy and compulsion to lead and organize.[31]

He seems to have had a real interest in trade unionism and popular education for adult workers, and he had links with the Edinburgh Trades Council which organized skilled workingmen in the city. He lectured to its members in November 1861 on the topic "Digging into the City Records", and when he was about to leave the city for London he offered his services if the Trades Council wanted to petition the Commons. In fact, as the historian of Victorian Edinburgh's 'labour aristocracy' states, he was one of a group of middle class men who "played key roles in linking the world of the respectable working class to that of the middle class". Some of these men were Liberal/Radical politicians on the Town Council, some were Volunteer officers, some were advocates with a social conscience; Gorrie, of course, belonged to all three categories. Besides his links to the Trades Council, he participated in a course of Saturday evening talks for working people of the city organized by a church mission. *The Age*, the paper which he probably helped to found, was said to circulate mainly among 'higher class tradesmen and artisans' and to advocate 'the rights of the working classes'. He also took part in the Society of Sons of United Presbyterian Ministers which held social functions and raised funds to help needy dependents of clergymen. In fact, he was an active churchman during these years in Edinburgh. He served his church as an elected elder, as a member of the Managers' Committee and of other special committees, and as an 'auditor'. When he moved to London he joined the English Presbyterian Church at Clapham. His religious belief seems never to have faltered. True to the traditions of his Church, his was a broadminded Presbyterianism, and his faith was always practical, "with wide sympathies with all religious bodies who are doing good work", evangelical yet tolerant, insistent that 'love and reason' were the hallmarks of the good Christian.[32]

Although we have no direct evidence for Gorrie's involvement in the Edinburgh antislavery movement, it is likely that he was at least interested in, and sympathetic to, its efforts to publicize the cause of the American slaves before the Civil War. As Lord Provost, McLaren welcomed Harriet Beecher Stowe, author of *Uncle Tom's Cabin*, to the city in 1853 and in the same year he conferred the freedom of the city on William Lloyd Garrison, the radical American abolitionist. In 1854-55 Gorrie's United Presbyterian Church founded the New Edinburgh Antislavery Association, which aimed at immediate and universal emancipation in the USA. Edinburgh's antislavery movement was galvanized by the outbreak of the Civil War, when Scottish men and women campaigned for emancipation and then, after the Emancipation Proclamation, mobilized to send help to the freedmen. All the branches of Scottish Presbyterianism were strongly pro-Union, and Freedmen's Aid Societies were established in several cities including Edinburgh. It seems likely that Gorrie followed these events and developed a strong antislavery commitment in Edinburgh; almost certainly his sympathies were with the radical wing of the movement with which he aligned himself when he went to live in London.[33]

Moreover, his interest in slavery, and in American affairs, could only have been reinforced by his journey to North America in 1860 which took him to Nova Scotia and New Brunswick, New England and beyond. This was on the very eve of the Civil War, and while in Boston he attended meetings on the Free Soil question (whether the new states springing up in the West should allow slavery or be designated 'free states') and election meetings for the presidential election which Lincoln won. Later he recalled:

> I was very glad that I had been there at that time because one was able to go to the meetings of both sides and hear the question discussed by the American orators, so that when the question of the war afterwards came up at home one was able to understand it and sometimes able to explain it to those who knew nothing either about America or about its politics.

This trip was a lucky break for a junior advocate; its purpose was to search for the heir to a large Scottish property who had disappeared in America.[34]

The heir search took Gorrie into some fairly wild country in upstate New York and Illinois, and nearly thirty years later he entertained a Trinidad audience with anecdotes about the rough types whom he encountered there and the perils of travel when one got beyond the railway network of the day. He also encountered a community of Shakers and attended their church services with their dance ritual of worship. While visiting the Shaker settlement, Gorrie stayed at a large hotel where people from all over the Union were spending their summer holidays. "The slavery argument was occasionally discussed, but it had to be done with great reserve because those gentlemen from the South were in an excited state at the time and were in the great habit of carrying revolvers . . . as a means of persuading people to adopt their opinions." (One of his colleagues, meeting President Buchanan at a levee, had publicly hectored him on the slavery issue – "he was not going to hide his Scotch free views for any President" – and when he was told by Buchanan that the slaves were happier as they were, he retorted: "You have no right to enforce happiness on any man who does not want it.") Gorrie visited Niagara Falls, which he described in a public lecture in Edinburgh, and then went into the wild prairie lands west of the Mississippi which were being opened up for farming. He told his working class audience that America was the place for those with experience in agriculture or 'handicrafts' even though it lacked the 'comforts' of the Old World.[35]

Emigration was probably on his mind by 1861; not, of course, to America, but to the metropolis of the South, where he went to live in 1862. By then he was a family man with heavy responsibilities. In December 1855, before qualifying as an advocate, he married Marion Graham, who was only 18. At the time of her birth in 1837 her father, Michael Graham, was described as "late jeweller residing at No.11 Charles Street"; perhaps he was ill, or unemployed, or even retired, and he died when Marion was very young, in 1841. The Grahams appear to have been a solid lower middle class family; according to Michael Graham's will, he owned two Edinburgh houses and shares in the Edinburgh Water Company. The young couple had their first child Marion (Minnie) in 1857, followed by Isobel Jane in 1861; another daughter had been stillborn in 1859. Besides the care of his growing family, Gorrie may have had to help support his widowed mother, possibly also his unmarried sister Isobel. We know that Marion had an unmarried sister (Isabella) who lived with the Gorries in Edinburgh and went with them to London, and then to Mauritius, though she probably had some income from the Graham properties in the city. Money must have been scarce even after Gorrie began his practice, and he soon fell into arrears of payments to the Advocates' Widows and Orphans Fund, from which he was later 'expunged' for nonpayment of dues. It is possible, too, that his support for McLaren in the city's politics was detrimental to his practice; a Fife newspaper hinted in 1866 that it meant 'professional starvation' for him.[36]

Gorrie and his family moved to London in 1862. He may have been promised a post on the *Morning Star* by Bright before he left Edinburgh; but in any case it seems likely that he was anxious to take an active part in the larger political and literary world which the capital offered, and he may well have begun to find the narrow round of an Edinburgh law practice and municipal politics somewhat confining, especially if he found himself blocked by a powerful Whig legal establishment hostile to his radical views. As for so many young Scots before and since, the lure of the great metropolis was too strong to resist. At the farewell dinner organized by his professional colleagues in Edinburgh, he remembered fondly twenty years later, all the political factions of the city were well represented, with the Whig Sheriff of Fife as chairman and the Tory Treasurer of the Faculty of Advocates as vice chair. He was then 33, ready to start a new life. But his worldview – his radical politics, his religious principles, his social egalitarianism, his belief in social and political activism – had already been formed, in Fife and in Edinburgh.[37]

Journalism in London

The move to London meant that journalism would be, for the next six years, his main source of income. Gorrie was never admitted to the English Bar, though two Scottish newspapers reported after his death that he had 'prepared' for the Bar, presumably by study and perhaps by 'eating dinners' in one of the Inns. He could not practise in the ordinary English courts, but he certainly did some legal work and maintained 'chambers in the Temple'. In London, Scottish advocates could appear before the House of Lords, the Judicial Committee of the Privy Council and Select Committees of either House; practice in these institutions was known collectively as the 'Parliamentary Bar'. The most promising opportunity for this kind of work occurred when a Scottish private bill was dealt with by a Select Committee enquiry at Westminster; the opponents and supporters of the bill would retain an advocate to argue the case before the Committee. A Scottish advocate could also be retained on English, Irish or colonial cases; his right to appear before the House of Lords, the Privy Council and Parliamentary Committees – all 'Imperial' institutions – was not confined to Scottish cases. Gorrie also apparently advised on 'foreign' cases; his knowledge of Scottish law presumably gave him a good grasp of continental legal systems.[38]

No doubt Gorrie took a keen interest in contemporary efforts to reform the English legal system; his Scottish training, and his political radicalism, both inclined him to be highly critical of many aspects of that system. One historian describes the law of real property then as "a lumber-room of pedantry and a rich source of income for lawyers; the establishment of a registry of titles [as had long existed in Scotland] in 1862 had little effect, partly because solicitors did not encourage their clients to use it". The criminal code was consolidated in 1860 and in 1863 Parliament began to repeal many obsolete laws. But no effort was made to simplify the language of the laws, or to compile a civil code similar to those of the continental countries, and "the English legal system in 1870, though far less of an anomaly and a hindrance to a reasonable social order than it had been in 1815, was still very far from an ideal code in which . . . processes like the buying and selling of land could be carried out easily and cheaply". This last issue was taken up by the Cobden/Bright radicals who argued that there should be 'free trade' in land, by which they meant the abolition of primogeniture, entails and 'strict settlements' which all had the effect of tying up land artificially, and changes in legal procedures so that the buying and selling of land should be no more difficult than with any other commodity. These issues were to become a lifelong preoccupation for Gorrie.[39]

But journalism took precedence over the law during Gorrie's London years. He held a salaried post with the *Morning Star* as a reporter and editorial writer, though he may also have contributed pieces to other journals and magazines. As his friend and colleague Justin McCarthy put it, he "had taken to journalism as the readiest way of beginning his career" in London.[40]

The *Morning Star* was a radical paper founded in 1856 specifically to articulate the views of the Cobden/Bright wing of British Liberalism. Both men took a keen interest in its progress and frequently suggested topics for articles or improvements in editorial policy. It was a cheap 'penny' daily meant for a wide readership, a product of a series of reforms for which Cobden and Bright had agitated: the repeal of the advertisement duty in 1853, of the newspaper stamp tax in 1855, and of the excise duty on paper in 1860-61. McCarthy, its editor-in-chief between 1865 and 1868, summed up the paper's political programme: It supported complete free trade, the abolition of all religious establishments and the principle of colonial self-government; it favoured the secret ballot and manhood suffrage, a national system of education, a nonaggressive foreign policy. He said further: "We were admirers of the American Republic; we refused to believe that all foreigners were our natural born enemies; we were against capital punishment; and, in fact, no one at any other period of the world anywhere was ever so anarchical as we were then." The paper suffered for its opposition to the Crimean War, a stand that was said to have adversely affected its financial prospects, and during the American Civil War the *Morning Star* and the *Daily News*, another Liberal paper, were the only two British dailies to support the Union consistently, an unpopular position with 'the classes'. As a sympathetic writer commented after its demise, the *Morning Star*, "able, earnest, and generous, enforcing unpopular opinions, and appealing to a limited class of readers, was a competitor to be sneered at by those who chose, but hardly to be feared". Its circulation was never large; at its height, the joint circulation of the *Morning Star* and its afternoon paper never exceeded 15,000 and had sunk to 5,000 by its last year (1869). Its politics must have made it unacceptable to the upper and much of the middle classes, and it made few concessions, in content, style or language, to working class readers.[41]

John Bright developed a warm relationship with the paper's editorial staff, especially when his brother-in-law, Samuel Lucas, was editor-in-chief (Lucas died in 1865). He routinely dropped in for 5 o'clock tea, "entered very freely into all our talk", and calmly discussed the great issues of the day, listening "with great good humour to our outbursts of levity, doing us the credit to believe that we had a serious purpose under all our attempts at frivolity"; he would come from the House at any hour to give the staff the latest parliamentary news. At times he objected to criticisms of opponents which he felt were harsh and would give pain: "Most of the men who wrote for the *Morning Star* in those days", McCarthy recalled,

> were young and had their fair share of youth's audacity and recklessness, and when they got a good chance of holding up some political opponent to ridicule and contempt they were not slow to avail themselves of the opportunity, and were not always overscrupulous in their manner of using it.

But Bright always objected to any unfair or exaggerated attacks and drew the line at 'below the belt' tactics. Until he became a minister in Gladstone's first government in 1868, Bright seems to have kept in very close contact with the paper's staff, including Gorrie.[42]

Lucas, who was editor when Gorrie first began to work for the paper, was described as "a man of great intellectual faculties and charming conversational powers" with a special gift for encouraging able young men to give their best; he was much loved by his staff. McCarthy was first House of Commons reporter, then foreign editor; he succeeded Lucas as editor-in-chief on the latter's death. Frederick Chesson, a prominent antislavery activist who became Gorrie's close friend, was editor of the evening paper. Also on the staff was Charles Cooper, later to become editor of *The Scotsman* and a correspondent of Gorrie's. All the members of the editorial staff met at a regular afternoon meeting at which views were exchanged and topics for leaders discussed. "Pleasant and genial gatherings", McCarthy recalled many years later: "I do not know that I ever listened to brighter talk or heard more original ideas or more startling paradoxes than those which used to enliven the more serious course of our disquisitions and our discussions on the subject of appropriate leading articles." Cooper cherished similar memories: "Those were pleasant gatherings. I think of them now [1896] with the kindliest remembrance."[43]

Gorrie must have blossomed, intellectually and socially, as one of such an assembly of talents, united by a common set of political views and sense of mission. The *Suva Times* reported that he recalled for an audience in Fiji that:

> he could tell many a story of the jovial times he had had in the gallery of the House of Commons, not as a reporter (for he was never able to do that work) but as a listener to the debate on which it was his duty to write an article for next morning's paper. The article would be penned there and then, and given to the – the devil – who were ready in relays to take 'copy' as it was furnished and then, that done, there was a call for Hackney or Hansom to get to bed as fast as the poor horse could drag them.

Besides his editorials and leading articles, always unsigned, Gorrie also wrote pieces for the evening paper, which featured little essays on various topics contributed by many well-known writers, and perhaps for other journals like the *Saturday Review* and the *Fortnightly Review*, both Liberal periodicals of the 1860s.[44]

The *Morning Star* never built up a large circulation and it was not a financial success. Bright ended his active involvement in the paper as soon as he became a government minister in 1868, and this led McCarthy to resign as editor. It also led several of the shareholders to voice their dissatisfaction with the paper as a business venture. Circulation was as low as 5,000 by 1869, and the paper was reduced in size early in 1868. John Morley, then a brilliant young journalist, was appointed editor of a declining paper; the proprietors refused to give him the funds to improve it, and though under Morley it did in fact begin to pick up both in circulation and in influence, they decided in October 1869 to merge it with the liberal *Daily News*. In saying farewell to his readers, Morley assured them that the paper had achieved two objects in its thirteen years of existence: "One of these was the advocacy and propagation of political principles which were then counted extreme in their Liberalism; the other was to establish the feasibility of providing journalism of the best sort under what were then the untried conditions of a penny newspaper."[45]

No doubt the decline of the paper in 1868-69, and its closure in the latter year, helped to persuade Gorrie that he should seek a colonial appointment. In fact, he left Britain just at the time when the closure of the paper was being carried out. Chesson commented in his diary on a farewell dinner given by Gorrie just before his departure:

> Rather odd that at that hour the notices terminating everybody's engagement at the *Star* were being issued. The ship is sinking; but it appears more than probable that the terms of amalgamation with the *Daily News* have been agreed upon – Morley to act as co-editor. The printers too have received a fortnight's notice. Gorrie goes to Mauritius.

During the paper's final week, a ceremony took place attended by "the principal members of the staff, now greatly attenuated". Chesson "in the name of the subscribers, made, quite unexpectedly both to him and to the majority of the company, a presentation to Gorrie who seemed to be greatly astonished, but as Morley afterwards said, soon recovered himself".[46]

The decline, and eventual demise, of the *Morning Star* dissolved the talented and congenial group of young journalists with whom Gorrie had worked and socialized. Cooper (who left in 1868 to join the *Scotsman*) wrote: "There was much that was painful in the severance of what had become old and dear ties"; "never were better comrades than these. Rarely could be found abler men, taking them all round." Cooper was especially close to Chesson and Gorrie, who would remain lifelong friends. He described Chesson as "the gentlest, most amiable, most earnest, and most persistent man I have ever known . . . a better man never lived". His view of Gorrie was less positive: "If he could have subordinated secondary considerations to those of first importance, he would have been a successful man. Being what he was, he seemed to be doomed to eventual failure" (a comment made after his old friend's death). But Cooper admitted to "a great liking for him [Gorrie]. There were not many questions on which we agreed; but he was a gentleman, and differed from you in the spirit of a gentleman."[47]

Antislavery and Politics

The *Morning Star* was a strong supporter of the Union during the American Civil War and represented antislavery opinion. Gorrie wrote many articles on the subject, in which he "enthusiastically took the side of the North and freedom", and was probably further encouraged in his views by Chesson, a leading figure in the radical (Garrisonian) wing of British abolitionism in this period. It is likely that Gorrie had already become interested in the antislavery movement in Edinburgh; in London he quickly aligned himself with the London Emancipation Society, the most important radical antislavery organization in the 1860s.[48]

British antislavery, in full decline during the 1850s, was galvanized by the outbreak of the Civil War and especially by the first Emancipation Proclamation of President Lincoln in September 1862. In 1859 George Thompson, the leading British Garrisonian, Chesson (his son-in-law), and others founded the London Emancipation Committee, which changed its name to the London Emancipation Society in December 1862 following the Emancipation Proclamation. Its stated aims, in a 1862 prospectus, were to combat pro-Confederate opinion in Britain and to encourage the Union government in its policy of emancipation. John Stuart Mill joined its committee, Cobden and Bright gave it their active support. It published several pamphlets and arranged lectures. The LES, like most of the American Garrisonians, supported Lincoln's policies from the beginning of the war, and was the most active pro-Union, antislavery British group in the first half of the 1860s.[49]

Within a few months of arriving in London, Gorrie began to take part in the work of the LES, whose office was situated, it seems, next door to the *Morning Star*'s advertisement office on Fleet Street (perhaps it shared premises with the newspaper). In January 1863 he made a statement to a LES meeting on the *Alabama* case. The *Alabama* was a disguised warship which had been constructed at the Liverpool docks. Once on the high seas, in 1862, it hoisted Confederate colours and preyed successfully on Union shipping until it was captured and sunk in 1864 (Britain was officially neutral in the war). The LES apparently decided to publish his statement but "without the name of the Soc[iety]". Later that month Gorrie presided over an antislavery meeting at Exeter Hall and helped to prepare a resolution "most tastefully engraved on vellum" for transmission to the Union Ambassador in London. He was a member of a two-man deputation from the LES which addressed the congregation of Clifton Church in Peckham on the subject of Negro Emancipation in April 1863, moving a resolution denouncing the government for allowing Confederate privateers to be fitted out in British ports. In May 1863 he was on the platform with Chesson at a large meeting held in Finsbury Chapel, Moorfields, with a crowd of over 3,000, and at another one in the Hanover Square Rooms to protest against the government's anti-Union policies. Later that year he lectured for the LES to the Whittington Club on the topic "Recent Northern Successes and the Prospects of the War". He told the audience that southerners had only one principle, slavery, and only one argument, the sword; they hated England, and at that moment 27 black British subjects (West Indians) were being held in jail in South Carolina under that state's infamous laws which assumed all blacks must be slaves. "The lecturer then proceeded to give a lucid and eloquent statement of the rapid and successful progress of the northern arms." He attended a great meeting at Exeter Hall to hear Henry Ward Beecher on the American situation; thousands were turned away disappointed, unable to get in because of the massive crowd.[50]

Once it was clear that all the slaves in the USA would be freed as soon as the Union's arms triumphed, the British antislavery forces began to mobilize to send money and materials to aid the freedmen. This Freedman's Aid movement was at its height between 1863 and 1866, with societies all over the nation. In London, the LES was associated with the London Freedman's Aid Society and its journal, *Freed-Man*. The same people ran the two groups, above all the tireless Chesson (who was also secretary of the Aborigines

Protection Society and would hold the same office in the Jamaica Committee). Gorrie and Chesson met frequently to discuss the American situation in 1864 and 1865; in December 1864 they were both part of a large deputation to Adams, the US Ambassador. In August 1865, with the end of the Civil War and the final end of American slavery, the LES was dissolved. Generally speaking, the Freedman's Aid societies and the LES, like British antislavery as a whole in the 1860s, were led by men over the age of fifty who had been part of the cause ever since its great days in the 1830s, but both Chesson and Gorrie, born in 1833 and 1829 respectively, represented rare new blood for the movement.[51]

In Edinburgh Gorrie had been actively involved in municipal politics – in London his political reporting for the paper in and out of Parliament must have sharpened his appetite for the fray. During the campaign for the November 1868 general elections, he offered himself as the Liberal candidate for the 'Border Burghs' seat in southern Scotland; unfortunately, there were at least two other Liberal aspirants, and Gorrie was late to stake a claim. At a lively election meeting in Galashiels, he delivered a lengthy speech. According to the *Morning Star*, he reminded his audience that when living in Edinburgh he had actively supported giving the borough vote to payers of the poor rates, which had become the law of the land under the second Reform Act of 1867. The newspaper report continued:

> Of late his lot had been cast in a different sphere, but the change had only enabled him to do a little more with his pen for the promotion of those measures of progress which were now ripening to the harvest (Applause). He had all his life maintained that it was the people who were to make the choice of the candidate, and it would be sufficient for him if he got the feeling of the people in any sufficient manner to induce him to take his course (Renewed cheers).

After these explanations, Gorrie settled down to expatiate on a number of topics so that, as he said, "the electors would be able to discover the bent of [my] politics". On Ireland, he favoured disendowment and disestablishment of the Anglican Church; he opposed protection in any shape or form; he wanted expenditure on the Army and Navy to be drastically reduced; and he called for an end to the 'little wars' on the frontiers of the empire. Gorrie's expatiation on other topics was reported by the *Morning Star*:

> He denounced the law of entail, and recommended the abolition of the law of primogeniture. The time had also come, he said, when the remnants of feudalism should be abolished from the Scotch system of title-deeds . . . Mr Gorrie concluded by saying that to the next Parliament would be given to . . . decide whether we are to adapt our legislation to the traditions, aspirations and the national distinctions of the Irish people, or to maintain the system of coercion in order to gratify the few who have mistaken political ascendancy for religion . . . The leaders of the Liberal Party are giants in intellect; and if the cause of progress does not gain the victory when the standard is upheld by Mr Gladstone and Mr Bright, then never is it likely to be borne higher or to float more proudly. I would therefore call upon the constituency, whatever representative they select, to choose the one who has faith in the great principles of which those leaders are the present types and representatives (Applause).

The meeting heard Gorrie "with every means of respect and courtesy . . . and cheered him warmly when he sat down". He was questioned about the Factory Acts and the 'nine hours bill', which he said he supported, parting company here with his mentor Bright who opposed any legislative interference between employer and employee. When he was asked if he was prepared to have the bishops withdrawn from the House of Lords, he replied drily that he was not "favourable to bishops, and would certainly oppose any more of them getting in; [but that he] could not promise to turn out those that are in". At last, however, an elector asked him the crucial question: was he prepared to retire rather than risk damaging Liberal interests in the seat? It was explained that the great majority of the electors had already committed themselves to the two other Liberal aspirants and that if he persisted he could only "endanger the triumph of true Liberalism". A motion was put inviting him to withdraw, whereupon "tremendous applause, hissing and confusion" broke out. Gorrie asked for a few days to consider the matter and to hold meetings in the other burghs. "At this stage of the proceedings the meeting became tremendously excited – individuals speaking in different parts of the room. Some time elapsed before order was restored." An amendment that Gorrie be asked not to retire was moved and seconded; "on the amendment being put a small proportion of hands were held up, and for the motion a large majority, at which there was immense cheering. The meeting broke up under high excitement." [52]

On the day after this confusing but clearly unsatisfactory meeting at Galashiels, Gorrie addressed electors of Selkirk. He spoke mainly on Ireland, the major issue in the 1868 general elections. Not only should there be disendowment and disestablishment; a Liberal Government must take up the question of land reform, which was as important as the question of religion. "But Irish grievances were not all to be settled in a moment; to satisfy and pacify Ireland must be a matter of time." Gorrie repeated his earlier call for reduction in expenditure on the armed services, and warned that the Army was getting out of control, illustrating his argument by referring to the excesses committed by the troops in suppressing the rising in Jamaica in 1865. As he had said the previous night, he insisted that he was ready to retire if his persistence as a candidate was likely to endanger the Liberal cause, and sat down after a speech lasting over an hour amidst 'loud and prolonged cheering'. The real situation must have been clear to Gorrie, however, and on the following night the Provost of Selkirk read out to the assembled electors a gracious letter announcing his retirement in order to avoid dissension and a possible Conservative victory.[53]

G.O. Trevelyan, his main rival, was duly selected as the Liberal candidate for the Border Burghs. He was returned for the seat in the great Liberal landslide of 1868 which brought the first Gladstone Ministry into power with a majority of 112. Gorrie's rejoicing at this famous victory must have been tempered by his own failure to enter Parliament, a failure which (along with the demise of the *Morning Star*) must have prompted him to contemplate a colonial career. It was a turning point in his life, which ruled out a possibly distinguished career as a Liberal MP with close links to John Bright; and led him to seek a position in the colonial legal or judicial service. There can be no doubt that he was better suited, by temperament, aspirations and experience, for a life in journalism or politics than for a seat on a colonial bench.

But other factors also pushed him to seek a colonial post. His family grew during the London years; his only son, Malcolm, was born in 1864, and his third daughter and last child, Jane (Jeanie), arrived late in 1865. With a regular salary from the paper and whatever income his legal work brought in, perhaps the young family was less strapped for cash than it had been in Edinburgh, though money can hardly have been abundant. It seems, though, that Gorrie was able to travel on the Continent, perhaps on legal business, perhaps as one of the new Cook's tourists, for he wrote in a letter from Jamaica in 1866 that he had visited the Rhine valley and 'the plains of Styria'.[54] In this letter he compared the Jamaican scenery favourably with the finest prospects in Europe or in his own Scotland; but his trip to Jamaica was no pleasure jaunt. It brought him face to face with the darker realities of British rule in the colonies, and forced him to work out his ideas about his country's imperial mission, before he actually took up a position in the colonial service.

CHAPTER TWO

The Jamaica Case, 1865-68

Gorrie was already in his mid thirties when he first came into sustained contact with a multiracial colonial society. His involvement with the 'Jamaica case' of 1865-68 – when 'Jamaican blood' engaged 'Victorian conscience' to create a *cause célèbre* which split the British political and intellectual community – was nevertheless a formative experience of his life. His political and social worldview had, of course, long been formed; he had been engaged in liberal/radical politics in Edinburgh and London since the early 1850s; he had taken part in the antislavery movement of the 1860s. But his visit to Jamaica in 1866, under the most dramatic circumstances imaginable, and his intimate involvement in the 'Jamaica case' over the two years following his return to London, irrevocably shaped his understanding of the dynamics of colonial societies, where small white elites ruled populations of another race, and of the proper role of the Imperial power and its servants in such societies. He was to spend the rest of his life serving in colonies of this kind, and his whole career after 1869 was powerfully influenced by his exposure to this Jamaican tragedy.

The Morant Bay Rebellion

The events which put Jamaica in the headlines of the British press towards the end of 1865 may be quickly summarized. In the eastern parish of St Thomas, a minor disturbance occurred during a session of the magistrates' court at Morant Bay, the county town, on October 7, 1865. Warrants were issued for the arrest of Paul Bogle and several others who had been responsible for the disturbance in the court house. When on October 10 policemen went to Stony Gut, a small hillside village near Morant Bay, to serve the warrants, they were surrounded and beaten by a large crowd and made to take oaths swearing to "join their colour . . . cleave to the black". Baron von Ketelhodt, the custos (chief magistrate) of St Thomas, asked the governor, Edward Eyre, for troops and prepared for possible trouble at the vestry meeting scheduled for the next day, October 11. The troops did not arrive until October 12.

At Morant Bay, the vestry met on October 11; while they were in session, Bogle and a large crowd approached the courthouse square where the custos had assembled about twenty militiamen. When they entered the square, the custos read the riot act while the crowd began to throw stones. The militia opened fire and several of the crowd were killed or injured. The mob then rushed the militia, who retreated into the courthouse, and a siege began. It

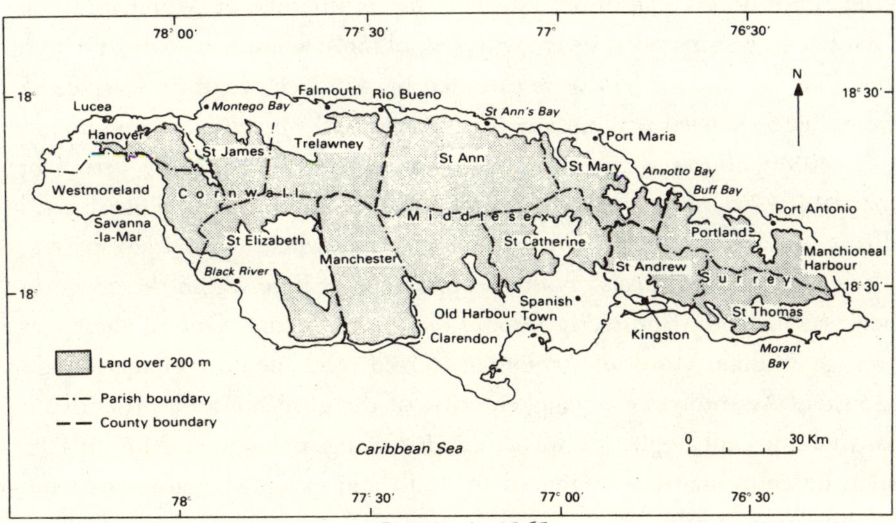

Jamaica in 1865

culminated in the firing of the building; as the vestrymen and militiamen ran out, several were beaten and hacked to death by the crowd, including von Ketelhodt, an Anglican curate, and other local notables. In all, the rioters killed 18 and injured 31 people on October 11. In the two or three days following, mobs attacked and plundered several neighbouring estates and one small town (Bath). During this phase of the disturbance, three or possibly four men were killed and three injured by the mobs; no women or children were harmed. They plundered about twenty houses and shops and burnt down a few buildings, including the courthouse, on October 11. By October 15 or 16 all violent activity by the rioters had ended.

The governor mobilized troops as soon as he heard of the disaster of October 11, and on October 13 he proclaimed a state of martial law to exist over the whole eastern third of the island except Kingston, the chief town. For the next two weeks, British troops and naval personnel, local militiamen and volunteers, and irregular armed men of the Maroon community (descendants of rebel slaves who had won their freedom and semi-independence in the previous century and had continued to live separately from the general black population) roamed through the disturbed districts carrying out summary executions and punishments under martial law regulations and also shooting a number of 'rebels' without formalities of any kind. Excluding the number killed by the militiamen at Morant Bay on October 11 (estimated at seven, with several more wounded, some of whom were later executed), 354 were executed by sentence of courts martial, 85 were shot or hanged without any trial, at least 600 were flogged, and no less than 1,000 houses were burnt by the authorities. During the period of martial law, moreover, Eyre had several men living outside the proclaimed district arrested and transported to Morant Bay where martial law existed. These were the 'politicals', political opponents of Eyre whom the governor believed had been indirectly responsible for the rising. One of these was George William Gordon, a coloured (mixed race) member of the island's House of Assembly, an outspoken critic of the governor and a friend and associate of Paul Bogle. He was arrested in Kingston, sent to Morant Bay, tried by court martial, sentenced to death and executed (with Eyre's full approval) on October 23.[1]

News of these events reached London in November. Eyre's first despatch to the Secretary of State for the Colonies (Edward Cardwell) showed no hint that he was nervous about official reaction to the measures he had taken. He took on himself "the whole responsibility for what has been done".[2] By the end of November, however, individuals and groups sympathetic to the Jamaican blacks had begun to mobilize. The 'Jamaica case' had begun.

As detailed information on the repression became available, the antislavery leaders prepared to put pressure on the Colonial Office to ensure that Eyre's interpretation of the events of October 1865 did not go unchallenged. The publication of his first despatch, along with reports from the field by military officers in charge of the repression and extracts from Jamaican papers gloating over the martial law punishments, was the signal to Exeter Hall – as the British antislavery and humanitarian movement was popularly known, after a favorite London meeting place – to swing into action. The defence of Jamaican blacks against official brutality was a cause dear to its heart, reviving memories of its glory days when it campaigned for the extinction of slavery in the British empire and then defended the ex-slaves against their enemies. The newspapers sympathetic to Exeter Hall, and notably the *Morning Star*, published disturbing documents from Jamaica, and Louis Chamerovzow, secretary of the British and Foreign Anti-Slavery Society (BFASS), who had excellent contacts there, reproduced a letter describing the troops "shooting and hanging the unfortunate blacks, men and women, with very little discrimination, and with a zest horrible to think of". Chamerovzow unequivocally defended Gordon, who would become the principal martyr of Morant Bay: "From a correspondence with him extending over many years, I believe him to have been incapable of encompassing conspiracy in any form." On reviewing the evidence of the repression, Chamerovzow asked: "On which side are the bloodthirstiness and savagery so recklessly ascribed to the long-suffering and badly governed negro population of Jamaica?"[3]

John Bright ensured from the start that the *Morning Star* would be an important organ for the campaign. Writing to its editor Justin McCarthy as early as November 13, 1865, he urged the paper to publish information about maladministration in Jamaica and "the injustice to the negro" and to call for a Commission of Enquiry. A few weeks later Bright wrote to McCarthy:

> The Jamaican affair deepens in horror; form a powerful committee and ask for funds . . . Let the committee announce their determination to have a rigid inquiry and to bring to justice in this country the Governor and his pliant and bloody tools . . . Able lawyers should be engaged; and the country should undertake to do what it is to be feared the Government is slack in beginning . . . If you could have the question discussed by some good lawyer in your columns, it would be well.

Bright played a leading role in the formation of the Jamaica Committee (JC) in December 1865.[4] In that month, several delegations visited the Colonial Office to protest against the repression and to demand an investigation. These groups combined with liberal/radical politicians to form the JC. Its office holders were all antislavery activists. Charles Buxton served as the first chairman, a man with an inherited interest in West Indian causes as the son of T.F. Buxton who had steered the Act of Emancipation through Parliament in 1833; Peter Taylor, also an MP, and treasurer of the recently dissolved London Emancipation Society, filled the same office in the JC; and Gorrie's friend and colleague, F.W. Chesson, served as Secretary. The best known founding members of the JC were John and Jacob Bright, J.S. Mill, Thomas Hughes, Chamerovzow, Samuel Gurney (president of BFASS) and Samuel Morley. The pressures from the antislavery groups and then the JC, combined with the Secretary of State's own growing sense of unease about the reprisals, had their effect. In December 1865 he announced that a Royal Commission would investigate both the riots and the repression and that its chairman, Sir Henry Storks, would supersede Eyre as Governor of Jamaica during its sittings and until further notice.[5]

Immediately after the announcement, Gorrie was asked to go out to Jamaica as one of two lawyers retained by the JC to represent the interests of those who had suffered in the reprisals, including Gordon's widow, and to help them to present their evidence before the Commission. It seems he received very little notice of this assignment. Chesson recorded that Bright had used his influence to raise the money needed to send Gorrie at very short notice: "Mr Bright then met Mr Morley who promised £500 and Mr Gorrie therefore bade us goodbye." Gorrie told an audience in Trinidad twenty years after the event:

> One morning, when I went to my chambers in the Temple, a gentleman came in and just said in an offhand way: 'Would you take a brief to go to Jamaica about those disturbances if it is sent to you?' I said 'Well probably I would, I don't know that there is any reason to prevent me'. But I was not sure that he was in earnest and I thought no more about it until a Saturday, when the brief itself came in, and I was asked to start by the steamer on the following day. So that the first intimation that my family got that I was going was when some of my outfit went home before myself on the Saturday night, and I was off for Southampton by the steamer on the next day.

No doubt he exaggerated somewhat, but he clearly had only a few days' grace. He embarked on December 18, 1865; two days earlier Bright had sent him a gracious note:

> I am very glad to hear that you are going out to the unhappy Island of Jamaica, in the capacity of legal inquirer, and adviser of the Central Jamaica Committee. I am sure all your sentiments will be in favour of what is just . . . There will be difficulties in your path – but I believe you will surmount them. You have my best wishes for your success, and for your safe return.[6]

Early in 1866, when Gorrie had already arrived in Jamaica, the JC submitted a 'case' for legal opinion from two eminent lawyers, one of them James Fitzjames Stephen. Seven specific questions were posed, relating to martial law, to Gordon's trial and execution, and to the proper modes for bringing to trial Eyre and any of his subordinates if they should have been guilty of illegal acts. In an elaborate 'opinion', the lawyers went into great detail on the purposes and limits of martial law in the English legal and constitutional system. On the case of Gordon, they stated:

> As to the legal powers of the officers sitting as a court martial at Morant Bay, we are of opinion that they had no powers at all as a court martial, and that they could justify the execution of Mr Gordon only if and insofar as they could show that that step was immediately and unavoidably necessary for the preservation of peace and the restoration

> of order. They had no right whatever to punish him for treason, even if he had committed it. Their province was to suppress force by force, not to punish crime.

This opinion was to guide the JC throughout all its proceedings as they related to the courts martial, and it was upheld eventually by the Lord Chief Justice. The lawyers advised that Eyre and his officers could be indicted in Middlesex or impeached in Parliament, and that any private citizen might prefer a bill of indictment.[7]

Soon after receiving this opinion, the JC retained William Shaen as its solicitor. He composed a Letter of Instruction for Gorrie and John Horne Payne, the second lawyer briefed by the JC. This document gave guidelines for what was, by any standards, a difficult and highly delicate assignment. The JC's object, the solicitor stated, was "solely to vindicate the supremacy of English law; and consequently . . . your duty will be not that of an advocate . . . but rather that of a commissioner on the part of the committee, to assist in ascertaining and placing in the clearest and most distinct light the facts". They were to obtain and organize the evidence on which the Royal Commission, "if they permit you to be heard before them", would base their report, and on which, "as an entirely separate and distinct proceeding", the JC would reach a decision as to whether to bring charges against any party. At all times they were:

> to endeavour to assist the Commissioners in making this inquiry complete and exhaustive; both by tendering witnesses on behalf of any claimants who may satisfy you that they have solid grounds of complaint, and also, if permitted by the Royal Commissioners, by cross-examining any witnesses produced or tendering themselves on the other side.

Independently of the Commission's enquiry, they were to procure any evidence of acts of illegality or cruelty which might justify indictments or private actions for damages, working through local attorneys who would collect evidence as agents of the JC.[8]

Besides his primary responsibility as counsel for the JC, Gorrie had a second mission in Jamaica: as the 'Special Commissioner' for the *Morning*

Star, he sent long, vivid reports to his newspaper which must have helped to shape anti-Eyre opinion in Britain in the first few months of 1866. He was not the only British journalist to go to Jamaica to cover the proceedings of the Commission; *The Times, The Daily Telegraph, The Morning Herald* and *The Daily News* all sent out reporters. Gorrie's first letter, written mostly on board ship, was published on January 30. He challenged the easy wisdom of the 'old hands' whom he met on the ship, the men who were "violent that the negro will not work; that he is not subject to the same ambition and desire of improvement as the white man; that he cares for nothing but to squat on his hams at the door of his miserable hut and bask in the sun". Gorrie recognized that "in the eyes of many West Indians, when a negro prefers to work for himself, in place of labour for a master, at any rate of wages which the master may choose to dictate, he is guilty of a crime deserving to be severely reprimanded".[9]

The Jamaica Royal Commission

Gorrie arrived in Jamaica on January 6, 1866 and the Commission opened its proceedings on January 23 at Spanish Town, the capital; he later reported that some spectators at the opening ceremony, seeing Gorrie and Payne in their gown and wig, said "Dem be real Queen Commissioner". At the start of the proceedings, the question of the status of the two counsel for the JC, and the rights to be accorded them, was put before the Commissioners. They ruled that they could cross-examine only when testimony against one of their clients was given. Using extracts from Eyre's official despatches, Gorrie showed that the ex-governor had considered Gordon to be the instigator of the whole rising; hence, as lawyer for his widow, and as defender of his reputation, *all* evidence as to the origins, causes and progress of the rebellion was testimony pertinent to his client. Besides the right to cross-examine, Gorrie asked to be allowed to see the official records of the trials under martial law. The Commissioners insisted on their original ruling on cross-examination, and refused to give Gorrie or Payne access to the records of the courts martial. They could, however, suggest questions to the Commissioners, who would decide whether to put them to the witnesses. When Eyre was examined on January 31, Gorrie reported, "the Commissioners did not permit a cross-examination of Mr Eyre . . . Indeed, the liberty of action accorded to the counsel who have come out from England has been extremely small . . . Mr Gorrie [for in his newspaper reports Gorrie referred to himself in the third person for obvious reasons] pressed for liberty to cross-examine, but this was rather tartly refused". Significantly, Commissioner Russell Gurney replied to Gorrie's exasperated question "Am I to understand that the Royal Commissioners will not allow me to put any questions to Mr Eyre relative to Mr Gordon at present?" by reminding him: "We are not here to try the guilt of any person."[10] It seems, however, that the Commissioners soon relaxed these restrictions on cross-examination by the counsel for the JC, and adopted the practice of questioning witnesses 'at the request of' Gorrie or Payne. It is clear from the voluminous evidence printed as an appendix to the Commission's report that Gorrie did take a most active part in cross-examining the key official witnesses (as well as interviewing victims of the repression and marshalling their evidence). For instance, General Abercrombie Nelson, the senior military officer actually in the field during the reprisals, was subjected to a severe and lengthy cross-examination by Gorrie, as the following extract reveals:

> *Q*. Had Capt. Adcock authority from you to carry out the sentence of death upon any persons he might see on the roadside by drum-beat court martial? – *A*. He went out to attack an enemy and he was authorized to do so, decidedly.
>
> *Q*. You gave him authority to try others than rebels in arms? – *A*. The whole were rebels, all were enemies.
>
> *Q*. The whole of whom? – *A*. The whole of those that he went out against. He went out against rebels.
>
> *Q*. Do you mean that he went out against the whole country? – *A*. Those he went to attack were supposed rebels.
>
> *Q*. Would you just explain what you mean by the term 'rebel' – do you mean a man in arms? – *A*. No, certainly not.

Q. Or a man that could be proved to have been in arms recently? – *A*. Decidedly.

Q. Do you limit the term to that? – *A*. No, I give it a general acceptation. I considered the whole of St Thomas in the East, till they came forward and proved otherwise, were all rebels, if they did not come in and proclaim their loyalty, and I considered myself employed against them.

Q. You considered the whole population of St Thomas in the East? – *A*. Under martial law.[11]

Several witnesses were cross-examined by Gorrie in order to bring out the reckless cruelty, amounting at times to sadism, of the military forces. A captain of the volunteer cavalry (a white Jamaican) was asked about the practice of subjecting persons who had just been flogged to a gauntlet of marines and sailors who hit at them and threw sticks or stones as they ran past:

Q. In what condition were the men when they were thus pursued, after having received these floggings; were they dressed? – *A*. They generally took their shirts in their hands.

Q. And ran? – *A*. Yes.

Q. With their bleeding backs? – *A*. Yes, or without.

At Bath, a small town not far from Morant Bay, evidence was brought to prove that men and women had been flogged with special cats which had piano wire twisted around the rope. A white overseer of the district who had served in the volunteers during the reprisals was asked by Gorrie:

Q. How many people did you flog with your own hand? – *A*. Very few, but I don't remember how many. It was no pleasant occupation. Now and again I did it.

Q. How were you selected for the purpose of flogging; did you volunteer for it? – *A*. Yes.

Q. Then you need not have flogged unless you liked this disagreeable occupation? – *A*. Unless we really liked it.

A white planter-magistrate of Port Morant, who had given evidence at the court martial of Charles Mitchell to the effect that Mitchell had told him, on the morning of October 11, "Oh, you are going to have your head chopped off at Morant Bay; I want a white wife and an estate myself", was asked by Gorrie:

> *Q*. And that is what he was executed for? – *A*. Yes, and the additional evidence of my overseer.
>
> *Q*. On the same affair? – *A*. Yes; the man went and cut off a bamboo, and said 'That is the way to cut off buckra's head'.
>
> *Q*. He did not cut your head off? – *A*. No.
>
> *Q*. Or your overseer's? – *A*. No.
>
> *Q*. Only the bamboo? – *A*. Yes.
>
> *Q*. And for that he was executed? – *A*. He was executed.[12]

Much of Gorrie's work in Jamaica took place outside the sittings of the Commission. Aided by the solicitors working with them, he and Payne interviewed large numbers of Jamaicans, heard their stories of suffering at the hands of the authorities, sifted through their testimony, and marshalled evidence. He wrote that he was "not two days in Jamaica" before he was "besieged from seven in the morning till late in the afternoon by people eager to detail to [him] their suffering"; crowds congregated on the verandah of his Kingston rooms waiting to make their statements about "the killing time of 1865". As he told a Trinidad audience twenty years later: "When I got to Jamaica I found that I had no less than 350 clients, every one of whom had lost a near relative by the excess of martial law". On one occasion he actually examined a man's back; this man had been flogged twice on orders from the Provost Marshal "to teach him manners". The experience was a sobering one. Payne went to Morant Bay and saw the great trenches where the corpses of the executed men and women had been buried; when he went on to Bath, scene of some of the most reckless punishments, "a perfect mob of witnesses" waited to tell him their horrible stories and to describe the infamous wire cats (one of which was actually examined by the Commissioners).[13]

Gorrie's attitude towards the Jamaicans whom he interviewed, and his opinion on "the credibility of negro witnesses", were characterized by a common sense humanity. He cited the case of a woman (*not* brought forward by the JC's counsel) whose evidence had been much ridiculed by the pro-Eyre forces. This woman, Sarah Robinson, had come before the Commission on her own initiative to tell about the execution of her husband and his brother. Under examination "she became excited, and began to speak of the soldiers killing babies, and to repeat a story which was current, but without the least foundation, of a woman in labour having been shot in her own house, as if she had seen it herself". When she was taken by Commissioner Gurney to Morant Bay, she admitted that she had no first hand knowledge of any such atrocities. This episode was seized on by the Jamaican *Colonial Standard*, not only as 'proof' of the complete unreliability of testimony from uneducated blacks, but as the inevitable result of the JC's agitation. In some districts, this newspaper claimed, the blacks believed that they would be compensated at four shillings a stripe and large sums to each relative of an executed man; hence "Quashie will swear to anything at all". But as Gorrie pointed out, the fact that Sarah Robinson's husband and brother-in-law had been executed, and that she had been compelled to watch (a standard practice during martial law), was abundantly proven. "Although it is very wrong of a negro woman to go crazy over the hanging of her husband, it occurs to me that any party which strives to base a doctrine on such an event is about as much to be pitied as the unfortunate woman herself." Despite exaggeration by witnesses for both sides – only to be expected granted the large numbers testifying and the nature of the enquiry – "all the leading acts of atrocity deposed to by the negroes were substantially corroborated by the evidence of the officers, or the white and coloured inhabitants".[14]

Though Gorrie came to understand something of the injustice and oppression faced by the black peasants and labourers of St Thomas, and to appreciate even if only dimly the frustrations which had driven some of them to the violent action at Morant Bay on October 11, he made it clear that he had no sympathy with armed resistance to authority or murderous attacks on individuals, whatever the provocation. He described the way in which the men fleeing from the burning Court House were beaten and hacked to death as "inhuman in the last degree" and "barbarous", "a work of destruction and blood [such as] in all countries and in all times must be put down and punished as sternly as the law allows". This was unequivocal; and the JC's counsel had been carefully instructed that they should do nothing to give the impression that they wished to shield actual murderers and rebels from justice. Gorrie never questioned the justice of executing known rebel leaders like Paul Bogle, though he did express his admiration for Bogle's courage at his end and he noted that everyone at Morant Bay spoke well of him as a prosperous farmer and local religious leader; everyone except "that bitter vestry set to whom he was opposed and to whom a prosperous nigger is an offence". In general, Gorrie argued that the rising at Morant Bay was a strictly local fracas of no great significance except for its unfortunate consequences. There is no doubt that he failed to grasp some of the dimensions of the rebellion and that, as a result, he downplayed its meaning and importance. It certainly was not what Eyre and his planter allies thought it was; but it was more than a purely local squabble which happened to turn violent.[15]

The events surrounding the riot and reprisals naturally preoccupied Gorrie while he was in Jamaica, but he took every opportunity to inform himself on some of the wider issues which, he recognized, lay behind the rising. On several occasions, he cross-examined witnesses to the Commission about wages and working conditions on the estates, trying to bring out the very common practice of docking wages for work which, it was claimed, was improperly done, and of paying them late and irregularly. He also recognized that the kind of justice which was dispensed to ordinary Jamaicans was a key cause of the rebellion. Impressive testimony by Allan Ker, a Jamaican judge, confirmed his earlier view that the system of unpaid planter-magistrates was a disaster and that the labourers of St Thomas had no confidence whatever in the administration of justice. Ker stated that at least half of the 270 JPs in the island were, in his judgement, quite unfit for the office. Moreover, it was so costly and difficult to appeal from the magistrates' courts that this form of redress was effectively beyond the reach of the ordinary Jamaican. "From very long experience", Ker said, "I have become convinced that if one thing is of more importance than another in dealing with a most ignorant and helpless population, it is to make the law of redress extremely simple" – advice which was to be confirmed again and again in Gorrie's subsequent career as a colonial judge. C.S. Roundell, secretary to the Commission, was correct when he wrote: "If any defect was conclusively established by the inquiry in Jamaica, it was the need of a stipendiary magistracy." In several of his colonial postings, Gorrie would encounter the problem of planter-magistrates dispensing doubtful justice to their own employees or tenants who belonged to a different race and culture to their own. It seems fair to conclude that his experiences in Jamaica early in 1866 strongly influenced his thinking about the administration of justice in plantation colonies where whites dominated nonwhite labourers, and he would often recall them in his subsequent career.[16]

The Commission sat over a period of 51 days, examined 730 witnesses of whom no less than 49,158 questions were asked, and eventually issued a report which, with the evidence and appendices, consisted of 1,162 closely printed folio pages. None could fault their industry or thoroughness. In his reports to the *Morning Star*, Gorrie warmly praised the Commissioners for their immense efforts, and Storks in particular for his patience and fairness as chairman. He noted that the Jamaican creole posed great difficulties for the Commissioners and for all the lawyers from Britain; the women, in particular, tended to get excited while giving evidence and to speak very rapidly. But the Commissioners had shown immense patience in extracting the truth from uneducated and simple people whose sufferings, combined with the awe they felt for the Commission and its trappings (it met in the Legislative chambers), often overwhelmed them. In their anxiety to hear everyone who had something to say, the Commissioners decided to split up; while Storks and J.B. Maule remained in Spanish Town, Gurney proceeded to St Thomas, along with Gorrie. At Manchioneal, near Bath, Gurney was obliged to hold a session in the ruins of the courthouse (it was one of the few buildings destroyed by the rioters). Gorrie described, to his readers at home, how "unable to get a spot for his briefs to rest on, because of the destruction caused by his clients at the moment of their folly, [he] laid them at his feet, and was subjected to the penance of all manner of draughts from all possible quarters through the paneless and frameless windows".[17]

The Commission's report was, with some reservations, acceptable to the JC and its supporters, and its conclusions were all the more weighty because its members were by no means men who might be expected to be hard on the authorities. So far as the reprisals were concerned, it concluded:

> . . . that by the continuance of martial law in its full force to the extreme limit of its statutory operation the people were deprived for longer than the necessary period of the great constitutional privileges by which the security of life and property is provided for. Lastly, that the punishments inflicted were excessive: 1. That the punishment of death was unnecessarily frequent. 2. That the floggings were reckless, and at Bath positively barbarous. 3. That the burning of 1,000 houses was wanton and cruel.

The *Morning Star* argued that, on the key issues, "the views originally adopted and insisted on by this journal have been emphatically borne out by the conclusions of the Commissioners, none of whom has ever been suspected of favouring the political principles which we advocate".[18]

Predictably, Gorrie's activities in Jamaica, both as counsel for the JC and as newspaper reporter, were strongly criticized by the pro-planter and pro-Eyre forces in the island. His identity as the *Morning Star*'s 'Special Commissioner' was an open secret both in Britain and Jamaica. His brother Daniel, in far-away Orkney, told him: "It seems to have leaked out somehow that you were the writer of the *Star* correspondence so that the attempts at disguise were not very successful." In Jamaica, no one doubted it. The local newspapers supportive of the planter interest, which had taken the line that Eyre had saved the colony from destruction and the white population from massacre or rape, found him to be a useful target. As Gorrie told his readers, his early despatches describing the horrors of the martial law period, especially the second one which he had headlined "Reign of Terror in Jamaica", had given great offence in the island; "the squalid ruffians of the planter press were especially exercised about it".[19]

The *Colonial Standard*, in particular, devoted an extraordinary amount of its columns in February and March 1866 to vituperative attacks on the 'Special Commissioner'. Its editor predictably made great capital of Gorrie's dual role as counsel for the JC and newspaper reporter. He advised the British public to discount Gorrie's 'Nancy stories' got up from hearsay, "especially as Mr Gorrie joins to the character of correspondent that of an advocate feed to uphold one side of the case". The *Colonial Standard* made a point of praising the 'able' and 'balanced' reports from the other British journalists covering the Commission's proceedings, and expressed its confidence that "whatever the negrophilists do, we are certain the British public as a whole will attach the proper value to the letters of these correspondents".[20]

Nothing infuriated the *Colonial Standard* more than Gorrie's piece "Reign of Terror", which Daniel wrote had "made a sensation" in Britain. Several editorials were devoted to this article alone. The paper's "London Correspondent" assured readers that "in literary circles in London, [Gorrie's] latest letter has caused no end of fun", but its editor clearly was not amused. Why had Gorrie ("we may as well call the mysterious 'Special' by his right name") not brought before the Commission the pathetic people who "crowded his verandah" with their horror stories? "Every line [in the article] almost expresses a falsehood, and it is impracticable to refute all . . . We cannot imagine that anyone, except Mr CHAMEROVZOW could feel otherwise than ashamed of owning belief in such absurd stories."[21] But Jamaica's leading 'liberal' paper, the *Morning Journal*, tried to defend Gorrie as well as the JC from these attacks. It published over four issues the "Reign of Terror" piece, which it called "able"; interestingly, its editor made no attempt to deny that its author was also the senior counsel for the JC. The *Morning Journal* believed that all the attacks on Gorrie stemmed from his determination to expose evils and uncover truth, a determination which could only be "hateful" to the "governing and propertied classes" of the island.[22]

The *Colonial Standard* bade farewell to Gorrie in a pleasant little spoof:

> Our Own Dear Special 'Morning Star'
> Twinkle, Twinkle, little Morning Star
>
> We learn with deep regret, that Concealer Gorrie, exhausted and regularly 'used up' from his sport among the 'Black Game' of Jamaica, returns in the next Mail Steamer. 'Joy be with him', and may Britannia rule the waves straight during his worthy Exporter's voyage . . . NB Trade mark, 'a Gull with a spoon in his beak'.[23]

During the four months that Gorrie spent in Jamaica, he was able to travel around the island to some extent, and he took an interest in Jamaican life as a whole. One or two trips into the countryside brought him into contact with rural Jamaicans; he found them to be good-humoured peasants delighted to talk with any friendly 'buckra', "absurdly and childishly loyal" to Britain. "And these are the people some of the terror-mongers of Jamaica would have us believe are ready to kill us all for the sheer love of the thing!" – so much so that "it has become fashionable with Jamaican persons of the official or planter class to carry revolvers". Gorrie understood that wages were at the root of the agrarian problem in Jamaica, at least so far as the estate labourers were concerned. The mountain settlers, who cultivated their own land, were more concerned with land issues, and with problems like the impounding of their stock by estate owners. Gorrie thought that the blacks of the St Andrew hills around Kingston were as well off as the 'lower orders' of the British or European agrarian population, and might become independent and prosperous, a prospect "by no means relished by many of the white people" to whom "a well to do negro is a standing offence". This attitude explained the island's tax regime, based on the "Lay the tax on Quashie" principle: "Quashie can stand it". The planters wanted the blacks "to remain landless, moneyless, horseless, and hopeless, in order that they may devote themselves for 9d or 1s a day to the cultivation of the estates". But the mountain settlers, more independent than the resident labourers, resisted; they began to feel "the spirit of a free citizen" and could not be held in "modified slavery": "Given sugar on the one side, and freedom on the other, I prefer to back freedom as the winner." Indeed, the events of 1865 would merely hasten the end of "the old sugar party, with all their semi-slaveholder notions of the Divine right in white men to govern black men wrongly".[24]

Gorrie recognized, too, that the administration of justice by planter-magistrates was one of the fundamental reasons for the alienation of rural blacks from the authorities. He saw that "it is absolutely necessary, as a first step to the regeneration of Jamaica, that a clean sweep be made of the bench of justice". He also recognized the need for fundamental constitutional change; he believed that the 'old class' of administrators who had run the island were prejudiced, inefficient, ignorant of the people they ruled. "Under the new Constitution it is to be hoped that the Council will be composed of the best men of all parties, and that the energies of the Government will be directed more to roads and bridges than to the erection of the gallows and the wielding of the cat."[25] Ironically, it was Eyre who exploited widespread fears of black insurrection immediately after Morant Bay and persuaded the House of Assembly to abolish itself, clearing the way for the introduction of crown colony government early in 1866. The governor who succeeded Storks was able, under the new constitutional arrangements, to sweep away some of the most flagrant abuses in the island's administrative and judicial system.

Reaction in Britain

Gorrie left Jamaica on 24 March 1866, arriving in London by the middle of April. As newspaper reporter and editorial writer, as polemicist and strategist for the JC, and occasionally as witness in court, he was actively involved in the efforts to prosecute Eyre and some of the military officers who served under him, efforts which began as soon as the Commission's report was published (June 1866) and continued into 1868.[26]

As soon as he returned, he briefed the JC on his work in the island. Chesson recorded in his diary:

> In afternoon attended JC meeting – Chas Buxton in the Chair . . . The meeting was held to meet Mr Gorrie who for an hour and a half passed through a running fire of questions and produced a most favourable impression. Mr Bright urged Mr Buxton to move for the production of all the Naval and Military despatches. I moved a resolution requesting Mr Gorrie to prepare a report with a view to its being printed, the precise mode of its publication being postponed as one part of the Committee in favour of a semi public meeting; while Mr Buxton thought that the report should be simply printed and circulated.

Later Chesson noted that the JC was "completely crippled as regards funds" because the "Jamaica lawyers bill has taken up all our reserves". Gorrie also briefed the Freedman's Aid Society in London, a body which had very close links to the men who formed the JC.[27]

Once the conclusions of the report became known, the JC had to decide how to proceed, and it was divided; one group felt that the Commission's condemnation of the excesses of the repression, and the recall of Eyre, were sufficient, while the militants wanted to prosecute him and others for murder. Buxton headed the first group, while Mill and Bright were the leaders of the second. Chesson's diary makes it clear that Gorrie took an active part in the special meeting of the JC which rejected Buxton's view and opted for prosecution. In July 1866, the House of Commons debated the issue; no fewer than 19 MPs, including Mill and Buxton, sat on the JC. Buxton's speech was especially effective precisely because he had broken with the militants of the JC; though he opposed prosecuting Eyre for murder, he wanted a clear Parliamentary censure of his conduct as proof to the nation and the world that England did not sanction such acts of illegality as had occurred in the repression. He, Mill, Thomas Hughes and W.E. Forster stressed the paramount need for Parliament to demonstrate unequivocally that no agents of the Queen were above the law; it was a question of the rule of law as against the arbitrary exercise of force. In a compromise move, a resolution deploring the excessive punishments was unanimously carried. In the Lords, the new Secretary of State (Carnarvon) said that Eyre had revealed fatal flaws as a governor; he had shown an inability to rise above the panic of the hour. The leaders of both Parliamentary parties, and Buxton, hoped that these events would defuse the JC's agitation for criminal prosecutions.[28]

This was not to be. Under Mill's leadership, the JC pressed forward to secure criminal indictments against Eyre. Its membership increased to over 800, with prominent new recruits joining, including Charles Lyell, Charles Darwin and T.F. Huxley, England's leading men of science. The JC publicly appealed for funds to meet the costs of a prosecution, explaining that it was the government's failure to do its duty which made it necessary to proceed with a private action. Public subscriptions were organized to meet the heavy expenses of bringing witnesses from Jamaica and supporting them in England, as well as legal costs.[29]

The *Morning Star* fully supported Mill and the 'militants' of the JC in their decision to prosecute Eyre for murder, and so did Gorrie, who had a thorough knowledge of all the facts surrounding the Gordon case. In September 1866 he wrote a letter under his own name criticizing the Marquis of Lorne's assertion (in a letter published in the *Daily Telegraph)* that Eyre's transfer of

Gordon to Morant Bay was done "on the stress of the moment". Lorne, who had visited Jamaica early in 1866, had concluded that Eyre had acted wrongly but in good faith: "No one can help being very sorry for him. He did what he thought his duty, and has avoided no responsibility." This was the view of many in Britain who believed nevertheless that Gordon's execution was wrong and the reprisals excessive. But in a detailed account of events, Gorrie showed that Eyre was fully aware that all resistance had ended by October 17, when Gordon was arrested in Kingston by the governor himself, and had been specifically cautioned by the head of the Executive Committee that the detainee should not be tried by a Morant Bay court martial. On October 20, at which date the governor informed the Secretary of State that the rebellion was 'crushed', he handed Gordon over to General Nelson to stand trial, in full knowledge that the court would be presided over by a young and totally inexperienced naval officer. Nelson delayed execution in order to secure the governor's approval, which was duly given after reading the notes of the so-called trial. "It was a cool, deliberate, well pondered deed." Lorne had referred to Eyre's characterization of Gordon as an immoral man as only reflecting the general view in Jamaica. Even if this was true, argued Gorrie, it could have no bearing on the illegality of his execution. In a courteous private letter to Gorrie, Lorne stood by his assertion that many in Jamaica who had known Gordon, including men "of his own colour", disapproved of his moral character, "whatever may have been their opinion of his complicity in the disturbances". "You and I will not agree upon the subject", Lorne told Gorrie, but to say that all the doubts about Gordon were false was "to speak rather too dogmatically", a justified rebuke.[30]

With Eyre's return to Britain in August 1866, the whole controversy entered a new stage; his friends established a formal body, the Eyre Defence Committee (EDC), to counter the JC. Its leading intellectuals were Thomas Carlyle, John Ruskin and Charles Kingsley. Carlyle, probably the leading British man of letters of the day, found all his great principles caught up in the Eyre controversy, and all his pet hates (democracy, radicalism, mob rule, lily-livered philanthropy and 'nigger-lovers', the industrial middle classes) somehow ranged against the ex-governor, a natural hero and upholder of order. No wonder he denounced, in a famous essay, the British government "who, instead of rewarding their Governor Eyre, throw him out of the window to a small loud group, small as now appears, and nothing but a group or knot of rabid Nigger-Philanthropists, barking furiously in the gutter". The *Morning Star* took him on in a spirited article written rather cleverly in a tone of grieving admiration for a great writer now revealing unexpected obtuseness. Hero-worship was noble, when the object was noble; "but when this worship became a blind idolatry of force", one must pause. But Carlyle was unquestionably the intellectual giant of the whole pro-Eyre movement, and his ideas "of governing minds, and superior races, and the right of strong men, and all the rest of the nonsense which he once made fascinating", as Justin McCarthy recalled many years later, lay behind it.[31]

The JC always insisted that the great issues which impelled them to prosecute Eyre were legal and constitutional; they centered around the question of martial law in the British system. This was the subject of Frederick Harrison's six letters to the *Daily News* (1867), later published as one of the JC's pamphlets. He argued that:

> English law is of that kind, that, if you play fast and loose with it, it vanishes . . . What is done in a colony today may be done in Ireland tomorrow, and in England hereafter . . . The precise issue we raise is this, that throughout our empire the British rule shall be the rule of law; that every British citizen, white, brown, or black in skin, shall be subject to definite, and not to indefinite powers.

Victorian wars against native peoples, and the Indian Mutiny, had corrupted the Army; in a striking phrase, he argued that they had "called out the tiger in our race . . . That wild beast must be caged again". C.S. Roundell made much the same point when he wrote that the Mutiny had engendered "the military spirit" among the English, of which the "first-fruits [were] the red anarchy of Jamaica martial law". Pride of race and of birth bred, among Englishmen in India and the colonies, a "caste-like spirit" which made possible terrible outrages against common humanity like those which occurred during the reprisals in India in 1857-58 and in Jamaica in 1865.[32]

The Jamaica case forced Britons to confront their deep-seated racial fears and prejudices. The middle decades of the century saw a deepening of racist thought in Britain and Europe targeted at all nonwhite peoples but especially at those of African origin. The earlier humanitarian enthusiasm for blacks as men and brothers waned, and pseudo-scientific racism became increasingly respectable in academic circles and filtered down to reinforce popular prejudices. The older liberal (if deeply paternalist) views on race were still held by many in the 1860s, but the 'harder' line was becoming more widespread among the upper and middle classes. As Harrison and Roundell had seen, constant 'little wars' against native peoples and especially the Indian Mutiny had contributed to this cluster of attitudes; and the events in Jamaica in 1865, coming so soon after the end of the American Civil War which saw the abolition of slavery in the South and which had itself divided the British political and intellectual elites, played their role in this development. For those already convinced of the innate inferiority of blacks, Morant Bay provided welcome confirmation. *The Times*, speaking no doubt for the great bulk of the upper and middle classes, editorialized with melancholy satisfaction: "It seems impossible, to eradicate the original savageness of the African blood . . . Whenever he attains to a certain degree of independence there is the fear that he will resume the barbarous life and the fierce habits of his African ancestors." Eyre himself, in a public speech in Kingston, described Jamaican blacks as "an ignorant and excitable population, in many respects little removed from savages".[33]

Supporters of the JC, many of them men long active in the antislavery cause and more recently in the movement to help American freedmen, saw from the start that contempt for darker-skinned peoples led inevitably to an acceptance of harsh and illegal measures taken against them by colonial officials, an acceptance that could slide into a positive enthusiasm for such measures (Harrison's "tiger in our race"). The *Morning Star* tried to place the events in Jamaica in a wider perspective:

> Much of the revolting levity with which 'niggers' are spoken of by military and naval men is doubtless due to the Indian mutiny. The deeds then perpetrated were too frequently applauded . . . and a desire to emulate the 'vigour' of those dark days seems to have entered into the thoughts of some of our officers in Jamaica. The proclamation of martial law was regarded as the abolition of all justice and mercy and the inauguration of a carnival of blood

– as had happened in India. The forces which gathered around the EDC naturally exploited deepseated British fears and prejudices about blacks in order to present their hero in a sympathetic light. No one did so with more authority than the scientist John Tyndall, who declared:

> I decline accepting the negro as the equal of the Englishman, nor will I commit myself to the position that a negro and an English insurrection ought to be treated in the same way . . . We do not hold an Englishman and a Jamaica negro to be convertible terms.

The *Morning Star* recognized that men who supported Eyre might cherish in all sincerity a conviction that blacks were subhuman; men holding such views would naturally "pardon Eyre because his error of judgement involves only negro blood, what would have otherwise been in our nation's eyes simply unpardonable".[34]

Actions in the Courts

In February 1867 the JC began to proceed in the English courts against General Nelson, Lieut. Brand and Eyre himself, and for the next year and a half these actions slowly worked their way through the legal system. Gorrie almost certainly wrote the lengthy reports which appeared in the *Morning Star*, as well as some if not all of the editorial articles on the cases; on one occasion he was called as a witness. But he did not appear as counsel for the JC (the prosecutors) since he had never been called to the English Bar.

The JC moved first against Nelson and Brand for the murder of Gordon because they (unlike Eyre) were residing in London and therefore under the jurisdiction of a Middlesex Grand Jury. The opening scene took place at the Bow Street court of the London chief magistrate, where applications for warrants against Nelson and Brand for murder were sought by Mill and Taylor of the JC, who acted as the private prosecutors. J.F. Stephen appeared for the JC, with Gorrie's colleague in Jamaica, Payne. Stephen set the tone for the prosecution from the outset when he told the court that the case was not brought "in any petty, party, or personal spirit towards the gentlemen . . . We wish to obtain a decision from the highest court in the land on a question affecting the lives and liberties of the people": whether Gordon was not killed in a "criminal violation of the English law". The chief magistrate issued warrants, and both men were charged with murder and given bail, after Stephen had made it clear that the prosecution had no wish to inflict any "personal indignity".[35]

A preliminary hearing on the murder charges attracted considerable excitement as large crowds tried to secure a seat in court and others milled around outside to get a glimpse of the accused. Stephen emphasized: "This is a legal not a moral inquiry, and all that can be said in a court of law is as to the legal character of the acts done." The core of his argument was concerned with the proper use of martial law, which he insisted was legal only as

> a military power used for the suppression of a revolt . . . Repression is legal – punishment, not necessary for repression, is illegal. It is legal to put a man to death to put down a rebellion; it is illegal to punish a man for his conduct, which may have contributed to that rebellion.

This definition of the limits of martial law formed the cornerstone of the JC's case against Nelson, Brand and Eyre with respect to Gordon's death. Despite efforts by the defence counsel to ridicule the whole prosecution as "a solemn and serious farce" designed only to extract from the magistrate "some statement which might be used to affect the trial of another person [Eyre]", the chief magistrate committed Nelson and Brand to stand their trial for Gordon's murder at the next sessions of the Central Criminal Court.[36]

With Nelson and Brand committed for trial, attention focused on Eyre. On the advice of the EDC and its solicitors, he had settled in rural Shropshire and avoided even brief visits to London where he would have come under the jurisdiction of the Bow Street magistracy. Eyre's behaviour, as the *Morning Star* pointed out, was hardly consistent with the moral heroism claimed for him by his admirers; at first, he had insisted on his sole responsibility for all the acts committed under martial law, but now he evaded it by staying "in the heart of a Tory County, where the great unpaid [*ie* JPs] would dismiss the application for a committal and any grand jury would ignore a bill against him". Nevertheless, the JC determined to apply for a murder warrant at the next petty sessions at Market Drayton, the town closest to Eyre's rural retreat.

Towards the end of March 1867 a small army of London lawyers, celebrities of the JC, witnesses (at least one of them black) and journalists descended on the little town. One was Gorrie, the *Morning Star*'s 'Special Reporter' at Market Drayton. Seeking to assess the state of public opinion among these "agrarian, nonpolitical people", he gathered that the citizens held Eyre personally in high respect because he was a friend of the local magnate in whose house he was living. "These rather primitive people", he wrote with all the condescending scorn of an Edinburgh man and an enemy of the squirarchy, could not believe in Eyre's guilt: "Why if Mr Eyre did anything so bad, sir, he wouldn't be up at the Hall."[37]

On the morning when the warrant was applied for and issued (Eyre did not appear), many of the local ladies arrived in splendid outfits to watch the proceedings and the courtroom was packed with the favoured (the lower orders were carefully excluded, according to Gorrie; his reports of the progress of the case at Market Drayton were lively and frankly partisan). The warrant was duly issued, and it was served at 'the Hall' under a special arrangement with the bench to ensure that Eyre would not be taken into custody, an arrangement clearly viewed with disgust by the Special Reporter. Preliminary hearings were then held before a bench of Shropshire magistrates to determine whether Eyre would be committed for trial. Stephen spoke for nearly five hours, but they refused to commit the ex-governor. When the decision was announced, church bells began to ring, and "the indecency of the bell-ringing" continued to a late hour.[38]

The *Morning Star* gave full vent to its sense of injustice and frustration. Not only would the episode totally discredit the administration of justice by unpaid and unprofessional local squires: "No living being will believe that Mr Eyre is innocent of the grave charges made against him because a bench of country justices . . . have declined to commit him." The proceedings at Market Drayton lasted for several days, the speeches of opposing counsel alone took eleven hours; yet the learned justices needed exactly fifteen minutes to decide on the weighty questions involved.

> Perhaps there never was a greater caricature of justice . . . The whole affair was a drawing-room performance, before a select audience, with a pre-arranged dénouement . . . To leave game-preserving squires to try

> poachers is anomalous enough, but to leave it in the power of blind and bigoted partisans to say whether or not a foul political murder shall be inquired into is going beyond the toleration of any civilised community.

The similarity in attitude and behaviour between the Jamaican planter-magistrates and these Shropshire gentry JPs must have struck Gorrie forcibly. Back in London, he wrote to the *Morning Star* under his own name rehearsing yet again the circumstances surrounding Gordon's death.

> And this is a case which five Shropshire justices refuse to allow to go to a jury, which has occasioned pious appeals to the Almighty by a Market Drayton clergyman, and set the bells a-ringing! As has been truly said, if it had only been a rabbit which had been unlawfully put to death, an inquiry would not have been refused.[39]

The events at Market Drayton meant that Eyre could not be prosecuted for murder. But the *Morning Star* pointed out that one other way to bring him to justice remained: to charge him under the Colonial Governors' Acts. These Acts provided for trials of governors only for misdemeanours; but cases under them would be tried by the Court of Queen's Bench without the need for a magistrate's committal. This was to be the procedure adopted by the JC, although some supporters had their doubts, and Stephen himself, who disapproved of any further action against Eyre, withdrew from the case.[40]

In April 1867 the JC won an important victory when the Lord Chief Justice, Sir Alexander Cockburn, personally delivered a lengthy charge to a Middlesex Grand Jury in the case of *Q* vs *Nelson and Brand* for Gordon's murder. This was an authoritative exposition of martial law in the English legal system. He argued that the law of England knew no such thing as martial law and that Gordon had been sentenced on evidence which was inadmissable both according to the rules of ordinary civil law and those of military law. His conclusions were much the same as those expressed by Stephen in the original legal opinion to the JC and those articulated by Harrison in his *Six Letters on Martial Law*. Supporters of the JC were jubilant, and the *Morning Star* believed that the charge vindicated the decision to proceed with private prosecutions in order to secure this kind of authoritative statement of the law. Cockburn had established once and for all that there was no power in martial law to try and punish civilians.[41] In the following month, Cockburn published an 'authorized' version of his charge along with additional explanatory notes and a statement at the end of the text in which he protested "with whatever of weight and authority belongs to the office I have the honour to hold, against the execution of martial law in the form in which it has lately been put in force". He insisted that Gordon's trial had been a travesty of the justice and fair play due to the worst criminal: "All I can say is that if, on martial law being proclaimed, a man can lawfully be thus tried, condemned, and sacrificed, such a state of things is a scandal and a reproach to the institutions of this great and free country". The *Morning Star* thought that by publishing the charge, Cockburn had "performed a public service only second in importance to the original delivery of the charge itself".[42]

The charge was a serious setback to the pro-Eyre forces even though Eyre himself was safe from a murder trial. In a famous essay, Carlyle denounced the charge as beneath contempt. And on the whole, Carlyle's view was more acceptable to the propertied classes in Britain than Cockburn's. The Middlesex Grand Jury chose to ignore a charge from the country's highest judge which virtually demanded an indictment for murder. Instead they threw out the bill, though they did recommend "that the martial law should be more clearly defined by legislative enactment". Nelson and Brand were discharged. The JC found consolation in the fact that they had secured an authoritative ruling that Gordon's death was illegal and unjustifiable, and decided to proceed against Eyre under the Colonial Governors' Acts. They first attempted to get the government to prosecute Eyre under the Acts for illegalities committed during the repression. Predictably, the Attorney-General (in a Conservative Government) declined to file a criminal information against Eyre under the Acts. This meant that it would have to be a private prosecution.[43]

When Eyre finally came to London early in 1868, the JC swung into action, reviving a public controversy which had faded somewhat over the previous months. Their new counsel appeared before a Bow Street magistrate seeking a summons against Eyre on charges under the Colonial Governors' Acts. These charges – misdemeanours – were for issuing an illegal proclamation of martial law and acts done under it; and for proceeding against persons residing in nonproclaimed districts. After lengthy legal manoeuvres, in May 1868 preliminary hearings took place at Bow Street for Eyre's committal under the new charges. Gorrie was summoned as a witness as "a barrister of the Jamaica bar" (he had been specially admitted to the island bar while he was there). He gave evidence that volumes produced by the prosecution were statutes of Jamaica for the last 200 years; he also answered a question about the organization of judicial districts in the island. Recalled on a subsequent day, he deposed that the statutes of Jamaica had the force of law from the time of their enactment until vetoed by the Crown; if they were neither confirmed nor vetoed they would continue to have the force of law. Other questions to which he responded related to acts of indemnity in Jamaica, Jamaican acts authorizing the governor to issue special commissions, and the office of Provost Marshal. Several Jamaicans appeared for the prosecution, brought to England by the JC. Counsel for Eyre took the line that the prosecution was undertaken merely out of "malign spite . . . to degrade a high-minded and honourable gentleman, a faithful public servant, by dragging him forward upon a criminal charge", but was ordered to desist by the magistrate, and then rested the defence on the assertion that Eyre "by his admirable promptitude, justice, and wisdom, had saved a valuable colony, and preserved the lives of all the respectable inhabitants of the island, whether white or coloured".[44]

The magistrate committed Eyre for trial and set bail at £1000. The ex-governor, breaking his long silence, made a moving little speech to the effect that the disgrace would fall on his prosecutors

> that a man who had served his country faithfully for 26 years . . . was now, after two years and a half of wearing and most rancorous persecution, about to be committed to a felon's dock, for having discharged his duty faithfully . . . saving indubitably a great British colony from ruin, and the people from massacre, or worse than massacre. He did not envy the feelings of those who, conspiring to ruin a public officer, now, at last, succeed in bringing this additional stigma upon him, but he did rejoice in believing that they formed but a very small section of the community.

He sat down to "tumultuous applause". There can be no doubt that his assessment of the state of opinion among the respectable classes was accurate. Clearly sensitive on this point, the *Morning Star* defended the JC's actions and motives against the allegations both of Eyre and of his counsel, and criticized the ex-governor for his "impassioned language". The magistrate had only done his duty: the evidence made a trial necessary, "for the honour of the country and the vindication of humanity and justice".[45]

The last act in the long drawn-out legal drama took place in June 1868 in the Court of the Queen's Bench before Justice Colin Blackburn. In a lengthy charge, Blackburn in effect argued that all Eyre's acts including Gordon's execution were undertaken in the genuine belief that they were necessary to save Jamaica and so could not be regarded as illegal. It was a charge which encouraged the Grand Jury to throw out the bill, and this they duly did. Eyre was free, and the JC had failed to bring him to trial.[46]

The supporters of the JC must have anticipated this outcome, and there seems little doubt that Eyre had acted out of a sincere (if misguided) belief that the safety of Jamaica required savage reprisals and Gordon's death. But the *Morning Star* expressed their sense of disappointment and frustration: "On the one side we have a catalogue of foul murders, such as cannot be surpassed by anything in modern history . . . on the other, the infallible grand jury with their NO BILL." These crimes would never be submitted to a British jury in open court. A letter to the editor signed "Jurist", which reads as if it was by Gorrie, argued that Blackburn's charge "blew away with a few breaths the legal privileges which the people of Jamaica have struggled to maintain for 200 years" and ignored the island's constitutional history, especially the fact that since 1728 Jamaicans had enjoyed all the rights of Englishmen including the great constitutional guarantees.[47]

Immediately after the Grand Jury threw out the bill, Eyre wrote to *The Times*: "Confident in my own integrity, and believing that truth would ultimately prevail, I have submitted in silence to the malignant and monstrous calumnies and misrepresentations by which I have been so unscrupulously assailed during two years of unceasing and most rancorous persecution." Now, two judicial tribunals, and a Grand Jury, had thrown out all the charges against him, a verdict which "will be endorsed and re-echoed by the large majority of my fellow-countrymen of all classes and politics". This was too much for Gorrie, who wrote in reply that:

> as Mr Eyre has written a letter to *The Times* assuming the airs of a martyr over his prosecution, I suppose we may all now consider ourselves unmuzzled by the failure of the criminal trial, and are free to appeal to that public opinion which Mr Eyre claims to be on his side.

Gorrie asserted that far from merely proclaiming martial law and leaving its implementation to the military, the ex-governor personally directed operations from the very first execution. Eyre, Gorrie charged, knew all about the atrocities committed under martial law; he pushed through an Act of the island legislature confiscating the provision grounds of the 'rebels', gardens which "alone were left to support the widows and children. When I arrived in Kingston, in the beginning of January 1866, the poor people came down in scores to say they were living in the woods without shelter, and with only such wild fruit for food as they had in common with the fowls of the air". Not until the news spread that Eyre had been suspended from office did they "gradually creep back to their ruined settlements".[48]

With the failure of the attempt to bring Eyre to trial, the leaders of the JC formally announced that their campaign was at an end. One further defeat lay ahead. Just before Eyre's case reached the Grand Jury, one of his supporters, a West Indian proprietor and MP named Lamont, presented a petition to the Commons calling for Eyre's reinstatement in the public service. It was claimed that this petition had been signed by over 30,000 people including peers, MPs, bishops and clergymen, generals and admirals, but later it became clear that under 11,000 had signed. Eyre was not reinstated, and here the matter rested until 1872, when a motion calling on the government (now a Liberal ministry under Gladstone which included former members of the JC) to defray all his legal expenses was debated in the House. Peter Taylor made a moving defence of the JC's motives and actions and urged the House not to sully itself with a 'contemptible vote' in Eyre's favour; but the motion was passed by a vote of 243 to 130. And in 1875 the new Disraeli government agreed to grant Eyre a 'second-class pension' as a 'retired', instead of dismissed, colonial governor.[49]

Gorrie's intimate involvement with the Jamaica case was not confined to his work for the *Morning Star* nor to his activities while in the island. In 1867 his lengthy pamphlet (over 100 pages) "Illustrations of Martial Law in Jamaica" was published as the sixth in a series of *Jamaica Papers* put out by the JC. Chesson had urged him to write this book and had arranged for its publication. It marshalled a great deal of material from the evidence presented to the Commission on the atrocities committed during the reprisals and on the Gordon case, and it demonstrates Gorrie's ability to synthesize a great mass of evidence, to argue a case forcibly, and to write in a lively style even on tragic events. He explained in the preface that the Commission's report

> while entering very minutely into the misdeeds of the negroes, and at a length which raises into a false importance the disturbances which occurred, scarcely touches, in its narrative portion, the incidents of the suppression . . . At the request of the Jamaica Committee . . . I have endeavoured to supply this information. I have tried to bring together under appropriate heads bits of evidence which lie scattered promiscuously about the pages of the bulky volume of evidence, or which are lost in the confused pages of the Blue Books.

On the whole he succeeded admirably; his pamphlet is a valuable guide to the massive volume of evidence on all matters related to the repression of the rising. It ends with this statement:

> My task has not been undertaken in vain if it tends to deepen the resolve of my countrymen to resist at all hazards the preposterous pretensions of colonial Governors and military officers, to deal with human life and property as they please, without responsibility to the laws which bind society together, or to the Nation which places the sword in their hands for the purposes of justice and mercy.[50]

Gorrie and the Jamaica Case

The JC failed to bring Eyre or any of his subordinates to trial for crimes committed during the reprisals of October/November 1865, and it is clear that it also failed to persuade the vast majority of the propertied classes in

Britain that these men had done anything unjust or illegal granted the circumstances which they faced at the time. In assessing their achievements and their defeats, the leaders of the movement concluded that they had, nevertheless, won important gains for the cause of justice, and one feels sure that Gorrie shared this view. J.S. Mill, Peter Taylor and Justin McCarthy, for instance, reflecting many years later on the movement, all argued that their efforts had made impossible the recurrence of the 'killing time' of 1865 in the British empire. "Never again in a British colony", Taylor told the Commons in 1872, "shall be enacted the policy of ex-Governor Eyre, nor the world stand aghast at the atrocities of a Jamaica massacre". And McCarthy wrote: "It is almost impossible that such things could ever be done again in England's name."[51]

Of course, Mill, Taylor and McCarthy were tragically wrong in their prediction that 'never again' would events like those of 1865 sully Britain's name; there would be more 'administrative massacres' in the name of the imperial government. Yet one can hardly doubt that the JC succeeded in sending a strong signal of caution to colonial officials, and that, as Goldwin Smith put it, the controversy over Jamaica at least taught "the world, and the official world especially, that the common cause of humanity is not yet abandoned, and that if a 'nigger' is unjustly put to death in Jamaica there are those in a distant country and of another race who will call for an account of his blood".[52]

For Gorrie himself, the events in Jamaica and the public controversy which took up so much of his time and energy in the three years that followed had at least two significant results. First, they brought him to the attention of several influential men in public life, some of whom became ministers in the first Gladstone government which came to power in November 1868. Granted the structure of patronage which governed official appointments in the empire, he would have found it difficult to secure a good colonial posting without influential friends. Bright (president of the Board of Trade in the new ministry) and Storks both recommended him for the position in Mauritius which he secured in 1869.

More important, the Jamaica case helped to shape his ideas about multiracial colonial societies and about the risks and potential benefits of imperialism. Neither of these subjects was entirely new to him in 1865, but his intimate involvement in Jamaican issues forced him to rethink his positions and confronted him with some of the realities of colonial rule. He acquired an interest in West Indian affairs which he never lost; he was to spend the last decade of his life serving in that part of the world.

Several editorials in the *Morning Star* on Jamaican issues, probably written by him, illustrate what may be described as the liberal position on West Indian problems. It was recognized that the abolition of the old Assembly and the introduction of crown colony rule in Jamaica could provide the opportunity for a radical change in the island's administration and, even more urgent, in the judicial system. When Provost Marshal Ramsay was set free by a Jamaican grand jury, despite overwhelming evidence that he was guilty of an especially revolting judicial murder, the *Morning Star* called it "a huge travesty of justice" and argued that the grand juries and the unpaid planter-magistrates needed to be swept away immediately. The new governor, Sir J.P. Grant, would see from this case "the nature of the ruling caste with whom he has to deal". Later, the paper congratulated Grant on his vigorous overhauling of the police force and the courts. He had ordered that procedures in the magistrates' courts should be simplified and that appeals to higher tribunals should be made cheaper and easier, a reform Gorrie had advocated when he was in Jamaica. Grant had also secured the appointment of salaried district judges from England to take over some of the cases previously heard by unpaid and untrained planter-magistrates, perhaps the most important of all his reforms, thought the *Morning Star*, and one advocated by Storks in 1866.[53]

An interesting editorial written in 1868 was prompted by the publication of the Colonial Reports for the British West Indies for 1866. They seemed to show that these colonies were "monstrously over-governed" while great abuses still prevailed in the simplest administrative arrangements and services. Heavy taxes were needed to support an army of officials and established clergymen; each island had its own tariff and there was little inter-island trade; smallholders were heavily taxed; so was imported food eaten by the masses. "Our administration of these regions is a caricature upon government, and has been designed apparently to crush down the population with taxation, for the purpose of providing places for the genteel unemployed at home." Parliament would have to clean out "this nest of jobbery and incompetence". The *Morning Star* proposed a comprehensive scheme of reform for these colonies. Federate all the islands into two or three colonies with the smaller ones treated like parishes with one salaried magistrate and a few police to represent government; abolish the ecclesiastical establishment; consolidate the judicial and civil establishments; have a single common tariff; tax land and income and free trade entirely; link the islands by cable and steamer service, subsidized if necessary, to stimulate trade; codify the laws and make them uniform; confiscate uncultivated lands and give them to small settlers; help the people diversify their cultivation and find markets for their produce.[54]

This represents the Cobden/Bright prescription for colonies which, because of old obligations and the weight of history, Britain could not simply abandon. These ideas were to lie behind Gorrie's actions as a colonial official over the next quarter of a century. The Jamaica case had helped Gorrie to work out his views on imperialism before he took up his first colonial appointment.

CHAPTER THREE

Planters and Immigrants: Mauritius, 1869-76

Appointment to Mauritius

It was Gorrie's involvement in the Jamaica case which made him well known in London's liberal/radical circles and which brought him to the attention of the Colonial Office. He had decided to seek a colonial appointment by the start of 1869, if not before, for at that time he enlisted the support of two well-known figures: John Bright, and Sir Henry Storks of the Jamaica Royal Commission. Storks seems to have readily agreed to "drop a word" to the Secretary of State (Granville) about an appointment to Mauritius, "for which you are so well fitted". Bright, on the other hand, may have hesitated at first to lobby on behalf of his Scottish admirer, for he told Gorrie "when I see you I can tell you why I cannot interfere on your behalf on this occasion". A few months later, however, he was writing in a different strain: "I have written to Lord Granville, and have said what you would wish in your favour. I shall be sorry if you are to leave the country, and yet I should be glad to hear that the appointment had fallen to you, for the sake of your family, and for that of the population of Jamaica".[1] By the middle of 1869 the decision was made: Gorrie was appointed to the office of Substitute Procureur-General (SPG) of Mauritius, with the right of private practice. Clearly, his influential friends had dropped the right words in the right places. Granville told the Mauritius governor, Sir Henry Barkly, that Gorrie had "been represented to me as being a good French linguist and an able man". The post carried a salary of £720 p.a., low enough to make permission to carry on private practice a necessary inducement to a British lawyer. The family embarked in mid October on a steamer en route to China, and Gorrie was sworn in office on December 15, 1869.[2]

The office of SPG was Gorrie's for only a few months, however, for in September 1870 he was appointed to the Mauritius bench as third puisne judge, and judge he remained for the rest of his years on the island. Barkly had advised that Gorrie "appears to me a man of ability and discretion, and I am told is far more deeply versed in the jurisprudence of several foreign states which, like Scotland, retain the Roman law as their basis, than most of his countrymen; and as he is daily acquiring out here practical knowledge of the laws of Mauritius, the presumption certainly must be, that he is better qualified . . . than anyone" likely to accept the post for the relatively small salary of £1200. On this recommendation, the Secretary of State (now Lord Kimberley) agreed to Gorrie's appointment as third judge; he accepted the post but asked to be allowed to "reserve his claim" to the post of Procureur-General (PG) should that become vacant.[3]

At this point, the PG (Jules Colin) died. The acting governor offered the post to Gustave Colin, his brother. He explained, reasonably enough, that he needed a man "of longer colonial experience than Mr Gorrie who has only been nine months in the island"; Colin was a Creole, and an eminent lawyer, "whilst Mr Gorrie has been here too short a time for his qualities to have been generally appreciated". Never one to take apparent injustices lightly, Gorrie penned a 'respectful protest' to the acting governor against Colin's appointment as PG instead of himself: "I was entitled, almost as a matter of course, to have the acting appointment as Procureur until the pleasure of the Secretary of State was known." He then termed the appointment as objectionable on the grounds that "he is a brother of the late Procureur thus

Comoro Is.
Mozambique
MOZAMBIQUE
MADAGASCAR
Tamatave
Tananarive
Antsirabe
Tulear
INDIAN
OCEAN
Pt. Louis
Reunion (Fr.)
Mauritius (Br.)
Round I.
Flat I.
Gabriel I.
Gunners Quoin
C. Malheureux
Grand Bay
Amber I.
Poudre D'or
MONT CHOISY EMERGENCY LANDING STRIP
Arsenal Bay
Tombeau Bay
PAMPLEMOUSSES
Pamplemousses
Mapou
RIVIÈRE DU REMPART
Rivière du Rempart
Grand River N.W.
PORT LOUIS
Coromandel
Petite Riviere B.
Albion
Rosehill
Moka
Quartier Militaire
Belle Isle
Medine
Curepipe
Magenta
BLANCHE MTS
Bel Air
Trou d'Eau Douce
Tamarin Bay
Tamarin
Black River B.
Mare Longue Res.
BLACK RIV. GORGES
Midlands
BAMBOU MTS
Grand River S.E.
Mare aux Vacoas
Nouvelle France
Cluny
Mahébourg
Fouquets I. de la Passe
PLAISANCE AIRPORT
Blue Bay
Union Vale
Rose Belle
Benitiers I.
LE MORNE BRABANT 1809
Choisy
Ruisseau Créole
Baie du Cap
Chemin Grenier
Souillac
Jacotet Bay
R. des Anguilles
Brocus I.
INDIAN OCEAN
Miles
Boundaries, District
Railways
Principal Roads
Other "
Administrative Headquarters are underlined in red
Heights in Feet
57°20′
57°30′ Longitude East of Greenwich
57°40′

Mauritius

making the office a family prerequisite", that he was related to several local lawyers, magistrates and landowners, and that these connections would make it impossible for him to "exercise with the same impartiality as a stranger" the wide patronage and influence on appointments enjoyed by the PG. Moreover, "the legal profession teems with abuses which cannot strike a Creole, who has himself been mixed up with them during a long practice, in the same light as they appear to others".[4] Nevertheless, Kimberley sanctioned these arrangements; Gorrie lost the "prize" of the Mauritian legal profession, much to his "mortification", as he put it, and served on the island bench between September 1870 and March 1876.

This turn of events was to have important consequences for him. His acceptance of a seat on the Mauritius bench virtually committed him to a career in the colonial judiciary rather than in the political or administrative branch of the service. Henceforward the promotions he could look for would be to chief justiceships in colonies of ascending importance. He was, in many ways, unsuited by temperament to the bench; his enemies who described him as essentially an 'unjudicial' man were right. He was always more interested in reforming abuses and changing laws than in dispensing justice according to existing codes. A policy making, political or administrative position would have given far greater scope for his tremendous talents, his abundant energy, and his reforming zeal; this is why, in each colony where he served, he became involved in political activities. When he was in Fiji he applied at least once (unsuccessfully) for an administrative post, in New Guinea. No doubt he had come to recognize that a colonial bench was not the ideal place for a crusading reformer.

Mauritius – the former Ile de France – a small island of some 720 square miles situated 1400 miles east of the African coast and 500 miles east of Madagascar, had passed from France to Britain by conquest in 1810. The capitulation provided that "les habitans conserveront leurs Religion, Loix, et Coutumes", and over the next sixty years island society had remained essentially French. The Roman Catholic church, the French language and the French derived creole, the Napoleonic Civil Code and French legal procedures, received official sanction and remained entrenched. Very few Britons emigrated as settlers in the decades after 1810, so that the landed elite was overwhelmingly French all through the nineteenth century; their influence was preponderant, only feebly modified by the few British officials, merchants and professionals resident in the island, many of them mere 'birds of passage'.

In 1871, the island's population numbered 317,069. Its strategic importance for the security of British shipping en route to India – the original reason for its capture – had long been eroded as a result of the Victorian pax britannica and, more recently, the opening of the Suez Canal. Economically, the island had long been dedicated to a monocultural regime of sugar production more extreme than anywhere in the Caribbean with the possible exception of Barbados. Immensely prosperous as a sugar producer between the 1820s and the 1850s, the island by 1870 was suffering some of the inevitable effects of declining yields caused by soil exhaustion and the lack of fresh lands for exploitation. Most of the French Creole planters were in debt to British firms which had advanced them credit in palmier days.

Yet the French Creoles formed a cohesive, self-conscious class in firm control of the island's resources and key institutions. A small group of families established in the island in the eighteenth century dominated the society well into the twentieth. This was an elite immensely proud of its past, royalist in politics (when Jacobin commissioners arrived on the island in 1794 they were chased away, and the island remained in a sort of unilateral independence from France until 1810) and profoundly rooted in the land. It was also an elite with a long tradition of slaveholding. When Gorrie arrived on the island, slavery had been abolished for only thirty years, and slaveholding traditions and values still flourished; indeed, the British decision to abolish slavery (1834) seems to have caused the French plantocracy far more grief than the capitulation itself. French Creole society was narrow and provincial, though it produced a few brilliant men; a pervasive complacency, an almost comic self-importance, characterized this group in much the same way that they did the Barbadian oligarchy. The chairman of the Royal Commission which looked into Indian immigration to the island in the early 1870s wrote of "how they [French Creoles] resent as treason anything that disparages the island or the planting interest and how double-dyed a traitor he is thought not only who exposes but who would not conceal at every cost all that might be reprehensible in any plantation". This was a trait which soon became only too obvious to Gorrie.[5]

Even before the final end of African slavery in March 1839, the planting elite had moved to ensure that they would continue to have access to unfree labour by importing Indian labourers under contracts to replace the blacks. Some 450,000 were imported between 1834 and 1907. As early as 1861, Indian labourers (whether still under contract or 'free') comprised some two-thirds of the island's population. The Indians – 'coolies' to all and sundry – served under stringent indentureship contracts which severely restricted their freedom. Even when they had served out their contracts, and were therefore in principle free of all legal restraints not applicable to other sectors of the population, iniquitous laws enacted since the 1840s (but especially in 1867-69) made it very difficult for non-indentured Indians to survive except as semi-serf labour on the sugar plantations. To all intents and purposes, therefore, Mauritius in 1869 was still a slaveholding society; only the legal framework, and the origins of the unfree labour caste, had changed.

A French Creole elite based on land and plantership but including merchants and professionals (especially lawyers) dominated a large Indian labour force which made up the bulk of the population. The descendants of the slaves, blacks whose ancestors had come from East Africa for the most part, lived in considerable poverty as peasants, hucksters or fishermen in the interior hilly districts or coastal villages, or as labourers in Port Louis, the capital. Virtually none worked on the sugar plantations. A small middle stratum of mixed race (African/European) people held white-collar jobs or were small businessmen; a few were well educated and prosperous. Britons served as colonial officials, ran businesses or worked as professionals, but few owned plantations. Sanitation all through the island, but especially in the capital, was notorious, and Mauritius was racked with epidemics of tropical disease in the 1860s; Gorrie acquired a malarial infection that stayed with him all his life. The colony's legal and administrative systems were inefficient and corrupt. This was the isolated little island society which gave Gorrie his first sustained experience of life in a multiracial plantation colony where entrenched whites dominated an alien and unfree labour force.[6]

Law in Mauritius

Service in Mauritius presented peculiar difficulties and challenges for a British official or judge because of the survival of French civil law and legal procedures. Indeed, the post to which Gorrie was appointed at the end of 1869, that of SPG, was unique in the colonial empire. Mauritius possessed an important department of government known as the Ministère Public which was headed by the PG and the SPG; the closest analogy in the conventional British system was with the posts of Attorney-General and Solicitor-General. The duties of the SPG were varied. In criminal cases either he, or the PG in very important matters, acted as prosecuting counsel for the Crown. As Ministère Public he appeared for the Crown in civil cases, and in all cases where minors were parties he acted as their special, court appointed counsel. In certain civil cases, he had the right to deliver 'conclusions' which were statements or recommendations to the Supreme Court. He appeared before the Land Court, presided over by the governor, which heard questions such as the use, division and deviation of rivers and canals between riverain landowners. In effect, the SPG was the government's advocate in all civil cases and public prosecutor (with the PG) in the Assizes.[7] On leaving office as SPG in 1870, Gorrie wrote an interesting memorandum on the duties of the post. He observed that any SPG "who does not comprehend the French law or is not able to give an opinion ['conclusions'] on the spur of the moment will rapidly lose influence". In Gorrie's view, the Ministère Public needed to act more firmly against petty corruption among the lower officials and the lawyers, for it "had great power without legislation to put a stop to much of this jobbery". Moreover the magistrates needed careful supervision. These responsibilities were delicate and difficult, and Gorrie believed they could not be properly carried out by "a Creole of the Island mixed up with the magistracy and the legal profession".[8]

The French Civil Code remained the fundamental law of Mauritius. This meant that the civil laws were based on Roman law, as was the case in Scotland but not in England. This is why a Scottish advocate was well equipped to serve there, particularly one like Gorrie who was (said the chief justice, Sir Charles Shand, who had practised with him at the Edinburgh Bar in the 1850s) "well known for his extensive acquirements especially with regard to foreign laws [and] well acquainted with the Roman law".[9] English was the official language of the courts, but French was frequently used by lawyers when they quoted the Civil Code or the opinions of French jurists, and a British judge unable to understand or read French would have been gravely handicapped. Even Gorrie, no friend to Creole lawyers, admitted that the Registrar of the Supreme Court should always be a 'French' lawyer. To complicate matters, however, sixty years of British rule had inevitably led to the introduction of certain English laws and procedures; in effect, in the words of a governor, "rival systems of jurisprudence have long contended for the mastery", pitting Creole lawyers against those appointed 'from home'.[10]

This diversity of laws and procedures, rich in its potential for confusion, petty graft and legal jobbery, presented an intellectual challenge to a man already well read in Scottish and Continental law and fluent in French. It soon kindled the reformer/crusader in him, and both as SPG and as judge he sought to expose and reform what he saw as legal abuses. In this he had little help from his colleagues. The man appointed PG in 1870, Gustave Colin, was a brilliant, agile jurist with little interest in changing venerable procedures or reducing traditional perks and emoluments enjoyed by the Bar. Shand, the chief justice, was generally acknowledged to be easy-going, anxious for a quiet life, and second rate as a lawyer and judge. Gorrie privately castigated 'the old gentleman' for his apathy and incompetence, and believed that his reluctance to take notice of abuses was at least in part due to his local connections (two of his sons were engaged in commercial operations in Mauritius). From the other side, the *Commercial Gazette* attacked Shand for his failure to check Gorrie, his junior on the bench, and to defend traditional legal practices; "by consenting to be the humble satellite of Mr Justice Gorrie", the editor believed, Shand had lost the respect of the community (read the French Creoles). Gorrie's other senior colleague, the first puisne judge (Bestel), was described privately as "an old Creole idiot, who . . . has been on the bench since 1832".[11] Very soon after his appointment to the bench in 1870, Gorrie seems to have dominated the Supreme Court and monopolized public attention, much of it critical.

The judicial style which Gorrie developed on the Mauritian bench, a style which was to characterize his performance as a judge for the rest of his life, was combative and interventionist. He believed that one of his duties was to expose abuses and to criticize public officers, lawyers and anyone else whose misdeeds (whether of commission or omission) were brought to his attention in court. This was a novel interpretation of the judicial role to the Mauritians, and they were not slow to react. As Gorrie told his friend Chesson in 1871,

> the papers give me credit for reforming some abuses already since I was placed on the bench, but the French organ complains that I am severe and harsh in language to those who require to be rebuked. My hand is rather heavy in the snaffle I suppose for a horse not accustomed to be ridden much. We will understand each other better by and by.

Here he was overly optimistic; the island press continued to attack his judicial style and actions all through his term of office. According to Barkly's successor as governor, Sir Arthur Gordon, there was "a sort of conspiracy of the newspapers against Judge Gorrie, which annoys him greatly". On at least one occasion Gorrie managed to persuade Shand to summon a newspaper publisher for contempt following an attack on the impartiality of the Assize Courts.[12]

One reason for the barrage of criticism was Gorrie's inveterate tendency to browbeat those who appeared before his court, whether jurors, counsel, plaintiffs and defendants, medical witnesses or even officials of the court. This habit seems to have stemmed from a certain irritability in his personality, a love for 'plain speech' carried often to an unjudicial extreme, and an anxiety to get to the truth of a case.

Jurors appearing before him were at times roughly treated for what he saw as a lack of respect for his court, and when they were prominent members of the French Creole community this was, of course, much resented. On one occasion he fined a number of jurymen who claimed they were unable to serve because of their imperfect English; these men were treated to a lecture on their duties to the community. At times Gorrie apparently bullied jurors into bringing the verdict he believed to be just, as when he told a jury that if they did not believe the evidence, clear as it was, he did not know what evidence could be adduced that would bring conviction to the minds of a jury in future.[13]

Gorrie's relations with the Bar were always stormy, to a large extent because of his efforts to end legal jobbery and excessive fees. Counsel appearing before him in court might be roughly handled. He frequently interrupted their cross-examinations and addresses to the court, often with considerable brusqueness. "On more than one occasion", intoned the editor of the *Commercial Gazette* in 1873, "we have had to allude to the abrupt and discourteous manner with which he has behaved on the bench towards the Bar." By 1874, his conduct had become "a standing offence to the Colonial Bar, unbecoming in a Judge, and scarcely consistent with the habits of a gentleman". The members of the Bar were not the only ones to be criticized by the judge; plaintiffs who he believed were seeking to deceive the court might be threatened with committal for contempt; and medical witnesses were on at least two occasions publicly accused of negligence and callousness in their treatment of murder victims.[14]

In its frequent editorial assessments of Gorrie's performance on the bench, the *Commercial Gazette*, the English-language organ of the landed and professional elite, generally gave him credit for high ability, profound learning, and a zeal for justice; but accused him of the unjudicial qualities of discourtesy, impatience, party spirit and a willingness to go beyond the requirements of the law in a mistaken pursuit of equity. Especially towards the end of his term in Mauritius, he was criticized "as a gratuitous insulter of advocates, attorneys and witnesses, and as an habitual trespasser on the rights and privileges of his colleagues on the bench and his brethren at the Bar, and on those of the Chiefs of the Executive and Administrative departments of the colony". The *Gazette* was sure that Gorrie's well-known political views had crept into his judicial acts; his "exaggerated philanthropy or eccentric theories, [his] political feelings and the party spirit which may animate them" were steadily undermining public confidence in the sound and impartial administration of justice in the colony. In sum, complained the editor in one of his parting shots, when Gorrie's imminent departure had been announced, the judge's great achievement was that he had:

> frightened some subordinate policemen out of their wits; tortured, morally, witnesses deposing before him; abused a few solicitors; silenced one or two advocates; threatened notaries; quashed the judgments,

> whether rightly or wrongly is not the question, of a magistrate or so; bearded the Protector of Immigrants; insulted the SPG; overborne his brother judges; dictated to the Ministère Public; and trifled with the governor in executive Council. [And] the final end of all his ardent, zealous, passionate and arbitrary efforts to remedy a few minor evils, common to all countries, has been the creation of greater evils.[15]

The Crusading Judge

But the abuses in the Mauritian legal system which Gorrie tried to expose and correct were hardly 'minor evils', and zeal for legal reform was one of the characteristic features of his term in the island. Not only was Mauritian law founded on the French Civil Code; the legal profession itself retained important features of French practice. The profession was divided into three branches: barristers who functioned as in England; attorneys who corresponded to solicitors; and notaries whose functions and duties were 'entirely French'. The notaries enjoyed a practical monopoly of the lucrative business of advising on family property matters, drawing up deeds and working out successions. A Chamber of Notaries, modelled closely on the French body of the same name, was the sole source of discipline or control over the 13 notaries practising in Mauritius in 1874. Extremely high fees were routinely charged by the notaries, sanctioned by an ordinance, and this naturally had the effect of encouraging attorneys especially, but also barristers, to inflate their fees.[16]

Soon after his appointment as SPG, Gorrie raised the question of notaries' fees. In August 1870, in two cases of deeds of partition under the French law of partition, cases in which minors were involved and therefore the SPG acted as guardian of their interests, he commented in his 'conclusions' that the notaries concerned had charged excessive fees. With uncharacteristic finesse, he began by praising the Mauritian notaries, but he argued that the local notaries had misinterpreted the 1856 Ordinance which regulated fees for deeds of partition and had come to charge fees far in excess of what the Ordinance intended, especially in deeds involving fairly small sums. This intervention met with the hearty approval of the editor of the *Commercial Gazette*.[17]

Although the Supreme Court upheld as lawful the fees charged by the notaries for the two deeds of partition on which Gorrie had commented, he continued to raise the question of legal fees from the bench, criticizing, for instance, a fee of ten shillings for taxing a bill of costs of only thirteen shillings, and a charge of £20 on a small deed of partition. On two occasions shortly after his elevation to the bench, he persuaded his fellow judges to refuse to 'homologate' (to confirm or register) a deed of partition because of excessive costs. At this point, when Gorrie had apparently persuaded or bullied his senior colleagues on the bench to take the fees issue seriously, the *Gazette* began to change its tune and editorialize darkly about illegal actions and changes in traditional practices. But Gorrie persisted. In *Sunkur* v *Tankoor*, in what was described as one of the longest judgments ever given before the Supreme Court, he noted that in a case involving disputed land worth $3,000, nearly $2,400 had been incurred in fees to notaries and attorneys, and directed that some of them (apparently a small army had got into the act) should refund part of their fees. This judgement included a bitter attack on the probity of several professionals involved, who by clear implication had exploited the plaintiff, a 'free' immigrant ignorant of legal matters. It was, predictably, severely censured by the *Gazette*, whose editor was especially upset by "public statements tending to show that Indians are not fairly dealt with before our courts of justice", as well as by the attack on the professionals who were simply "doing what the existing law required them to do".[18]

With the encouragement of the governor, Arthur Gordon, Gorrie wrote a report on the notaries and attorneys which recommended major changes in the organization of the legal profession in Mauritius. As Gordon commented when transmitting the report to London: "Many serious abuses exist in these branches of the legal profession, and I fear that Mr Gorrie's honest efforts to effect reforms, which must touch many powerful existing interests, will be the means of exciting against him much bitter and dangerous enmity." After detailing some of the excessive fees charged for deeds of partition involving small properties, or for changes in partnerships, Gorrie noted how the high fees guaranteed by law to the notaries had an inflationary effect on all legal costs. He recommended the establishment of a unified branch of the profession combining attorneys and notaries, each equally entitled to carry out all the functions hitherto divided between them. A table of fees and professional rules should be enacted, Gorrie thought, binding on the united branch, so as to give fair remuneration while protecting the public interest; he was clear that the profits of the leading notaries would have to be drastically cut if worthwhile reforms were to be made. This report was favourably received by the officials in London, who thought its author had ably demonstrated that the notaries were expensive and useless and had made the right recommendations; but the Colonial Office decided that a local commission could better expose the abuses he had pointed out and that its report could lead to a comprehensive ordinance reforming the entire legal profession.[19]

Another feature of the legal system in Mauritius which came under fire from Gorrie was the 'family council', an assembly of relatives who were called together to give advice or authorization to the guardian as to the sale of a minor's property. This system, based on Roman law, was applied even to minuscule properties, "to heap up costs upon the sale of the half acre of some ex-apprentice, whose relatives can scarce be distinguished, or on the sale of the petty garden of an Indian cultivator, whose only blood relatives are far away on the banks of the Gadavery or the Ganges". For most of the population, Gorrie was convinced, "the system of family councils is a pure farce": in nearly all cases involving small properties, the relatives were outnumbered by strangers hauled in to complete the necessary numbers. Even when large properties were concerned, the council was purely formal; its real purpose seemed to be to increase legal costs on the sale of minors' properties. In one case coming before the Supreme Court in 1873, Gorrie ruled that the Master had no power to order a family council without a previous reference to a judge in chambers, who could direct that the step be bypassed if the minor's property was small or for any other reason. An ordinance incorporated this change in procedure, but Gorrie wanted to go further, and recommended to the governor in 1874 that family councils should be abolished for all properties worth less than £600.[20]

Right at the end of his term, Gorrie challenged another aspect of the

French system, the so-called Law of Recusation, article 378 of the Civil Code. This article allowed an appellant to challenge a judge as unqualified to sit on the appeal court because he had given the original decision. The appellants in *Bestel* v *Joly* challenged Gorrie under article 378; as required by a 1830 Ordinance, the validity of the challenge was upheld by the governor in council. Gorrie argued that the Law of Recusation might be used to intimidate an impartial judge and that, as a purely French procedure, it should not be held to bind a British judge. A flood of challenges, he argued with considerable hyperbole (in fact, according to the governor, only three or four Recusations had been made since 1830), could paralyse the courts: "It is not pleasant to reflect that although one holds the Commission of the Queen to hear and determine causes, I may after all be sitting purely by the good will of the parties." His arguments, however, failed to persuade the governor in council (where they were countered by a masterly defence of the Law of Recusation by PG Colin) or the Colonial Office, and the law was left intact.[21]

The mistrust of Creoles which Gorrie revealed in his attack on the Law of Recusation, and his belief that French Creoles in the final analysis would seek to protect their vested interests even when these involved abuses and injustices, were even more strongly manifested in his attitude towards the magistracy. From his experience as SPG and as judge, he concluded that Creoles could not be trusted to deal fairly and firmly with all parties in the magistrates' courts (where virtually all minor criminal cases were heard). On many occasions Gorrie criticized magistrates' decisions (or inaction) from the bench. In one typical case, a trial of eighteen Indians for assaulting an overseer, he noted that the Indians had complained to the local magistrate (a Creole) of illegal cutting of wages by the estate, but he had dismissed their complaint after a superficial hearing. The assault would probably not have happened, Gorrie believed, if he had done his duty and carefully investigated the situation. He told Chesson of a case where

> a Coolie [was] brought to a Magistrate by the Inspector of Immigrants with his back cut up by a flogging and the Magistrate says he would not take the evidence of the Coolie (plus his back) against that of the respectable Creole gentleman who denied it. The Magistrate (a Creole) is an idiot fit for any absurdity.

But Gorrie also blamed the higher officials of the legal department for failing to monitor and correct negligence by Creole magistrates:

> Unless you have a very good man indeed to examine the Magistrates' Returns they are practically left to themselves. Returns of cases and sentences are sent to the PG and a good man in this office, zealously bent on checking abuses, could easily have checked all that was going on. Unfortunately . . . the first and therefore chief person to see these Returns is the Crown Solicitor . . . He is a thorough Creole, and would not see what was amiss simply from his want of understanding of what justice is in questions of this kind.

His superior, the PG, who should have taken this responsibility on himself, was also a Creole. Though the Colonial Office had been persuaded that in future Creoles should not be appointed to the magistracy, "it would evidently be better to have an English PG with a partially Creole staff of Magistrates than English Magistrates with a Creole head. In the latter case there would be constant wars. As it is I have great difficulty in preventing my judicial action being interfered with."[22]

The problem of negligent or incompetent magistrates was compounded by a police force which was both inefficient and corrupt. Over and over again, presiding in the Assizes, Gorrie felt obliged to criticize the force for its incompetence and its abuse of the law. Almost immediately after his elevation to the bench, we find him condemning the police in a murder trial for "carelessness that almost passed belief" and criticizing the Inspector-General (the police chief) for failing to take down in writing the prisoners' confessions. In another murder trial in 1873, he accused the police of gross carelessness in carrying out the investigation, and noted that the lower ranking officers were left to conduct an important case on their own. Gorrie also criticized the practice of allowing police officers with little knowledge of law to prosecute: "Some ancient mariner is taken from a vessel in the harbour, the Police uniform is put on him, and he is then sent to prosecute people upon serious charges." Miscarriages of justice were frequently the result. No wonder that he acquired a well deserved reputation as the scourge of the Mauritian police, or that the editor of the *Gazette* felt obliged to exhort senior officers that "no fear of being 'hauled over the coals', or insulted by an irritable judge, relieves them from their obligation to perform their bounden duty".[23]

Gorrie had a life-long interest in land laws; in each of his colonial appointments he made a substantial and lasting contribution to the development of laws governing the transfer of real property, and he built up a formidable knowledge of the subject. Practical experience as SPG and on the bench revealed both the strengths and the weaknesses of the French legal system as it related to the transfer of land. During the court vacation at the end of 1873, he wrote an elaborate report on the Mauritian land laws. After a clear exposition of the history of land law in Mauritius since the eighteenth century, which is generally appreciative of the French system as well suited to the social and economic realities of the island, Gorrie concluded that the existing land laws "have permitted the fullest possible development of the industry and enterprise of the Island". They presented no obstacle to the concentration of land into large properties for efficient sugar production or to the use of those properties "to the fullest possible extent as a fund of credit" through the system of 'hypotheque' (mortgages secured by registration in a public office, as in Scotland). Land could be held and worked in partnership "as freely and perhaps more freely than a colliery, a quarry, or a cotton-mill at home". Yet the laws were flexible enough to satisfy the demands of ex-slaves and 'old immigrants' for small plots for petty cultivation. The main defect of the system lay in the excessive formalism of the French law which led to high costs and unnecessary complications in effecting judicial sales under the Civil Code, worsened of course by the existence of three distinct branches of the profession. Ordinance 19 of 1868 was an "honest and able" attempt to reduce the excessive costs and complications in judicial sales, and to simplify procedures relating to minors' properties. Unfortunately, the Ordinance in effect removed jurisdiction over judicial sales from the Supreme Court and handed it over to the Master, an error which weakened the reforming intent of the law. It was difficult for the Master to enforce those parts of the law which were designed to cut legal costs and to minimize appearances by barristers or attorneys. Gorrie proposed that all applications for judicial sales be to the Supreme Court, to be dealt with by a judge in chambers.[24]

Sales or partitions by 'licitation' (a French legal term meaning sale by auction) took place when a co-proprietor or co-heir of a property sued to have it partitioned or sold in order to get his share in land (partition) or in cash (sale). Any owner or heir could begin proceedings without a judge's permission. Too often, unscrupulous attorneys persuaded people to sue, without any serious intention, merely to obtain costs, and this might happen repeatedly. When the property was small, as in the 1873 case of *Sunkur* v *Tankoor* already referred to, repeated sales by 'licitation' might result in nearly its whole value being absorbed in legal fees. Even with larger properties, and even when there was no dishonest intent, fees might be so high as to eat up the profits of the sale. Gorrie proposed that no 'licitation' proceedings should commence without the permission of a judge after a preliminary hearing, and that procedures for sales and partitions (when allowed) should be simplified in the case of small properties. He criticized the "exaggerated importance given in the French system to the family councils" and recommended that these be abolished entirely in the case of minors' properties worth under £600. Finally, he advised that forms of title deeds should be enacted to "restrict legal discursiveness", and that the forms for the registration of mortgages should be simplified. "The basis of our system here", he concluded, "both of Land Rights in general, and of registration of them, is very good. It is only the superstructure of forms and formalities which requires vigorous pruning."[25]

This able report was sent to the Colonial Office along with comments by Gordon and Colin. Colin, as we might expect, was generally hostile, arguing that Gorrie's proposals were "too general and sweeping" and arose more from "exceptional cases" which could be dealt with by the courts rather than from "the general working of the law". He advised against a wholesale implementation of the recommendations in the report. But Gordon defended Gorrie's report and believed that Colin had misunderstood the scope of his proposals and missed his strong support for most features of the French system. In Gordon's view, he had made a good case for returning control over judicial sales of land to the Supreme Court, for controlling costs for unnecessary legal work, for simplifying procedures, and for abolishing compulsory family councils for small properties. Colin, Gordon noted, had a "natural bias" in favour of the local system, while Gorrie approached the issues with an open mind. The Secretary of State, after instructing Gordon to "inform Mr Gorrie that I have read his report with much interest", decided to seek the comments of the Mauritian judges on the reports by both Gorrie and Colin.[26]

The three judges – Chief Justice Shand, easy-going and near retirement, N.G. Bestel, venerable and unassertive, and Gorrie – reported, to no one's surprise, in a sense generally supportive of Gorrie's report, though some of the specific suggestions for amendments were milder than those in the report. They advised more power for the Supreme Court over judicial sales of land; careful consideration of the question of costs and more power for the judges to determine them; no 'licitation' without permission of a judge in chambers; abolition of family councils for properties under £200; and the revision and reduction of notaries' fees, pending the likely abolition of the Chamber of Notaries. But these recommendations, along with the other proposals in Gorrie's report, seem to have been shelved for several years; perhaps the departure of both Gordon and Gorrie took the heat off the issue and allowed Colin's conservative views to prevail. Only minor changes to the law were made in 1875-76. Finally, in 1881 an Ordinance was enacted which changed the procedures for judicial sales in the ways advocated by the report and the judges' recommendations.[27] Much of the credit for these belated reforms should go to Gorrie for his persistent, and unpopular, efforts.

Government and Politics

Mauritius was Gorrie's first colonial posting, and it was here that he established a leading trend of his career: his active involvement in a wider public life. Gorrie was both judge and politician; he was on the bench, but he frequently came down from it to behave like a political activist and a policy maker. By far his most important political activity concerned the treatment of Indian immigrants in the island; but, before we analyse this, it may be useful to consider his emergence as a political figure and some of the other issues in which he became engaged.

The most important person Gorrie met in Mauritius was Arthur Gordon, who arrived in the island as governor early in 1871. In him Gorrie found a patron, an inspirational leader, and soon a friend. Gordon's views on colonial affairs, especially on the proper relationship between white employers and black or Indian labourers and on the government's responsibilities towards the latter, were close to his. Though their social backgrounds were vastly different (Gordon was a scion of one of Scotland's greatest aristocratic families, the son of an earl and a former prime minister), they soon developed a mutual respect for each other's qualities, helped perhaps by their common Scottish origins and by that country's relatively democratic and egalitarian social structure. Both were close to the Liberal Party, albeit on very different levels – Gordon was an intimate family friend of the Gladstones and corresponded with the Liberal leader for many decades – and both believed strongly in liberal imperialism and British trusteeship on behalf of the 'subject races'. Within months of Gordon's arrival in the island, a close working relationship between the two men had developed, and Gorrie became one of the governor's inner group of advisors.[28]

It seems that initially Gorrie made a somewhat poor impression on the Scottish aristocrat, who described him in a private letter as "cleverer than his colleagues [on the Mauritius bench], but rough and vulgar in manner – tres cassant [gruff] – and not a man to inspire confidence". But as they came to work together, Gordon grew to appreciate his "courage, his thick-skinnedness, and his facile pen" while deploring the way that 'his zeal in the discovery of abuses [sometimes] misled him and induced him to exaggerate the importance of very small matters". By the time Gordon left Mauritius in 1874, after a stormy governorship, he admitted that he would miss Gorrie, along with a handful of others, as fellow workers. He correctly predicted that his "friends" would "have a rough time of it" after he left, and that "Gorrie . . . especially will have great difficulties to encounter. A sort of conspiracy has already been formed to secure [his] removal, which the planters hope to effect much as Beaumont's was effected in Guiana." Back in London, he spoke very highly of Gorrie to their mutual friend Chesson, much to his gratification when he heard of it.[29]

For his part, Gorrie was immediately impressed with the new governor, who came with a considerable reputation for successful colonial administration, especially in Trinidad (1866-70). Within a few months of his arrival, Gorrie was telling Chesson

> our new governor Sir Arthur Gordon is going to be very useful. He has already infused greater vigour into the administration and he will certainly be more favourable to the Indian element of the population than his predecessor. Probably his measures will lead to Planter discontent but better that than servile outbreaks. There are a good many abuses to correct, and these I think stand a better chance of being corrected in the right manner than I had at one time believed possible without a row.

The correspondence between the two men makes it clear how much Gorrie admired him and how close (allowing for the difference in official position and social status) they became. He wrote to Gordon, home on leave in 1874,

> I confess that when I got your letter from Scotland, kind and cordial far above my deserving, that I felt somewhat 'lonely'. But that very selfish reason soon gave way to one of satisfaction that you had been relieved of a most irksome and ungrateful task. May your next government be as pleasant as your sojourn here has been the reverse. You will permit me to say, however, that your absence is felt and deeply regretted by a great many more warm friends than you think, and I sincerely believe that the population in general had a perfect confidence that so long as you were governor no wrong would pass without a remedy. What can anyone expect more than this? It is easy enough to win the approbation of the rich, who have no grievances to redress; it is a very difficult thing to earn, and to earn justly, the title of the friend of the poor and the needy.

No doubt precisely the kind of title he himself would most have appreciated.[30]

Inevitably, perhaps, Gorrie found Gordon's successor, Sir Arthur Phayre, much his inferior in understanding, energy and zeal for justice, a judgement which was not altogether fair. Gorrie believed that Phayre was too complacent about abuses which still flourished even after Gordon's efforts to expose them: "If a man be unsuspicious here, he will be fooled completely, and if he be not of a searching and enquiring disposition, abuses will go on under his very nose without his detecting them. The new governor I doubt much," he wrote to Chesson pessimistically, "is too old to enter keenly into reforms, and my present strong impression is that he funks giving the planters umbrage. I fear it is to be five years of Sir Henry Barkly again" – a gloomy prediction indeed, as it was during Barkly's regime that most of the worst abuses against the immigrants originated and flourished. The villain of the piece, Gorrie believed, was his enemy, Colin; "the new governor is in his hands I very much fear like soft wax". Later, however, he wrote more sympathetically: "I cannot make Sir Arthur Phayre out . . . He is personally very agreeable but I fear he will shrink from Colonial unpopularity and if so he will do no good. But I may be judging wrongly and hope for the best."[31] In fact, though Phayre was no crusading reformer like Gordon, he was a conscientious and thorough administrator, and under him many of the more important recommendations of the Royal Commission on the immigrants' situation were gradually implemented.

Phayre's qualities were not such as to be appreciated by a man like Gorrie, but Gorrie clearly liked him as a person and never quarrelled with him. Such was not the case with Gustave Colin, by all accounts far and away the ablest Mauritian in public life and scion of a prominent Creole clan. Colin's political views, his passionate admiration for the French legal system, warts and all, in which he had been trained, his excellent mind and facile pen, allied to a temper which seems to have been as touchy as Gorrie's, all guaranteed that the two men would collide, especially once Gordon's restraining influence had been removed. It is to be recalled that Gorrie had been a disappointed aspirant to the PG's post in 1870, and that Colin had criticized his proposals for reforms in the land laws. No wonder that Gordon confided to a friend shortly before leaving Mauritius: "I am sorry to see that my very able and agreeable, but not altogether very high principled PG, Mr Colin, will be quite ready to turn on [Gorrie] *when my back is turned*, though he does nothing hostile *now* except try to make me think ill of him."[32]

In a private letter, Gorrie described Colin as "a Creole who from formerly being pretty liberal, at least he pretended so, has come back imbued with all the notions of the old Planter clique, and is evidently disposed to carry things with a high hand". With Phayre as governor his influence was paramount, and he was using it to stave off real reforms. "The governor of this Colony at the present moment", Gorrie wrote on the day he left the island for good, "is the PG, Mr Colin, and will be so long as Sir Arthur [Phayre] is here. Now that

I am gone there will be no influence whatever to cope with the old party." There were frequent skirmishes between the judge and the PG in 1874-75. One, in 1875, reached the Secretary of State. It concerned the respective powers of the Supreme Court (Gorrie) and the Ministère Public (Colin) to discipline lawyers. The voluminous correspondence between the two men reveals a deep personal hostility, and for once, the language used by Gorrie's opponent was more offensive than his own.[33] Gorrie was not to encounter an opponent as able as Colin until he came up against the Trinidad politicians at the end of his career.

Like Gordon, Gorrie believed that the powerful planter clique which dominated affairs in Mauritius was unfit to be trusted with anything like responsible government, because of its slaveholding traditions and values, its contempt for nonwhite races, and its determination to monopolize power and resources in the island. In the 1870s, there were no elected members in the island's Legislative Council, which consisted of official and unofficial members nominated by the governor; the latter were private citizens supposed to speak for the community, and they outnumbered the officials by fourteen to seven. "The unofficials are nearly all – with two exceptions I think – either planters or lawyers who are the mere agents of the planters, or themselves planters also", wrote Gorrie. He continued:

> Four of them are connected with one estate . . . The trouble experienced in governing the Colony is from these men who think that every proposal for reform is a personal insult to them or their class. In all Colonies where there is such a preponderance of Coolies the official element ought to be in the decided majority and the minority ought not to be purely planters or in the planter interest

– here Gorrie echoed the time honoured justification for crown colony government. Like many others, he noted the typical complacency and self-satisfaction of the island elite: "They have a confirmed belief that they are immaculate, that the island is paradise and that if any new laws are passed it is simply to satisfy a political enquiry and not intended to be obeyed."[34]

In less contentious spheres of civic life, Gorrie threw himself into Mauritian affairs with characteristic energy. The island's sanitary conditions had long been notorious, and this was a subject that interested him deeply, as well it might considering the implications for his and his family's health (his wife's sister died within weeks of their arrival in Mauritius). A fever epidemic in 1873 prompted him to write to Gordon to tell him that the Port Louis sanitation service had virtually collapsed so that filth accumulated just at the time when it was most dangerous. He urged the governor to deal with the 'useless' Sanitary Boards: "A board is the best possible method to have things neglected and to shield everyone from responsibility." After a destructive hurricane in 1874, he complimented the city authorities for their efforts to remove debris, "but it already begins to send forth odours. Any amount of money would be properly spent in cleaning up the town, for the risks of epidemic among these poor creatures [the people who had lost their huts] seem so great." He also contributed to secondary education on the island by serving on the Council of Education from as early as 1870, later becoming its president. Among its responsibilities was supervision of the Royal College of Mauritius, then the island's only government supported secondary school.[35]

The Police Inquiry Committee and the Indians

Gordon's major achievement as governor of Mauritius (1871-74) was to expose abuses in the treatment of Indian immigrants, both the indentureds and the 'old immigrants' (those who had completed their first indentures), and to set in motion a long drawn out process which eventually led to substantial reforms. In this effort, Gorrie was actively involved to an extent highly unusual for a man who was, after all, a judge of the Supreme Court. He had early indicated his sympathy for the Indians from the bench, and Gordon (who was desperately short of able men who shared his views) in effect drafted him as one of his advisers and assistants. In particular, Gordon appointed him to the Police Inquiry Committee (PIC), whose report he effectively wrote; this was the first searching exposure of abuses against the Mauritius immigrants, and it led directly to the appointment of a Royal Commission whose recommendations for reform were gradually implemented. Gorrie's active involvement in the effort to publicize and correct the many injustices suffered by the Indian labour force made him, more than anything else, a prominent public figure and *bête noire* to the planting interest: Public Enemy Number Two, as it were, second only to Gordon himself.

Indian immigrants made up two-thirds of the island population by 1861, and they accounted for virtually all the plantation labourers. All immigrants had to serve an initial five-year indenture and the indentured labourers were controlled by stringent laws restricting their mobility. In 1853, the Mauritius planters had secured the abolition of the right to free repatriation to India; this meant that most of the 'old immigrants' had little realistic chance of leaving the island. Many abuses relating to the treatment of Indians under indenture had crept into the system by 1870. But perhaps more flagrant was the treatment of the old immigrants who should have enjoyed all the rights of free subjects in a British colony. Under Governor Barkly, an ordinance enacted in 1867, strengthened by Regulations in 1869, sought to reduce them to a semi-serf status by forcing them back to the plantations where they had little alternative but to work as fulltime resident labourers. Free Indians who had set up on their own as peasants, carters, small traders or casual labourers were harassed by the police, under the enactments of 1867-69, rounded up as vagrants, charged iniquitous fees and licenses, all in an effort to get them back under the planters' control. The 1867 law, modelled on practices in neighbouring French Réunion, made the old immigrants carry a livret or pass book at all times. Failure to produce a valid pass at any time meant that the Indian could be sent to the Immigration Department at Port Louis; if he was found outside 'his' district he could be arrested, convicted and imprisoned; if he was found to be unemployed he was 'deemed to be a vagrant'; if he lost his pass there was a £1 fee for replacement (a large sum in relation to income); to move out of 'his' district required reporting to the police in both the old and the new districts.

Severe as these provisions were, it was the manner in which the police enforced them, between 1867 and 1872, which gave rise to flagrant abuses. Peaceable, inoffensive and often industrious free Indians, once they had 'escaped' from the plantations, were branded as vagrants, and the police conducted organized 'vagrant hunts' (like big game shoots) in which almost every Indian who could be run down was arrested. In 1869 alone no fewer than 30,824 free Indians were arrested for vagrancy, over twenty per cent of the total Indian population. The treatment of the old immigrants under the 1867-69 enactments was the most serious issue to be tackled by Gordon, but in general the condition of all the immigrants, indentured and free, was deplorable. The suicide rate among Indians was alarmingly high. Casual abuse of Indians by plantation personnel was routine. The Commission recorded the death of at least 50 Indians from severe beatings between 1869 and 1872. Worse, neither the magistrates nor the Protector of Immigrants' office intervened effectively to protect them; the police authorities were their principal enemy. This was the situation which began to engage Gordon's attention soon after his arrival early in 1871; Gorrie had already, by then, come to understand something of the facts.[36]

Two court cases in the first half of 1871, one of them heard by Gorrie, helped to direct the enquiries which Gordon initiated. A trial of three Indians for arson at Moka revealed that the police had abused the prisoners in order to extract confessions. Gorrie informed the governor about this case, stating his belief, based on his experiences on the bench, that the police habitually used "foul play" against Indians to gain confessions, arrested them on mere suspicion, and tampered with evidence. A formal letter followed, and this allowed Gordon to begin enquiries into police conduct which led directly to the appointment of the PIC. Gordon later acknowledged publicly, in his evidence to the Commission, that he decided to appoint the PIC "in consequence of certain statements made to me by Judge Gorrie as to the conduct of the Police towards prisoners".[37]

The Moka case, and the conclusions which Gordon and Gorrie drew from it, convinced the governor that the conduct of the police towards the old immigrants was the abuse which needed investigation most urgently. His hand was greatly strengthened when he received, in June 1871, a petition signed by 9,401 old immigrants, complaining of their mistreatment by the police and by the Immigration Department under the labour laws. These Indians had been aided in drawing up their petition by Adolphe de Plevitz, the French manager of a remote interior plantation where many hunted immigrants had apparently found refuge in the past. The petition complained of the ticket of leave and the pass-book, the close police surveillance of their movements and constant harassment. Even a respectable, landowning old immigrant, who lost his papers, might be condemned to hard labour as a vagrant. The police habitually arrested immigrants in batches of fifty or so, and there was no redress for false arrest. The petition cited 18 particular cases of discrimination and harassment. Gordon decided to appoint a local committee to investigate the conduct of the police and to refer the petition to it. Unfortunately, he felt unable to set up this committee (the PIC) until several months had passed. The delay in constituting the PIC, which did not start work until December 1871, led directly to the publication by de Plevitz of his famous pamphlet "The Old Immigrants of Mauritius".[38]

De Plevitz's pamphlet reprinted the petition and added his own 'observations'. These amounted to a harsh indictment of the Immigration Department, the magistrates, and the police. "If [the Protector's] office was instituted to facilitate the oppression of the Immigrants", wrote de Plevitz, "it has certainly answered its purpose". The 1867 labour laws "have almost wholly deprived the poor Indian Immigrant, even when he has completed his engagement, of the rights of citizenship; have almost put him without the pale of humanity, and reduced him to the position of a Helot". Between the police and the Creole magistrates, justice for the immigrants was impossible. The publication of this pamphlet (August 1871) unleashed a storm; Creoles were outraged at this public castigation by an outsider (much was made of his German sounding name and the local press enjoyed calling him "von Plevitz"). His "villainously ingenious observations", thundered the *Gazette*, probably included "a thin thread of fact" and one or two of the isolated and exceptional cases which he cited might be substantiated; but the colony would have to bear "the burden and reproach of the whole of his false and scurrilous charges". A petition signed by 950 injured sons of Mauritius called for de Plevitz's deportation, which Gordon ignored; then in time honoured Creole fashion de Plevitz was horse-whipped in the streets of Port Louis by a young man, the hero of the hour, especially when (on express instructions from the governor) a charge of assault was laid against him.[39]

Gordon saw that the publicity generated by the de Plevitz affair gave him a unique opportunity to push ahead with investigations on several levels which might, at last, lead to real reforms; the 'conspiracy of silence' created by the

Mauritians about immigration abuses had been broken. He decided on a three-pronged strategy. First, he asked for a Royal Commission to investigate the whole system, modelled on the recent British Guiana Commission. He pointed out that any enquiry by local men would be made difficult by the kind of harassment de Plevitz was suffering, and asked for commissioners with Caribbean experience, ideally some who had served in the Guiana enquiry. Second, before the commissioners arrived, he pushed specific reforms through a reluctant legislature. Third, he went ahead with the local PIC. It was to investigate all allegations of police misconduct towards Indians, especially those cases highlighted in the Old Immigrants' Petition. The PIC was chaired by General S. Smyth, the officer commanding the local troops, and consisted of Gorrie, Captain Blunt of the Police, Celicourt Antelme (a planter), J.Fraser (a banker), and J.A. Robertson (a merchant). From the start Gorrie, the only unequivocal critic of the immigration system on the PIC, dominated proceedings. "Such was the determination of Gorrie", the historian Hugh Tinker notes, "that his imprint was largely given to [their] report".[40]

Attention now focused on the work of the PIC. It took evidence between December 1871 and February 1872, sitting on twenty-three occasions and examining one hundred and thirty-five witnesses, and reported in April 1872. The two main issues investigated were the methods used by the police to gain confessions, and the old immigrants' grievances as detailed in their petition. As the PIC proceeded, it soon became clear that the complaints of the petitioners related to the labour laws of 1867-69 rather than to the action of the police under them, and the main thrust of its report was to criticize those laws and call for their repeal or substantial amendment.[41]

So far as police conduct was concerned, the PIC reported that violence was still occasionally used to extract confessions, though trickery and spying had come to be employed more often than actual physical abuse. People were arrested merely to extract 'evidence' from them; prisoners were kept on poor diets and frequently moved; fictitious cases of robbery were brought up to involve 'bad characters'; accepting bribes to refrain from bringing charges and extorting money by threats were still prevalent. Turning their attention to the Petition, the PIC concluded: "Most of the grievances complained of have a real and substantial foundation." Of the eighteen special cases appended to the Petition, a few were unfounded, several were not serious, but the chief cases were substantiated, revealing that much hardship had been inflicted on old immigrants by arbitrary police actions. The PIC attacked the Immigration Department for its relentless exaction of fees – for photographs for the pass-books, for the pass-books themselves, for the annual £1 licence paid by all 'free' labourers unattached to an estate – fees which, it believed, had been illegally imposed by the 1869 regulations. Though the police were generally acquitted of having acted illegally with regard to the old immigrants, the PIC was clear that they had made a harsh law even more oppressive by their modes of enforcement, and the 'vagrant hunts' were severely censured. It stopped short of stating that the real intention of the enactments of 1867-69 was to force old immigrants to re-engage (though Gorrie's cross-examination of witnesses makes it clear that such was his own conviction), but it believed that this was their inevitable tendency. The PIC recommended the amendment of the laws especially in two crucial respects: the repeal of the vexatious restrictions and fees to which only old immigrants were subjected, and the restoration of free return passages to India after a certain period of 'agricultural residence' in the colony. The police were to be ordered to cease their irregular modes of obtaining evidence, and to relax their general harassment of immigrants not attached to estates.[42]

There is no doubt that Gorrie's role in the outcome of the PIC was critical; he was, as Tinker notes, the only member clearly opposed to the laws of 1867-69, sympathetic to the immigrants, and unafraid to attack prominent personages or hallowed local institutions. The printed evidence to the PIC makes it clear that he dominated the cross-examination of all the most important witnesses; he was also the only lawyer on the Committee. Public opinion (which, of course, was strongly hostile to the report) was convinced that Gorrie was the effective author of the document as well as (along with Gordon) its guiding inspiration. The police chief did not hesitate to state publicly that the Committee "allowed itself to publish the opinion of a single member in the report submitted as the work of the whole". Gorrie told the Colonial Secretary that

> an attempt has been made . . . to deprive my colleagues . . . of the credit due to them for their anxious labours by representing me as the sole

> author of the report, whereas it was a joint report carefully prepared by the Chairman from the separate drafts, and adjusted paragraph by paragraph by all the Commissioners who signed.

This was the actual procedure: Smyth as Chairman asked for drafts from each member and used the drafts he received (from Gorrie, Blunt and Robertson) to draw up a document which was then discussed by all the members who eventually signed the majority report. But much of the language of the final report was, by the admission of the Chairman, Gorrie's, and it seems clear that his was the mind, and the will, which dominated proceedings and shaped the report. His detailed letters to Gordon between December 1871 and April 1872 make this clear.[43]

Public reaction to the PIC and its report was predictably hostile. So was the response of the police chief (O'Brien). In his letter to the Commission attacking the report, he went so far as to accuse Gorrie of deliberately tampering with evidence (police order books) before the PIC in order to prejudice his colleagues against police officers. This outrageous insinuation, which was made public by the Commission, triggered off a dispute which simmered for months. As Gorrie said in a private letter to the governor, "it is a little too much that one should be subjected to a charge implying personal baseness and malignity simply for having acted as one of a Commission charged with a public duty". His official reply was both dignified and (for him) restrained. Only strong pressure from the governor persuaded O'Brien to make a grudging apology to Gorrie, which he, rather uncharacteristically, accepted.[44] Planter reaction to the PIC's proceedings was reflected in the *Commercial Gazette.* It branded the report as perversely onesided; everything favourable to the magistates, the police, the Immigration Department and the planters had been ignored, exceptional incidents were taken to be the norm, evidence had been distorted. Moreover, the "real author" of the report was definitely not the chairman. And after many similar editorials, the *Gazette* concluded "we know *of a certainty* that General Selby Smyth did not compile the report at all". Hostile opinion was absolutely clear that Gorrie was the author, and Gordon the inspiration, of the report; and hostile opinion seems, in this respect, to have been almost entirely correct.[45]

The Royal Commission

By the start of 1872, when the PIC was still taking evidence, the Colonial Office had accepted Gordon's advice to appoint a full scale Royal Commission, modelled on the 1871 British Guiana Commission, to investigate the whole immigration system in Mauritius. The Commission arrived in April 1872. Partly because of the immense thoroughness of the Commissioners, partly because of the chairman's illness, it did not finish its work until November 1874, and its massive report was not published until April 1875, a full three years after that of the PIC had appeared. One must agree with Gordon's judgement that although the report was "a monument of laborious research, and of carefully weighed and balanced statement . . . it would have been far more effective and more useful if it had been shorter, less diffuse in its phraseology, and above all, if it had appeared sooner". Yet it remains, as Tinker notes, "the basic document on the Indians in Mauritius". And it completely endorsed all the main findings of the PIC (whose report it adopted as its main working document); indeed, Gordon noted, "the Royal Commissioners went much further than the Police Commission" in attacking abuses and advocating thorough going reforms. Its report was a vindication of the PIC and of its dominant member.[46]

Gorrie followed the Commission's work with great interest and not a little anxiety, and he kept Chesson fully informed. He was impressed with the industry and fairness of the Commissioners: "They have most honestly industriously and thoroughly performed their work of investigation." When, at last, the report appeared, Gorrie told Chesson, with pardonable self-importance: "So far as regards the particular matter with which my credit as a public servant was somewhat bound up – the acting of the Police – I understand the report to be very condemnatory of their mode of acting and showing a state of things much worse than that brought forth in our PIC."[47] On the whole, the report was a thorough indictment of the immigration system in Mauritius, which was shown to be quite as vicious as Gorrie had long concluded. But it had been written by men whose position and appointment by the Crown placed them beyond the kind of local abuse and insinuations which he had suffered for his part in the earlier enquiry.

The Commission's findings fell into two main categories: the situation of the old immigrants, and the treatment of the indentured and estate resident Indians. On the former, it harshly criticized the operation of the labour laws of 1867-69 and found the de Plevitz Petition amply justified by the facts. It recommended the end of 'vagrancy hunts' and the amendment of the vagrancy laws, severe punishment for any policemen who subjected old immigrants to false or malicious arrests, and the abolition of the £1 licence for day labourers. On the latter, it concluded that the laws for the protection of the indentureds were inadequate, and poorly enforced; the Commission condemned magistrates, police, doctors and planters alike. Its recommendations closely paralleled the Resolutions which Gordon had forced through the Mauritius Legislative Council in 1872: strengthening inspections, prompt payment of wages, doctors appointed and paid by government, greater powers for the Protector and the governor to withdraw labourers, cancel contracts and refuse further allotments, no re-indenture for more than one year, an independent magistracy. The Commission did not recommend the restoration of free repatriation (it was split on the issue), but in the event the Secretary of State instructed Phayre (who had succeeded Gordon) to push for this crucial reform which had already been grudgingly endorsed by the Council.[48]

The implementation of the major recommendations of the Commission, as modified by the Secretary of State's instructions, fell to Phayre, who was too cautious and too trusting, in Gorrie's judgement, for the task of pushing through reforms in the teeth of universal opposition. Gorrie lamented to Chesson in 1875:

> It is ridiculous after two Commissions to wait until a new man has got hold of the right end of the string . . . Another year gone – and not one single abuse which we pointed out in 1872 corrected. This is caution with a vengeance. But it makes all the difference who it is who feels the sting. The fact is when I meet a band of 'vagrants' on the road, knowing as I do that at least one half of them have been condemned for trifling inaccuracies of papers etc. which the Commissions have condemned, I feel humiliated that one should be so powerless to remedy a flagrant wrong. As the Anti Slavery Society put it, the almost impossibility of

> getting the local people to move in the way of reform of abuses is the great difficulty in the Coolie question.

In a private letter to Gordon, he complained that "things will drop, and are dropping back into their old groove . . . I doubt if the Governor can 'spot' what is going on". Abuses exposed and denounced in 1872 were in "full vigour" in 1875.[49]

Nevertheless, between 1876 and 1878 Phayre moved slowly but methodically towards a new labour law which would incorporate the needed reforms, against fierce opposition from the Creoles and lukewarm support from his own officials, especially Colin. The law was finally enacted in October 1878 (Ordinance 12 of 1878). Gordon believed that it was a useful and generally satisfactory ordinance, and in retrospect he considered that the abuses exposed by the two Commissions were, in subsequent years, "effectually checked and well nigh altogether removed". A substantial share of the credit belongs to Gorrie.[50]

But the truth was that in a 'Coolie colony' like Mauritius, a society where the employing class had relinquished few of the traditions and values of slavery, most planters assumed a right to treat their labourers, alien by race and culture, if not with outright cruelty then at best with a kind of contemptuous indifference mixed with rough-and-ready benevolence from time to time. The few British officials who, like Gordon and Gorrie, made their abhorrence of this kind of attitude clear met with persistent harassment in the island press and elsewhere. In 1874 J.G. Daly, the only British magistrate serving in Mauritius in the early 1870s, sentenced an Englishman (Piddington) to 14 days in jail for abusing and kicking Indian labourers. The response was predictable:

> As the *kicker* is an English engineer and the *kickees* Indians, [wrote Gordon,] the white population are naturally furious. What! is a white man not to swear and kick at an Indian if he does not understand orders given as to the placing of a piece of machinery? Is it not one of the rights of a freeborn Briton to 'walk into' a stupid 'nigger'? The papers are of opinion that 'L'incident Piddington aura peut-être des suites graves'.

A question was asked in the House of Commons about this affair, hostile to

Daly's action, and Gorrie wrote to Gordon: "If the government at home don't support Daly in his honest action as a magistrate, then farewell to equal justice on the island. The backs of the Creole magistrates are sufficiently weak already."[51] These deeply racist attitudes towards a semi-serf labour caste, of a different race and culture, were first encountered by Gorrie in Jamaica, and he was to meet them again in Fiji, the Western Pacific, the Leeward Islands, Trinidad and Tobago; in each place he used all the powers of his position, and all the force of his personality, to counter them.

The leaders of the old immigrant community were, of course, well aware of Gorrie's sympathy for them, and grateful for his support and practical concern for their interests. When he left the island, he was presented with a address signed by 366 Indians. It described his departure as "a heavy blow and discouragement to us in particular". His presence on the bench had been seen "as a guarantee that the progressive policy pursued by the Local Government [*ie* by Gordon] would be continued, and would encounter no check, and the events of the last five years have fully answered our expectation". Gorrie's judgments, said the address, "have been founded on strict principles of law and equity, and have never been influenced, in any way whatever, by considerations of caste or creed". In reply, Gorrie stated: "I have striven to act impartially – to know in the seat of justice no class of society, no race of men, no caste, no creed." He expressed the hope that the imminent addition to the Queen's titles of 'Empress of India' might mark a new era of progress in India and greater solidarity between India and the British Empire as a whole.[52]

Leaving Mauritius

Gordon left Mauritius in 1874, and was offered the challenging post of governor of Fiji; he would be the first substantive governor of the islands which were ceded by their King to Britain in that year. As an inducement to accept the post, which would mean serving under difficult and even dangerous conditions, he was given an unusually free hand in choosing his key officials. Recognizing no doubt that Gorrie was just the man for the kind of 'rough work' that would be needed in Fiji, he suggested that he accept the chief justiceship early in 1875. Gorrie was delighted at the idea, admitting that he had thought of telling Gordon that he wanted the post but had hesitated through a "stupid want of frankness". He promised Gordon "what I know will please you best – work like a brick". The initial plan was for him to receive twelve or eighteen months' leave from Mauritius to accept a temporary appointment in Fiji; he would receive half salary from Mauritius as well as the (small) salary of the Fiji post.[53] This plan miscarried, however, and Sir William Hackett was appointed first Chief Justice of Fiji with a temporary commission. Gorrie was philosophical, confident probably that Gordon would get his way in the end: "These contretemps will happen when one is not on the spot." Gordon did get his way, and early in 1876 Gorrie was offered the position following Hackett's return to his substantive post. He left Mauritius at the end of March 1876, taking a sailing ship to Adelaide. As he told Chesson:

> Long before you receive this I shall be on my way to Australia in a little Danish schooner en route to Fiji. Lord Carnarvon has telegrammed to me my appointment as CJ and to go at once if accepted. I accept and go . . . I am to have the same salary at present as in Mauritius viz. £1,200 but of course when the Colony becomes a little more prosperous they will 'draw' better. I am however going on leave with the three months full pay and as many months half pay as Lord Carnarvon will allow consistently with the Treasury of both Colonies. This puts me down 'free of expenses' which is a great thing in these days.[54]

Alas, this arrangement to cover his expenses in the period between his leaving Mauritius and taking up duties in Fiji was to cause him endless worry in years to come, and the Colonial Office much heartburning.

Once it became known that he had accepted the Fiji post and was to leave immediately, the island press swung into action with editorials denouncing his misdeeds over the last six years. The *Gazette* affected to believe that the move was a demotion ("*relegated* to the Fiji islands") – though perhaps for loyal Creoles *any* move out of Mauritius was by definition a demotion – and congratulated the island on the happy decision to send Gorrie packing after his mentor. Its editor seized the opportunity to tell Gorrie "what the public mind really is as to his merits and demerits", at considerable length, and had fun denouncing a complimentary address being "hawked about for signature by 'maroon brokers' and individuals of similar standing". However many signed it, said the editor, hedging his bets, it could never represent public opinion in the recognized sense, only the distorted views of "those who hate attorneys or advocates or notaries or policemen or police magistrates".[55] From Fiji, Gorrie struck back, telling Chesson: "The statement in the Mauritius *Commercial Gazette* about my being sent to Fiji for bad behaviour!! of course was quite in the old style of Planter spite." The *Gazette* could be easily dismissed, and the congratulatory address (which was in addition to the one presented by the old immigrants) gave Gorrie pleasure. It was signed by the Mayor and Town Council of Port Louis, along with lawyers, planters, merchants and others, over 2,000 in all. As he commented to Chesson: "Better public sentiment has for once aroused itself and testified that when a man does his duty he forces people to respect him."[56]

We can believe Gorrie when he told Chesson that he regretted leaving Mauritius, unlike Gordon who made no secret of his loathing for the place and his anxiety to get away. He had lived there with his family for over six years and he was clearly fascinated by the society. He liked the tropics: "How you must envy us our perpetual sunshine!" he told Chesson. "Really I enjoy that part of exile and I fear would be apt to grumble if my lot were cast at home for any length of time now. This Colonial life is certainly not without its discouragements, although not without its comforts and pleasures." He was sincere when he told a Port Louis deputation, just before he left: "I have enjoyed my residence in Mauritius very much; I like the people."[57]

Gorrie's health while in Mauritius was variable. He was apparently subject to bilious attacks, and had several bouts of malaria. One, in early 1872, was quite serious, prompting Gordon to suggest that he take a prolonged local leave in the cooler and healthier hills: "Very many thanks for your kind suggestion of leave. I am too weak yet to think of going anywhere. But I think Reid [his doctor] has expelled the disease from my unhappy liver, and that all I need now is to gain strength". The children suffered from several illnesses in Mauritius, including whooping cough, then a very serious childhood disease, and his sister-in-law died there. But for most of the time Gorrie apparently enjoyed his usual abundant energy: "I am thankful to say my own health is now perfectly reestablished and that I feel up to anything . . . from pitch and toss to manslaughter. If things keep as they are, I shall probably work off a little steam by going to Madagascar during our next winter (July!) vacation" (he did not, to his subsequent regret). In 1875 he reported that his health was "perfect".[58]

As Gorrie said just before he left, "My wife and children will always regard [Mauritius] as their second home." His eldest daughter Marion (Minnie) had grown up there, and he told Gordon in 1875:

> It will amuse Lady Gordon to know that my eldest girl has already gone through the ceremony of getting a proposal, and declining it, so that the sooner her piano lessons are finished the better! I thought the age was fast when I married before being called to the Bar, but we are improving even in this respect.

Minnie was then 18. It was decided that the family should not go out with him to Fiji, but should spend some time 'at home': "I am anxious to give my girls a final polish, and my boy must go to school." Moreover, conditions in Fiji were quite unsettled in 1876, and very few white women lived there. His wife and children returned to Britain by a long voyage in 1876, and spent a year in Edinburgh and London, joining him in Fiji in 1877.[59]

Gorrie enjoyed a vigorous life outdoors in Mauritius, taking a keen interest in its flora and fauna, its weather and its varied countryside. He frequently stayed in the mountainous interior and walked a great deal in the cool hills, a great contrast to hot, smelly, unhealthy Port Louis. Indeed, like nearly every other reasonably affluent resident, he actually lived, not in the capital but 'up in the country', at Beau Bassin in the low hills above the town, and travelled up and down each day by train. Ten years after he left Mauritius, the two experiences which he focused on in a lecture to a Trinidad audience on memories of many lands were its hurricanes, and its hunting parties. He vividly described his experience of a bad storm in 1874, but his most amusing anecdote was about a 'Mauritius chasse', a genial hunting expedition in the interior stalking wild deer:

> The rule in Mauritius is that there is nothing to be shot at but a stag, so the does surround the finest stags . . . and if you hit a doe you are never

> asked back to a chasse – you are supposed to be a duffer who has disgraced himself. Then at night when we all come in to the great dinner that is usually given in the roughly put up place in the forest, each man recounts his exploits. Sometimes there are fifty or sixty fine stags shot. It is regular butchery. It is not the regular way of taking sport, but still we all did it . . . [60]

Moreover, Mauritius inspired him to exercise his literary talents in new ways. He wrote poems, at least one of which he thought good enough to seek a London publisher, asking his old journalistic colleague Justin McCarthy to suggest one ("he will think I have got sunstroke!"). He would have loved to have written the sort of lively polemic about Indians in Mauritius that Edward Jenkins had so successfully penned on British Guiana, *The Coolie, His Rights and Wrongs*, and even suggested a title, "The New Paul & Virginia", after the romantic legend set in the island. "I would rejoice to do the thing myself, and my fingers tingle at the very thought, but", he admitted regretfully, "of course I must not."[61]

Not satisfied with his work on the bench and all his many extracurricular activities, Gorrie wrote a full-length romantic novel, set in the island and full of his likes, dislikes and prejudices about its society. Never published nor even, apparently, titled, the work is competently written and contains many good descriptions of scenery and Creole lifestyles. But the characters are stereotypical (frank, manly English soldier; corrupt, proud, touchy, passionate French Creole; beautiful, shy yet charming Creole girl with a 'touch of the tar brush') and fail to come to life as rounded individuals. Gorrie's crusading zeal for justice, his hatred of oppression, his stern moralism and didacticism, are all to be found in his novel, and he constantly breaks into the narrative to deliver lectures on diverse topics: how duelling could persist for so long in a British colony; how the police arrest and convict unscrupulously and how the higher officials fail to stop this; how oppressive laws made life difficult for poor but honest black fishermen. We can, perhaps, glimpse Gorrie's ideas about race and colour from this work: he condemns high Creole society for its ostracism of the heroine's family because of its "slight touch of the tar brush" and portrays Sgt Stocks of the local police, who has all "the contempt which the low Briton entertains for the rights of the coloured race, and especially for a coloured race which was additionally contemptible by speaking French", and Amirantes, the Creole rake who is careful "never to show by his manner that contempt for the black race which he so profoundly felt", as thoroughly despicable characters. But this was a work of fiction; its author actually describes the Indian labourers on the heroine's estate as being "as happy as any peasantry in the world"; can this be the pen of the scourge of the Mauritian planters? Yet the work contains many carefully observed and detailed descriptions of island life, sympathetically presented, suggesting a real appreciation for Creole society at its best, an empathy for the cultured French families who constituted a local elite of more refinement than could be found, perhaps, in most British colonies. It does not suggest any deep prejudice against the French Creole planters or their traditions, and it does indicate that Gorrie liked the island, had learned much about it, and had come to appreciate its unique qualities.[62]

CHAPTER FOUR

The Frontier Colony: Fiji, 1876-82

In February 1876, Gorrie accepted the chief justiceship of Fiji. For as long as Arthur Gordon was there, Gorrie was one of a small group of men who helped him to create the Crown Colony of Fiji and to shape its fundamental social and legal institutions. In effect, Gorrie was a member of Gordon's inner cabinet as well as sole judge. Gordon inspired extraordinary devotion and loyalty from the men who served with him, including Gorrie, whose relationship with him combined profound respect with friendship and a camaraderie based on common principles and shared goals. His influence was immense: he moderated Gorrie's impetuous personality and kept him out of major difficulties so long as he was governor; and in return he received outstanding service from his Chief Justice.

Fiji was a frontier colony which had just been annexed to the Crown. The fundamental questions about its future development had not yet been settled when Gordon, and then Gorrie, took up their respective offices. This was no mature, settled plantation colony like Mauritius, there was no self-confident, long entrenched white landowning elite, there was no legacy of plantation slavery. In Fiji Gorrie had a chance to help mould a new society and to determine future relationships between the indigenous Fijians, the European settlers and the immigrant labourers from other Pacific islands. His years in the Pacific offered abundant scope for his immense energies and his political and legislative skills. In many ways this was the most creative period of his career.

Fiji in the 1870s

The new Crown Colony consisted of many islands. The two largest were Viti Levu and Vanua Levu, but the chief centre of white settlement in the 1870s was on Ovalau, a much smaller island to the east of Viti Levu. In 1874, the year of annexation, the population of the whole group may have been around 135,000. The great majority were of course indigenous Fijians. In addition, there were many Tongans settled in the Lau or Eastern group of islands under their powerful chief Ma'afu, an increasing number of people brought in as labourers from other Pacific islands known collectively as Polynesians, and a few hundred whites from Britain, Australia, New Zealand, America and Europe. White men first stepped ashore on Fijian soil in 1804; they were escaped convicts from New South Wales. Various adventurers, beachcombers, shipwrecks, derelicts and more runaways came to live in the islands in the decades that followed, but no systematic settlement occurred until the late 1850s. Far more influential than these early visitors were Methodist missionaries from Britain. From around 1840, a small group of men and women, unshakable in their conviction that Christianity and western ways were immeasurably superior to Fijian religion and culture, worked to convert the islanders. By the time of annexation nearly the whole population had abandoned the religion of their forefathers and had accepted the *lotu* (Christianity). Accepting the *lotu,* of course, meant the rejection of traditional ways of life, including intercommunity warfare and much of the indigenous culture in general. The extraordinary success of the missionaries entrenched the Methodists as a potent influence on Fijian affairs, and made the islands relatively safe for white incursion and settlement.

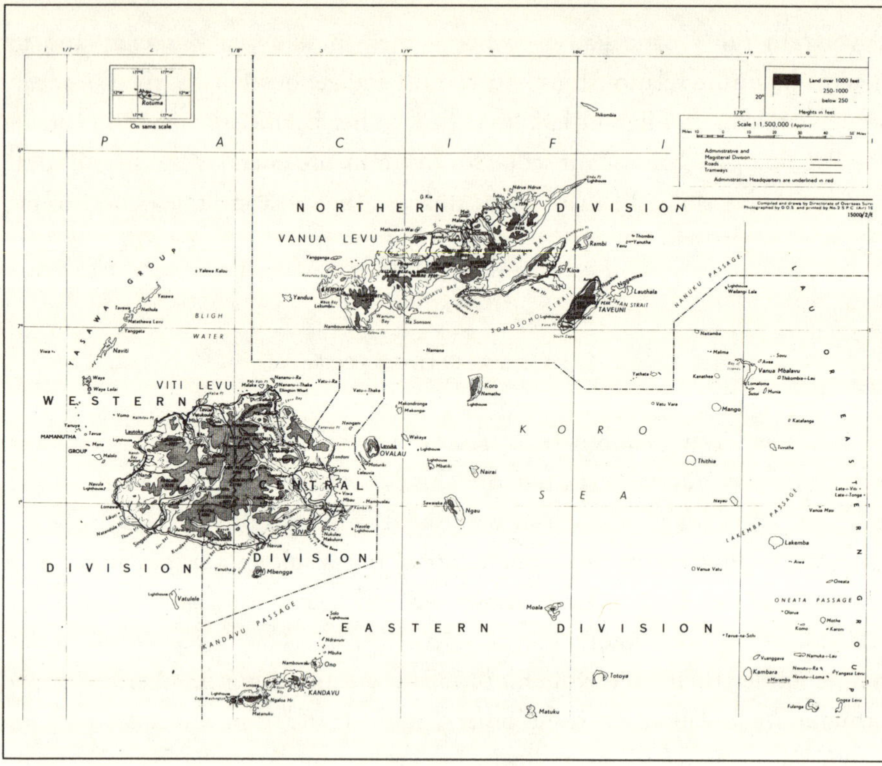

The Fiji Islands

White settlers flocked to Fiji starting from the late 1850s, but especially between about 1867 and 1872. Most were from Australia and New Zealand; many were penniless adventurers; a few were out and out criminals. They came to 'buy' land from native chiefs and establish plantations of cotton, sugar or coconuts. The American Civil War had caused a sudden rise in world cotton prices, and Fiji was thought to be especially suited to cotton cultivation. Hence the "great Fiji rush" of the late 1860s: the white population, estimated at around 800 in 1867, had crossed 2000 by 1870, and in 1870 and 1871 alone, 1508 whites arrived, some 350 of them women. Considerable areas of land were acquired from the chiefs, sometimes bona fide purchases, but often through fraud or coercion. The cotton boom was short lived, as prices collapsed in the early 1870s, but sugar and coconuts became important crops; the first sugar mill was built in 1872 at Suva in Viti

Levu, the site of the future capital. Since the chiefs were reluctant to let Fijians work on the new plantations, except for very short spells, a traffic in more or less kidnapped Polynesians developed, the notorious blackbirding trade. These men, from many Pacific island groups, were recruited by professional kidnappers and shipped to Fiji for work on the white owned plantations.

The centre of white settlement, and the first capital of colonial Fiji, was Levuka on Ovalau. By 1874 its population was a few hundred, and it had developed into a regular little township. Levuka before annexation was a somewhat raffish place, predominantly male, with an atmosphere of impermanence, lawlessness and adventurism; its tone was set by rough types anxious to make a quick fortune and not overburdened with scruples about the means. Outside the little town, whites were scattered round the coasts of the larger islands carving out plantations and coexisting more or less peaceably with their Fijian neighbours.

Nearly all the white settlers were British subjects. But London had rejected in 1858 an early offer by prominent chiefs to cede the islands to the Crown, and in 1870 no action was taken in response to fresh appeals for annexation from Fiji and from the Australian colonies. In 1871 a formal "native government" was set up. Cakobau, the leading chief, was proclaimed King (Tui Viti) with white and Fijian ministers, and a constitution was enacted. The most powerful man in the new government was John Bates Thurston, an English settler who as Cakobau's chief minister did what he could to protect Fijians both from their chiefs and from the planters, and was hated by the settlers as a result. But Cakobau's government soon became unviable because of the hostility and lawlessness of most of the white settlers. Moreover, it became deeply indebted to Australian debenture holders, who became anxious as Fiji slipped towards anarchy. In Britain, public and Parliamentary opinion was agitated about the horrors of the blackbirding traffic, a cause taken up by Chesson and his Aborigines Protection Society (APS). These combined pressures led a reluctant Gladstone ministry to agree to a Commission to examine the Fijian situation and make recommendations. Commissioners J.G. Goodenough and E.L. Layard arrived early in 1874, and reported that virtually all the whites, the Tongans living in Fiji led by Ma'afu, and most Fijian chiefs favoured annexation. Cakobau himself announced his willingness to cede sovereignty. Accordingly, the Commission strongly recommended annexation. Sir Hercules Robinson was sent to negotiate an unconditional cession to the Crown by the Cakobau government. He signed the Deed of Cession with Cakobau and leading chiefs on October 10, 1874. Fiji had become a Crown Colony. [1]

Gordon was appointed the first substantive governor of the new colony, and took up his post towards the middle of 1875. But before his arrival, an appalling tragedy took place: Cakobau and his sons, returning from a trip to Australia, introduced measles to the Fijian population early in 1875, through the negligence of the officials who should have insisted on quarantine procedures. Lacking all immunity, and naturally suspicious of any advice about treatment offered by the whites, Fijians succumbed in enormous numbers all through the islands. It has been estimated that about a quarter of the total Fijian population perished in a few months. Though most Fijians accepted this tragedy with resignation, it is hardly surprising that some chiefs and commoners, especially those in the interior of Viti Levu who had not yet accepted Christianity or had done so reluctantly, concluded that the old gods had wreaked a terrible retribution and that British rule meant death and disaster for the people of Viti.

British rule could hardly have commenced under more difficult circumstances. Gordon had to work to overcome the fears and suspicions of Fijians in the wake of this tragedy, and to persuade white settlers that their interests would be protected in the 'crown colony of a severe type' which he was instructed to establish. Moreover, with the collapse of the cotton boom, and with sugar not yet established as the main export, most white settlers were poor and despondent, and the revenue base of the new colony looked precarious. The Colonial Office had made it amply clear that Fiji must become self-supporting as early as possible and that no lavish funding from Parliament would be forthcoming.

The main issues of Gordon's government centred on native administration, land, and immigrant labour. He believed that his mission – and that of British rule in Fiji – was to preserve and protect the Fijian population from the rapacity of white settlers and from the demoralization inseparable from working on their plantations and absorbing their 'civilization'. Fijians should be left to live as much as possible in the old ways and under their traditional leaders; it must be recalled that nearly all of them were already Christians and that most of their chiefs had renounced intercommunity warfare and practices like infanticide. Gordon confirmed and developed provisional arrangements made by Robinson to set up a special native administration under which the Fijian population would be governed. Fiji was divided into twelve districts, each under a leading chief styled *Roko Tui*; ex-King Cakobau was given the honorary title *Vunivalu* and treated with great deference by Gordon and his men. The districts were further divided into smaller units under *Bulis*, or minor chiefs. Besides the *Rokos* and *Bulis*, who were invariably chosen from the chiefly or aristocratic caste, there were native magistrates with jurisdiction over Fijians only. *Rokos, Bulis* and native magistrates all received stipends from the colonial government, administered 'native regulations' not British law, and were loosely supervised by a Chief Native Commissioner responsible to the governor. The apex of the system was the *Bose vaka Turaga*, the annual council or parliament of the *Rokos* and some of the *Bulis*, which deliberated on problems affecting the indigenous population and made recommendations to the governor. In effect, this was an early system of indirect rule, with the Fijians largely under the control of their traditional leaders.

This system was strengthened by Gordon's decision to replace a poll tax, imposed on the native population by Cakobau's government, by a community tax levied in produce not cash. A poll tax had the effect of forcing male Fijians to work on the plantations for wages with which to pay the levy. But Gordon wished to prevent Fijians from leaving their communities, abandoning their gardens, and becoming dependent plantation labourers. Instead, each district was assessed for a certain sum to be paid each year; the local *Roko* and *Bulis* then had the responsibility of ensuring that produce to the value of the sum was delivered at the appropriate times. The produce (yams and other root crops, coconuts, bêche de mer – *ie* sea cucumber, a delicacy in China which was one of Fiji's early exports – and other crops traditionally grown by Fijian farmers) was sold to dealers at market prices. This tax, loosely based on Dutch methods in Indonesia, kept most Fijians in their communities engaged in farming under their chiefs; it also made them keenly aware of the real market value of their produce, to the chagrin of white dealers accustomed to buying Fijian goods for the proverbial song. In time, the community tax became firmly established as the principal tax on the indigenous population and as a sound basis for the colonial revenues.

If most Fijians were to be kept away from the plantations, how was labour to be supplied? Gordon recognised that the islands had started on an irreversible process of plantation development and that this could only accelerate as capitalist confidence grew after annexation. He believed that immigrants should be the main source of plantation labour, recruited and protected under stringent regulations. Polynesian immigration, once the abuses of blackbirding had been suppressed and the recruits were protected in Fiji by careful laws and regular inspections, should continue. But Gordon, influenced by his experiences both in Trinidad and Mauritius, believed that indentured Indian labour was the better solution in the long run; he thought that Indian immigration could be conducted both efficiently and humanely, in the interests both of their employers and of the immigrants themselves. He therefore took the fateful decision to begin Indian labour immigration to Fiji; the first recruits arrived in 1879. In effect, Gordon wanted to use Polynesian and Indian immigrants as substitutes for Fijians, in order to protect the latter from the rigours of the plantation regime and to preserve the indigenous civilization.

Plantation development required both labour and land. In the years before annexation, many whites had claimed and, much less frequently, actually cleared and cultivated lands throughout the islands. Should all these claims be accepted by the new colonial government, and should whites be permitted in the future to 'buy' land from chiefs? Traditionally, land in Fiji was held by communities, by groups of families or clans, and it was unthinkable for a chief to sell land to anyone; alienability of land, or individual ownership, were concepts unknown to Fijian society. In very many cases, whites had 'bought' land through fraud or coercion. Gordon believed that each claim should be carefully investigated by a special commission (not a regular court) which should proceed on the basis of equity and substantial justice to all parties. Once a claim had been approved, the Crown would grant an indefeasible title to that land; if a claim was disapproved, the aggrieved claimant should have no recourse to the law courts. All land not granted to whites in this way would be considered as belonging forever to the Fijian chiefs and communities (except for some reserved to the Crown for special purposes) and would be inalienable in the future. This policy was to be the cornerstone of Gordon's administration in Fiji; it had fateful consequences for the development of the colony over the long run, while in the short term it was the most controversial aspect of his regime.[2]

Law, Legislation and Government

In February 1876, the governor of Mauritius received a telegram from the Secretary of State: "Offer Gorrie chief justiceship Fiji present salary £1200 Must proceed to post by earliest opportunity." The decision to offer Gorrie the post was the result, not only of Gordon's lobbying, but also the Colonial Office's evaluation of his performance in Mauritius. "Mr Gorrie has the character of an able lawyer", noted one official, "and is a man of a good deal of force of character, well able to cope with the rough elements with which he will be brought into contact in Fiji. His temper is said to be somewhat hasty but this is perhaps of less importance as he has always managed to keep on good terms with Sir A.Gordon."[3]

On receiving news of the offer, and noting the advice that he should proceed to Fiji as soon as possible, Gorrie decided to go almost immediately, forgoing the home leave to which he was entitled after six years' service in Mauritius, and instead going directly to Australia and thence to Fiji. At the end of March 1876, he took passage with a small Danish schooner destined for Adelaide. The run from Mauritius to Adelaide took five weeks (a distance of over 4,000 miles) and Gorrie was the only passenger on what was essentially a cargo boat. He became good friends with the captain and crew, though they spoke no English, and helped the captain work out the latitude and keep his records. His first exposure to Australia was at Adelaide, where he was impressed by the cheapness of food and the dearness of all services, and by the prosperity of the working class. While at Adelaide, he did some research on the Torrens system of land titles by registration, which had first been implemented in South Australia by Sir Robert Torrens, but he cut his stay short when he heard by telegram of the outbreak of a rising in the interior of Viti Levu. The cable suggested that this was a rising against white settlers, and Gorrie assumed that his presence would be needed. He proceeded by train from Adelaide to Melbourne, then Sydney, where he took ship for Fiji, some 1800 miles away.[4] After this heroic journey, he arrived at Levuka on June 10, 1876; to his dismay, he found that his predecessor, Sir William Hackett, was still there carrying out his duties and drawing his salary. Hackett did not leave until July 7, the day on which Gorrie took up his duties.

Unfortunately for Gorrie, his decision to depart for Fiji so quickly, forgoing his entitlement to 'home leave' and leaving Mauritius before the details of the transfer had been worked out, and then his arrival before Hackett had left, involved him in a protracted dispute with the Colonial Office about money, which was not finally resolved until 1880, and then in a manner calculated to embitter him. The details are unimportant; but the whole unpleasant episode undoubtedly increased Gorrie's sense of being an 'outsider' in the colonial service, without influence or powerful friends to win favourable consideration for his claims, and he certainly believed (probably unjustly) that Gordon had not fought hard enough on his behalf.[5]

Meanwhile, the family had returned to Britain by a long sea voyage via St Helena, taking just over three months. They had no news from Gorrie until they reached London early in August 1876. Here they received a long letter from Fiji, which somewhat dismayed the eighteen year-old Minnie:

> Fiji seems a very wild sort of place. The houses are not very good, and very dear. In some parts the people are still cannibals. At dinner only Sir Arthur Gordon and Papa sat on chairs, the others on mats. There are no roads and altogether it seems a very rough sort of life. I don't think I should like it.

Minnie was pining for Mauritius, which she had loved, and where she had left a young man whom she thought she liked. Perhaps, though, she cheered up a little when Papa wrote saying "[he thinks] we will be the only young ladies there [Levuka]"; and when she read that "Papa has been asked to two dances but only went to one, he said it was rather slow but thought he was the better of having gone", she was willing to concede: "I don't suppose we will find it such a bad place after all". The family arrived in Fiji in the middle of 1877, after a separation from their husband and father of over 16 months. He greeted their arrival with a touching poem to his wife:

> So murmuring thus soft words of love,
> The light will wane, the stars above
> Shine from yon cloudless dome:
> A sacred joy will fill each breast,
> And thus caressing and caressed,
> My wife I welcome home.[6]

When Gorrie arrived in Levuka in June 1876, Gordon was preoccupied with the suppression of a rising by chiefs in the mountainous interior of Vitu Levu. These 'mountain people', the *Kai Colos*, had not accepted Christianity, nor had they abandoned the old practices of raiding villages, seizing women and killing men. They fiercely resented the new religion, the annexation, and the measles epidemic, but their rising was not directed against the British, nor the white settlers, but against the Christian communities and chiefs of the coastal districts of Viti Levu. Though the rising was limited in terms of the numbers involved, it was menacing enough, and Gordon decided to suppress it by the use of levies of 'volunteers' contributed by the majority of *Rokos* and *Bulis* who were loyal to the Crown and to the *lotu*. This was brilliantly successful; the Fijian troops responded with enthusiasm to the governor's call, and the *Kai Colos* were subdued in a few weeks with little loss of life on either side. Gordon personally supervised the campaign, and he took Gorrie up to the hills with him on his last trip "just to see something of the mountain tribes before they become civilized, like those of the coast". By an extraordinary twist of fate, also accompanying Gordon on this trip, as his private secretary, was young Charles Eyre, son of ex-governor Eyre of Jamaica. As another former associate of Gordon commented, many years later, "Could he have had two stranger companions, when he had to shoot and hang natives who had committed atrocities?" Gordon admitted that when he recognized that some trials and executions were unavoidable, he "sent Gorrie away" on a long walk to Nadi, and had them carried out by one of his officials under a proclamation which exempted the disturbed districts from the jurisdiction of the Supreme Court. Neither Gorrie, nor Hackett (who was still Chief Justice when the trials took place) played any role in these events.[7]

With this first-hand glimpse of old Fiji, now passing away, Gorrie wrote a lively article about the "little war", as Gordon referred to the rising and its suppression, and about Fiji in general, which was published in the *Daily News* (successor to the *Morning Star*) in August 1876. It was unsigned, but a letter from Rachael Gordon confirms his authorship; she told her sister that "he was with the Governor at the time, so it is quite correct. No one knows here [in Fiji] who wrote it". The long article gives a vivid description of the *Kai Colo*s, and offers a thoughtful, generally approving assessment of Gordon's policies on native government and his conduct of the campaign against the rebels. Noting that 14 men had been executed for murder and other crimes, on the governor's authority, he explained: "Sir Arthur Gordon apparently thought that to leave these chiefs [those found guilty of murder] to escape . . . would simply be to run the risk of a repetition of the outbreak. He is too true a friend of native races to be suspected of any colonial antipathy to these mountaineers. He is too firm a ruler to be suspected of panic." By no stretch of the imagination was Gordon an Eyre, nor were the rebel *Kai Colos* Jamaican peasant farmers.

Until Gordon left Fiji at the end of 1880, Gorrie functioned, along with a handful of others, as an adviser on policy, as his main assistant in drafting legislation, and as his legal consultant. In effect he acted as cabinet member, attorney-general, legislator and confidant, as well as sole judge. This was only possible, of course, because his relations with the governor were close and mutually respectful. Gorrie never quarrelled with him, and he was perhaps the only man who could check his temper and make him reconsider.

In the small white society of Levuka, Gorrie and his family were on intimate terms with the Gordons. Rachael Gordon told her sisters how pleased her husband was at Gorrie's appointment "as he liked him very much in Mauritius, and it was his own suggestion"; she herself liked the new Chief Justice "extremely, far better than Sir W. Hackett". During his first weeks in Levuka, he stayed at Nasova, the governor's house, and became an adopted member of the family: "We all like him very much. Nevil [the Gordon daughter] has taken possession of him, and obliges him to read to her and play draughts with her." Even after he moved into his own house, he continued to dine at Nasova; and when his wife and children arrived, they were frequent guests there.[9]

The voluminous correspondence between the two men during and after Gordon's term as governor makes it clear that this was a relationship of equals. Gordon frequently sought advice from his Chief Justice on all sorts of topics, and Gorrie was confident enough to criticize his superior freely and banter with him. There was both respect and affection between them. Gordon often took Gorrie with him on his trips to the islands and districts, even when there was no judicial work to be done, and asked his advice on such matters as whether he (Gordon) should consent to serve as 'patron' of races planned for Levuka. No wonder that Gorrie, congratulating him on an article in *The Scotsman* which praised his achievements, wrote teasingly "you *have* done a good work here, although, of course, if you had taken the advice of a certain person on *every* and *all* occasions it would have been much better!" Gorrie wrote the truth when he told Gordon:

> both in Mauritius and here, our relations have been very different from the merely formal ones which usually subsist between Judges and Governors in the Colonies. Had you been a Governor of the ordinary type, and had not attempted to remedy the great abuses in Mauritius, I have no doubt I should have despaired and left the service; and here, what pleasure or profit would it be to spend one's years at the antipodes did I not constantly feel that if I have anything to propose that would help to strengthen the foundations you are laying that you are willing to hear and consider favourably, whether it affects my own peculiar work or not. If therefore I regard such a letter as you have sent [thanking him for his work while Gordon was on home leave] as something to be treasured, it arises from a feeling much higher than mere pleasure at official recognition of duty performed.[10]

Gorrie did not always agree with all the details of Gordon's native policies, and criticism from him was keenly felt by the governor, proof of the importance he attached to his views. But such disagreements were minor, as Gorrie reminded him when he was about to leave Fiji: "Upon the native policy, I need not say my sympathy has been entirely with you; any trifling leaning this way rather than that way being as nothing." But much as Gordon respected his friend, he was too shrewd a judge of men not to recognize that Gorrie had serious personality flaws. This is why he advised the Colonial Office to appoint William Des Voeux to act as governor during his year's home leave in 1878-79; if it was Thurston, who as Colonial Secretary had the 'right' to act, the Chief Justice would be "mortally offended", but Gorrie "would not be a good Governor". Gorrie had hoped to be named acting governor, and he expressed his disappointment quite bluntly, telling Gordon "I am just as ambitious as other people, and certainly don't intend to stick where I am."[11]

Gorrie was not the only ambitious and forceful personality close to Gordon. A small group of men devoted to the governor made up his official 'family'. The most important were J.B. Thurston and William MacGregor; Thurston was certainly the most remarkable. An early settler in Fiji, he had served as Cakobau's chief minister; he had been 'demoted' after annexation but had won Gordon's confidence and was appointed Colonial Secretary in 1877. He probably knew Fiji and Fijians better than any other white man, and he thoroughly sympathised with Gordon's native policy. Gorrie admired him, recognised his abilities, and was almost certainly jealous of his friendship with Gordon and his unique status in Fiji. He told his friend Chesson, rather ruefully, "Thurston is certainly an able man – and between ourselves with a fine sense of the importance of No.1. You and I would have been none the worse of some of it at an earlier period of our career." Thurston did not have a high opinion of Gorrie, and tried his best to prejudice both Gordon, and Des Voeux as acting governor, against him. He wrote to Gordon, soon after he had gone home on leave in 1878, "Gorrie is certainly piqued at not having the temporary administration . . . Then at heart he is dead against our native policy, and death upon a *Roko* or any native chief. Native Magistrates are an abomination in his eyes, and the name of a native Court stinketh in his nostrils." Thurston sent Gordon lively and immensely detailed accounts of the skirmishes between Des Voeux and Gorrie during the governor's home leave, always putting Gorrie in a bad light, or sometimes damning him with faint praise: "So far as Gorrie is concerned, I really don't believe he means mischief, but he is not prudent in his language, nor is he careful to whom he expresses his opinion . . . I like him immensely in many ways, but if he was somewhat more reserved and dignified, and less extravagant in his language, I would like him better." It was MacGregor's view that Thurston was deliberately seeking to worsen relations between Des Voeux and Gorrie, and to prejudice Gordon against the latter.[12]

MacGregor, a Scottish doctor who was close to Gordon and had risen to the position of Receiver-General in the Fiji government, was Gorrie's ally. Indeed, the two men had much in common: both were Scots from humble backgrounds, both were quintessentially self-made men, both revered Gordon, both felt that they were outsiders vis-à-vis the colonial establishment in London; and it no doubt helped their relationship that MacGregor could not stand Thurston. MacGregor believed that Gorrie was a loyal colleague and friend. He told Gordon that he was "the most genuinely honest of your followers, the one of all others that has his heart with you in your work here", a man of "candour, sincerity and straightforward action". He warned Gordon not to allow himself to be prejudiced against Gorrie; if he did, he would find "only one official of importance [Thurston] in a contented mood on your return". One can agree with MacGregor's biographer when he writes of "the jealousies and incompatibilities which are almost inevitable in a small group isolated in remote colonies".[13]

Gorrie drafted many ordinances for the Legislative Council between 1876 and 1882, amended his drafts after discussions with Gordon, and often introduced and defended the bills in the Council. This was especially the case with ordinances forming part of the civil law code, and those related to land transactions. In 1877, he drafted a Native Debtors' Ordinance, and a Bankruptcy Ordinance which Gordon described as "of Gorrie's manufacture – not a bad one". He had begun to work on this law almost as soon as he took up office, using an earlier draft by his predecessor, and attempting to "get rid of the greater bulk of the confused English law of Bankruptcy, and make a short, pithy, complete system". Under the Ordinance, bankruptcy cases were to be taken as part of the ordinary business of the Supreme Court.[14]

It was the Chief Justice's intention to produce a whole series of ordinances which would constitute a complete civil code for the new colony, adapting English law to its special circumstances. In 1878 he completed a draft law on joint stock companies, which the Secretary of State called "a well considered and ably prepared compendium of the law on the subject". Gorrie himself took the bill through the Council, delivering an elaborate speech which included a detailed historical account of the evolution of the law of partnership and joint stock companies. He told the Council that he intended the bill to be "an additional step towards a commercial code, which was begun by the Bankruptcy law".[15] And between 1878 and 1881, a stream of ordinances relating to the civil code flowed from his pen. One of the most important was Ordinance 11 of 1879, to provide for the registration of deeds and other documents. It did not merely adapt English law, but sought to introduce innovations specially designed for Fijian circumstances. These innovations were carefully explained by Gorrie in lengthy memoranda, which pointed out that similar provisions existed in the codes of British colonies which had a French legal tradition (Mauritius, Quebec, and St Lucia), and in Scotland, and argued that in a brand new colony, there was no difficulty in adopting nonEnglish forms if they seemed to be helpful. The men in the Colonial Office were so impressed (or overwhelmed) by these very long documents by Gorrie that they waived their earlier objections and sanctioned the Ordinance without modification. Similarly, an ordinance on bills of sales (8 of 1879) was confirmed with only minor changes after the Secretary of State declared he was satisfied with the Chief Justice's explanations as to why the English law on the subject had been so substantially modified.[16]

In 1880-81 Gorrie produced ordinances on contracts, on the administration of intestate and vacant estates, on contract of agency and on indemnity guarantee and bailment. These were all part of a series "which is being introduced by Gorrie with a view to its ultimately forming a complete Code of Civil Law". The Colonial Office's legal experts, headed by Edward Wingfield, gave his work high marks. His ordinance on contracts was described as "an elaborate and ably and carefully drawn up chapter on contracts for a Code". All these laws were sanctioned with only minor changes.[17]

In addition to his labours in drafting, introducing and defending legislation, Gorrie at times gave legal advice to the government. This was partly due to the incompetence of J.H. Garrick, Attorney-General during most of Gorrie's time in Fiji. Garrick was lazy as well as incompetent. A clearly exasperated Gorrie informed the Colonial Office that he drafted and took charge of many legal ordinances "simply because if they had been left to Mr Garrick they would never have seen the light". Worse, Garrick had an extensive private practice which often involved him with clients who were engaged in conflicts with the government. As Gordon put it: "The plague of having one's Attorney-General the private solicitor of every one who has interests against the Government is almost intolerable, and must justify my sometimes asking you [Gorrie] questions I should otherwise ask him."[18]

The extent of the work performed by Gorrie, over and above his normal duties as sole judge, was illustrated by a letter from Gordon in 1877, sending

> a sort of table of all you have been kind enough to undertake for the Government! – Ordinance to provide for arbitration in cases of land taken for public purposes under the Deed of Cession; Ordinance making debts by natives above a certain amount irrecoverable; Amended Land Transfer Ordinance; Late Government Liabilities Commission; Woods and Forests Committee; Mrs Blair's case; Friendly Societies Ordinance Select Committee.

Gorrie amply deserved the various tributes paid to him by Gordon, and later by Des Voeux, for his legislative efforts. Gordon told an assembly of white settlers early in 1878 that the laws then being introduced or framed by the Chief Justice "would not only reflect credit on their author, but go far to make the Statute Book of Fiji respected and admired beyond the narrow limits of the Colony". When he left on his home leave later that year, he told a 'levee' that "the sensitive independence of the Bench would be alarmed were the Governor to express himself as obliged to a Judge, but as a member of the Legislative Council and as a friend he trusted the Chief Justice would accept his thanks for much efficient help".[19]

The Chief Justice sat on the Legislative Council (which was wholly nominated, but included four 'unofficials' to represent the white settlers) throughout his stay in Fiji. He frequently piloted bills, often drafted by himself, through their stages. In the absence of the governor or acting governor, he presided, as he did in December 1879 when he introduced two legal bills. As Fiji was a Crown Colony 'of a severe type', the Council had an official majority and no elected members, meaning, of course, that the governor could push through any measure he wanted. Gorrie was as convinced as Gordon that the Crown needed to keep complete legislative control over the new colony. He was a valuable official member of the Legislature, and he was certainly a very active participant in its proceedings.

Land Issues

Land questions lay at the heart of Gordon's administration in Fiji, and Gorrie was closely involved in these issues. In 1875, whites claimed some one-fifth of the total area of the colony, though only a fraction of this land was actually under cultivation by them. The Colonial Office was disposed to give Gordon absolute discretion to settle the whole matter. Article IV of the Deed of Cession vested in the Crown "the absolute proprietorship of all lands not shown to be now alienated so as to have become the bona fide property of Europeans or other foreigners". Gordon moved quickly: ordinances enacted soon after his arrival in 1875 prohibited suits over existing white claims to land in the colony's law courts, forbade all alienation of native lands for the time being, and set up a Lands Commission (LC) empowered to investigate land claims under Hackett as chairman. Its recommendations on specific claims were considered by the Governor in Council (*ie* the Executive Council) and, if approved, the governor then issued Crown titles.

But how would the bona fides of land transactions between whites and chiefs be determined? All the experts on Fijian society agreed that chiefs could not alienate land without the consent of their people (*taukeis*); many thought that Fijian land was communally held, strictly entailed from one generation to the next, and therefore completely inalienable. If the latter view (held by Gordon) was taken by the LC and the Governor in Council, no sale of land by Fijians to whites could be considered bona fide and the Crown could disallow all such claims. Actually, the LC was much more flexible. It generally approved claims once it was satisfied that no coercion or fraud had been involved, that a 'fair price' had been paid and that both parties believed it was a reasonable transaction; at times it recommended an *ex gratia* grant on the basis of actual occupation by whites. Each case was taken on its merits. On the basis of the LC's recommendations, the Governor in Council either disallowed a claim, or issued an indefeasible Crown title for the amount of land recommended. Finally, Ordinance 21 of 1880 declared that all native lands were inalienable except to the Crown, and then only for 'public purposes', and were vested forever in the traditional Fijian communities or clans (*mataqali*). The *mataqali* could, however, lease lands under certain restrictions. This law confirmed native titles to land, discouraged the development of individual ownership by Fijians, and meant that new investors would be obliged either to lease land, or buy it from settlers who had been issued Crown grants after their pre-Cession claims were upheld.[20]

In succession to Hackett, Gorrie was appointed a member of the LC, a responsibility which involved travelling all through the islands and hearing complex evidence from white claimants and Fijians. As he told Chesson, this work gave him "a thorough insight into the condition of society both now and previously". It is not clear whether he was formally appointed chairman of the LC, but he certainly behaved as if he was. On joining the LC in July 1876, Gorrie heard claims on the island of Taveuni. The *Fiji Argus* was pleased: "His Lordship seems to have a thorough go ahead spirit about him, which, we trust, will aid the Land Commissioners in getting along a little smarter than hitherto." On the completion of the Taveuni hearings, the editor noted that he had "given great satisfaction in his manner of dealing with the claims"; seventeen cases were got through in one day. He was then involved in cases at Ovalau, where Levuka was situated. These were described by him as "small potatoes", but claims by ex-King Cakobau complicated matters, and finding a Fijian interpreter who was both competent and honest was a problem.[21]

In November 1876, the LC went to Viti Levu to hear claims in the fertile Rewa district. Some of these claims were difficult. He told Chesson "at Rewa I spoke very sharply of the action of certain Wesleyan Ministers who had purchased land cheap of a Chief and sold it dear, in the most approved style of land sharks". Writing to Gordon from Navuso on the Rewa, he said: "The country around is open, rich, and interesting, as you know. The mosquitoes day and night simply – (put in any strong adjective) . . . A New Zealand resident claims the ground on which the town and plantations of Navuso are, and an immense tract besides – the original purchase having been made with 'trade' not worth a rood of ground." He added a poetic report on the hearings at Navuso:

> We sat in Adi Kuila's house
> We slept upon her mats;
> But, oh, the swarm of mosquitoes,
> And, oh, the rush of rats.
>
> The planter came with his land claim,
> He swore that white was black;
> The pious missionary too,
> Swore black was white – alack!
>
> . . .
>
> And Mitchell bathed, the Judge made puns,
> The Colonel tried long naps,
> Young Eyre, I swear, with brown legs bare
> Worked hard and late – perhaps!
>
> And when the oaths had all been sworn,
> The lies in form recorded;
> What could we do but make report,
> That men were mean and sordid?[22]

Not long after the Rewa hearings, Gorrie abruptly resigned from the LC. Gordon wrote in his journal: "Chief Justice made a foolish speech at the meeting of the LC which will not assist the progress of that body, and a yet more foolish move in resigning his seat in a pet." He told Gorrie that he "sincerely regretted the public statement, the consequences of which will, I fear, be far more serious, and far more mischievous than could have been anticipated by you". Gorrie defended himself in two long letters, now lost, to which Gordon replied: "You must excuse my not writing argumentative answers to your letters. What is done cannot now be mended, and I have no desire to enter publicly or privately on discussions which have no longer any practical bearing." Perhaps chastened, Gorrie wrote: "your letter re the LC is certainly not argumentative. But from its very brevity I can learn much, and, as it is clear this must have come sooner than later, it is better to have come sooner, so that I can make my bow and retire without bitterness and with a grateful sense of relief – *Sa oti* [Fijian for 'it is finished']." Rather cynically, the governor anticipated trouble from his volatile chief justice after this episode, confiding to his journal: "I am afraid he is going to be 'nasty', owing to my having taken him at his word as to quitting the LC. I never allow people to play with announcements of resignation. If they make them, I assume they mean them."[23] The real reasons for Gorrie's resignation from the LC are unclear, though Gordon may have been correct in thinking that he acted in a 'pet' and had hoped that his resignation would not have been accepted by the governor.

Though Gorrie was no longer on the LC, he was still intimately involved in the settlement of claims because he was invited to attend all meetings of the Executive Council which considered the LC's reports and made the final decisions. And he was frequently consulted by the governor. Difficulties arose both from disappointed white claimants, and from Fijians unwilling to sell lands which were not being used by chiefs or communities. Gorrie argued that Fijians should not be encouraged to block transfers of lands which they did not use or need:

> As to these little 'blethers' and hitches stopping the progress of the country by refraining to sell lands not in the occupancy of the chiefs and tribes, that will never do. It is the only way to prevent squatting, and to provide a revenue sufficient to permit the country to be governed at all. Any disposition on the part of the natives to resent reasonable and proper settlement must be put down just as firmly as sedition among the whites.[24]

Neither Gorrie nor Gordon, in fact, was an enemy of white settlement or plantation development in Fiji; they merely wished to protect the Fijians and their civilization. But this was never grasped by the planter interests, who bitterly attacked the governor's land policies.

Partly as a result of such attacks, the Colonial Office felt some unease at cutting off all opportunities for rehearing or appeal to disappointed claimants; as one official minuted, "even Sir A. Gordon may make a mistake". Both governor and Chief Justice were convinced that it would be fatal to allow claimants recourse to the ordinary courts. A lengthy memorandum by Gorrie written in March 1877 argued that it was much fairer to the claimants to say to them: "Come to me and show me that you acquired your lands fairly and for a fair price from the natives, and I will not only admit your claim, but give you a new title with the guarantee of the Crown, which will be worth more to you than all your land was worth in the old times." The situation required 'executive enquiry' before the issue of a Crown grant, not a court process. Moreover, the LC should not act like judges who heard only the evidence actually brought before them. Native testimony must be sought out, the circumstances of the sale must be investigated, and the LC must in effect act as protector of native interests in ensuring that all relevant evidence was available. But the LC did not decide, it only reported; the decision by the Governor in Council should always be made on grounds of equity and public policy. Speed was of the essence, "as the title will be granted in a very great proportion of the claims, and until granted the Colony is paralysed".[25]

This memorandum was useful support for Gordon. But both Gordon and Gorrie had to concede that a few cases of unusual difficulty might require further legal investigation before final disallowance; for instance, cases where white claimants were in dispute over a piece of land, or where a vast tract was claimed (as by the Polynesian Company, a large Australian concern) by virtue of sale by a chief when his people rejected his right to sell. After much discussion, the outcome was Ordinance 25 of 1879, drafted by Gorrie. It stated that any claim not yet sent in must be submitted within six months, or meet with absolute rejection. Investigations of claims would continue to be heard by the LC, but now with a full-time legal member sent from England as its chairman (he was Victor Williamson, who had served on the Mauritius Royal Commission and was a friend and ally of Gordon). On the basis of its reports, decisions would be made by the Governor in Council. Any aggrieved claimant could petition for a rehearing within a given time. The rehearing would be before a special board comprising the Governor in Council plus the Chief Justice and Chief Native Commissioner. Its decisions were to be final, and Crown grants were to be indefeasible.[26] Gordon and Gorrie had won an important victory. There was to be no recourse to the courts; and appeals would be heard by a body effectively dominated by the two men.

The first appeals under the Ordinance were heard in January 1880. Dissatisfied claimants soon began to grumble that it was futile to appeal from the Executive Council to the appeals board, that the native witnesses were led, that Fijians believed the government was their ally against white settlers. At a meeting with the Agricultural Society which spoke for the white planters, Gordon acknowledged that complaints had been made, but pointed out that the board had been set up by the Crown as a court of final appeal and could not be lightly set aside. Like Gordon, Gorrie found the work of the appeals board interesting and important. He told Chesson:

> I wish I could give you an idea of the nature of the work we are doing in the Land Claims Court [the appeals board]. I am sure it would give you satisfaction. We have the native owners represented and they are regarded exactly in the light of white persons having land rights of the same nature. The claimant must prove that he has got a good title (meaning by that not a technical bit of paper) from the actual owners before we will give a decision which may dispossess them. Last evening we threw out a claim to 30,000 acres which is covered by native towns and would probably have required force to turn out the people if we had granted the claim. On the other hand, as the claimant is a Queenslander who cannot comprehend the first principles of fair dealing with a native race, he will probably make a great howl.[27]

The enormous task of investigating land claims in Fiji was completed by the end of 1881. Between December 1875, when the LC first met, and December 1881, it dealt with 1683 applications and sent in 1327 reports. 517 claims were granted in their entirety; 390 were disallowed as of right but were granted *ex gratia* wholly or in part; 361 were disallowed; 56 were withdrawn; and 11 remained to be decided in the appeals board. In its final report, the LC stated that virtually all the relevant information on the cases it had investigated had been considered, and that any move to reopen the question of land claims, after the Fijians had been told that the settlements were final, "would be fraught with grave danger to the future relations of the whites towards the native subjects of Her Majesty in this Colony". And the Colonial Office set its face resolutely against all pleas for reconsideration or redress, whether from British subjects or from Germans. The settlements of 1876-81 were, indeed, to be "final and irrevocable" as both Gordon and Gorrie had insisted.[28]

Gorrie was the main author of legislation to govern the transfer of land in Fiji (those lands granted by the Crown to individuals, which were fully alienable). This was Ordinance 34 of 1876, "to provide for the transfer of land by the registration of titles". The issue of a Crown grant was to be taken as the first title, the starting point of the Ordinance; subsequently, all transfers were to be by the public registration of title. This was the Torrens system of land titles by registration, a system which Gorrie had long studied and admired. He told Chesson that: "In passing through S. Australia I took care to enquire into the subject as having had to study the French Land Laws, the Land Laws are now a hobby." In a long despatch, Gordon described the Ordinance as "among the most important, if not the most important, of those which have as yet been submitted to the consideration of the Legislative Council". He explained how it differed from the Torrens system on which it was based. First,

> the Australian Land Laws all contain sections which create a machinery, more or less elaborate, for bringing lands under their operation. Though requisite in a long settled community, where land has already been granted and dealt with under other systems, such provisions are unnecessary in a new colony, where not a single Crown grant of land has yet been issued, the issue of the grant itself ensuring its registration. [Second,] it is provided that the only estate in land shall be an estate in fee simple. [And third,] the mortgagee, instead of being empowered to take possession of the estate on foreclosure of his mortgage . . . is only enabled, as under the French code, to compel its sale.

The Ordinance was the result of intensive discussions between Gordon and Gorrie, and the two men also conferred frequently on the amendments requested by the Colonial Office before it was finally sanctioned later in 1877.[29]

In a pamphlet on Fiji published in 1882, Gorrie carefully described how Ordinance 34 of 1876 actually worked. Title to land originated in the indefeasible Crown grant. One copy was retained for registration. Thereafter, all transfers could only be by registration, with a new Certificate of Title granted as often as the property was transferred, "so that the title consists of one deed simply, and is always kept clear and distinct, without any accumulation of papers and deeds so puzzling to non-professional persons, and so fruitful a source of expense in lawyers' charges and otherwise". The key to the law was registration: "The transfer or mortgage only becomes effective when registered." After explaining the rights of mortgagees under the law, and discussing such matters as entail and encumbrances, Gorrie concluded: "It will thus be seen that the European titles to land in Fiji are absolutely secure, each Crown grant or Certificate of Title upon transfer, which is in effect a new grant from the Crown, being indefeasible."[30]

Judicial Work

Despite all Gorrie's nonjudicial activities, he was first and foremost Chief Justice of Fiji and the colony's sole judge. Gordon was instructed to establish a Supreme Court consisting of one judge. Criminal trials were to be held by him with the aid of 'assessors', not a jury, in cases where any of the parties was not white, a procedure in use in India for the protection of the local people. Civil proceedings were to be as simple as possible, and the Chief Justice was empowered to frame rules which might later form the basis of an ordinance embodying a complete code of procedure. In suits between Fijians or in which they were involved, and in any criminal prosecution of a Fijian, the Chief Native Commissioner was to serve *ex officio* as assessor. A special ordinance would be needed to provide for the admission of unsworn testimony from Fijians in civil and criminal cases, and to empower the Supreme Court to admit evidence of local customs "not repugnant to justice and morality" especially relating to marriage, wills, land titles and transfer of property, and to deal with such cases "in accordance with natural equity and good conscience". Though the chiefs and native magistrates were to retain their jurisdiction over the Fijians, the Supreme Court was empowered to hear any case where a party so desired or where the Chief Justice saw it fit. Gorrie played an important part in advising on regulations and procedures relating to the courts.[31]

As in Mauritius, Gorrie became known as a judge who never hesitated to criticize officers of the court, government officials or lawyers when he believed that they had failed in their duties. Very few lawyers practised in the colony in the 1870s, and perhaps their calibre was not especially high. Unquestionably, he had to put up with a great deal of incompetence and even dishonesty from officers of the court and from the Bar. One lawyer's clerk, for instance, was convicted of forging a certificate of title and a bill of exchange in 1878. J.H. Garrick, the colony's Attorney-General until 1880, routinely represented clients whose interests were in conflict with the Government's, even in cases where he might be called on to advise the Crown. W.J. Thomas, the Registrar of the Supreme Court up to the end of 1877, was thoroughly incompetent, and worse. In three months in 1876, Gorrie was obliged to decide two cases against his own Registrar, one "of a very shady kind". By 1877 the situation had not improved, and he confided to Gordon :

> I have been much worried with Thomas the last two days, and for the same reason as before, he helping to dig pitfalls that I might tumble into them, in place of being my right hand and remembrancer . . . I wish you could transfer him. I have no confidence in him, and it is a perpetual worry to be on your guard against your own registrar.

He was in fact eased out of his post by the end of 1877.[32]

Gorrie's experiences in Jamaica and Mauritius had convinced him that the magistrates were the key to the administration of justice in multiracial colonies, and he was unsparing when he believed they were negligent. In 1879 he subjected magistrate Heffernan of Colo (Viti Levu) to "an awful dressing-down in court". But if Gorrie was quick to castigate delinquent magistrates, he was equally energetic in defending them against pressures from white settlers. In 1880 the magistrate in Taveuni, Archibald Taylor, became unpopular with the planters of the island, especially J.E. Mason (a member of the Legislative Council), because of his firm rulings in cases arising from mistreatment of Polynesian or Fijian labourers. Some of these cases involved Mason. In January 1880, Mason's overseer (Drummond) was charged with a savage assault on a seventeen year-old Solomon Islander. Drummond had previously been convicted on several charges of common assault on labourers. Taylor found Drummond guilty and sentenced him to six days imprisonment with hard labour, a sentence which Taylor admitted was inadequate in view of the offence. Nevertheless, to Mason and his cronies in Taveuni, this meant that Drummond, "an English gentleman, is put to work on the roads with Fijian prisoners for six days". Mason quickly persuaded his friends to write letters to Taylor threatening to cut off all social relations with him and his family. These letters were, as Taylor told Gorrie, "a decided attempt to intimidate a magistrate in the discharge of his duties". Gorrie reacted strongly, drawing Gordon's attention to "the supreme impertinence of these men . . . This is purely and simply intolerable, and the firmest action must be taken to put it down."

Mason was not content with organizing threatening letters to Taylor; he also petitioned the governor to "assist the Taveuni settlers" in their "present troubles" caused by the magistrate's conduct. In this petition, Mason made serious allegations against Taylor. He claimed that "great insubordination is caused in plantations" by Taylor's actions; that planters had no confidence in his court and felt they could not prosecute their labourers; that in consequence planters "cannot get an honest day's work from their labourers" and had been forced "to relinquish, in most cases, the employment of Fijian labour"; and that, generally, "distrust and antagonism" among the labourers had arisen from Taylor's conduct. Gorrie believed that this case highlighted a serious problem. He told Gordon that it was vital that "the Magistrate should receive the full support of the Executive in the discharge of his functions. Indeed, placed as he is in the midst of a planting community, unless the Magistrate is to feel that he acts with the full support of the Executive he will be practically useless as a protection of the native labourer." The allegations in

Mason's petition were dismissed in a long and severe letter by Gordon, and he and his friends were more or less ordered to withdraw their letters and apologize to Taylor.[33]

The Taveuni magistrate fell foul of the white settlers of his district because he tried to protect Polynesian and Fijian labourers against mistreatment by their employers. Some of the most important cases which Gorrie heard involved relations between whites and 'natives'. Inevitably, he acquired a reputation (along with Gordon) of being 'pro-native'. One of the most persistent enemies of both men, the Australian based pamphleteer who wrote under the pseudonym "The Vagabond", described him thus:

> His delight is to work himself into an apparent fury of virtuous indignation anent 'the inhuman manner in which the poor Natives are treated'. He gets these absurdities printed in the Fiji papers, and sends copies home to his friends of the Aborigines Protection Society. Then Exeter Hall cries, 'Oh, what a good man is Gorrie'. He is the biggest bubble in the Pacific, and the most dangerous, as he invariably takes the part of the Natives against the white settlers.[34]

In 1877 Gorrie heard an important case, *Aromasi et al* v *G.B. Evans and J. Rannie.* The plaintiffs were labourers from the Kandavu islands, in the eastern part of Fiji, who had been fraudulently persuaded to work for a planter on Taveuni. They sued for cancellation of their labour contracts and damages on the grounds that they had been tricked into entering those contracts by Evans, the labour recruiter, and Rannie, their employer. Gorrie found for the plaintiffs and awarded them six months' wages, substantial damages, the cost of their passage home, and legal costs. This suit had a history: Aromasi and the others had previously complained to the Kandavu magistrate, who had dismissed the case because of alleged discrepancies in the evidence. But another magistrate, who had earlier reported Evans' misdeeds as a recruiter, felt that justice had not been served, and he enabled the labourers to bring the case to the Supreme Court as a suit for cancellation of their contracts and damages, with support from Gordon and Gorrie.[35]

As Gorrie pointed out, this case was important because it was "the first civil cause at the instance of Fijians tried in the Supreme Court, and they succeeded in their suit". But his ruling infuriated the white settlers, not only the award of damages and costs, but also Gorrie's severe language against the defendants and his insistence that Fijian evidence was as valid as that of whites:

> Men like Rannie must be taught that they must honestly carry out their contracts with the native labourers in the same way as they must do to white men . . . I have no sympathy with what seems to have been the ground of the decision in the case before the Magistrate . . . that we are not to believe the evidence simply because it comes from native witnesses. I have heard that often argued in regard to negroes, and Indians, as well as now in regard to Fijians, and if a Judge were to allow himself to be led away by such arguments, it would simply mean that the native races were to be left as the prey of white men.[36]

Immediately after the ruling, a notice appeared in the pro-planter *Fiji Times,* addressed to "Planters, Merchants and Residents" and appealing for subscriptions to pay the "harsh damages inflicted" on Evans and Rannie, "it being the universal opinion of the subscribers that they are deserving of some mark of sympathy, under the trying circumstances, from their fellow settlers". Characteristically, Gorrie decided to cite the *Fiji Times* owner, G.L. Griffiths, for contempt. Gordon urged caution, reminding him: "Your enemies both here and at Mauritius are fond of insinuating that you lose your temper on the bench, and of course will do their best to make out that the proceeding results from personal feelings." But Gorrie was determined "to put the thing through", and Griffiths duly appeared for contempt. The Chief Justice took the opportunity to "put in some truths":

> I felt that if the Supreme Court did not take notice of the contempt, Magistrates in the out-districts, living in the midst of the antagonistic elements, and where the bitterness of race is fierce, would be deterred from doing their duty, by fear of a public clamour against their decisions whenever they happened to be in favour of the natives. I am resolved that justice shall be freely administered in this community to white and native alike.

As Griffiths apologized "fully and completely" he was discharged; "but I warn him, and those who are at the bottom of these affairs, for the law has long arms, and can reach them as well as those of whom they make tools – that if I have to punish for this offence the punishment will be very severe".[37]

Another important case involving white-native relations came up in 1877. Patrick Scanlon, a planter or overseer, was charged with the murder by flogging of a Polynesian labourer. The Attorney-General requested a jury trial under the Criminal Procedure Ordinance; the Chief Justice believed (wrongly, it turned out) that he had no option but to agree. Although the evidence against Scanlon was clear, and Gorrie's summing up was strongly adverse to him, the all-white jury acquitted him, and the Chief Justice discharged him stating "the verdict had not the assent of the presiding judge". In reporting this "miscarriage of justice", Gordon noted that:

> it was to meet such cases that provision was made for the substitution of assessors for a jury under the Criminal Procedure Ordinance, 1875, and I am inclined to agree with the Chief Justice in expressing regret that any option was left between the two modes of trial. It is not too much to say that whatever the evidence, a jury composed of white settlers in Fiji will never find another white settler guilty of murder if the murdered man be a native.

Gorrie explained that as the Ordinance was then written, "in cases of murder, a motion either by the Crown or by the prisoner's counsel for a trial by jury would be held by most Judges as a sufficient special reason for granting that mode of trial in the case of a white man". This interpretation of the Ordinance, however, was incorrect.[38]

It was ironic, in view of Gorrie's solid record as a judge committed to the defence of natives' rights, that the Colonial Office chose to issue a severe reprimand to him and the Attorney-General for permitting a jury trial and thus causing a miscarriage of justice. "While in Mauritius I never got one word of encouragement or sympathy all the time I was there trying to do justice", he complained to Chesson, "but the moment they thought they had me on a slip here some base snob in the C.O. thought it would be fine fun to give me a slagging for not protecting a native." Not surprisingly, Gorrie was angry at the rebuke; but the governor pointed out that he had, in fact, overlooked the relevant section (70) of the Ordinance and could only be at a disadvantage in any 'wrangle' with the Colonial Office. He defended his action in a long, formal letter to the governor, and he recommended that Section 70 of the Criminal Procedure Ordinance should be amended to take away the judge's discretionary power to allow a jury:

> I am clearly of opinion that the Ordinance as it stands places the judge in a most difficult and invidious position, that if trial by jury was intended to be taken away by the Ordinance it should have been done openly and clearly by a special section, and that no option should be left in the hands of the judge, when, as may not infrequently be the case, the determination of that point will really mean whether the prisoner is to be acquitted or condemned on the gravest cases known to the law.[39]

This recommendation does not appear to have gone forward. But in the following year, Des Voeux as acting governor forwarded a similar proposal. It arose out of *R* v *Walker*, in which a white man was charged with the unlawful wounding of a Fijian boy. His counsel asked for a jury trial, but did not press home the constitutional arguments presumably because it was not a capital case, and Gorrie refused a jury under Section 70 of the Ordinance. "But I feel more strongly than ever the false position in which a judge is placed by having to decide in each case whether there are special reasons, connected with a case he has not heard, to determine whether a British subject shall be tried by jury or not." There was no doubt that trials with assessors were necessary, granted the state of Fijian society; the problem was the responsibility placed on the judge. Gordon, at home on leave, strongly supported Gorrie's recommendation to delete the words in Section 70 granting the judge discretion to allow a jury in special cases. But the Colonial Office decided otherwise, overriding Gordon's protest. Of course, the denial of a jury in criminal cases involving whites and natives was a grievance to the colonists. The *Fiji Argus*, usually sympathetic to the government's 'native policy' and to Gorrie, believed that it was "monstrous" that Englishmen were denied their right to trial by jury. Towards the end of 1880, an unofficial member of the Legislature (appointed to represent the whites) raised the issue in two speeches in the Council, calling for the amendment of the 1875 Ordinance to permit jury trials in all criminal cases where whites were charged with serious crimes; but he failed.[40]

A case which became even more celebrated came up in July 1880, when Lieutenant Chippendall of the Navy, a planter at Savu Savu Bay in Vanua Levu, was tried for manslaughter of a Polynesian boy. He had brutally kicked the youth, who was in poor health; but the assessors (substituting for a jury under the Ordinance) found him not guilty because the cause of death was the prior illness rather than the assault. In his summing up, Gorrie made it very clear that he considered that the magistrate at Savu Savu was only doing his duty in committing Chippendall for trial, and that he believed that the violence of the assault had been greater than the assessors had stated. He told Chippendall: "I am sure you regret now, and will continue to regret, the circumstances which have led to this trial. I hope it will be a warning to yourself and all others to abstain from every kind of violence towards your labourers." But in the view of the planting community, the point was not that Chippendall had been acquitted; he should never have been committed for trial for so trivial an offence as kicking a Polynesian labourer. He had been persecuted; his trial was the culmination of a systematic policy of harassing the planters of Fiji. As the *Fiji Argus* put it, "It was a case that not so much affected the interests of an individual, as it did the planting interests of this colony." The kick was nothing; as the *Fiji Argus* calmly explained, Chippendall "coming down to the sugar mill one morning, and seeing this boy slow at some work he was doing, gave him a kick to help him along faster". For this trivial and routine action, he was committed by officials who "do not hesitate to try to ruin and damn the name and character of a fellow citizen upon the very slightest evidence".[41]

Chippendall's father was well connected; he published a pamphlet calling for an enquiry into the case, and lobbied the Colonial Office, John Bright and other MPs. He succeeded in getting a MP to ask a question in the Commons about the case and Gordon's conduct in relation to it, much to the latter's fury. In an indignant letter, Gordon rejected the allegations that Chippendall had been improperly committed for trial or that he had anything to do with it, and insisted that all such cases had to be prosecuted according to the law precisely because, to the Fijian whites, "a native life is looked on as a matter of infinitely small value". Naturally Gorrie endorsed this view:

> In a community the material success of which depends upon the introduction of native labourers from Polynesia and India, there must be no flinching from a firm carrying out of the law. Upon this the whole success of the experiment depends, and if any encouragement is given at Home to interested clamour the experiment will prove a failure alike for whites and natives. I trust therefore that Peers and Members of the House of Commons will not hastily give credit to charges against public officers, who, from the peculiar conditions of the society among which they are placed, are apt to be most bitterly assailed when most deserving of approbation.[42]

Prosecutions against Fijians and Polynesians for serious crimes, which were taken to the Supreme Court, often presented difficulties for Gorrie. In 1877 he tried Otawata, a Polynesian, for the murder of a Fijian. Otawata said that he had killed the victim because the Fijian had stolen his execrement to do him harm, to charm his life away, and his counsel therefore argued for a manslaughter plea as Otawata saw his action as self-defence. Gorrie disagreed: "We cannot allow our law to be broken down to meet the superstitious notions of these Islanders, or we shall soon become as lawless and savage as themselves. The law is a great teacher, and all men who are within our bounds must be taught that fantastic notions like these cannot be listened to as excuses for crimes." Otawata was sentenced to death with a recommendation of mercy because of his beliefs. A letter to the *Fiji Argus* in 1879 drew attention to similar problems in the conviction of islanders for serious crimes. A Polynesian had recently been sentenced to death for murdering his wife, a crime he had certainly committed; but in his home island it would not be a crime and might even be a duty in certain circumstances. Was it right to impose a death sentence on a man who was not a British subject and who was only temporarily under British jurisdiction? In another case a Fijian had been sentenced to five years' imprisonment for rape. But the evidence suggested that the accused and his victim were cousins and that traditionally Fijian men had sexual rights over their female cousins who were considered potential wives. In each case, the verdicts and sentences were fully in accord with the law of the land; but there were special grounds for mercy which the governor should consider, a view which Gorrie would certainly have endorsed.[43]

Fijians charged with serious crimes were tried in the Supreme Court, but many officials, including Gordon and Thurston, believed that in certain circumstances it was better to deal with them in the magistrates' courts to ensure swift justice and summary punishment of a kind which the population could understand. This argument was not always acceptable to Gorrie, who was jealous of any reduction in the jurisdiction of the court and sceptical about the ability of the colony's magistrates to try difficult cases properly. This issue was highlighted by an incident in 1878. Some Fijians living along the Ra coast in Viti Levu had raped several women. Rape was a crime which normally required a Supreme Court trial; but the local magistrate, with encouragement from Gordon and then Des Voeux as acting governor, had tried them in his own court, in order to ensure speedy justice and swift punishment and to avoid the expense, difficulties and uncertainty of a court trial. Gorrie was furious; he decided to make a fuss, though well aware that Gordon would not support him. He asked to see the court returns sent in by the magistrate, which Des Voeux refused; he then wrote a formal letter of protest to the acting governor. Sending a copy to Gordon in England, he wrote:

> I am glad there are 10,000 miles between us, as I know you will be very angry; but if you think calmly over it, you will see, I am sure, how unworthy I would be of my office if I allowed it to be trifled with, as was done in this instance; and imagine the fellows who thought themselves competent to exercise supreme jurisdiction! I have stood with perfect patience the mountains being taken out of my jurisdiction, – but no poaching on the plains![44]

Gordon, however, strongly supported the acting governor who had (on his advice) authorized the trial by the district magistrate. The relevant Ordinance (14 of 1875) empowered the governor to exempt districts or classes from the jurisdiction of the Supreme Court expressly to meet difficulties such as those in the Ra rape case. To back up his argument, he sent the Colonial Office an extract from a letter from Thurston, who disapproved entirely of Gorrie's actions, and went so far as to write: "One thing is very clear to me, and that is, if *all* criminal cases were to be tried in the Province by the European and Native Justices, more substantial justice would be done than by the Supreme Court with all its wisdom." Thurston instanced a recent case where a Fijian woman had been killed by two Polynesians. The facts seemed pretty clear, but the Supreme Court trial led to their acquittal because the witnesses could not give their evidence properly:

> I believe that if the trial had been held quietly in the Province, the evidence would have been much better. No semi-civilized man, much less a comparative savage, can stand being taken into Court, and put by himself in a box – white men all round him, all glaring at him. One awful man in a red robe, of severe aspect, on one side of him, another awful, bumptious, hectoring turaga [chief] in a mystical black garb in front of him – other persons whom he has just seen, clad in the white man's customary dress, entering the precincts of the Court, now arrayed in strange costumes . . . When just as he is about to falter out his first reply, the policeman in attendance roars out 'Silence!' he breaks down, and becomes for the time an idiot, who can be made to say anything, or contradict himself ten times in five minutes.

The result was a miscarriage of justice, heavy expenses, indignation among the Fijians, especially the victim's relatives, and probably "the mysterious disappearance of a Polynesian or two ere long".[45]

It seems that Gorrie came to accept the view shared by Gordon, Des Voeux, Thurston and most of the other Fiji officials about the difficulty of securing justice in the Supreme Court in criminal cases involving Fijians or Polynesians; but he nevertheless objected to the decision to exempt Rotumah from the court's jurisdiction. Rotumah was a small island to the north of Fiji which was 'ceded' to the Crown and annexed to Fiji in 1881. Before leaving Fiji, Gordon issued a Proclamation (November 1880) stating that Rotumah was exempted from the jurisdiction of the Supreme Court of Fiji; the Resident Commissioner's Court was answerable only to the Governor in Council, with death sentences referred to the Governor and Chief Justice.

Gordon wrote to Gorrie just after he left: "I did not suppose you would like this for though you are freer from legal prejudices than almost any other judge I ever met you are not, being mortal, wholly untouched by the maladies which cling to the seat of justice." The Resident Commissioner was given exclusive jurisdiction over both natives and whites, with no power of appeal to the Supreme Court, except that capital cases were reserved to it. This, of course, was over Gorrie's protest.[46]

Gordon's 'Native Policy'

In general, Gorrie supported the various facets of Gordon's 'native policy'. He told Chesson soon after his arrival in Fiji: "I like what I have seen of the natives although I am not quite so enthusiastic as Sir A. Gordon . . . He has them heartily with him already – as you would see from the way he has been able to put down the outbreak in the mountains." But Gorrie was uneasy about some aspects of the Fijian 'native administration'. Thurston, for his own reasons, tended to exaggerate the extent of these disagreements in his letters to Gordon. He told Gordon, at home on leave in 1879, that "if you were not to return . . . Gorrie would have tried to upset the native policy . . . Gorrie does not believe in any native officer. He does not affect to hide his opinions; they have been expressed to me often in anything but judicial language."[47] But the evidence suggests that he was generally 'sound' on 'native policy'.

In 1877 he was appointed a member of the Native Regulations Board, and in this capacity – and as one of Gordon's main advisers – he helped to shape the regulations and laws which applied to Fijians. The correspondence between the two men makes it clear that they worked very closely together to frame the various regulations issued by the Board, and to draw up ordinances affecting the Fijians such as the Native Debt Ordinance (1877) and the Native Lands Ordinance (1880).[48]

But Gorrie did have his doubts about the capacity of many of the Fijian magistrates (of course, he was often scathing about the European magistrates too). And he was unenthusiastic about the annual *Bose vaka Turaga*, the assembly of great chiefs, which was the keystone of Gordon's Fijian administration. As he told Gordon in 1879, "I am not very competent to advise as to anything connected with the Bose, as I never saw one"; but he thought the governor should take steps to "make these meetings for business rather than orgies". Gordon gently rebuked him: "Pray don't run away with the utterly false and mistaken notion that it is from any apprehension of the Bose giving rise to 'orgies' that I resort to this measure [to limit attendance] . . . I am very sorry you did not go to the Bose last year at Bua, and I hope you will come to that at Bau. You will not be the witness of any 'orgies', but you will see native life under a very curious and attractive phase." He did not go to the 1879 *Bose* at Bau; and he was still sniping away the following year. But the governor succeeded in taking Gorrie to the *Bose* at Loma Loma, in the Lau or Eastern group of islands, in November 1880, "being determined", he noted in his diary, "that he should see for himself what a *Bose* was really like, and not any longer indulge in suspicions bred of his own fancies and nourished by malicious misinformation". The Chief Justice wore his grandest official robes at the formal opening and the *meke* (ceremonial dance) which followed. In a talk on Fiji delivered in London in 1883, he said :

> I was at the annual council of chiefs just before Sir A. Gordon's departure, where he explained to them what had been done to secure the recognition of the title to their lands, and there could be no doubt, from the manner in which they received it, that the announcement was another tie by which these men, unless in future they be grossly misgoverned, have had their loyalty riveted to the Crown of England.[49]

Like many Europeans who were not entirely blinded by prejudice, Gorrie admired the Fijians of the chiefly caste for their physical presence and their dignity. Many years after he left the Pacific, he told a Trinidad audience that he had known ex-King Cakobau well:

> That was a fine man, upwards of six feet high, and in his bronze skin he looked remarkably well. No one could ever doubt that he was a chief, from his bearing and his manner. I have seen chiefs from all parts of the group. They have sat down at table and never committed one single mistake of etiquette. They watched quietly and in a dignified way to see

> how others would use spoons or knives and forks . . . They sat with the utmost composure and grace. They were men who had come from the remote islands and had never sat down at a European table before.

And even if he had doubts about the Fijian magistrates or the annual *Bose*, he was a staunch defender of Gordon's 'native policy' against its many critics. In his 1883 talk to the Royal Colonial Institute, he justified Gordon's efforts to allow the Fijians to work out their destiny on their own lines. In the following year he replied to an anti-Gordon letter to *The Times* with an impressive defence of his former chief's policies: "I, who have been against slavery of all kinds since I was able to take part in public questions, and who know the conditions of the native Fijians thoroughly, venture to say that the policy of Sir A. Gordon saved them from deterioration, promoted their material comfort, guaranteed to them their tribal lands, and in every way advanced them as a race."[50]

The other side of Gordon's 'native policy' was the continuation of Polynesian immigration, as well as the introduction of indentured Indians. Ordinance 24 of 1876 laid down regulations for the conduct of Polynesian labour immigration to Fiji. The Government arranged for the recruiting to be done by licensed ship captains supervised by Government Agents on board. Ordinance 11 of 1877 governed relations between the Polynesians and their employers in Fiji. Repatriation after five years was guaranteed, and a minimum wage was fixed. But the question of Polynesian labour immigration remained controversial. The APS followed it closely; Chesson wrote two papers on the subject, and the Society lobbied the Colonial Office. Although the measures taken in 1875-77 did something to end the worst abuses, violence still sometimes occurred during the recruiting process, and mortality among the Polynesians in Fiji was appallingly high even in the early 1880s, due to illness, a sort of depression and (above all) a grossly inadequate diet.[51]

Gorrie wrote to Chesson that the protection of the Fijian population required Polynesian immigration:

> So far as I can see at present there is no reason why Polynesian labourers should not be brought under strict Government supervision (we send a Government Labour Agent in each vessel) and my own views go further,

> to have the whole duty of recruiting done by Government – that will benefit the Polynesian and relieve the pressure on the Fijian whom we hope to see preserved as a Race.

Of course, planter opinion was hostile to the regulations and restrictions placed on Polynesian recruitment and employment by Gordon's government. The *Fiji Times* complained in 1877 that Navy cruisers still roamed the Pacific "built specially for the prevention of that system of kidnapping which does not exist", while repressive laws governed the employment of Polynesians in Fiji. "The party at home is strong and influential, and must be kept in good humour"; the APS still saw "the kidnapper in the respectable trader, the slave-holder in the struggling, hard-working planter".[52]

Gorrie firmly believed that Gordon's 'native policy' was essential if the Fijians were to survive into the twentieth century and to preserve their civilization. Like Gordon, he knew that most whites in Fiji despised the Fijians and Polynesians and saw them merely as potential serfs for the plantations. He would heartily have endorsed Gordon's remark to a friend, "You have little idea how skin-deep, how purely superficial, is in most cases the conventional 'due regard for the interests of the native races' even among well intentioned and honourable men in Fiji"; and he would have agreed with Thurston when he wrote:

> The fact is that the Trader looks upon the Native as an ignorant being born to sell at the cheapest and buy at the dearest, to, or from him the Trader. The Planter regards the Native as a being specially adapted if not specially intended by Providence to work for him the Planter.[53]

These were attitudes that he had fought against since the 1860s, and he was convinced that only Gordon's policies stood between the predatory white settlers and the indigenous population.

Difficulties with the new Governor

Gorrie admired Gordon and worked closely with him. But his relations with William Des Voeux, who acted as governor for a year in 1878-79 and was then given the substantive post late in 1880 when Gordon was transferred to New Zealand, were extremely troubled, and complicated quarrels with him darkened Gorrie's last years in Fiji. Des Voeux was a quick tempered, insecure, impulsive man, often ill, and prone to fits of petulance; he saw slights everywhere, and could react almost irrationally at times. This was the view of nearly everyone who worked with him in Fiji, including Thurston and Gordon. Collision with Gorrie – also quick-tempered and impulsive, self-confident, devoted to Gordon – was almost inevitable. Gorrie wrote to Gordon soon after Des Voeux's appointment as acting governor in 1878:

> He does not seem to wish for any assistance, but is rather jealous, I should imagine, of interference with the Executive, forgetting how we have been jumbled up together, and what a nice kettle of fish it would have been if you had commenced, or I had originated, jealousies and nonsense of this kind. However, I think I am bound to humour him in every way, and to keep on cordial terms with him at all hazards; and you may be sure that I will act on these principles. Out of school he is famous.

But keeping on cordial terms proved impossible; and Gordon in England was soon bombarded with letters, from Gorrie, Thurston, MacGregor and others, giving him their differing versions of the skirmishes between the two men.[54]

Thurston, no friend of Gorrie, believed that he was annoyed at not being appointed acting governor himself and was determined to give Des Voeux a hard time; MacGregor, no friend of Thurston, argued that Des Voeux was piqued that he had not been made acting High Commissioner for the Western Pacific instead of Gorrie. Probably both men were right. The most serious collision occurred over the Ra rape cases in 1878, and the subsequent episode in the Legislature early in 1879, when Gorrie made some critical remarks on the subject and was sharply reminded by Des Voeux that he was an official member of the Council. Des Voeux wrote an extremely intemperate letter on this issue to Gorrie; to his credit, Gorrie took this calmly, and did not reply. MacGregor told Gordon: "It must have caused a fearful mental struggle to the C. J. to take it in the way he did . . . In this affair Gorrie has shown himself more devoted to yourself and to your work than any man I have ever known serving under you".[55] He had certainly been hurt by this 'crisis', however, and he reacted strongly to a letter from Gordon warning him to mend his ways because the Colonial Office believed he was in the wrong:

> As if I were a kind of firebrand who ought to be removed from the service! . . . I dare say I may have enemies, that is possible, but I have also friends, and if any enemies imagine they can Judge Beaumont me, or try it with impunity, they are mistaken. Long disuse, and natural laziness, may make me less of a speaker and writer than before, but if [illeg.] by a sense of injustice I feel I could smite to powder a good few enemies still, be they who they may.[56]

After Des Voeux's troubled year as acting governor in 1878-79, it is not surprising that Gordon had forebodings when he was appointed to the substantive post at the end of 1880. He told a friend, "Most of the public officers who have efficiently supported me will resign. Probably the Chief Justice (who cannot abide Des Voeux) will do so." But Gorrie greeted the news of his appointment calmly and even generously:

> I am glad Des Voeux is coming, in some respects, he is personally genial, and we will find, I doubt not, a *modus vivendi.* But he has already grievously offended some people, as you know, and others of whom you probably don't know; and unless he can curb his temper, he will not be on a bed of roses.

By Des Voeux's own account, he returned to Fiji determined "to make every sacrifice consistent with my duty to the public to maintain friendly relations with [Gorrie]"; but "he seemed to think himself entitled to address me on any subject in the capacity of either Judge, member of the Legislative Council, or amateur adviser". During the first year an open rupture was avoided, according to Des Voeux, "by means of conciliatory replies and social amenities". But by the end of 1881 Gorrie was very critical in his letters to Gordon: "I am quite sure the best interests of the country are suffering by the want of power in the present man to undertake the business and the extraordinary uncertainty of his views . . . Not only has he no power to deal with the work, he has no taste for it."[57]

Open conflict between the two men was precipitated over the move to Suva. Some time in 1880, the government announced that the colonial capital would definitely be moved from Levuka to Suva, in Viti Levu, and that the removal would be carried out in stages in 1881-82. Public officers would be offered free grants of land in the new township on which to build their houses. This decision led to a protracted serio-comic skirmish between governor and Chief Justice which ended only with the latter's departure from Fiji late in 1882. Gorrie's house in Levuka was seriously damaged by a hurricane early in 1881, and he decided that he must move to Suva immediately, during the Supreme Court's vacation in March. Like other public officers, he was offered a free grant of one-third of an acre as a house lot; he indignantly rejected this and asked for five acres, which was refused. He then decided to buy land from a private owner and build a house at Suva at his own cost. This he did, and he took up residence in October 1881, long before Suva had been proclaimed the capital and before most public offices had been transferred. The new court building in Suva, under construction during 1881, was taken over by the Chief Justice before it had been handed over to the government by the contractors. After October 1881, he did not visit Levuka regularly to conduct judicial business, and the merchants of that town complained to the governor. When Gorrie failed to satisfy Des Voeux that he would continue to hold court at Levuka until the capital was officially moved, the governor took the extraordinary step of enacting an ordinance which empowered the Governor in Council, not the Chief Justice, to fix the place of sitting for the Supreme Court. The Colonial Office sanctioned this ordinance over Gorrie's protests, and he was obliged to visit Levuka at stated intervals until Suva became the official capital in the second half of 1882. This episode caused a scandalous and public breach between the two highest authorities in the colony.

During the first months of 1881, as MacGregor told Gordon, "there [was] an intermittent guerilla strife between Nasova [the governor's house] and Vagadace [Gorrie's]". MacGregor, who was his sincere friend, was forced to admit that Gorrie's letters at this time to Des Voeux on the Suva issue were "marked by a coarseness, a tone of disrespect, and recklessness, that, coming from any other officer, would probably have led to his immediate suspension". MacGregor's judgement was entirely correct; Gorrie's letters to Des Voeux in the first half of 1881, all duly scrutinized by the men in the Colonial Office, were disgraceful. He amply deserved Des Voeux's dignified rebuke regretting that such letters should have been written by one of his position and standing "who has rendered such unquestionably valuable services to the Colony". Gorrie must have realised that he was hopelessly in the wrong, for he replied to this rebuke in a letter whose tone was, if not exactly apologetic, rueful and conciliatory:

> Some people cannot write feebly if they tried. I felt I was being not merely hardly, but almost contemptuously treated with that third of an acre. And I see no reason why I should not speak out either to Your Excellency, or the Secretary of State, or the Queen in Council. I am not ashamed of being poor after 11 years' service as a Judge. I would be very much ashamed if it were otherwise, for I would not have made rich [*sic*] honestly. I am not ashamed to try to prevent myself getting into heavier liabilities than I can stand in a place where I am the sole Judge, and thus I speak as I feel. I am sure also Your Excellency will admit that the reply before me is not mealy-mouthed, and thus, I think, we may cry quits.[58]

Nevertheless, he proceeded to move to Suva in October 1881 without notifying the governor, to take over the Supreme Court building there without authorization, and to decline to go regularly to Levuka to hear cases. For these rash actions he was scolded by Gordon, who felt it was "too heartbreaking to see two men who have the same cause really at heart, and are hated by the same enemies, tearing each other to pieces (to the delight of those who bear no love to either) and wasting, in miserable disputes, time which might be better bestowed". But any chance of reconciliation disappeared with Des Voeux's decision to enact Ordinance 11 of 1882, which provided that the Governor in Council should fix the place for court sittings and that, until Suva was proclaimed the place for such sittings, the Chief Justice should be obliged to reside in Levuka for six days in each month. Gorrie's letters early in 1882 reveal that he was deeply worried at the impasse. He appealed to Gordon to intercede with the Secretary of State and to protect him from Des Voeux's 'violence':

> You are quite right as to the folly of men who have the same principles tearing each other to pieces, but I beg you will not imagine that I am in a wild state. He tears at me or rather rushes at me like a wild bull as my presence here is offensive to him, because he dislikes you and thinks I pay more respect to you than I do him, which is perfectly true for who can respect a man who so acts?

At the same time he told Chesson:

> The fact is no one knows what [Des Voeux] would do next. He is getting wilder and wilder, and as he has taken a special spite against myself at present I quite expect he will go to any extremity. I think the position so serious that I have written to Mr Bright and asked him to speak to Lord Kimberley . . . You cannot have any idea of the dangerous and fantastic fool he is to be shut up with.[59]

Relations between governor and Chief Justice were made even worse (if that were possible) by a case heard in 1882, *Everett* v *Crown*. Everett claimed some lands which the Crown argued were in the possession of Fijians. Gorrie was dissatisfied with the statement put in on behalf of the Fijian owners by the Attorney-General, and issued an order in July 1882 that this statement should be withdrawn and that the Fijians should be represented by a lawyer other than the Crown's counsel (the Attorney-General), because he believed that the interests of the Crown and the Fijians were not identical and that the Crown had not properly looked after the latter's interests. The governor did not obey this order, believing it to involve fundamental questions of 'native policy'. In an interlocutory judgement delivered in October 1882, Gorrie castigated Executive defiance of the Supreme Court and ordered the defendant (the Crown) to pay damages on a daily basis to Everett for as long as the order continued to be resisted. He did not mince his words:

> If I were to permit the judgements and orders of this Court to be defied and resisted, I should undo the work of years, betray the trust that has been confided in me, and transmit to my successor a heritage of difficulty and humiliation. I prefer rather to leave this Court as I found it, with its just authority undiminished, and the reputation of its Judges for independence in the discharge of their duties untarnished.

Des Voeux bitterly resented this judgement, which he regarded (with some reason) as an attack on the government and on himself personally; he was charged with neglecting the Fijians' true interests and defying the Supreme Court, while the government had been punished by the damages awarded Everett. Moreover, the judgement had been exploited by dissatisfied land claimants, whose association had printed thousands of copies of the document, which they believed greatly strengthened their case. He asked permission to appeal to the Privy Council, but the Colonial Office ruled this out on grounds of cost.

The breakdown in relations between Des Voeux and Gorrie is revealed in the voluminous correspondence on *Everett* v *Crown*. Told that Des Voeux intended to seek an appeal to the Privy Council, Gorrie replied: "It is not unusual when persons in my position leave a Colony, to be threatened with consequences for having done their duty . . . I can only say I am ready to meet Your Excellency whenever and before whomsoever you may make your charges." For his part, Des Voeux told the Secretary of State:

> It would seem only fair to the governors of the Colonies in which Sir John Gorrie may serve in the future that he should be apprised as to there being some limit to his licence of language on the Bench and to the embarrassment which he may cause with impunity to the Executive Government.

He concluded: "I believe the true explanation of his conduct on various occasions to be that having unusually strong personal prejudices and a natural proclivity against power other than his own, he is unable, and entirely unaware of his inability, to divest himself of these feelings on the Bench." This wretched affair continued to exasperate the Colonial Office long after Gorrie had ceased to be Chief Justice of Fiji. Not until May 1883 did the Colonial Office declare the correspondence closed, with the fate of the case left to Gorrie's successor.[60]

In view of the state of their relationship by mid 1882, it is to Des Voeux's credit that he went out of his way to involve Gorrie in the successful suppression of a minor disturbance on the Driketi River in the interior of Vanua Levu. He exempted the disturbed district from the jurisdiction of the

Supreme Court and then persuaded Gorrie to go there as Special Commissioner, telling the Legislature "The acceptance of so disagreeable a duty, outside of his ordinary functions, is the more honourable to Sir John Gorrie, in as much as he is, on principle, opposed to the exclusion of Supreme Court jurisdiction." The trouble turned out to be a squabble between two chiefs and was easily suppressed without loss of lives by 100 armed Fijian constabulary and the Special Commissioner. Though Des Voeux told the Secretary of State that Gorrie's enquiry into the causes of the affair was thorough, and his conduct of the trials admirable, he could not resist a dig; he censured Gorrie for making one or two gentle criticisms of the *Roko* in charge of the province, the Chief Native Commissioner and the district magistrate in his address to the assembled people following the trials. Gorrie replied to this last, rather silly complaint quite mildly:

> I hope it is possible for a public officer, and especially one who had just been employed as a Special Judicial Commissioner, to give a hint about what seemed to him a looseness of executive organization or want of touch between the higher authorities and the local native questions, without meaning to cast personal reflections on the governor.

The Secretary of State declined to give Des Voeux any support; Kimberley minuted rather severely: "Acknowledge only. Mr Des Voeux is too prone to take offence at trifles." But it was clear even from Des Voeux's own despatches that Gorrie had acquitted himself well in Vanua Levu, and we may believe him when he wrote that the Chief Justice returned "highly pleased with the result of the expedition".[61]

By the middle of 1882, all the parties involved – Des Voeux, Gorrie and the Colonial Office – had recognized that the only solution to the breakdown in civility between governor and Chief Justice was the latter's promotion out of the colony. In July 1882, he was offered the Chief Justiceship of the Leeward Islands at £1500 p.a. But it took some hard bargaining on Des Voeux's part to get him to agree. Gorrie claimed all sorts of entitlements; to induce him to accept the offer, Des Voeux proposed a grant of land worth £307 to cover all possible claims either for passage or for compensation. But this was on the express condition that he resigned his appointment in Fiji as soon as his six months leave were up, "certain circumstances having led me to think it possible that he would claim the right to return here, if before the end of his leave he should prefer to give up the appointment in the Leeward Islands". This he would regard as "seriously prejudicial to the interests of this Colony". On this ground, as well as on the general principle that a sole judge should not stay in any colony for too long, "I have no doubt whatever that it is well for him to be transferred to another sphere of duty, though at the same time acknowledging the good service he has on several occasions rendered to the Colony and retaining nothing but respect for his courageous efforts to suppress the anti-native spirit which is so prevalent among Australasians of European descent". The Colonial Office sanctioned the land grant in satisfaction of all his claims whether valid or not. Des Voeux had gotten rid of his Chief Justice.[62]

Life in Fiji

Gorrie was an intensely gregarious and social being, and his family soon became leading members of Levuka society. In 1876, the little town was home to perhaps six hundred whites. It was described in 1880 as

> a straggling town of one principal street which, extending along the beach almost at high-water level, is bordered on one side by the sea. In this street are the shops, merchants' offices, stores etc . . . The dwelling houses are perched upon the rocky mountainside above the town, and are approached by steep winding paths, over rocky slopes, or by stair-like ascents. A worse site could not be chosen for a town.

It was this location – squashed up against mountain slopes, with no room to expand, and without a good harbour – which ensured that the capital would be moved to Suva. But from all accounts the town was extremely picturesque. Its heart was Beach Street, nearly a mile in length, a succession of stores and drinking places. The stores were said to stock nearly everything needed for 'colonial life', except for fresh food which was bought from the Fijians, while all the gossip of the Pacific, especially planter grievances, could be picked up on the verandahs of Beach Street's leading hotel. Most of the houses occupied by the whites were crudely built and unsuited to the climate. A relative of Gordon described them as very inferior to those in India, built of wood, with corrugated iron or zinc roofs, and usually without bathrooms; most people took their morning shower in the open air at a deep pool about a quarter of a mile behind the town, though some householders used streams plunging down from the hills where their houses were situated. In 1876 Levuka had no vehicles of any kind and very few horses; the first wheeled vehicle appeared in 1878, and by the following year ex-King Cakobau was taking drives in his carriage.

The social amenities of a colonial town were not lacking in Levuka. Writing in 1880, one enthusiast assured his homebound readers:

> When I say that, in a population of some 600 souls [*ie* whites], there are two boat and yachting clubs, besides cricket, archery, and shooting clubs; that Levuka possesses an admirably conducted mechanics' institute, with a capital reading room and library; that concerts, professional and amateur, are neither few nor far between; and that the *valse à trois temps* is thoroughly appreciated – I fancy my readers will agree with me that emigration . . . to 'cannibal' Fiji is not altogether such a miserable prospect as they perhaps imagined.

Levuka had regattas, balls, bazaars, picnics, sports meetings, church functions, public dinners; tennis, cricket and croquet were all played in the 1870s, and picnic excursions to nearby bathing spots, both rivers and the sea, were popular. All this in a town which boasted only 120 'ladies' in 1880, thirty of them single (and three of them young Gorries). Levuka was the metropolis of Fiji, and dress was important:

> What is quite good enough for the planter on his estate is hardly the thing for the capital. Suits of good white drill, of white flannel, or of thin serge, are the correct thing, while a sun helmet is the best protection for the head. White canvas shoes are generally worn, while a waterproof coat and a pair of leggings are indispensable. An umbrella is required both for sun and rain . . . Evening dress of the 'complete waiter' order is anything but unknown, though spotless white drill is generally considered a permissible substitute.

Though most writers on Levuka in the 1870s were at pains to stress the gentlemanly tone of the town, Des Voeux considered that 'non-official' white society was poor, and he found entertainment no pleasure. Though most whites who came to Nasova, the governor's residence, behaved decently, Des Voeux thought that several might well have imitated the dignity and good manners of the Fijian aristocrats "whom they were pleased to despise as inferiors".

In contrast to Levuka, Suva in the 1870s barely existed. At the end of 1875, Rachael Gordon wrote that it consisted of three or four houses, a disused chapel, an abandoned sugar mill and a deserted hotel. But it had an excellent harbour and abundant room for expansion, and it was situated on the main island. By 1881, when Gorrie moved there, a town of sorts existed, though it was "very much a shanty town" well into the 1880s. When it became the official capital in 1882, it was a run-down, unhealthy place. Des Voeux commented rather sourly that the move was a relief in one sense: far fewer whites lived in Suva than in Levuka, so the burden of entertaining people was less. Gorrie himself told Gordon, shortly before he moved there, "I like Suva better the more I see of it, and so does everyone who comes down."[63]

On Gorrie's arrival at Levuka, he stayed for some weeks at Nasova with the Gordons, and then rented a house. Early in 1877, Gordon told his wife, Gorrie

> hired a piece of ground at Vagadace, and is going to build a native house there: not a pleasant welcome for Mrs Gorrie [who had not yet come to Fiji with the family]. Moreover I am vexed that she and you will be separated by the whole length of Levuka, and only able to visit one another in boats. I am very sorry to lose them as neighbours.

Vagadace was a small bay to the north of Levuka, at the opposite end of the town from Nasova; a wide open expanse fronting the bay became the venue for all the town's sporting activities, especially cricket. The Gorries lived at Vagadace from mid 1877 until October 1881, and during this period it became a fairly well populated suburb; the *Fiji Times*, noting at the end of 1877 that several new houses had just been built near Gorrie's, thought that Vagadace "will no doubt become the spot chosen by the upper ten in times to come".[64]

Early in 1881, Gorrie's house was severely damaged by a hurricane. This made him determined to move to Suva immediately. He bought some twenty acres on the Tamavua river, about three miles from the little town, and built a large house called Vatunivalu, with a spacious garden sloping down to the river. He told Chesson he had:

> the most glorious view from my garden than can possibly be conceived. I can see from the middle of the drawing room, from the mouth of the Rewa to the mouth of the Navua, a distance of nearly 50 miles of coast line and closer to me I look down on the river Tamavua from a height of 400 ft and away back on an immense panorama of hills clad with the richest vegetation.

At around the same time he told Gordon, "It is a sight worth seeing to look down on the river from the house. We are now tolerably well settled." He was especially pleased with the "really good library" in the new house. It also contained three bedrooms and three "public rooms", a large kitchen, a modern bathroom with "plunge and shower bath" and a water supply "never less than 3000 gallons". When the Gorries left Fiji after only one year in the new house, the extensive gardens were "already planted with fruit and ornamental trees"; they sloped down to the river Tamavua, where there was a landing-place for boats and a zigzag path up to the house. The house was advertised for sale or rent: "either as a private residence, a bachelors' club (the River Tamavua being excellent for boating), or a private hotel, the position and premises are admirably adapted". It must have been a wrench for the Gorries to leave such an attractive place.[65]

The family threw themselves into the social and sporting life of Levuka. Gordon was told by one of his correspondents, when he was home on leave, "their Saturday afternoons have become a regular lounge for the young unmarried people in the place"; everyone attended in black coats and lavender gloves – "it is not considered correct now to take off your coat before ladies, even in the hottest of lawn tennis games". The Gorries came to Nasova every Tuesday afternoon to play tennis; the gig from Nasova was sent to Vagadace to fetch them, "and I am afraid they now look upon it as a matter of right, for if by any chance it is late at all, they make all kinds of remarks to me about it".

Vagadace was the venue for all sporting activities, and most of the town's population went there on Saturday afternoons. At Christmas 1879 there was a great athletic meeting "under the patronage of the Gorries"; "all the fashion of Levuka was collected", Gordon informed his wife, "displaying some amazing toilettes". The Gorries played tennis, took up archery, and (at least Gorrie himself) rifle shooting. At the prize shooting of the Fiji Archery Club at Vagadace in 1879, the Gorries were in full control: Malcolm won the second prize for gentlemen, Minnie the first for ladies, and 'Charlie' (Isobella) tied for second place. Their father was the president of the Fiji Rifle Association. The family often went boating, attending the Suva Regatta at Christmas 1878, and visited many of the islands of the Fiji group during the court vacations; an article by Gorrie published in the *Contemporary Review* described several of these trips.[66]

Very few balls took place in Levuka without the Gorries. Before the family had yet joined him, Gorrie attended the Regatta Ball and, it was noted, "took a most active part in the evening's amusement, showing an amount of energy worthy of emulation by all the young men present". At the Christmas Masonic Ball in 1880, hosted by the Masonic Fraternity, all the Gorries except young Jeanie were present. In Suva, the family went to the Queen's Birthday Fancy Dress Ball in 1882; the outstanding costumes were those of the two older Miss Gorries, as La Marquise and the Girl Graduate. Their father wore evening dress, but made up for this by "his thorough enjoyment of, and abandonment to, the pleasures of the evening". But unquestionably the high point of the Gorries' social career in Fiji was the visit of the two oldest sons of the Prince of Wales, teenaged naval officers on a round-the-world cruise. At two balls in their honour, Minnie Gorrie opened the dancing with Prince George, the future George V.[67]

Gorrie took his duties as a leading citizen seriously. He showed a keen interest in the work of the Wesleyan Mission, by far the largest Christian body in Fiji, and often presided over their various functions, including tea meetings, dinners and lectures. On these occasions he rarely missed the opportunity to make a speech. In 1880 he inaugurated a series of monthly lectures at the Mechanics' Institute with a talk on "Reminiscences of Travel". He led the effort to establish the first public school in Levuka, taking the matter "vigorously in hand", and presiding over the first prize-giving of the Levuka Public School at the end of 1880, warning the (white) pupils to look to their laurels if they did not wish to be overtaken by the Fijian school at Mua Levu whose examination he had recently attended. As the leading Presbyterian in the colony, he told Gordon in 1881 that he was thinking of calling his co-religionists together to consider whether they should take a block of land at Suva to build a church, but it does not seem that this happened before he left Fiji. He was also involved in efforts to set up a Suva Athenaeum, a kind of literary and debating society, just before he left the colony. The *Suva Times* commented, when the news of his departure became known:

> Socially Sir John will be much missed. The hearty, cheery salutation with which he met all, and the interest he took in everything that was going forward, put him on good terms with everyone . . . His eminently good neighbourly qualities have called forth pleasant remembrances in the minds of every class of society, and even the most extreme of his critics is ready to confess to his thorough bonhomie in the social circle.[68]

Marion and their three daughters had joined Gorrie at Levuka in 1877, and a few years later their son Malcolm, having finished school in Britain, also came out to Fiji, working with his father as unpaid private secretary and aide. The second Gorrie daughter, Isobella or 'Charlie', married Hamilton Hunter, chief police magistrate at Levuka, in April 1882. As a Winchester old boy, Hunter was considered to be one of the most 'socially eminent' of the Levuka residents; he had lived in Fiji since 1874, and must have worked closely with his new father-in-law as chief police magistrate and also as Deputy Commissioner for the Western Pacific. When the family left Fiji at the end of the same year, Charlie stayed behind with her husband.[69]

It seems clear that Gorrie was happy in Fiji, and enjoyed the challenges offered by his work in the colony and with the High Commission for the Western Pacific, as well as the opportunities for travel in the region. But he was much troubled by disputes with the Colonial Office over money, originating in his rather unorthodox departure from Mauritius, and compounded by disagreements over his salary as Judicial Commissioner for the Western Pacific. On two separate occasions, he was forced to refund considerable sums. This certainly embittered him. He told Gordon: "Where a man is a trifler with his public duty, and permits all manner of abuses to remain unchecked, he appears always to get promotion and salary. If a man tries to do his duty up to some kind of high standard, he is generally shunted as regards both." It also strained his relations with Gordon:

> I somehow think that you, who can generally manage things you have a mind to, could have backed me up better. However, the thing is finished, but the recollection or rather reflection – what a fool I am to bother about public business I am neither paid nor thanked for – has left a bitter taste in my mouth.

Gorrie's irritation with Gordon was momentary, but his resentment at the Colonial Office was real. As he told Chesson, "There is some influence at work against me in the C.O." By 1880 he was beginning to get restless and to think of a change. One possibility was promotion to a governorship rather than another judicial post. He told Chesson:

> If anything of that kind is *offered* then all I would have to consider would be whether it was my public duty to accept, if the Secretary of State thought I was the best man for the post, but it is a great responsibility to seem to seek a change which may turn out to be unfavourable to the health of wife and children. If they were to offer me the Governorship of Hong Kong I would accept at once.[70]

But Gorrie's thoughts were also turning to Scotland. After asking Chesson to give him all the news on the 1880 elections in Britain, especially details about the "new men of promise", he commented wistfully "my old friend John McLaren will now be Lord Advocate if the Liberals got in and I suppose I will be forgotten because I am absent". And he wrote to Gordon, who had just taken up his new post in New Zealand (which he hated),

> I wonder when my turn will come for a change – Not that I don't like Fiji as much as you do – but that one fears to be lost sight of, and be left to be buried here for ever. I would not care for any other Chief Justiceship even at a considerable rise in salary . . . but I am casting longing looks back to Scotland. Why should one who has learnt much

> more of his profession than if he had remained at home, not be eligible for a judgeship in his own land? The fate of Chief Justices is a most melancholy one – To return home with not large pensions and to find themselves out in the cold . . .The bold plan would be to chuck up and jump into the Parliament House [in Edinburgh] one fine morning, where I know I would be a 'power'! . . I think that because I have been in the Colonies I ought not to be cut off from the natural rewards of the profession.

He asked for Gordon's opinion, "as one of a Scotch noble house, and as a man and a brother!"[71]

Gorrie's grievances about money (which were not unfounded) and his sense of persecution in high places must have been somewhat alleviated by his knighthood. Gordon had first recommended him for that honour when he was on home leave in 1878-79. Sir Robert Herbert of the Colonial Office noted in the middle of 1879: "Sir A. Gordon is anxious that Mr Gorrie should be knighted and retained for a further period in Fiji instead of being offered any promotion which he may be thought to have earned. I think he has earned knighthood". But the Secretary of State felt unable

> to recommend any more judges for knighthood at present. When Sir A. Gordon returns to Fiji, he will be able to judge how matters have gone in his absence. If he then thinks Mr Gorrie worthy of knighthood, and would recommend him officially for that honour, I should not be unwilling to consider it.

Early in 1881, Gordon told him "I have written privately to Lord Kimberley strongly urging your knighthood." Chesson seems to have heard of the knighthood as early as April 1881, when he wrote congratulating his friend, but the Letters Patent were not issued until May, and Gorrie himself was informed at the end of that month by telegram. The *Fiji Argus* announced the Chief Justice's new style early in June 1881.[72]

In October 1882, it became publicly known that Gorrie would soon leave Fiji to take up his new post in the Leeward Islands, and each of the colony's newspapers, the *Suva Times* (which had succeeded the *Fiji Argus*) and the *Fiji Times*, published assessments of his work. The former was favourable though by no means uncritical. In a very long editorial, the *Suva Times* admitted that there were times when the "terrors" of his cross-examination did not help elicit the truth, and that he was often "brusque" to the members of the Bar. Hence "for a time Chief Justice Gorrie was as unpopular a representative of the judicial faculty as we could well have had". But "as he became better known, the residents of this colony began to appreciate his stern honesty of purpose, and to credit him with an anxious desire to judge fairly in every case"; though a few prejudiced people never changed their opinion of him, "the voice of the people is against them, and the Chief Justice would carry a very large majority with him if it were possible to bring the question to the arbitrament of numbers". But the *Fiji Times*, always an enemy, would have none of this. Its proprietor, G.L. Griffiths, had been summoned on a contempt charge in 1877, and its editor, W.F. Parr, was a confirmed opponent of Gorrie and Gordon. (The *Suva Times* assured its readers that "Parr is making arrangements to follow Sir John to Antigua, as he fears that his life will be lonesome without anything to stir up his bile occasionally".) Parr categorically rejected the rival paper's claim that his conduct was approved by the majority of the white population, and ended his editorial: "We wish Sir John every success in his new sphere of operation, but in the general interest we can neither regret his departure, or complacently regard the chances of his returning in any other capacity than that of a private citizen."[73]

Some Suva residents who were well disposed towards Gorrie organized a farewell dinner for him, and the speeches at this affair were elaborately reported in the *Suva Times*. Replying to the toast in his honour, he confined himself to genial reminiscences of his career before Fiji and his love for the colony, its climate and scenery. Only one speaker alluded to his conduct as judge, a lawyer who responded to a toast to the Bar:

> Mr Winter said he was indeed alarmed when he first came to the colony from the reports he heard of Judge Gorrie, but it was an alarm soon dissipated. He found himself listened to in Court with more than patience, and, as a professional man, he considered himself fortunate in having belonged to the Bar of Sir John's Court.

The *Fiji Times* ridiculed the dinner, saying that the 23 gentlemen present represented "a large proportion of those whom, in his public capacity, the recipient of their homage had *not* gratuitously insulted".[74]

At the last sitting of the Supreme Court over which he presided, speeches were made by the new Attorney-General, by P.S. Solomon of the Fiji Bar, and by Gorrie. The Attorney-General "believed that in no court in Her Majesty's dominions could the two systems of law and equity be said to be more completely fused and blended than in the Supreme Court of Fiji". He praised Gorrie's work as legislator: "The fruits of His Lordship's labour remained permanently fixed in the Ordinance Book of the colony", with "masterly" laws on guaranty, bailment, agency "and other ordinary common law subjects", as well as the Real Property Ordinance which had been such a boon. Solomon, who had practised before Gorrie since 1876, emphasized the enormous change for the better he had wrought in comparison with "the chaotic conditions which prevailed ere an English Judge sat on the bench . . . when Victorian [*ie* Victoria, Australia], Hawaiian, and every sort of law which might apply to a case was read". Thanks to Hackett and Gorrie, "simplicity, regularity, and consistency of procedure" had been established. "As to the relationship between bench and bar, although he must in all candour urge that the Bench sometimes sat upon them severely . . . whether as a cultivated gentleman or a genial host, His Lordship had always shown the Bar that they had his friendship". Gorrie replied in a lengthy speech. Among other topics, he discussed the difficulties presented by cases involving Fijians, Polynesians or Indians and the principles that had guided him in these cases, "the Judge, in my opinion, having a much more direct responsibility cast upon him in such countries as these to see that the truth is discovered than where the administration of the law is the outcome of the traditions of generations of a civilized people". The magistrates had also had their difficulties as in all places "where the white race are the employers of labour and the native races are the servants, under strict Government protection and supervision."[75]

It seems that Gorrie had hinted that he intended to return to Fiji after his retirement from the colonial service and make it his permanent home. Of course, he had a link to Fiji in his married daughter Charlie. But when he left Fiji for Sydney and then England in November 1882, it was to be for good.

CHAPTER FIVE

Outrages and Reprisals: the Western Pacific High Commission, 1878-82

In 1877-78 the British Government created the Western Pacific High Commission (WPHC) in order to control the often lawless activities of British subjects in the Pacific islands which were not in the hands of any 'civilized' power. The governor of Fiji was appointed High Commissioner (HC) and the Chief Justice was to serve as Judicial Commissioner (JC) in the HC's Court. This gave Gorrie an interesting but difficult jurisdiction in addition to his work in the crown colony of Fiji, and involved him closely in the formation of British policy with respect to the Pacific territories outside the boundaries of Australia, New Zealand and Fiji.

Creation of the WPHC

The WPHC was created primarily to control the Polynesian labour trade. British subjects kidnapped islanders to work on the plantations of Queensland and Fiji. This provoked violent retaliations which came to be known as 'outrages'. The victims of such 'outrages' were usually officers and

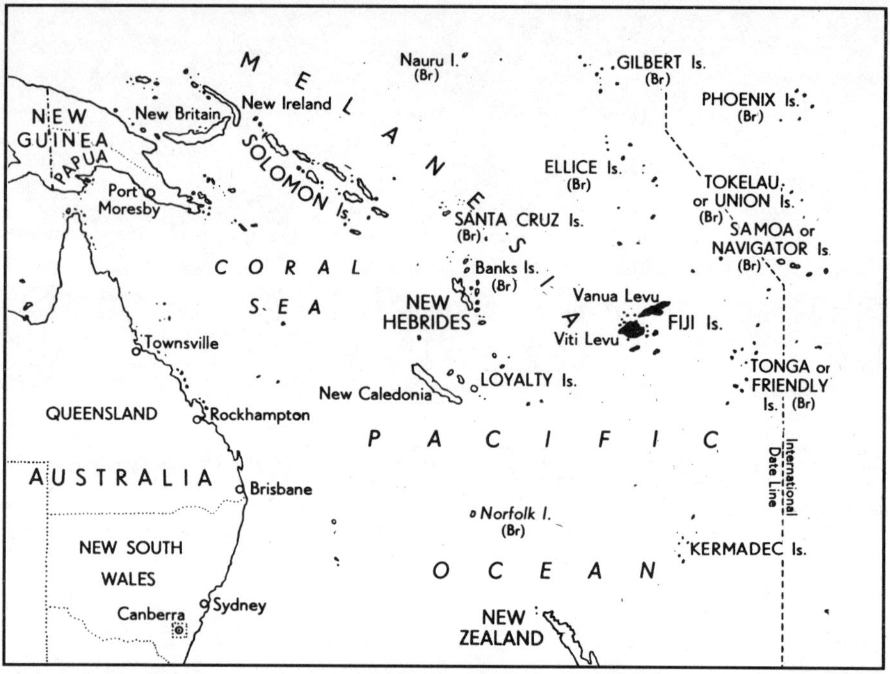

The Western Pacific

men of the labour ships, but occasionally persons wholly unconnected with the trade were killed, most notably Bishop Patteson in 1871 and Commodore Goodenough in 1875. It was the objective of the WPHC to subject the labour trade to strict controls, to eliminate the abuses and thus prevent reprisals, and to bring lawless British subjects in the Pacific to book.

The labour trade to Queensland and Fiji began in 1863-64 and ended in 1904 and 1911 respectively. There was also a smaller trade supplying the French colony of New Caledonia, German concerns in Samoa, and British planters and copra traders in the New Hebrides. Most of the 'recruits' were obtained from the New Hebrides and the Solomon Islands, though many other island groups in the South Pacific were also drawn into the trade, which was at its height in the early 1880s. At least to the mid 1870s, actual kidnapping was routine, and the use of trickery and coercion was the norm. The Queensland trade came under loose government supervision in 1868, but it was not until the later 1870s that this was made effective; the traffic to

Fiji was gradually brought under control by Gordon. But even after 1880 abuses persisted in the Queensland and Fiji branches of the labour trade, always by far the largest; the trade to Samoa and New Caledonia was notorious; and the small schooners which recruited for the New Hebrides planters and traders, often flying the French flag, were under no supervision whatever. Government agents were required by law to be present in all vessels recruiting for Queensland or Fiji, but their performance varied considerably. The Queensland newspapers frequently reported murderous attacks on the crews of labour vessels from the colony in the 1870s and early 1880s: "We do not believe", one editor wrote in 1876, "there is a trade in the colonies which, for its term of existence, has been so terribly marked with savage reminiscences."[1]

Bishop Patteson's murder provoked an outcry in Britain, and the result was the Pacific Islanders Protection Act (also known as the Kidnapping Act) of 1872. By this law, the kidnapping or decoying of islanders was made a felony; all British ships engaged in the trade were to be licensed; consuls and naval officers were empowered to seize suspect vessels and to enquire into alleged cases of kidnapping. But the Act did not purge the labour traffic of abuses. For one thing, its application to Fiji was extremely doubtful until annexation in 1874; even then, making one small area of the Pacific a crown colony could not solve the problems of the trade as a whole, nor could it curb lawlessness by British subjects roaming through the islands free from any kind of control. The way forward was pointed out in the report of Goodenough and Layard recommending the annexation of Fiji in 1874:

> We think that the commission of the Governor of Fiji should give him authority over the persons and acts of British subjects in the New Hebrides and the Solomon Islands, or the islands of the Pacific south of the equator and west of the meridian of 168° West longitude (except New Caledonia and the Loyalty Islands which are under the French flag) . . . The formation of a centre of law and order could not fail to have a good influence in this part of the South Seas, where the number of adventurers in various pursuits is yearly increasing.

This was the genesis of the WPHC.

Gordon was anxious to be given some kind of consular authority over British subjects in the Pacific, and he pressed the idea on the Colonial Office while he was in Britain in 1874-75; he probably suggested the rather grandiose title of HC. There were protracted disputes with the Foreign Office about the extent of the consular authority which should be granted to the HC and the division of control between the Foreign and Colonial Offices; but the 1875 Act which extended the Kidnapping Act to Fiji provided the legal basis for the WPHC. It empowered the Queen to "exercise power and jurisdiction over Her subjects within any islands & places in the Pacific Ocean not being within Her Majesty's dominions, nor within the jurisdiction of any civilized power, in the same and as ample a manner as if such power and jurisdiction had been acquired by the cession or conquest of territory". By Order in Council, the Crown could create the office of HC, vested with consular authority and jurisdiction in his own Court.

To Gordon's dismay, the Order was not issued until August 1877, two years after the enactment of the enabling measure. The long awaited Order, which became effective in February 1878, constituted the office of the HC, with jurisdiction over British subjects in Tonga, Samoa, the Union, Phoenix, Gilbert, Ellice, Marshall, Caroline, Solomon and Santa Cruz Islands, Rotumah, New Guinea east of 143°E, New Britain, New Ireland, the Louisiades, and all other islands of the Western Pacific not within the jurisdiction of Fiji, Queensland or New South Wales, or any other 'civilized' power; the New Hebrides were not named to avoid offending France – they were closely connected to New Caledonia through the labour trade – but were always considered to be within the HC's jurisdiction. This was an area of about nine million square miles of sea and land. The HC was empowered to make regulations to force British subjects to obey any treaty between Britain and a local ruler; he could exclude from the islands any British subject judged to be dangerous to peace and good order and deport such a person if his orders were disobeyed. The Order made the Chief Justice of Fiji a JC for the Western Pacific; ad hoc JCs, persons of legal knowledge, might also be appointed. The HC, the JCs, and the Deputy High Commissioners (DHCs) constituted the HC's Court for civil and criminal jurisdiction, which could be exercised by the HC or the JC either in Fiji or elsewhere. The Court was to be aided whenever possible by assessors, British subjects of good character appointed by the HC. But it had no jurisdiction over the indigenous people of the region, whose sovereignty in their territories was specifically recognized. Nor did the HC enjoy any jurisdiction over the subjects of other 'civilised' powers in the Pacific.

The weakness of the Order was that it "thought too much in terms of courts and not enough in terms of executive authority", in the words of Deryck Scarr. It attempted to make Fiji a centre from which law and order might diffuse through the unannexed Pacific islands. But the HC lacked executive or treaty-making powers; he could not make regulations for the treatment of labourers working for British subjects outside Fiji; his powers to deal with complaints by British subjects against islanders were shaky. He could punish Britons for crimes against the latter; he could not punish islanders for crimes against British subjects, which inevitably made the judicial machinery seem one-sided and unfair to whites in the Pacific and to Australasian opinion in general. The Order concentrated on *judicial* machinery with which to punish abuses in the labour traffic at the expense of *executive* authority which might have prevented abuses by controlling British subjects engaged in it. Nevertheless, it did bring the problems of the labour trade closer to solution, and it was a credible attempt to bring lawless British subjects to book without assuming the responsibility and costs of administering more Polynesian communities. In the minds of its makers, the WPHC could curb abuses which threatened to cause chaos in the Pacific, chaos which would inevitably (and had already) led to pressures for further annexations. It was an instrument devised to avoid fresh annexations for the time being while asserting Britain's "special position" in the vast region.[2]

The First Cases

The HC's Court was inaugurated in Samoa when Gordon and Gorrie went there in February 1878. The application of the Order to Samoa, and to Tonga, required special measures since each had an organized government which had entered into treaties with 'civilized' powers (Germany and the USA). Gordon negotiated a treaty with the ruling chiefs of Samoa, known as the Taimina and Faipule, which allowed the HC to exercise jurisdiction over British subjects there. He concluded a similar treaty with the King of Tonga later in 1878, seeking to counteract German influence in that group of islands. Ironically, the HC's authority was strongest in Samoa and Tonga because a DHC with consular authority was normally resident in each, a decision made by the Foreign Office because of the German and American presence; but Tonga had no labour traffic at all, and the Samoan trade was in German hands and therefore beyond the HC's reach. Tonga and Samoa were precisely the places where lawless acts by British subjects were least likely to occur.[3]

In an interesting letter to Chesson, Gorrie described his trip to Samoa

> to inaugurate the jurisdiction of the High Commissioner's Court . . . To show that it will be useful I may add that we tried a British subject for conspiring to murder and murder in connection with a brutal lynch case which took place at Apia [Samoa's chief town]. As the case is under appeal (from myself as J.C. of the H.C. Court to myself as C.J. of Fiji) I will say no more about it at present.

This was the case involving W.J. Hunt, and the origin of a complicated series of actions which was still worrying Gordon and Gorrie in 1882-83. In addition, the governor, as Consul-General, tried to persuade the ruling chiefs to pay certain claims insisted on by the Foreign Office as compensation for the death of some British seamen, and a number of private claims by British subjects against the Samoan government "for all sorts of things from damages for broken heads to damages for not getting them back their whores"! These private claims were referred to a Commission consisting of a Samoan chief and Gorrie:

> We went very carefully over the claims and disposed of about 40 of them and laid down principles upon which the investigation of the others could be carried out. The Samoans I am glad to say were perfectly satisfied with this, and they have since offered to settle all British claims upon the principles I laid down.

But the chiefs, advised by the US consul, made difficulties about paying up the compensation required by the British government, and Gordon felt obliged to seize an armed schooner belonging to the Samoan authorities and take it off to Fiji to sell. An additional fine of £1000 – imposed by the Foreign Office for the same skirmish which had resulted in the death of the British seamen – was extracted only after a threat to shell Apia by a Navy vessel.

As Gorrie told Chesson, with some understatement,

> the little tiff we have thus had with the Chiefs will prevent all notion of cession to Gt Britain for some time. But if the question should turn up I hope you [the APS] will see your way to support it. [Samoa] is becoming a settlement of white men and the chiefs can never control such a community . There is practically no law and the whites are mostly low class ruffians who live with the native women, and spend their time in drinking . . . There is a strong German Colony, and in especial one house Godefroy & Co of Hamburg who go in for planting as well as commerce. Some British subjects are also planters. They go off to the Polynesian Islands for labour, a ship came in from the Gilbert Group with labourers while we were there for Godefroy and of course none of our Polynesian Acts can touch this kind of traffic, or even in Samoa look after the interests of the labourers when they are hired to a British subject. Under the Order we could enquire into assaults and such like, if we heard of them, but we have no powers to inspect and superintend the carrying out of contracts or officers to do it.[4]

W.J. Hunt was an Englishman who enjoyed the confidence of a leading Samoan chief, Malietoa, the main rival of the Taimina and Faipule who were in power in 1878. In 1877, an American (Corcoran) had murdered another US citizen at Apia, and Hunt had taken a prominent part in a public meeting which proceeded to hang him instead of sending him to the USA for trial. When Gordon and Gorrie went to Samoa, Hunt was indicted and tried for murder and conspiracy to murder. The JC acquitted him of murder, but found him guilty of conspiracy to murder with persons unknown, and sentenced him to one year's imprisonment. The Order provided for appeals from the HC's Court to the Supreme Court of Fiji, and Hunt appealed. The main grounds were that the Order creating the HC's Court came into force in February 1878 and that its jurisdiction could not be exercized retroactively in respect of a crime committed in 1877, when the hanging of Corcoran took place. In May 1878 Gorrie heard the appeal as Chief Justice of Fiji, and dismissed it. Hunt was placed in the Levuka jail. He petitioned the HC for a pardon, and so did the foreign residents in Samoa, both unsuccessfully.[5] Three years after this trial, Gorrie observed that it had greatly impressed 'natives' and whites alike:

> Our going down to Samoa to try Hunt for the lynching business and bringing him away in a man of war to Fiji had great effect upon even the natives here [Fiji]. On being introduced to a Chief afterwards he said to the magistrate introducing me, 'Is this the law dispensing chief who went to Samoa and punished a man there and brought him to gaol here?' On his being told yes, he said, 'A strong Chief, a powerful chief!' – simply because it had hitherto been unheard of that anyone had jurisdiction out of his own territorial limits, and the mean whites have been similarly affected.[6]

But the Colonial Office was distinctly uneasy about the retroactive application of the HC's jurisdiction. Sir Robert Herbert felt that the Court's jurisdiction was dubious and advised taking the opinion of the Law Officers. They ruled that the Order did not allow for retrospective jurisdiction and that the HC's powers were founded exclusively on it. This was certainly embarrassing, since the appeal had already been heard, the sentence confirmed, and Hunt was in jail. It was decided to remit the rest of Hunt's sentence without giving a specific reason or referring to the Law Officers' ruling, in other words, a 'free pardon' from the Queen after he had served about eight months of his term. While in England on leave, Gordon secured an indemnity for himself and Gorrie against any action by Hunt for false imprisonment.[7]

Hunt believed that the whole prosecution was political; he had opposed Gordon's 'politicking' in Samoa. Malietoa's confidence in him was asserted when he was appointed Chief Secretary to the Samoan Government in May 1880. Gordon decided, not without grounds, that his intrigues were helping to cause chaos in Samoa; the Order empowered the HC to deport British subjects from the Western Pacific if he was satisfied that they threatened "peace and good order". Hunt then renounced his British citizenship and declared he was a citizen of Samoa. Gordon went to Samoa in August 1880. The consuls of Britain, the USA and Germany at Apia all swore that Hunt's presence was "dangerous to peace and good order"; Gordon invoked the Order, declared his Samoan citizenship invalid, and ordered his prohibition from Samoa for two years. Hunt went to Fiji and entered an action against the HC for £2000 for losses and damages. It was heard by Gorrie as Chief Justice of Fiji. Gordon was worried by this case, asking Gorrie (rather improperly): "What am I to do in this matter, or shall I do *nothing*? I presume he will try to show that he is a *Samoan subject*, but he never put that forward in his application to or interviews with me. As I read the Order, there is no *appeal* against an Order of Prohibition." But as he must have anticipated, Gorrie, in a lengthy judgment, dismissed Hunt's suit and allowed costs to the governor. He held that, as a judicial officer, the HC was not liable for any error committed in a judicial capacity, which disposed of Hunt's argument that as a Samoan citizen he was beyond the HC's jurisdiction.[8]

This was far from the last of Hunt, however. He determined to return to Samoa in defiance of the prohibition. Arriving there in August 1881, he was promptly arrested by the DHC and jailed for 19 days. He was returned to Fiji, where he filed a suit against the DHC for damages; Gorrie dismissed it early in 1882. Hunt went off to New Zealand and brought an action against Gordon for damages of £8000 in the Supreme Court of New Zealand where he was now governor. Gordon was justifiably anxious, writing to Gorrie:

> That infernal nuisance Hunt, or rather [W.F.] Parr who backs him up and gives him money for the sake of annoying me through his means, has brought a fresh action for damages against me here [Wellington], and, I fear, a Wellington jury is likely to give a verdict, in all cases, against the Governor . . . How well one gets rewarded for trying to do a little good in the world, and not swimming with the stream.

Despite his anxiety, the case (which was not heard until 1883) turned out quite well for Gordon; Hunt was awarded only £100 damages for the few days imprisonment in Samoa.[9]

Acting High Commissioner

In the middle of 1878, Gordon went to Britain on leave, and instructed Gorrie to discharge all the functions of the HC. In effect, he was left as acting HC for over a year. This represented his first real taste of 'executive' authority. He was an extremely active *locum tenens*, earning praise from the Colonial Office and from Gordon, although he sometimes alarmed them with his zeal for action which they often felt was precipitate.

Unfortunately, and largely through Gordon's carelessness, there was some doubt in the Colonial Office about whether Gorrie had been formally appointed acting HC and what powers he could exercise. The Order made no provision for the appointment of an acting HC, and the Secretary of State had merely

> assumed [that] the duties of the High Commissioner would, to a great extent, be performed in his absence by the principal Judicial Commissioner, Chief Justice Gorrie [who] is not, strictly speaking, acting High Commissioner at all, though, as acting *for* the High Commissioner, it is very difficult to give him any other designation.

This was Gordon's understanding of the situation, at least. Gorrie called it "glorious uncertainty", but told Gordon: "I saw the difficulty from the first, but as the Crown directed you to give me the deputation to act, I am quite easy to consequences otherwise." But the Colonial Office felt that he did not understand his legal position, and the Secretary of State issued a rather severe rebuke towards the end of 1878. This despatch prompted Gorrie to explain the situation caused by Gordon's departure from Fiji more fully, and to insist that: "I did not take upon myself duties without warrant." Moreover, since all his actions were carried out in good faith, and with what seemed ample authorization, "I have the confident hope that all acts so done will be supported by the Crown, and any necessary indemnity granted to the person who has been placed in this position of difficulty and responsibility". The men in the Colonial Office recognized that the uncertainties surrounding Gorrie's position were not of his doing, and decided to offer him a little encouragement: "I have not failed to observe that the difficulties of your acting appointment during Sir A. Gordon's absence presented themselves to you before you assumed it", wrote the Secretary of State, "and I fully appreciate the zeal and ability which you have brought to the discharge of your functions under the Western Pacific Order in Council."[10]

The legal difficulty, that the Order did not provide for an acting HC or for the delegation of his powers, was remedied by an amending Order, issued in August 1879, which stated that the Chief JC would act for the HC whenever he was absent from the Pacific. But the new measure was issued only a few weeks before Gordon returned to Fiji and resumed his duties as HC. Moreover, the Colonial Office turned down his reasonable request for some remuneration for his fourteen months' service as (*de facto* if not *de jure*) acting HC. No wonder he commented bitterly to Gordon:

> The Acting High Commissionership has brought me, first, a hard slap in the face from the govt denying that I am acg Commr, second, a great deal of trouble and worry and work, third, the necessary assumption of responsibility which may hereafter cost me dear in a legal way; fourth, your disapprobation for my restless energy . . . fifth, the displeasure of two great departments of State [the Foreign Office and the Admiralty], sixth, Des Voeux's temporary dislike leading to difficulties in Fiji, seventh – no half salary eighth – no salary at all – ninth promotion stopped – pretty good that for a man who has tried to do his duty honestly and well – ay, and who knows that he *has* done it well, impugn it who so list.[11]

Deryck Scarr has written that:

> to leave Gorrie without special instructions to put in force the powers of an Order in Council which had only recently been received, and which was completely untested in action, was a curious lapse of judgment on Gordon's part, for Gorrie was precisely the kind of man the possible effects of whose being let loose with the Order had caused concern in the Colonial Office when it was being issued.

He is correct in stating that "Gorrie aspired to be a colonial governor" and that he believed (like Gordon) that the HC should be "the overriding authority in the Western Pacific". There is no doubt that some of Gorrie's pronouncements and (less often) actions as *de facto* acting HC worried the Colonial Office; but on the whole they appreciated his efforts to make the HC's jurisdiction effective and treated his many proposals to strengthen it as serious and well-considered recommendations.[12]

He alarmed the Colonial Office at the start of his stewardship by proposing to leave Fiji and go off to New Guinea. Gold had recently been discovered by Australian adventurers, and a 'rush' was thought to be imminent. He was thinking about going there even before Gordon left him in charge, as he told Chesson as early as April 1878: "I think I will go up to New Guinea as expeditions are organizing in Melbourne and Sydney to go there and if not looked after they are sure to get into rows with the natives." Gordon wrote from Australia, telling him that Queensland was agitating for colonization of northeast New Guinea, and suggesting that he request a Navy ship if he thought a visit advisable. Encouraged by this advice from the HC, he informed the Secretary of State that he believed it was his duty to go there, as soon as the Commodore of the Australian Station could provide a ship, in order to maintain law and order among the whites and to frame 'regulations' to ensure peaceful relations between the gold-diggers and the locals. The Colonial Office took fright. "I sincerely trust", minuted Herbert, "that the Commodore will have said that he was unable to take Judge Gorrie to New Guinea. I think it a very injudicious and meddlesome act on the Judge's part to propose to leave his Court in Fiji and go on a vague errand to New Guinea." Gordon's lieutenants in Fiji took a similar view; Thurston thought Gorrie would "make a very nice kettle of fish" if he did get there, but told Gordon that "He intends going simultaneously to Samoa, New Britain, and New Guinea. Happily, therefore, he will go nowhere."[13]

The office fired off a telegram to the governor of New South Wales (Fiji could not yet be reached by cable) telling him to order Gorrie to stay in Fiji; but his plan of going to New Guinea had already been foiled by Des Voeux, acting as governor of Fiji, and by Commodore Hoskins. Des Voeux tried to dissuade him from going, and was relieved when the Commodore declined to provide a ship. Gorrie entered only a mildly worded protest, to the effect that the demands on the small Australian squadron hindered the HC's effectiveness in dealing with urgent matters. He told Gordon:

> As the want of a ship gives a breathing time, I have written a longish despatch . . . I have put the legal difficulties down in black and white, and come to the general conclusion that if a rush takes place, or the European population in New Guinea get numerous from any cause, annexation will be the only remedy; but that if annexation is contemplated at any time, it had better take place sooner than later, so that the treatment of the natives might start fair from the first; but that the rule could only be retained in the Crown, and not given to any of the Australian Colonies.[14]

The suggestions put forward in this (and other) letters from Gorrie on the affairs of New Guinea met with warm approval from Gordon, who was asked to comment on them during his home leave. In a generous tribute to his friend, he wrote:

> I have occasionally felt it my duty to comment on exaggerations or indiscretions of language on the part of Chief Justice Gorrie which have caused me all the more regret because his unflagging energy, zeal for the public service, and unvarying intolerance of wrong or oppression, are at all times such as to merit the warmest acknowledgment.

Herbert commented: "Although C.J. Gorrie has been too eager to sail forth and redress wrongs throughout the Western Pacific, he has considered the various difficult questions . . . with much care and ability, and I think he should be thanked for his despatches and told that his views are receiving the fullest consideration." An encouraging note to this effect was duly sent, which must have been some compensation for the rather severe letter in which he was chastised for wanting to go off to New Guinea and told that he was not the acting HC.[15]

To decide to visit New Guinea merely because gold had been discovered and a rush of lawless whites might be imminent was imprudent, and it was probably fortunate that the Commodore squashed his plan. More reasonable, perhaps, was his wish to proceed to New Britain, a large island north of the Solomons, because of events there in April 1878. Four Fijians and Tongans, Methodist 'native ministers' or teachers, were killed by people from the interior of New Britain. The head of the Methodist Mission to New Britain,

George Brown, believed that all his Polynesian and European staff in these islands were in grave danger unless swift punishment was inflicted on the guilty chiefs and villages. He organized a war party which burnt many villages and killed a number of people, perhaps as many as fifty. He justified himself on the grounds of self-defence, arguing that many months would necessarily have passed before the Navy, or the HC, could have undertaken investigations and action. Brown sent an account of his proceedings in some indiscreet letters to his superiors, which were published in Australian newspapers and thus came eventually to Gorrie's notice.[16]

He believed that it was unacceptable for any British subject to take into his own hands the right to 'levy war' against the people of the Pacific, whatever their crimes had been, and that it was especially objectionable in a missionary. To ignore such an action was to condone it. As he told Gordon:

> This is the first time a missionary has attempted such work – so different from the spirit of [murdered Bishop] Patteson. If passed over, every trader in the Pacific will see a necessity to go and burn and slay. On the other hand, the public opinion here and in Sydney will be wholly favourable to Brown.

At the same time he informed the Colonial Office of these events, stating that if the case seemed to require a 'judicial' response it was his sole responsibility to take action, otherwise it was for the Office to determine whether Brown's proceedings were justifiable.[17] By November 1878 he had decided that it *was* his responsibility to take judicial action against Brown. He told Gordon: "I have given orders to have the martial missionary tried for manslaughter." His first idea was to try Brown in Fiji, but the Methodist authorities wanted the trial to take place at New Britain, where he could produce witnesses who would testify to the danger which he and his people had faced. This meant that Gorrie would have to go there. Here again, he was foiled by the Commodore, who said he could not produce a ship, and as he rather plaintively wrote to Gordon: "Of course if I go as J.C., I could not go in a schooner – for the time, the space, the dignity of the office, and the effect upon the natives." Not only did the Commodore prevent him getting to New Britain; the Colonial Office cabled him twice, ordering him not to leave Fiji unless positively instructed to do so. For the time being, he was unable to deal with Brown. He did, however, alert the APS through Chesson by giving him an account of the affair and sending him a copy of one of Brown's letters published in a Sydney paper. He also wrote to the Secretary of State, discussing the wider issues raised by Brown's actions: how the islanders should have been punished, and whether (as he thought) the HC's Court should not be given jurisdiction over 'natives' who committed crimes against British subjects. He conceded readily that the murder of the teachers required investigation and punishment, but not through "retaliatory war" waged by a private citizen.[18]

Although the Colonial Office was determined to stop Gorrie from going to New Britain and trying Brown for manslaughter, it recognized that some kind of action was necessary, especially as the APS had begun to lobby. Gordon's opinion was sought. He thought that, even taking the most favourable view of Brown's situation and motives, his conduct required further investigation, and he proposed that he should carry out a formal enquiry on his return to the Pacific. He believed that Gorrie's proposal that the HC's Court should be granted jurisdiction over crimes against British subjects deserved serious consideration, but that it was a difficult question full of legal complexities. The Office decided to instruct Gorrie to do nothing further in the Brown case until Gordon was able to carry out a formal enquiry. But the Commodore found it impossible to make a ship available to the HC when he returned to the Pacific in September 1879, and Gordon never held an enquiry in New Britain. Instead, the captain of HMS *Danae* went there and conducted an enquiry of sorts, which on the whole was favourable to Brown.[19]

But Gorrie still believed that Brown should stand trial on a criminal charge as a warning to others, and when he heard that the missionary was likely to pass through Levuka, he told Chesson "if he comes I shall certainly cause him to be tried". Brown arrived early in November 1879. Gordon and Gorrie were at cross purposes as to how to deal with him: Gordon wished only to question him (in order to carry out the 'investigation' ordered by the Colonial Office) while Gorrie summoned him before the HC's Court for a preliminary hearing on a manslaughter charge. As Gordon told his wife, "a very pretty quarrel" between the two men seemed imminent, but a rapid-fire exchange of letters between them brought a solution. Gordon, as HC, would conduct a *pro forma* 'questioning' of Brown and then write stating that he did not wish the prosecution for manslaughter to be proceeded with. Gorrie gave in reluctantly, for, as he told the governor, he believed that "there should be no difference in Brown's case from that of any other, and that the same course should be followed with him as has been followed with others, justice always showing best when it is no respecter of persons"; but, said Gordon, "I must do Gorrie the justice to say, that when once he had caved in, he behaved well and handsomely in facilitating an arrangement". Under this 'arrangement', the HC held an 'enquiry' which amounted to his informing Brown that he did not think that a crime had been committed and he hoped that the court proceedings would lead to a similar conclusion and Brown would be freed. Gordon made it clear, however, that he was not expressing approval of Brown's actions. As he later recalled, Brown was still anxious, "as it was well known in Levuka that . . . the Chief Judicial Commissioner was declared to have asserted his right to conduct the inquiry, and his determination to do so . . . He was, at all events, considered by most, if not by all the foreign residents of Fiji to be primarily, if not solely, the instigator of the action." But when he appeared before the JC two days later, the 'arrangement' was carried out. Brown was told that the HC had expressed his opinion that he should not be prosecuted, and so he was "free to depart".[20]

The Colonial Office was correct to call this *dénouement* "rather ludicrous"; a New Zealand paper described it as "a fiasco". Gorrie persisted in believing that the course of action imposed on him by Gordon was an error: "It will weaken our hands in dealing with the lawlessness of the Pacific", he told Chesson; but he had been left with no option "but to put the best face on it publicly that I could". Brown, in his memoirs, speculated as to Gorrie's motives in seeking a criminal prosecution: "He had always been *persona grata* with the APS . . . and it was thought that much of the zeal which he manifested was due to his desire still to occupy the same good position in the opinion of the members of that influential and useful Society." Gordon put it down, rather meanly, to Gorrie's dislike for the missionaries.[21] In fact, his actions in the Brown case were perfectly consistent with all his proceedings in relation to the WPHC. He believed that Brown had been directly responsible for the death of several islanders and that this was a case of unlawful killings; hence, a charge of manslaughter was appropriate. The fact that Brown was a missionary and had powerful friends would certainly have strengthened his resolve; but neither dislike of the entrenched Methodist body in Fiji, nor anxiety to 'keep in' with the APS, lay behind his actions. Of course, Brown's actions were thoroughly approved of by public opinion in Australia and New Zealand. An article in a Queensland newspaper headlined "Three Cheers for George Brown!" – which jovially regretted that no more than "50 or 60 natives" were killed – probably expressed the general Australasian reaction, and Gorrie's proceedings against Brown formed part of the indictment against him in that part of the Empire. Brown himself claimed that he enjoyed the "full sympathy [of] the whole of the residents in Fiji [during his] ordeal" in Levuka. This, however, is more dubious. The *Fiji Argus* argued that Brown's "retaliatory massacre" was indefensible and illegal and stated categorically that the "public" in Fiji approved of Gorrie's actions in the Brown case and believed that he was merely discharging his clear duty.[22]

The Brown affair attracted both publicity and controversy because of the scale of his reprisals and because he was a prominent missionary. Other cases dealt with during Gorrie's period as acting HC were more routine. Early in 1879, Captain J. Daly of *Heather Belle*, a labour ship, was charged with a kidnapping at Ocean Island; after trial in the HC's court, he was found guilty and sentenced to six months in jail and a fine, and was ordered to post a security of £500 for future good behaviour, failing which he was to be deported from the Pacific under the Order. This was, of course, precisely the kind of offence that the Order was designed to deal with. The Colonial Office sanctioned Gorrie's decision to carry out the sentence, and the Secretary of State called his proceedings in the Daly case "judicious and correct".[23] Another case arising from abuses in the labour trade concerned the *Stormbird*, but here the outcome was less satisfactory. This ship had been involved in irregularities while recruiting labourers under the British flag; but it had recently started to fly the flag of Hawaii, presumably to escape the jurisdiction of the HC. When it docked in Levuka in 1878, Gorrie proposed to seize it. Since the *Stormbird* was now of foreign nationality, such an action might have caused a collision both with the government of Hawaii, and with the USA, which had an informal protectorate there. As acting governor, Des Voeux believed that the responsibility of seizing a foreign ship in Levuka harbour would fall on him because Fiji itself was not within the HC's jurisdiction, and he "with great difficulty" persuaded Gorrie to desist. Both Gordon in England, and the Colonial Office, expressed their approval of Des Voeux's action, and their relief that the vessel had not been detained.[24]

When recruiters used trickery or coercion to obtain labourers, the result was often 'outrages' against the men of the next boat seen in the vicinity, with consequent pressures for reprisals. A good (or bad) example occurred in 1879. C.S. Kilgour, captain of the Queensland labour ship *Mystery*, destroyed a village in Aoba, New Hebrides, in retaliation for the murder of the mate and crew of a boat belonging to his ship the year before. The village he destroyed was *not* the guilty one. Kilgour was tried in the HC's Court, fined and ordered to post a bond of £250. Gorrie's charge to the trial assessors stressed the need to impress on British subjects that:

> a private citizen has not the right to go to war on his own private account . . . It is the sovereign power alone which has the right to say when a recourse shall be had to arms, and when a people or tribe shall be punished . . . So long as the whites continue to perpetrate offences, so long will the Pacific be unsafe, for I need not tell you that assaults breed assaults and crime breeds crime.

Kilgour's conviction, and the moderate fine imposed on him, were precisely what the WPHC was designed to achieve; but the Commodore of the Australian Squadron complained that the fine was excessive and "much to be lamented as likely to discourage a trade which . . . must often have to rely on its own powers of defence . . . Our struggling Traders in these Seas" would be discouraged by such a heavy penalty for "acts of indiscretion" like Kilgour's. But the Colonial Office rightly ignored this "ill conceived" attempt to make Kilgour a martyr and approved Gorrie's actions.[25]

One of the reasons for the vicious circle of 'outrages' and reprisals arising out of the labour traffic was the practice of paying part of the recruits' wages in firearms, which were taken back to their home islands when their three years in Fiji or Queensland were up. The murder of George Simpson, mate of the Fijian labour vessel *Agnes Donald*, by armed men on Pentecost Island after he tried to take three men against the will of their chief, prompted Gorrie to take up this issue. Taking the commonsense view that "it seems to be a self-evident proposition that a savage with a more formidable weapon becomes a more formidable savage", he recommended the prohibition of payment by firearms, and the general banning of all traffic in firearms in the area under the HC's jurisdiction. The Secretary of State agreed with this advice, and asked the HC to make regulations prohibiting both. Gordon issued a regulation prohibiting the traffic in arms, but it could be enforced only in Samoa (and, of course, in Fiji). It was easy to stop the payment by firearms in Fiji, but much of the Polynesian labour traffic was controlled by the Queenslanders, and they proved uncooperative. It was not until 1884 that their government agreed to support a regulation banning the arms traffic and payment by firearms all through the Western Pacific.[26]

The cases discussed so far arose from the well-known abuses in the labour trade. Another problem was the tendency of unscrupulous whites to assert specious claims to land in the islands and then try to make good on those claims. Two such cases, involving islands in the Ellice Group (Vaitapu and Funafuti), engaged Gorrie's attention when he was acting HC. As he wrote, "It is a fact that claim-mongering is a recognized business among a certain class of traders and settlers in these seas." In such cases, he thought it was necessary for the HC to shield the islanders from British subjects out to make money at their expense. He wrote stern letters to the white claimants, expressing his disapproval in very blunt language: "I hope you will let the fact be known as widely as you can, that the HC's Court will take cognizance of all attempts to defraud, and that the perpetrators if they continue to trade in Polynesia will not escape the jurisdiction of the Court." The Funafuti claimant was told: "I would advise you in all kindness to try conciliation and fair dealing, or if that is too much opposed to your feelings of contempt for the coloured races then it would be much better to remain at home." On this occasion, Gorrie wrote to the Chief of Funafuti, and his letter may be worth quoting in full as an example of the style thought appropriate in communications with indigenous rulers in the Pacific:

> Do not fear the visits of men of war. It is the desire of the Great Queen whose servant I am, and whose servants the officers and men of the ships are, to do you good and not harm. We will prevent the traders and everyone else doing you harm, and you must do no harm to them. Let there be peace and when you have a complaint do as you have now done, write to me. Let us love each other as God commands us, and do each other good and not evil. Farewell.[27]

The question of further annexations by Britain, and her relations with the other powers active in the Pacific, also engaged Gorrie's attention while he was acting HC. Rotumah was a small island to the north of Fiji. In 1879 its chiefs approached the acting governor of Fiji asking him to accept their offer of cession. Des Voeux dealt with this matter on his own, not even informing Gorrie even though Rotumah was specifically named as being within the HC's jurisdiction. Gorrie advised acceptance of the cession offer, in order to bring the people of the island under "good order and firm rule" and to increase British trade there; but he told Chesson that Des Voeux had put some pressure on the Rotumah chiefs – "he sent HM Schooner *Conflict* to Rotumah and got a cession of the Island" – and that in his view "when islands like that really desire to be annexed I would accede to their wish, but I would think any pressure utterly wrong, and at all events it should be the Government at home and not local officers to say whether any islands should be accepted." Moreover, "both Germany and France may be jealous if they hear we are extending". Des Voeux himself seems to have had some doubts about his action, and no decision was taken until late in 1881; Rotumah was formally annexed to Fiji early in 1882.[28]

Rotumah was a simple proposition in comparison with Samoa. The internal politics of Samoa were extremely complex, and Germany, the USA and Britain all had interests there, while the indigenous government struggled to control events. In 1879 it signed a treaty with Germany. In transmitting a copy of the treaty, Gorrie criticized it as offering no real advantages to the Samoans; it was a classic example, he thought, of a treaty imposed by a strong power on a very weak state. But there was also a party of chiefs in favour of annexation (technically, cession) to Britain, and Gorrie thought that the Colonial Office should give this serious consideration; he believed that the resident Germans would welcome cession as offering security for their property and trade. When the white 'Director of Laws' to the Taimua and Faipule (the ruling chiefs) wrote asking for a treaty with Britain, Gorrie urged them to avoid civil war, and pointed to the peace and prosperity enjoyed by Fiji: "I implore the Samoan chiefs not to shed blood. Let them seek out the ways of wisdom. Let them not waste their wealth in buying guns and powder from the white strangers with which to kill each other, and leave no land for themselves in their old age."[29]

But civil war seemed inevitable; the Taimua and Faipule were overthrown and replaced by a party dominated by Malietoa which was thought to be favourable to British annexation. Writing to George Turner, a Scottish doctor resident in Samoa and close to Malietoa, Gorrie advised that if the Samoan chief really wanted British rule, "the only possible way that can be obtained is by an unqualified cession of the sovereignty to the Queen as in the case of Fiji . . . but a cession made by a portion only of the Chiefs, or one of the two parties into which the country is divided, would not be accepted". He himself would strongly recommend acceptance of a satisfactory offer, but "a great deal would depend upon how the event would be viewed by the German Government for of course no home Government would be disposed to risk a rupture with Germany for fifty Samoas". In an interesting despatch, Gorrie analysed the Samoan situation for the Colonial Office. The chief European settlement, Apia, was much like Levuka before the cession of Fiji with "all the corrupting influences of the contact of the one race with the other in full operation". Germans dominated trade, but British subjects were more numerous. The Samoans had been Christians since the 1830s, and the new religion and white settlement had eroded traditional chiefly authority.

> By means of the teachings of the missionaries we have already in a certain sense morally annexed the country, and when affairs come into such a position that the chiefs feel they can no longer pretend to govern, they naturally turn to the country from which these teachers have come . . . It is no sinister influence acquired by war or intrigue, but a righteous influence.

Gorrie believed that any offer of cession should be accepted and Samoa governed as part of Fiji. But civil war did break out in the middle of 1879.

Malietoa's government was overthrown, he was made a prisoner, and by August Gorrie reported that no effective government existed. This meant that no offer of cession to Britain was now likely. Instead, the situation amounted to

> native anarchy presided over by three Consuls [of Germany, Britain and the USA] having different interests, aims, and masters, and no revenues . . . Better a thousand times that one of the Powers should by agreement take charge of Samoa and be done with it, than that the three Great Powers should be tearing this fragile creature asunder.[30]

Perhaps the most important issue which Gorrie took up during his service as acting HC was the question of criminal jurisdiction over islanders who committed crimes against British subjects. Could Britain rightly exercise any such jurisdiction over people who lived in their own communities subject to their own chiefs and customs? Did the Navy have the right to punish crimes against British subjects by 'acts of war', and if so, could the HC restrain or stop such reprisals? The Order gave the HC the power to try Britons for outrages against islanders; but if it was impossible to punish them for outrages against whites, the HC's jurisdiction would always seem unfair to whites in the Pacific and Australasia.

A case in point occurred in 1878. An "unmitigated ruffian", Henry Townsend, was killed in Ugi in the Solomon Islands; it seemed that he deserved his fate. But HMS *Beagle*, under the command of a young lieutenant, went off to punish the islanders by destroying the 'guilty' village. This disturbed Gorrie. He told Gordon, "It is quite clear these erratic Lieutenants cannot be allowed to fly about burning and hanging"; some kind of jurisdiction would need to be granted to the HC, perhaps in conjunction with senior naval officers (as in the case of pirates), over islanders committing crimes against whites: "It is clear that natives ought not to be hanged without trial – that they ought to be tried if they commit crimes – that their own rulers can't or won't – and that at present we have no authority." The truth was that the Order could never be properly worked "so as to carry public opinion along with us, without a jurisdiction over the natives for offences".[31]

Gorrie proposed to the Secretary of State that the Order should be amended to allow the HC's Court to try islanders committing outrages against British subjects. He thought this would be far better than punishing whole villages by 'acts of war'. Though both Gordon and Herbert thought the proposal worth serious consideration, the Secretary of State felt that it amounted to "an assumption of sovereignty over the natives within the HC's jurisdiction" which was quite undesirable. A month later Gorrie returned to the same point, arguing that the Brown case made the jurisdiction question even more salient. "Retaliatory war" by a private citizen was even worse than by the Navy. The Colonial Office submitted Gorrie's proposal to the Crown Law Officers: could the Queen confer on a British court jurisdiction to try "savages" not living within her dominions for offences against her subjects? They reported in the negative; such a move would involve a "serious infringement of international jurisprudence" and "would be a very mischievous example of a State attempting to legislate for those beyond its jurisdiction. If savage tribes inflict violence or injury, the only alternative is to treat those acts as acts of war, and vindicate justice accordingly." This seemed to rule out jurisdiction as proposed by Gorrie.[32]

Both Gordon and Gorrie believed that Navy officers, when taking action to punish 'outrages' against British subjects under the 'acts of war' doctrine, should be under some general supervision by the HC. This view raised difficult questions about the respective powers and jurisdiction of the Commodore commanding the Australian Squadron and the HC. As Gordon put it in a private letter to Gorrie, "I am sure that you will be as stiff as I am about admitting Lt de Hoghton [of HMS *Beagle*], and such like, to an equal and conflicting jurisdiction to ourselves!" Though Gorrie told the Colonial Office that he and the Commodore agreed that there should be no reprisals without patient and careful investigation, and that indiscriminate shelling of native villages was futile and wrong, there was a fundamental difference in their interpretation of the Order. Gorrie believed that the HC held an executive office under the Order and that he "was entitled to be consulted *as the superior authority* before any act requiring force was done within the limits of his jurisdiction". Naturally, the Commodore disagreed, and the Colonial Office doubted whether the Order gave the HC "a general authority over all the men-of-war in the Pacific".[33]

But Gorrie's correspondence with the Commodore makes it clear that he did, in fact, see himself as the superior officer so far as punishing 'outrages' was concerned. For instance, he told the Commodore that he approved of his decision to inflict only a moderate fine on Solomon Islanders who had killed a seaman guilty of interfering with their women. In another letter, he lectured the Commodore on the need for thorough investigation before any action was taken against a village; to destroy a whole settlement because of the actions of one or two men was "as useless as it is barbarous and certain to breed further acts of violence"; the officers of the Navy should discourage in whatever way possible "private wars" carried on by ship captains. The Colonial Office was correct to note that Gorrie's tone was that of "a superior", and needless to say, this was also the Commodore's view.[34] Relations between Commodore Wilson and the acting HC deteriorated swiftly. The Commodore took exception to the letters just cited "in that they assume a right to criticize and comment upon my actions, which I must not allow to pass unchallenged"; he hoped that future correspondence would reflect the fact that "we are independent departments without authority the one over the other". Gorrie denied that he had ever attempted to give the Commodore 'orders' as to his course of action, but he reminded him that the Admiralty had agreed that naval officers should consult with the HC (except in emergencies) before taking action to punish outrages. Sending this rather silly correspondence to the Colonial Office, Gorrie asked the Secretary of State for a ruling on whether the HC was, or was not "the officer more directly responsible to the Crown for the conduct of affairs in the Western Pacific". A 'ruling' was not forthcoming, but the Office insisted that the HC did *not* exercise any authority over Navy officers in their actions against islanders unless they actually committed a crime.[35] When Gordon returned to the Pacific in September 1879, he strongly supported Gorrie's view of the proper relations between Navy officers and the HC, and this issue continued to simmer until 1881.

Just before Gorrie's period as acting HC ended, a new Order gave the HC some additional powers, though it fell far short of what both Gordon and Gorrie had hoped for. The new Order increased the judicial powers of the HC when he was away from Fiji, and gave him extended powers to make regulations for the government of British subjects in the Western Pacific, and for the maintenance of friendly relations between them and local authorities. It provided for the discharge of the HC's duties in case of his death, incapacity or absence from the Pacific, removing the difficulty which had plagued Gorrie's exercise of authority. But it did not clearly define the position of the HC in relation to the Navy officers, nor did it confer criminal jurisdiction over islanders guilty of crimes against British subjects. Moreover, the Order did not change the basic difficulty: the HC still depended in the last resort on the naval forces to make his jurisdiction effective. In other words, neither the Order of 1877 nor that of 1879 provided the *means* to exercise jurisdiction. On the eve of Gordon's return to Fiji, Gorrie wrote his "valedictory Despatch" as acting HC. The men in the Colonial Office took the opportunity to draw up a sort of balance sheet on Gorrie's year in charge of the WPHC. One wrote:

> The slight reproofs which have been conveyed to him have, I believe, been *much taken to heart*, and in consideration of the fact that his sins of commission (if any) never went beyond the stage of intention, and that the difficulties under which he was at first placed were partly owing to a defect in the Order (since remedied), the Sec. of State will perhaps . . . say a few words in acknowledgement of the zeal and ability which he has brought to bear in the difficult position in which he has been placed. The 'difficult position' is I believe undeniable.

Another concurred: "I think he is fairly entitled to a compliment: he has acted with energy, more so than a *locum tenens* generally does; and his errors have been owing more to excess of zeal than anything else." Herbert minuted: "He has done well"; and the Secretary of State wrote a gracious note of praise. It was a fair-minded and generous assessment, which must have done something to compensate for the disappointments related to money and promotion.[36]

The Judicial Commissioner

Gorrie's involvement with the work of the WPHC was at its height during 1878-79 when he was more or less in charge, but after Gordon's return to the

Pacific, he continued to serve as JC and frequently advised Gordon on its affairs. This was still the case even after the latter left Fiji to become governor of New Zealand, as Gordon insisted that he should be allowed to combine the new post with that of HC. When he resumed his duties as HC in September 1879, he immediately took up the issue of the conflicting jurisdictions of the HC and the Navy, an issue which was left unresolved by the amending Order.

He sent the Colonial Office a memorandum by Gorrie on the subject. Gorrie argued that senior officers like the Commodore were likely to hold balanced and sensible views about "native races"; but such was not the case with junior officers

> who are not only apt to hold their opinions about the 'nigger' pretty strongly, but who are naturally much more liable to allow themselves to be influenced by the tone of opinion which prevails in colonial society . . . all, or almost all, in favour of strong measures – of burning villages on trifling provocation, of scourgings, of hangings, and therefore of encouragement to the very class of criminals among the whites whom it will chiefly be the duty of the HC's Court to punish.

If such a junior officer punished a village, and the HC considered the punishment unmerited, a serious collision of authority between the Navy and the HC might result. The only remedy was to give the HC power to determine the course to be pursued in each case of 'outrage'. In a lengthy despatch (which Scarr terms "hysterical"), Gordon supported the position taken by his JC in the conflict with the Commodore. As Gorrie told Chesson:

> My last act as acting H.C. was to give [the Commodore] a broadside with double shotted guns, and I am glad Sir A. Gordon thinks I was right, and is determined to follow up my action. [The Navy] in short meant to rule the Western Pacific as if the H.C. had not been established – but we are quite determined not to allow the young gentlemen in charge of the cruising schooners to take the law into their own hands.[37]

Meanwhile, the Admiralty bestirred itself to defend its officers in the Pacific: "My Lords think it is to be regretted that Chief Justice Gorrie should have entered into a Correspondence with the Commodore and asserted a jurisdiction which is admitted to be untenable, in a manner which could not fail to be offensive to Naval Officers." Having made the point, the Admiralty offered a significant concession: it would instruct the Commodore that in all cases where immediate punishment of natives did not seem necessary, the naval officers on the spot should simply investigate and report to the senior officer who would then consult with the HC on how to proceed. Where urgent action seemed called for, the officers were to act on their own responsibility, but would then be obliged to state their reasons and report on their actions both to the Admiralty and to the HC. The Colonial Office felt that this concession, though unlikely to satisfy either Gordon or Gorrie, was "quite as much as can be expected". It led to a 'truce' between the HC and the Commodore, although this 'solution' left the HC's capacity to deal with 'outrages' still dependent on the Navy.[38]

In 1880-81, the frequency of attacks on whites, including naval officers, increased markedly. A popular young officer, Lt Bower, was killed along with several of his men in 1880. As Gorrie told Chesson:

> the affair was caused by his own want of prudence in sauntering along the coast of an island not knowing the disposition of the barbarians who inhabited it. Of course a white man to an islander who has not become familiar with the race is just what a gorilla would be to us – a beast to be shot. Of course we must take our 'vengeance' and the play goes on.

In a thoughtful letter, Gorrie analysed the situation and made recommendations: "As long as savages are savages, and they are irritated and alarmed by the approaches of civilization, so long will there be that desultory and irregular warfare we term outrages." It was important to probe the causes of these attacks so as to reduce provocations from whites in the islands. An absolute ban on trading in firearms, and on the payment of immigrant labourers in guns, was essential. The labour traffic had to be more strictly policed, since abuses still rife in the trade were the cause of most outrages. Captains should be told to be far more wary when dealing with 'strange' islanders and traders should be informed (through Regulations issued by the HC) what they could legally do in self-defence, and what they could not.

Deputy Commissioners should visit the islands often and advise traders which were dangerous; two should be based at central points in the New Hebrides and Solomon Islands, where most recruiting took place. Some kind of jurisdiction over the islanders would need to be assumed so that justice, rather than indiscriminate vengeance, could be meted out to the guilty. In this last plea he was flogging a dead horse; but the Colonial Office judged his letter to be an "able contribution" to the discussion on the issue.[39]

The question of criminal jurisdiction over islanders committing crimes against British subjects was raised again in the 1880 Aratuga case. Aratuga was a native of Aoba, New Hebrides, who was accused of murdering the mate of the Queensland labour ship *Mystery*. Some evidence suggested that the blow was struck on board one of the *Mystery*'s boats – on "British territory" – and on this basis he was brought by the Navy to Fiji and lodged in the Levuka jail while the jurisdiction issue was considered. The Colonial Office believed that the HC's Court could not try him, but Gorrie, supported at first by Gordon, saw it as an opportunity to construct a criminal jurisdiction over islanders. As Gorrie told Gordon, "The case against Aratuga depends on jurisdiction, jurisdiction depends on facts – did he or did he not kill when on board a British boat as an enlisted labourer." The evidence on this point turned out to be very shaky. At the preliminary hearing, Gorrie noted that the evidence could not establish that the crime was committed in the recruiting boat and that, consequently, Aratuga could not be put on trial in the HC's Court. In a lengthy and rather rambling judgement, he discussed the question of whether Aratuga could, in any case, be held responsible for a crime in which his whole community had participated and his chiefs had sanctioned. He concluded that he was merely in the position of a common soldier who obeyed his superior's orders. The community and chiefs had already been punished (by a fine imposed by the Navy), and there were no grounds on which to proceed against Aratuga as an individual, or to hold him amenable for any offence against British law. He was accordingly discharged. This, of course, was a setback from Gorrie's point of view.[40]

There was no legal difficulty in bringing British subjects to trial for offences committed within the HC's jurisdiction. In 1880, Gorrie went to Rotumah, which had not yet been annexed to Fiji and was still therefore under the WPHC, to try a half-aboriginal Australian (Thomas Simpson) for murdering a Rotumah man. He told Chesson:

> [It] is a typical Polynesian island, small and not lofty but a perfect cocoa-nut grove from end to end, with white sand beaches and azure sea . . . I held the Court on board the steamer and it was a very fine sight to see the native witnesses and onlookers coming off boats and canoes all well dressed and taking their place with perfect propriety.

Simpson was convicted and sentenced to death.

> Immediately after the trial the anchor was raised and the *Ocean Queen* was on her way back to Fiji . . . leaving the healthful impression behind that the arm of England is a long one and that crime will now be punished in the most distant island of the Pacific as well as in any of the Australian Colonies.

This trial provided the subject of an anecdote which Gorrie told an audience in London some three years later:

> It was my duty as Judicial Commissioner for the Western Pacific to go to Rotumah to try a murderer, a half-caste Australian named Tom. He was found guilty, condemned to death, and brought back to Fiji, as the High Commissioner had to sanction his execution. Many months after . . . I was coming into Suva when at a very solitary part of the road I came full upon a sight which, if I had believed in ghosts, would have made my blood run cold. There stood Australian Tom, exactly as he appeared when I condemned him. 'Are you not Tom?' I said to the spectre. The spectre grinned and said in Fijian 'Yes, sir'. 'But', I said, 'I thought I had – I had – I thought I had –' 'Yes, sir', he said, helping me out; 'but you perhaps forgot that my sentence was commuted'.[41]

The labour traffic continued to give rise to abuses which required investigation by the HC. One reason for the increase in 'outrages' in 1880-81 was the activities of labour ships operating from New Caledonia, a French territory; this trade, and the men engaged in it, were beyond the jurisdiction of the HC. Early in 1881 evidence emerged of flagrant cases of kidnapping in the New Hebrides, especially at Pentecost Island, by the French vessel *Aurora*. Gorrie briefed Chesson on these events, and suggested that the APS could usefully alert the French government and public to what was going on. As he put it:

> We by appointing a H.C. and a H.C. Court have put a stop very nearly to outrages by British subjects, while these are the kind of French outrages which are proceeding because there is no such Court for French subjects . . . It is very curious how the action of the H.C. Court has affected these men [British traders]. I think I have only punished 5 or 6 of them, and very gentle punishment compared to what they would have got at home. But there is something in the idea of one and the same Court having jurisdiction everywhere in the islands which has struck them with terror.[42]

Gorrie did not greatly exaggerate when he declared that the office of Chief JC for the Western Pacific was

> perhaps the most unpopular seat of justice in HM's dominions – The wanderers and adventurers of the sister Australian Colonies had been accustomed to do as they pleased in the Western Pacific, and so soon as the powers of the Order were begun to be put in force, I have been assailed in every possible way, simply for doing the duties imposed on me by the Crown, from Cooktown in the North of Queensland to Dunedin in the South of New Zealand.

As he told a Suva audience just before he left Fiji, he had been "represented in the neighbouring colonies as a kind of ogre, hanging traders by scores, and like the cannibals of the islands, picking their bones afterwards". The actions of the HC and his Court were closely followed in the Australasian Press, and by those interested in Pacific trade and settlement. The *Brisbane Courier*, for instance, Queensland's leading newspaper, devoted several editorials and articles in 1878-82 to the WPHC and its Court, taking a generally critical stance, particularly with respect to the punishment of 'native outrages'.[43] Gorrie was also attacked in pamphlets and books, sometimes in a highly personal style. In one such book, he was addressed directly:

> How about the innocent white men butchered by the natives, as many have been? Is there to be no thought for the widows and families of these men left destitute and mourning in every Australasian city? Has it not been laid down authoritatively that over these natives your court has no jurisdiction, and that against these natives a British subject must seek redress in vain?

Gorrie's most persistent opponent (and Gordon's) was the American who wrote for Australian papers under the pseudonym 'The Vagabond'. This is an example of his style:

> The noble savage has, without exception, been allowed to slaughter and plunder England's pioneers, and has been patted on the back by the decisions of the Judicial Commissioner, Sir John Gorrie, to this effect, 'Good boy, I can't flog you, you're only a child' . . . The effect of the High Commissioner's policy has been that our people are murdered, our labour and other vessels are plundered, our trade destroyed, and all this has been permitted *unavenged* . . . a wholesale hecatomb of human victims offered up on the altar of those pests of colonization, the Aborigines Protection Society and Exeter Hall.[44]

This kind of journalistic abuse was given semi-official sanction early in 1881, when the Inter-Colonial Conference of delegates from all the Australasian colonies, meeting at Sydney, printed some of 'The Vagabond's ' newspaper attacks on Gordon and Gorrie as an appendix to its report. The delegates also resolved that appeals from the HC's Court in capital cases should lie to the Supreme Court of one of the Australasian colonies *other than* Fiji. Both Gordon and Gorrie were incensed. Gordon called the appendix "disgraceful" and told Gorrie:

> You have really no conception, I did not till I came here [New Zealand] – of the virulence of the attacks on both of us, which every mail from Levuka scatters broadcast through the Colonies. They are printed, circulated, and I suppose believed by the ignorant who read them [and] accepted as the voice of the 'people' generally.

For his part, Gorrie described the delegates as "rascals" and told Chesson that it was surprising to anyone who did not know Australian public opinion that "a body like the Delegates should accept and publish gross libels against a Judge at the hands of a worthless rascal".[45]

Both men wrote formal rebuttals; Gordon's was later published for Parliament. In a generous tribute to Gorrie, he wrote:

> It is not my intention to enter into an examination of Chief Justice Gorrie's proceedings, or to attempt to review, extra-judicially, the sentences deliberately pronounced after full and careful inquiry by a competent court, presided over by a fearless and enlightened Judge; but I think it only right to record my own grateful appreciation of the services he has rendered as Chief Judicial Commissioner, and my entire conviction of the correctness of the judgments he has pronounced.

Gorrie's rebuttal was couched in stronger language than Gordon's; it "had some of the Vagabond's vinegar about it", as he put it. He was especially concerned to scotch the notion of appeals from the HC's Court to the Supreme Court of an Australian colony. He pointed out that there was no jury trial in the HC's Court (assessors were used) and that the unsworn testimony of natives was accepted and given as much weight as the judge believed it merited. "An appeal accordingly from the High Commissioner's court to such a tribunal would be from a Court which in these particulars administers justice from a higher standpoint, to one which does not, and cannot." Gorrie then launched into a spirited personal attack on 'The Vagabond', ending: "Here we have a resolution of a meeting of colonial delegates supported apparently by nothing better than anonymous libels, or the random charges of an alien adventurer! I must enter my protest against the character and good name of Judges, who have grown grey in HM's service . . . being thus trifled with". Both Gordon and Kimberley felt that the denunciation of 'The Vagabond' was over-emphatic, but they also agreed that he had made out a good case against allowing appeals to Australian courts.[46]

Gorrie summed up the situation as he saw it to Chesson:

> In their own Colonies [Australians] would surely get off if they committed any crime against natives as they would be tried by a jury and their political friends could bully the judges. But what they are most bitter with myself for is that if they commit a crime they know they

> won't escape . . . I have seen from time to time the most absurd stories about myself in the colonial newspapers, showing how the extent of the jurisdiction has affected the imagination of the traders and sailors. I take it as proof that the Court has been a decided success . . . I believe it has done great good and deserves support from every friend to native races.

The Australasian Press certainly took Gorrie's rebuttal (which was published) seriously enough. 'The Vagabond' wrote indignant letters to the *Auckland Weekly Star* and the Sydney *Daily Telegraph* attacking him and vowing revenge; the *Fiji Times* sardonically noted "on both sides it is a veritable Homeric duel". And both the *Daily Telegraph* in Sydney and the *New Zealand Times* in Wellington published editorials criticizing Gorrie's memorandum.[47]

Nearly two years after Gorrie had left the Pacific, he was asked to make suggestions on the future of the WPHC following a report on the subject mainly written by Gordon. In a wide-ranging memorandum, which was printed for the Cabinet, Gorrie argued that the WPHC had not been given a fair trial, especially after Gordon left Fiji in 1880, and that wider powers were needed. As he had done on so many occasions, he advocated the extension of British jurisdiction over islanders who had entered into agreements with whites, or had committed crimes against them: "This is the only way to keep the peace." A second High Commissioner was about to be appointed for New Guinea and the Solomon Islands, and Gorrie advised that the New Hebrides should be included in his jurisdiction because of the importance of the labour trade in all three places. More Deputy Commissioners would be needed, and they should be given the duty of licensing all labour ships recruiting in their districts and exercising a general supervision over the process of recruiting and returning the labourers. No recruiting on new ground should be allowed without the HC's consent. Payment in arms, "and all traffic in arms, and spiritous liquor, ought to be simultaneously stopped by Rules and Regulations". Above all, adequate funds and ships were crucial for the HC to work effectively. "There is no earthly use in passing Orders in Council, or in appointing Officers great or small, if they are doomed to inactivity by the want of funds." It was better to spend money to enable the HC to prevent crimes and offences, than to pay for punitive 'acts of war' by the Navy.[48]

At the same time that he wrote this memorandum, while he was on leave from the Leeward Islands following the death of his wife, he asked to be considered when the High Commissioner for New Guinea was appointed. He told the Secretary of State:

> I applied to Lord Kimberley [his predecessor] to have my name considered for political, rather than judicial promotion, and his Lordship placed me on his list of those who sought the appointment of Governor of a Colony. My service extends now over 15 years and what with Coolies in Mauritius, natives in Fiji, and the Western Pacific, and negroes in the West Indies, I presume I must have as much experience as most men in dealing with native races. In consequence of a recent bereavement I should be glad to get away from the Leeward Islands, and as my home is now broken up it is of little consequence to me whether the sphere of my service be among savages or civilized men – whether I reside chiefly on board ship or in a house . . . What I did [*ie* in the Pacific] ought to be well known in the department and I am quite sure your Lordship will do me justice in this – the only application I have ever made for promotion.

Lord Derby, the Secretary of State, saw Gorrie at the latter's request; but Herbert commented: "I do not think Sir J. Gorrie would make a good H.C. He is too quarrelsome by nature & has been in collision with the naval authorities. New blood will be better." This was decisive.[49] Gorrie was to receive further promotion, but only to a more senior chief justiceship; he never received the governorship or High Commissionership which he aspired to, and he never returned to the Pacific.

CHAPTER SIX

From the Pacific to the Caribbean: The Leeward Islands, 1883-86

The Leeward Islands in 1883

In June 1883 Gorrie arrived in Antigua to take up his appointment as Chief Justice of the Leeward Islands. Though he had visited Jamaica briefly seventeen years earlier, this was his first official sojourn in the Caribbean; he was to remain in the Leewards for just over two and a half years.

The Federation of the Leeward Islands had been established in 1871. It consisted of five 'presidencies': Antigua, its headquarters; St Kitts-Nevis, amalgamated in 1882; Dominica, situated 100 miles from Antigua between the French colonies of Guadeloupe and Martinique; Montserrat, which was very small; and the (British) Virgin Islands, a group of equally small islands. There was a single governor resident in Antigua with administrators in the four other presidencies reporting to him, a federal legislature (the General Legislative Council) and a single Chief Justice and Supreme Court. The powers of the federal legislature were quite limited; there was no separate federal revenue and no federal control over local taxation. Each presidency

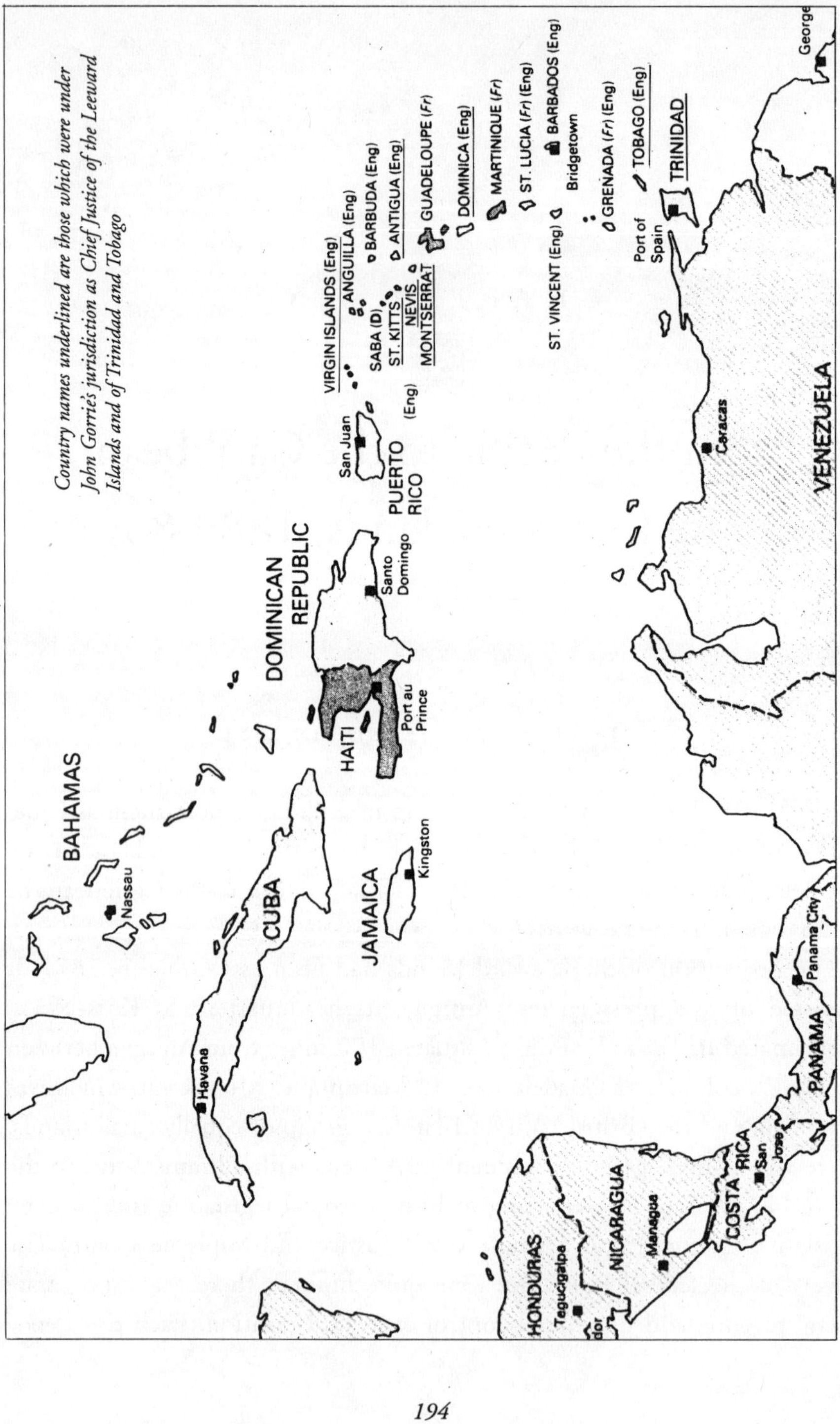

The Caribbean Islands

had its own local legislature, differently constituted; in the larger units (Antigua, Dominica, St Kitts-Nevis) the local legislative councils consisted of both elected and nominated members, with the latter in the majority. The creation of the Federation was a British strategy designed to reduce the costs of government and to secure greater uniformity and efficiency in administration; it was not a response to popular demand, and though some prominent landowners supported it, influential sectors of the island societies resented the inevitable loss of autonomy. In the words of Sir Benjamin Pine, who negotiated the Federation in 1869-71, "a spirit of self-importance and narrow patriotism which may seem ludicrous but cannot be ignored" was characteristic of the elites of each island. Complaints about the Federation persisted after the 1870s, and proposals to strengthen it were often resisted.[1]

Insular patriotism was not diminished by economic decline. Some of the islands had been in serious difficulties ever since the late 1700s, and particularly since the end of slavery in the 1830s, and they were all gravely affected by the depression in the sugar industry which became acute in 1884-85, coinciding with Gorrie's term of office. This depression was caused by competition for the British market from beet sugar grown in Europe; European governments paid growers bounties or subsidies on each ton exported, and artificially subsidized beet sugar flooded the UK market, especially after 1874, when all duties on sugar entering Britain were abolished. In 1884 increases in these bounties worsened the crisis, causing a serious glut and pushing prices down to unheard-of lows. The inefficient cane producers of the Leewards, still manufacturing the crude type of sugar known as muscovado, simply could not withstand this competition. Antigua and St Kitts were both wholly dependent on sugar. In these islands nearly all the people (descendants of the former slaves) worked for the sugar estates and most lived in huts on estate land. Wages were low, and were cut to a bare minimum during the depression; the labourers eked them out by growing provisions on little plots of land. Their survival skills were severely tested by the 1884-85 crisis which resulted in layoffs and arbitrary wage reductions.[2]

In the small islands of Montserrat, Nevis, and the Virgin Islands group, sugar had either disappeared as an export crop by the 1880s, or was rapidly going under. The blacks became peasants growing provisions, raising stock, making charcoal and lime and fishing, combining these occupations where possible with part-time work for cash wages or as sharecroppers for the few estates which struggled on cultivating sugar, limes or arrow-root. These peasants/labourers were desperately poor, and their relations with the estate owners were semifeudal.[3]

Dominica was very different from the other presidencies and the Dominican elites had opposed federation more bitterly than their counterparts in the other islands. It was situated 100 miles away from the federal headquarters and had been a separate colony with its own Lieutenant-Governor. Originally settled by French planters, French Creole was the language of nearly all the people and Roman Catholicism the popular faith; in these respects it was completely different from all the other Leewards. It was relatively large (three times the size of Antigua) but very underdeveloped. The production of coffee, the main crop during slavery, had declined markedly by the early 1880s, though several coffee estates struggled on. Sugar replaced it as the leading export crop by mid-century, and Dominica producers were hard hit by the crisis of 1884-85. Cocoa and limes were becoming important too. But estates of any kind were declining, in numbers, in the size of their labour force, and in their share of production. A fiercely independent smallholding peasantry had emerged since emancipation in the 1830s, and by the 1880s the peasant holding had become the dominant unit of production, even for export crops, including sugar, through various forms of sharecropping or metayage, a system which Gorrie would encounter again in Tobago. Wage labour was relatively unimportant to the local blacks by the 1880s, and the island was desparately short of capital; most estates were heavily indebted.[4]

It did not take Gorrie long to record some first impressions of social and economic conditions in the Leewards. Typically, it was the situation of the people which most interested him. He was struck by the frequency of funerals in St Johns, the capital of Antigua, and on checking the statistics was horrified to learn that mortality in the town was about 65 per thousand per annum "so that my first rough guess of decimation in the hot season was not far off mark", he told Chesson. "If you make a remark here to anyone about these things they answer it is infant mortality caused by the neglect by the blacks of their offspring", but most of the funerals he witnessed were of adults.

> As to the neglect by the blacks of their children, I have not seen enough yet to be able to determine, but I did send a few days ago a good looking young mother to one of the Attorneys to see that justice was done her – she complaining that by means of dragging her before the magistrate to compel her to work when her baby is ill and required her attendance, the child would die. The magistrate I see is a fat fool who wants common sense and does not know enough of law and morality to be aware that a mother's duty to a sick child is a more important obligation than a contract to hoe canes at 3/- a week (women's wages)!

One of the great hardships of the poor in St Johns was the scarcity of water, at its worst during the hottest and driest season. "In my peregrinations through the town I have seen young women washing their faces in tea cups so precious was the water only got with labour in small quantities and bad quality. The supply is now open again . . . but how many have gone meantime to fatten the Churchyard?" Noting that the Antiguan estate owners imposed "long contracts at miserable wages" on their labourers, Gorrie explained that "the estates are too small to work sugar profitably except on the condition of getting labour at a rate which is a scandal at the present age. The negroes here are not the stalwart race like the Jamaican yam and coffee fed mountain freeholders, but are under-fed and puny."[5]

On the whole, he found the labourers of St Kitts "notwithstanding the ordinary scale of wages of 1/- a day for men, looking comfortable. They seem to be better fed than Antiguan people . . . But as in Antigua the death rate is much too high – and I cannot understand what Governors, Doctors and all these fellows have been doing for the 45 years since emancipation." As in Antigua, water was a major problem:

> I saw people waiting by the scores in queue at the only well in the town [of Sandy Point] to get water to cook their evening meal after working all day. The legislature bestirred itself at length to bring in water, but their scheme was knocked on the head by some miserable wretched clerk in the C.O. and the population must go on dying because some ass who knew nothing about it must scribble something.

In Dominica, he was impressed by the poverty of the people and the lack of employment, which was driving them to emigrate to Venezuela and Cayenne to work in the gold mines, and the urgent need for an injection of capital with which to open up the interior and create new estates and jobs. On a trek across the forested interior from coast to coast, he saw for himself the magnificence of the island's resources: "I have strongly recommended that [Crown lands] be offered to any capitalists who will make certain absolutely necessary roads in the Island for it is a lamentable fact that after a hundred years of British rule there is not a public road in the Island fit for wheeled traffic."[6]

Even before Gorrie arrived in Antigua, strenuous efforts had been made to discredit him by his old enemies. Pamphlets attacking his doings in the Pacific were sent to the editors of the little Leeward Islands newspapers , half a world away. As the editor of the *Antigua Observer* wrote, "batches of pamphlets violently reflecting upon him have been forwarded to us, of course for publication"; especially prominent was "South Sea massacres" by 'The Vagabond'. The editors who received these effusions were admirably fair-minded, pointing out that much of the outcry against Gorrie in Fiji and the Western Pacific was the agitation of disappointed litigants who had tried to exploit the indigenous people and had been checked by Gordon's policies and Gorrie's firmness in upholding them, and advising their readers to keep an open mind. W.F. Parr, along with 'The Vagabond', Gorrie's most persistent opponent in the Pacific, fired off no fewer than four enormously lengthy epistles detailing his misdeeds to the editor of the *Dominica Dial* during 1884 and 1885 (these letters took on average four months to reach Dominica). The editor pleasantly headed the second of these, which occupied four closely printed columns, "ONE OF PARR'S PILLS (A dose for the C.J.)".[7] Parr and 'The Vagabond', the professional litigants and pamphleteers, ensured that Gorrie's recent history would be thoroughly re-hashed in the Leewards. But it is interesting to note that a much earlier episode in his career was also remembered. The *Dial*'s editor believed that Dominica's coloured men owed a debt "of grateful remembrance [to] the man who was Mrs GORDON'S counsel after the Jamaica official murders", who was one of those "who in the long past were content to be spent in their service".[8]

Law and Justice in the Leewards

The administration of justice in the Leewards presented several problems which were, in the main, the result of the federal structure and the strong tradition of insular separatism. In 1883, the federal judicial establishment consisted of a Chief Justice and two puisne judges; the former resided in Antigua, the first puisne judge in St Kitts, the second in Dominica; the Attorney-General and the Solicitor-General usually lived in Antigua. There was one Supreme Court for the federation, but it sat (in circuit court) in any of the presidencies; in other words, its seat was not fixed, and any one (or more) of the judges constituted this court. It heard serious criminal cases, appeals from the magistrates' courts, and civil causes. As the resident judge in Antigua, the Chief Justice presided over the Antigua Assizes for criminal trials; he might also join one of the other judges to hold circuit court in St Kitts and Dominica; he, or either of the judges, would travel to Nevis, Montserrat or Tortola (British Virgin Islands) to hold circuit court there. On the other hand, the Court of Appeals (comprising all three judges) sat only in Antigua, although the original intention was for it to sit in the presidency where the court of first instance had given the ruling being appealed.[9]

The elites of the 'out islands' believed it was necessary to have regular circuit courts in each. This was opposed both by Gorrie and the Attorney-General, Stephen Gatty. They argued that all the higher judicial business of the federal colony should be concentrated in Antigua, where all three judges should permanently reside, and that circuit courts should be held infrequently, and only in St Kitts and Dominica, not in the smaller islands. If the permanent seat of the Supreme Court was established "once and for all" in Antigua, Gorrie argued, barristers based in the other islands would move there, to the benefit of all:

> With the Court and Bar broken into fragments there is stagnation of business, stagnation of intellect, and a nursing of petty local grievances and partialities, in place of that healthy competition and those higher aims which are found amid a good legal society at the seat of a Supreme Court worthy of the name.

While circuit courts in St Kitts and Dominica for criminal trials and for such civil suits as could more conveniently be heard by a judge who was temporarily on the spot should continue, the Supreme Court should have an original criminal (as well as civil) jurisdiction, with the right to try accused from all over the colony if deemed advisable. But holding circuit courts in the smaller islands was undesirable: "It is little short of a humiliation for the Judge and Attorney-General to be forced to put up with the miserable accommodation which alone the wretched village in Nevis can give." And the claim that local planters were always happy to offer hospitality "only indicates the danger of holding circuits in such places, as the Judge cannot or ought not to accept hospitality when on such duty and there is neither hotel nor boarding house which contains accommodation fit for anyone above the rank of a black labourer". More important, Gorrie believed that "the clamour for circuits is perhaps an expression of the insular jealousies of one locality against another which ought in every way to be discouraged".[10]

Not surprisingly, these views were strongly opposed by public opinion in the 'out islands' and by the other two judges, Semper and Pemberton, who were white West Indians; before the establishment of the Supreme Court of the Leeward Islands in 1871, these judges held the rank of Chief Justice of St Kitts and Dominica respectively. It was pointed out, very reasonably, that the costs and difficulties of interisland travel (which Gorrie himself experienced first hand) made it hard for litigants and witnesses to travel to Antigua, that the periodic visits of a judge to the smaller islands were useful socially and politically, and that St Kitts and Dominica were sufficiently important to merit a resident judge. This was also the view of the Royal Commission which reported on West Indian affairs in 1884. These arguments persuaded the Colonial Office, and circuit courts in Nevis, Montserrat and Tortola, as well as in St Kitts and Dominica, were retained, while the two puisne judges continued to reside in the latter islands.[11]

Moreover, Gorrie suffered a further defeat with the enactment of a measure requiring the Appeal Court, instead of always sitting in Antigua, to hold annual sessions in St Kitts, Dominica and Nevis, as well as Antigua, and in Montserrat and Tortola when necessary. This act, he wrote, should really have been called "An Act to increase the business of the small attorneys in the

Leeward Islands by the multiplicity of courts and the impoverishment of the people". He went on to illustrate the probable operation of the measure by looking at cases he had recently tried on circuit in Nevis; "delicate and all-important points [such as] whether a Coolie woman had sold two-pence of rum on a Sunday morning . . . I have a very strong opinion", he continued, "that to encourage such questions to be litigated from court to court is the worst thing that can be done for the people who are poor as it is, and whose little means in this way would go into the pockets of the leeches who promote such measures". Petty cases already determined by a judge on circuit would now be appealed to three judges on circuit (*ie* an itinerant Appeal Court). The Colonial Office, however, recognized the existence of strong local opinion in favour of the measure, which was passed by the legislature with only one dissentient (an Antiguan member), especially since up to 1877 the Appeal Court had met in each presidency. The Royal Commission had heard several complaints early in 1883, from prominent residents of the 'out islands', that the cost of appeals which had to be heard in Antigua was prohibitive. The act was therefore sanctioned in 1885.[12] It is, perhaps, surprising that Gorrie was so unsympathetic to the view that a Court of Appeals with exclusive appellate jurisdiction and sitting only in Antigua caused hardships to the people of the 'out islands'. There is no doubt that this was the view of most spokesmen for island opinion.

Gorrie's experiences in Mauritius and Fiji, as well as his knowledge of the causes of the Morant Bay rising in Jamaica, had convinced him that the magistrates were critical to the whole administration of justice. Of particular concern to him were the untrained lay magistrates, invariably local landowners, merchants or professional men with close ties to the island elites. He recommended the appointment of good men, either with legal training or commensurate experience, on decent salaries, and then the enlargement of their powers. "The present system of weak magistrates on small salaries with large powers is the very worst which could be devised." After two years in the Leewards, he came to the conclusion that "the weakest part of the present system is that we have magistrates of a low type, and the Attorney-General as public prosecutor does not take that command of the business of public prosecution which I think he ought to do."[13]

On more than one occasion, Gorrie came into conflict with magistrates in the various islands. In 1885, he refused to try a petty offender while holding circuit court in St Kitts, sending the prisoner back to the magistrate after asking in court "what's the use of magistrates in the Colony?". But the magistrate in question had declined to take the case upon the grounds that the law precluded a magistrate trying an 'old offender' who had several previous convictions. This developed into an impasse: the magistrate, insisting that his reading of the law was correct, refused to try the man (whose offence was chicken stealing), the Chief Justice refused to take the case, with the result that "a felon of the worst type" (said a St Kitts editor, with typical hyperbole) was set free without trial. Hearing an appeal from a magistrate's decision in Nevis, Gorrie deplored "the idea of the Magistrate inflicting a fine of 40s. on a woman whose wages could not be more than from 3s. to 3s.6d. per week" merely for a squabble between two women; he reduced the fine to 5s. He formed the view that too many of the Leewards magistrates were callously indifferent to the poverty and ignorance of most of the petty offenders who passed through their courts. In an Antiguan case, he

> had to come down upon the Magistrate for fining a poor creature who sells ice creams and such like 10/- for pissing in a quiet corner, there being no public privies, urinals, or conveniences in the town [St Johns], the Police having dodged her to get a chance of laying a complaint about something . . . I dressed the fellow down, spoke kindly to the woman and on her promise to behave well in future, let her off. The poor woman sobbed and you could have heard a pin drop at this, to them, novel mode of dispensing justice. It is by the action of the lower officials of the law that the poor are most likely to be oppressed in our day.

In St Kitts, a magistrate fined a six-year-old child for trespass and sent him to jail when his mother was unable to pay; when the infant was brought before the Chief Justice as a criminal, Gorrie discharged him and severely rebuked the magistrate.[14]

It did not take long for Gorrie to impose his vigorous personality on the Leeward Islands Bench, and his performance as a judge soon attracted public interest and comment just as it had in Mauritius and Fiji. In October 1883, he went to St Kitts to hold circuit court, where he dealt with 17 cases. A local editor wrote:

> Everyone is satisfied with [his] uprightness and impartiality; in the Criminal Court he has been severe in his sentences on three or four 'old offenders' . . . on the Civil side of the Court he has displayed a readiness of conception, of what is generally termed the intricacies of a case, so that Counsel as well as clients are all satisfied with his impartial rulings.

But in reporting these glowing public endorsements to Chesson, he added, with a realism born of long experience, "Of course you know as well as I do how all this would change if I trod upon the toes of the local cliques."[15]

In Fiji Gorrie had felt that one of his paramount duties was to protect the indigenous people from injustice; in the Leewards, he felt a similar obligation towards the poor and generally uneducated black population. In an interesting case in which an Antiguan woman was charged with the murder of her infant, under a new act requiring a coroner's inquest in the death of all infants under one year, Gorrie sharply cross-examined two medical witnesses:

> *Q*: Do you ever go to the houses of these people? . . . Do you expect a mother to leave her sick child and come and report to you? . . . Why did you not send the child to the Hospital? – *A:* It never occurred to me to do so for such is not the practice – *Q*: Well in future let it be and get rid of the bad practice . . . Had you sent this child to the Hospital do you think it would have been alive now? . . . Do you think the child would have had a better chance for its life had you sent it there?

He asked another doctor:

> *Q*: Would a woman labouring have any effect on the milk? . . . If a woman brought an emaciated child to you would you not examine the breast of the woman? - *A*: No, I would be liable to be had up for an assault – *Q*: Then Doctor, the Magistrate or the Judge would be a fit inmate of the Lunatic Asylum (Roar of laughter in court) – Who supplies the medicines? – *A*: The usual practice is to obtain medicines from government under a requisition – *Q*: Do you ever make a requisition for food? – *A*: No, the government does not supply food – *Q*: So a child can be well supplied with medicines but no food.

After the summing-up, the jury returned a not guilty verdict without leaving the box.[16]

A very different case involving the Antiguan sugar industry was heard by Gorrie towards the end of 1884. A cane farmer, whose canes were ground by an estate mill in return for a cash payment and one quarter of the produce, sued the estate manager for losses caused by negligence during the grinding process. The canes in question were ground 14 days after they had been cut; naturally, the sugar was found to be totally spoilt. The manager claimed that the delay was due to bad weather, and disclaimed any responsibility, in which he was backed up by several owners or managers who testified that they were not responsible for this kind of losses to cane farmers. The Chief Justice had no difficulty in establishing that the acceptance by a millowner of a cash payment and a share of the sugar from a cane-farmer, in exchange for grinding his canes and boiling his sugar, meant that he was legally bound to grind those canes with a proper degree of care and skill; and even in Antigua, "a colony, speaking generally, of archaic sugar manufacturing", leaving canes lying around for 14 days could not have been the ordinary custom. The excuse given by the manager, that rains prevented him from getting dry megass for the engine, "betrays a helplessness which I do trust and believe is not common in the Island – but if it be common, it would be better for such millowners not to enter into contracts". Gorrie found the owner guilty of negligence and awarded damages and costs to the cane farmer.[17]

In Dominica, he took up the issue of a peasant's right to compensation for growing crops when evicted by the landowner. Most Dominican peasants were *metayers* (sharecroppers) of one kind or another, whether the crop was cocoa, coffee or limes, and it was a longstanding metayer grievance that the planters would find some excuse (taking advantage of the vague, usually verbal contracts) to take over the land and confiscate the peasant's 'improvements' without compensation. In a 1884 case, Gorrie ruled that if a tenant was evicted, he must be compensated for his tree crops before the eviction could be carried out. This ruling was praised as affording protection to the cocoa peasants who were beginning to extend this cultivation; but a Dominican editor feared that it might open the door to vexatious claims for 'improvements' of a kind which the landowner neither wanted nor had agreed to.[18] Gorrie was to encounter many similar cases both in Trinidad and Tobago involving cocoa contractors and sugar metayers.

The other side of Gorrie's anxiety to protect the poor and ignorant was his insistence that the privileged should not escape the penalties of the law when they transgressed. In his last few weeks in the Leewards, he heard an appeal by two young Antiguan whites against a sentence of 30 days imprisonment imposed by a magistrate for a fracas with the police on Christmas Eve 1885. Though the evidence was clear that they had been fully involved in the fracas and in resisting the police, their counsel "made touching appeals to the Judge to spare their clients the disgrace and public ruin which would be theirs if the sentence was confirmed . . . The Judge however was inexorable, stating that he believed the appellants were ringleaders of a most disgraceful riot." He not only upheld the sentences, but stated that the magistrate should have sentenced them to hard labour. The *Antigua Standard* felt that the sentences were harsh and asserted that the public "of all classes" deeply sympathized with the two young men and their families. "Several gentlemen" interceded with the governor on their behalf, who refused to pardon them; at least, thought the *Standard*, their sentence should be reduced, as even a few days in jail would have a profound moral effect "on young men of the class" of the prisoners, and "a long period [30 days!] might be a physical injury to them". Though the governor resisted the lobbying for a reduction of sentence, no doubt encouraged by Gorrie, he did order them to be treated as debtors in jail, which brought them special privileges.[19] This episode provides a good illustration of the influences of "caste and colour" against which Gorrie fought throughout his colonial career.

Circuit Court

At the circuit court in Dominica in January 1884, Gorrie's determination to protect the poor and uneducated people who came before him did not escape criticism. He was accused of trying "to improve his self-created reputation as an upright judge whose aim it is to administer law and justice on principles of equity". This Dominican critic was convinced that

> let two litigants, one white, the other not, appear before the Chief Justice, the primary notion in his mind is that the white man is the oppressor. Let the parties be of the same class, caste or colour, but of different social status, and, according to his pet theory, the one of inferior position is a fitting object of sympathy. All this takes the fancy of the ignorant, who immediately say 'at last we have a judge who is above the prejudices of caste or colour', and he is forthwith dubbed in the vernacular 'a we jedge'.[20]

Attacks on Gorrie's administration of justice accelerated during the course of 1885. His circuit court in Dominica in January of that year attracted an extraordinary amount of newspaper comment, and the *Dominica Dial*, previously a cautious supporter, joined the campaign against him; it is probably no coincidence that he ruled against the *Dial*'s proprietor, William Davies, in an important civil case during this court session. The *Dial* began its attack with a spirited editorial: "The chief topic of conversation in Roseau this week was the extraordinary manner in which Sir John Gorrie presided over the late session. Our Chief Justice may be congratulated on having created a profound sensation in this small community." He rushed through the cases; successful litigants rejoiced that the weaknesses of their cases had been obscured by the judge's speed, those who were unsuccessful felt that they had been denied justice. He shamelessly bullied counsel and the Registrar, and his whole conduct was such that "our ideas of the dignity of the Bench have been rudely dispelled by the display of thunder and lightning vehemence from Sir John Gorrie during the last Circuit".[21]

The *Dial* backed up its accusations by a highly partisan account of the cases heard at this celebrated session, an account which was spread over four separate issues of the paper. In one of these, *R* v *Estanie Jacques* (for wounding a bull), the defendant ("a pre-possessing and well-dressed young woman"), stated that neither of Dominica's two barristers would defend her. "You are much better off without either of them", the Chief Justice said cheerfully; "I shall see that you don't lack a defender". When both barristers tried to explain why she was without counsel, he snapped: "When I was at the Bar we did not squabble about retainers but defended ANY poor unprotected person!" As the case proceeded Gorrie cross-examined witnesses on behalf of the woman, and directed the jury to acquit her once it was established that the bull was in her provision ground. "She exited, bowing to her counsel-defender-Judge." When it came to the civil cases, the reporter claimed that Gorrie paid no attention to the attempts by counsel "to raise legal niceties or to argue any knotty points of law"; he rushed through 15 civil appeals in three hours. Among these appeals was one by Davies of the *Dial*, involving his right as the owner of an estate to keep trespassers off the stream which ran through it. Gorrie upheld the magistrate's decision, stating that Davies had no ownership in the stream – "a startling dictum . . . that a man may not have the exclusive enjoyment of his own property!" It is hard not to connect this ruling with the *Dial*'s change of heart about Gorrie. Not content with its highly coloured account of the session, the *Dial* published a witty skit on its proceedings entitled "Justices Injustice".[22] But the *Dial*'s rival, the *Dominican*, traditionally the island's liberal paper, took up Gorrie's defence. The truth was, it stated, the public in Dominica felt nothing but

> gratitude towards a JUDGE who does not belie the reputation of philanthropy and freedom from antiquated formality which preceded him . . . Sir JOHN GORRIE is doing a noble work in these islands, which has already secured grateful recognition in Dominica, and it is in the name of the people of this Presidency that we denounce the insults levelled at him by the *Dial* newspaper.[23]

From his controversial circuit in Dominica, Gorrie moved straight to St Kitts, where he held a session in February 1885. "An almost universal epidemic of Sir John Gorrie on the brain is prevalent among our fellow citizens", reported a local editor; "his way of conducting the Supreme Court seems to have thoroughly astonished the natives of St Kitts". He was accused of rushing through cases, handing down inconsistent rulings, showing improper leniency towards hardened criminals convicted of crimes against property, bullying jurors, counsel and medical witnesses, attacking magistrates' proceedings in such a way as to undermine their authority, and generally behaving in an undignified and unprofessional manner.[24]

The *Antigua Standard*, in a thoughtful editorial, reviewed the evidence of public dissatisfaction with Gorrie's conduct at his recent sessions in Dominica and St Kitts and contributed its own views based on his doings in Antigua.

> Sir John's manner on the bench is at one time jocose and familiar, and at another extremely austere, summary and rough. He never loses the chance of making a joke . . . His distemper is always displayed with as much suddenness as his good temper, and one can see that while he gives a spurt to his wit, he is not to be trifled with . . . His examination of witnesses is clever, and his aptitude in eliciting the truth by a familiar manner of addressing the witness is amusing. Medical and Police witnesses he handles in a manner that may be considered ungentlemanly. He allows no legal points to overthrow his opinion as to what is 'substantial justice'. All the authorities produced backed up by eloquent argument ends in 'Mr ——, don't you think we'd better deal with the case on its merits'. It is just as well for Counsel to desist, for to press the argument will be to invite a curt, harsh remark, or a stop put to his law . . . The idea exists that he is a strong advocate of a certain class of people and thus he has been styled 'a' we judge', but we must confess we see little reason for this . . . It is true he is apparently on the defensive and strongly so when a prisoner is not defended, but he does not forget to administer to the prisoner FOUND GUILTY, a severe sentence . . . It is to be regretted that the Chief Justice takes advantage of his position to the extent that he does on the Bench. He is undoubtedly a fearless, honourable and able man . . . There is such a contrast between Sir John as a Judge, and in his ordinary intercourse with people, that one is at a loss to understand how he can ever be so bluff.

The editor concluded this very fair assessment with the hope that his frank criticism would make Gorrie amend the unfortunate aspects of his conduct.[25] The evidence certainly suggests that his temper while on the Bench deteriorated markedly between 1884 and 1885, and it seems reasonable to link this to the illness and death of his wife in the middle of 1884.

His actions on the Bench at the start of 1885 prompted a St Kitts member of the federal legislature, Thomas McNish, to attempt an extraordinary 'impeachment' of the Chief Justice at a sitting of the Council in April 1885. This took the form of a motion asking the Council to note that certain accusations had been made against him and detailing eleven of them: four related to cases at the Dominican circuit in January 1885 (including *Q* v *Estanie Jacques*); four to St Kitts cases heard in the following month; two to cases in 1883 and 1884. Gorrie was accused of disregarding the facts or the law in his determination of these ten cases. The eleventh charge was that

> the general conduct of the said Chief Justice when on the Bench has been such as to provoke the indignation not only of the Bar, the Magistrates, Officers of Court and professional men, but suitors and witnesses who appear before him; and . . . has given rise to great popular dissatisfaction tending to bring the Bar into disrepute and thereby engendering a feeling of insecurity in the proceedings of the Courts of Justice in the Leeward Islands. Be it resolved therefore that this Council is of opinion that it is expedient that the proceedings and doings of the said Chief Justice be brought to the notice of HE the Governor, to be dealt with as to him may seem fit.

No one seconded this resolution, and McNish withdrew it, claiming that "every word of his resolution was true, and hon. members knew it".[26]

It was not to be expected that this episode would go unchallenged by Gorrie. He chose to take up McNish's gauntlet in an elaborate address to the jury convened for the Antigua Assizes in May 1885. He accused McNish of attempting to interfere with the administration of justice: "I need not tell you what would follow if, in Colonies and Islands like these, Judges were subject to be dictated to by the political Bodies, but I am glad to think that this attempt was that of one individual alone." No man or body of men, said the Chief Justice, would ever dictate how he dealt with judicial matters; but in the public interest, he was prepared to show how far from the truth were the 'accusations' made in the Council. He then proceeded to refute each one to his own satisfaction. Gorrie told the Antiguan jurors that he knew

> that in endeavouring to keep cases within bounds, in weeding out trifling charges, and in carefully investigating the very truth of all matters brought before me, I have your support as I have the support of the juries in the other islands.

If the episode stimulated magistrates and Crown law officers to improve their preparation of cases for the Supreme Court, then some good might come of it.[27]

This address prompted several responses from newspapers in the Leewards and further afield. The *Dial* published an even longer counter-blast, entitled "*The Dial's* address to the gentlemen of the Antigua jury". It lamented the fact that McNish had stood alone in the Federal Council and warned its members: "Let them beware that if the law can be set aside in the case of a fowl or a bull, it may be equally set aside in a question involving £10,000 or the title to a sugar plantation." The *Dial* found support from the *St Christopher Independent*, which published a lengthy editorial, probably written by a lawyer, setting out in detail the specific laws set aside by Gorrie in some of the celebrated cases referred to by McNish. It believed that the Chief Justice proceeded as if he had a right to override laws that he thought were bad, instead of faithfully executing the laws as they were, and advising the competent authorities to amend those that needed it. Granted the rumours and accusations about his doings circulating so freely in St Kitts and Dominica early in the year, McNish had every right to take steps in the Council to promote some enquiry by the proper authority, and Gorrie's 'address to the jury' was a waste of time and effort. The *Antigua Standard* agreed that in his address he did not "deal with what THE LAW IS, but what in his mind IT SHOULD BE, and all we can hope for is, that His Honour will recommend to the Executive such amendments in our laws as will be better suited to our social state". On balance, weighing his "peculiarities or eccentricities" against his good qualities, the *Standard* came down in the judge's favour: "We have had many Chief Justices . . . but we venture to say that none of Sir JOHN'S predecessors have been abler men or better lawyers than he."[28]

Perhaps this torrent of public controversy about his conduct on the Bench chastened Gorrie, for the *Dial*, reporting on the Dominica circuit in September 1885, stated that his behaviour was much improved. But this evidence of reformation did not mollify the *Dial's* editor/proprietor, William Davies, who had once again been an unsuccessful litigant. He was the defendant in an appeal by a woman against a magistrate's conviction for stealing limes from an estate he leased.

> Said His Honour to the respondent [Davies], while turning over the appeal papers: 'Why don't you make the poor woman a present of a few baskets of limes?' 'Because, Your Honour', he replied, 'that is not a profitable mode of conducting an estate'. 'Not in this world', said the Judge, 'but in the next' . . . Sir John Gorrie proceeded, after a transparent show of reading over the evidence, to keep his memory green in the hearts of hardened offenders of the stamp of the appellant, by quashing the magistrate's conviction.

The result of this was one of the *Dial*'s thunderous editorials against Gorrie. Returning to what was by now a familiar theme, the editor claimed that in his court, all landowners were "cast in the role of principal villain; the local barrister, the aider and abetter of villain No.1; and the criminal in the dock . . . is made to represent persecuted and suffering innocence". Gorrie was using the Bench "as the platform whence to disseminate his Fenianesque views".[29]

The *Dial*'s reporter was not the only one to note an improvement in Gorrie's conduct on the bench after the 'impeachment' episode. An article in a St Kitts newspaper concurred:

> Sir John Gorrie is beginning to understand us, and we him. His Honour has considerably toned down in his judicial demeanour since he last presided over the Circuit Court of [St Kitts] . . . Opponents as well as friends are admitting . . . the honest intention, the lofty integrity, the generosity and good humour, the love of freedom, right and justice.

His firm rulings, and his habit of checking frivolous questions put by counsel to frightened or simple witnesses, were commendable.[30]

Land Questions

As in Mauritius and Fiji, Gorrie took up questions which were political rather than judicial. In the Leewards, the main political issue with which he became involved concerned titles to land and mortgages, which had been of special interest to him since his days as a young advocate and journalist in Britain. Only a few months after his arrival, he told Chesson

> there is a beginning of a small freeholder class [in Antigua] but men are anxious to get land while estates are lying wasted. The Torrens system of land titles was introduced here by Sir B. Pine in 1873 but it has never been put into practical operation. I am tackling that and if supported may stir up matters a bit.[31]

Early in 1884, he wrote a long memorandum incorporating his ideas and recommendations. His first, and most important recommendation was the introduction of the system of title by compulsory registration, the Torrens system, which he had helped to establish in Fiji. The 1873 act which he referred to in his letter to Chesson had provided for the Torrens system, but as an optional matter; it had remained a dead letter. He proposed that the Registrar of Deeds in each island should issue a certificate of title unless he found any difficulty or unless a caveat was lodged, in which cases a Judge in Chambers would try the matter. Once the Registrar had issued a certificate of title, Gorrie proposed to bring in the system of title by registration compulsorily: all future land transactions would have to be preceded by a certificate under the Act, and after a period of three years nothing but a certificate of title under the Act would be received as evidence of land ownership. He explained the advantages of the system of title by registration, concluding that "the system does not suit the tricky and fraudulent, but it is invaluable to the honest and enterprising". The Leeward Islands, he believed, were "a fine Colony which only requires to be stirred up by the confidence of capitalists . . . to take a new lease of prosperity, until each separate island shall be as prosperous in proportion to its size as Barbados and I trust more so in many important respects". What the islands needed was capital lent on the security of land, and to secure this a safe system of land titles was essential. Under the Torrens system, "a title deed means that all the necessary inquiries have already been made, that the holder is without question the genuine proprietor, and that nobody can challenge his title to the land".[32]

The other proposals made in this 1884 memorandum were, on the whole, more controversial. Gorrie recommended that the Supreme Court should be given full powers over matters relating to mortgages and the sale of encumbered estates, taking over all the functions of the special Encumbered Estates Court so far as the colony was concerned. This court had been set up by an Act of Parliament in 1854 and was located in London. Its function was to facilitate the sale of land held by insolvent proprietors in the West Indies. Though most transactions were adjudicated in London, local courts, offshoots of the central court, also operated in the colonies with the colonial judges acting as commissioners. The Leeward Islands came under the jurisdiction of the Court in the 1860s. Most of the sales through the Court had been to British firms which enjoyed the exclusive right to market the produce of the estate in question and held the principal mortgage over it, known as the consignee's lien. Thus in Antigua, nearly all the estates sold under the Court went to the consignee firm, which petitioned for the sale and was given priority under the consignee's lien, usually paying a low price for a clear title to the heavily indebted property. By the 1870s, the general view in the Leewards (and elsewhere) was that the Court and its operations, especially the priority it accorded the consignee's claim, played into the hands of British merchants and damaged the interests of local planters and their dependents. The argument was that the consignee was able to snap up at a giveaway price properties still actually cultivated by the nominal owner, though heavily indebted; he petitioned for sale to the London Court so as to prevent a bid from any local resident who knew the true value of the property. In this view, the Court and the consignee's lien beggared the resident proprietors, gave British firms a near monopoly of plantation property and thus encouraged absenteeism, and prevented the influx of new capital to the islands.[33]

Sir T. Graham Briggs, who owned substantial properties in the islands, wrote in 1882 that

> the question of the abolition of the Encumbered Estates Court is of the most vital importance to everyone who has property in the West Indies, and above all to the wives and children of such, for at present they are liable to be shamefully robbed . . . without any chance of safety or redress.

In 1883 he told the Royal Commission, then hearing evidence in Nevis, that the Court with its insistence on the consignee's lien would inevitably wipe out the resident proprietors. Several other planters and merchants expressed the same view in each of the islands, and the Commissioners recommended the abolition of the lien and the repeal of the Encumbered Estates Court Act. Gorrie soon appreciated the force of these arguments. He came to the conclusion that the functions of the Court could better be exercised by the colony's Supreme Court, and he proposed to abolish or at least modify the priority given in the courts to the consignee's lien. The consignee's claim, he proposed, would be registered along with all the other charges on the property, which should be ranked according to priority of registration, and all creditors should enjoy the same security.[34]

Even more controversial, he recommended that the government should form a guaranteed insurance fund to secure the repayment of mortgages, in order to restore the confidence of capitalists in the Leewards. "I am quite conscious that the proposal of the Guarantee Fund is a bold one", he wrote, "but I believe the condition of some of these islands requires strong efforts to lift them up into prosperity, and that it is by this means that Planters and people alike will be most surely aided and stimulated." Finally, he proposed that dealings with land issued under Crown grants in disregard of the 1873 act should be validated, and the act amended to provide for registration of titles in all future Crown grants and the issue of a certificate of indefeasible title to the grantee without any preliminary examination of title.[35]

The memorandum was favourably reviewed in the Colonial Office, and the governor was instructed to proceed with a bill to introduce land titles by compulsory registration and to submit to the legislature the questions relating to the Encumbered Estates Court and the consignee's lien. This despatch naturally gratified Gorrie, who told Chesson that it

> accepted most of the proposals I had made for the simplification and indefeasibility of titles and although not yet absolutely authorized I believe a despatch will come next month authorising the transfer to the Supreme Court of the powers of the Encumbered Estates Court in London. These do not appear very great things in themselves but they go to the root of the security of capital advanced on land and therefore of the whole prosperity of these Colonies. They [*ie* the Colonial Office] could not accept my further proposal to create an Insurance of Mortgages Fund but I am thankful for what has been conceded and the latter may be managed in some other way. Certainly things are very low

> at present – I am hurrying on with the bill to give effect to these changes which I have been asked to draw up in case I may be wanted elsewhere before long.[36]

At the request of the Secretary of State, Gorrie produced a draft bill to introduce the system of titles to land by registration. He included an 'optional' Part IV providing for bringing encumbered estates to sale in the colony's Supreme Court and for abolishing the consignee's lien after a defined period, in the event that these changes were approved. The main part of the draft bill provided for the introduction of the system of land title by compulsory registration. This system, he noted, had been adapted to the actual conditions of the islands. No real problem existed with the estates. In the case of small properties, which he was glad to note were numerous, Section XXII provided that when deeds were deficient or obscure, certificate of title should be given to the apparent owner who had been in undisturbed possession for seven years, unless there were other means of finding out whether other claimants had a better right to the land:

> When I began to work at this scheme a year and a half ago, I thought mainly of the advantage it would be to the proprietors of estates, but I have since seen that the titles of the small properties are in a very loose condition from the ignorance of the peasantry and the excessive law costs, and that the title by Registration will be even a greater boon to the small peasant proprietor.

It would be essential to keep the schedule of fees for issuing titles to the small owners "to the proper level. Everything here in the shape of fees and fines is scandalously high compared to the incomes of the population." The draft bill received meticulous attention from the Colonial Office, and the Secretary of State informed the governor that he approved of the bill, including Part IV, in principle; some detailed amendments were proposed, and Gorrie was to be invited to revise the draft for re-submission before final approval.[37]

By December 1885, Gorrie had completed the work of revision and the draft bill was resubmitted. "The Bill is hailed as a boon by all ranks", he wrote, "and I may confidently say, as I have taken the opportunity of explaining the system widely, that the General Legislature which has been called together in

January will pass it unanimously if it be laid before them." He hoped that the Secretary of State might give the governor authority to lay the bill before the Council immediately; "I sincerely hope that after all this labour I may have the satisfaction of seeing the measure passed by the Legislature before removing to another colony", as he had already been appointed to Trinidad by the end of 1885. The governor was duly authorized by telegram to introduce the Land Titles Bill in the legislature in January 1886 as Gorrie had hoped.[38]

The Land Titles Bill successfully passed through the federal legislature in January 1886, after final revision by Gorrie (for which he was specially asked by telegram to remain in the Leewards instead of proceeding to Trinidad to take up his appointment there). While in Committee it was amended in several places, but he felt that little damage had been done to his bill. As he told Chesson, on the day before he left the colony:

> My Title by Registration Act was passed yesterday in the Legislative Council of the Leewards Islands with a note of thanks to myself. As I am not in the Council there was at one time great danger that it would be lost from the hostility of some of the lawyers and especially of the Attorney-General Gatty who had charge of the measure but the good sense of the majority prevailed and there is not much of the cloven hoof in the amendments. It is something we have accomplished.[39]

The debate on the Land Titles Bill, which was described by Gatty as "the most important measure that had been brought before the Council for some time", was long and thorough. After the bill was safely passed, the Council resolved "to offer to His Honour Sir John Gorrie its thanks for the great trouble and care he has taken in preparing the Title by Registration Act which was submitted to and passed by this Council during this Session". Act 2 of 1886, Title to Land by Registration, was assented to by the governor in February, after its author had left the colony.[40] It was an achievement in which Gorrie could take legitimate pride.

The other major issues taken up by Gorrie, closely related to the Land Titles Bill, were the transfer to the Supreme Court of the powers of the Encumbered Estates Court; the abolition of the consignee's lien; and the provision of mortgage insurance. In 1884 the governor had been instructed to take the first question to the legislature. The Federal Council passed an act (17 of 1884) conferring on the Supreme Court the jurisdiction of the Encumbered Estates Court. However, this act was disallowed as *ultra vires* and insufficient for its purpose. In April 1885, the Council passed a resolution stating that the Court should no longer operate in the colony, that jurisdiction over sales of encumbered estates should be vested in the Supreme Court, that the consignee's lien should be ranked in order of date with other claims registered against the property, and that any legislation on the question should not be retrospective. Gorrie told Edward Wingfield of the Colonial Office that "the unanimity of the Council was marvelous". The decision to disallow Act 17 of 1884 was taken purely on technical grounds, and the Colonial Office made it clear that it had no objection to a provision in the Land Titles Bill to the same effect; but an Act of Parliament would be necessary to exclude any colony from the operation of the Encumbered Estates Court Acts, and the Office wanted to ascertain the views of other West Indian colonies on the issue.[41]

In the end, Gorrie was asked to include provisions for the Supreme Court to acquire jurisdiction over the sale of encumbered estates in the Land Titles Bill. But since it was *ultra vires* for any colonial legislature to abolish the Encumbered Estates Court, which had been established by an Act of Parliament, the Colonial Office decided to seek a Parliamentary Act empowering the Queen by Order in Council to put an end to the operation of the Court in respect of any colony. This was done in 1886. In fact, all the colonies signalled their intention to transfer the Court's jurisdiction to their respective Supreme Courts, and were permitted to do so, on condition that they enacted a law for a simple, inexpensive system of land transfer, mortgages, and sales of mortgaged estates, such as Gorrie's Land Titles Bill.[42] His efforts to take the Leewards out of the jurisdiction of the Encumbered Estates Court had succeeded.

The abolition of the consignee's lien was an important, related issue. Since the consignee was always a British sugar firm, and since this claim took priority over all other debts, local creditors such as suppliers, shopkeepers and tradesmen, as well as resident investors and labourers owed arrears of wages, might all suffer when an estate was foreclosed. Gorrie believed that the priority given to the consignee's lien inhibited the investment of local capital in land and therefore hindered the development of sound, working estates owned and managed by residents. In a judgement which he delivered as local commissioner for the Encumbered Estates Court, he strongly reiterated his view that the Court invariably gave more weight to the consignee's claim than the law really warranted, to the injury of planter interests. He regretted that a case testing the question of the lien as applied by the Court had never been appealed to the Privy Council for an authoritative ruling; but he was clear in his own mind that the Court gave far too much weight to the consignee's lien and that this had operated to the detriment of local creditors of all kinds, as well as to the sugar industry as a whole. This judgement was praised by the *Agricultural Reporter* of Barbados, which noted that Barbadian planters had fortunately escaped an attempt to subject them to the doctrine of the consignee's lien, and hoped that the ruling would prove "the last nail required in its coffin" so far as the Leewards were concerned. The abolition of the consignee's lien, thought the *Antigua Standard*, would mean that London merchants would no longer come in before all other creditors, and that anyone, including locals, could advance money on crops and have first claim on the crops when ready for market, which its editor believed would have a beneficial effect on the business life of the colony.[43]

As we have seen, the federal legislature resolved early in 1885 that the consignee's lien should be ranked in order of date with any other claims registered against the estate, that is, the consignee's prior lien should be abolished, and this resolution was made effective by Part IV, Section 4, of the Land Titles Act.[44] This represented another success for Gorrie.

In his 1884 report on the Land Titles system, he had advocated a Guarantee Mortgage Insurance Fund backed by the government, which the Colonial Office vetoed. His scheme had considerable support among the islands' estate owners, many of whom were in desperate straits as the depression in the sugar industry deepened. The Vice-President of the Federal Council, Captain Berkley, wrote to Harris of the Colonial Office asking for re-consideration of the matter. He stated that he had consulted most resident planters, many merchants, and several landowners living in Britain, and nearly all favoured the scheme. "The local merchants, tradesmen and mechanics are strongly in favour of it, and as the labourers are entirely dependent on the prosperity of the planting interest, they are also in favour of the scheme." If the colony offered a guarantee against loss, capitalists would be willing to advance money immediately to keep the estates going. The Colonial Office remained unimpressed. Harris admitted that if a bill based on Gorrie's scheme was passed by the federal legislature with a large majority, it would be difficult to disallow it, but he felt that such a course would be necessary: "As Sir J. Gorrie originally put the scheme it seemed a most dangerous proposal; and Capt. Berkley does not suggest any improvements." Wingfield thought that the scheme "was sure to tempt some of the more hard pressed landowners – but I don't suppose it is likely to be seriously taken up".[45]

Wingfield was wrong. Gorrie decided to draft a bill to establish a system of guaranteed mortgages. In a memorandum accompanying the draft, he explained that London had not approved his earlier proposal in 1884, but since then the crisis in the sugar industry had become more acute and the colonies were agitating for 'remedial' measures. The purpose of the bill was to encourage capital to flow more easily and quickly to the sugar estates of the islands once the consignee's lien had been abolished; he had decided to prepare a separate bill, rather than adding the scheme to the Land Titles legislation, to give the Colonial Office a free hand to allow or disallow it without affecting the substantive measure. His scheme called for a Mortgage Board administered by a secretary who would be a salaried public servant and a Guarantee Fund controlled and invested by government officials. The bill was carefully considered by several senior officials, including the Permanent Undersecretary, Sir Robert Herbert, who commented "the language of the Bill needs to be put into better SCOTCH". The decision was a compromise. The Office felt that the inclusion in Gorrie's draft of a clause expressly declaring that holders of guaranteed mortgages should have no claim upon the general revenues of the colony made it less objectionable than the earlier proposal. But the Secretary of State could not sanction an act which would give the colonial government any responsibility for the security of mortgages, and therefore he could not approve of the provisions which made the secretary of the Mortgage Board a public officer and placed the management of the Fund under the governor. However, if the members of Council favoured a system of guaranteed mortgages, under a Board independent of government, he would not object to the government aiding the scheme by an annual contribution to cover administrative expenses. A version of Gorrie's bill was introduced in the Federal Council in January 1886 by an elected member, but, partly through the opposition of Attorney-General Gatty, it was thrown out on the motion for a second reading.[46] Despite this failure, Gorrie took up the issues of loans to estates, crop advances and mortgages again in Trinidad after 1886.

Social and Civic Life

In addition to his work on legislation relating to land issues, Gorrie found scope for his "superfluous energies" (in the words of a local critic) in various 'extracurricular' activities; as in Mauritius and Fiji, he plunged into the social and public life of the Leewards almost from the moment of his arrival. He frequently took part in religious and educational functions. He presided over a Wesleyan missionary meeting in St Johns, giving an "eloquent and masterly speech" to a crowded chapel. He had clearly done his homework, for he spoke on the history of Methodism in Antigua before going on to review the achievements of the missionaries in Fiji and the Western Pacific, concluding by reading a Gospel verse in the Fijian language. The fact that Gorrie, a Presbyterian, had presided over a Methodist meeting was favourably commented on as proof of his broadminded Christianity. He also spoke at the prize-giving function of the Catholic Convent School for girls in St Johns. After telling the gathering that he had seen the good work of teaching nuns in the Pacific, and in Mauritius where Catholicism was the majority faith, he said he was "sure they had nothing to fear about being converted . . . If there were no other schools in the Island where such education could be given he strongly advised his hearers to make use of this, and not to be afraid of the bogey of proselytism", for Antigua was strongly Protestant. No doubt his early exposure to the liberal Presbyterianism of his father's Relief Church, among other influences, had helped to shape his broadminded approach to religion.

Gorrie also took an interest in the colony's schools; one of his first public appearances was at the annual meeting of the Mico Charity, a body which ran schools and a training college in Antigua. Later he presided over the annual prize giving of the Antigua Grammar School, the main boys' secondary school; "by his geniality and well-timed remarks [he] gave éclat to the proceedings".[47]

Two recreational activities which he had pursued in Fiji, tennis and gardening, were taken up again in the Leewards. The newly fashionable game of lawn tennis had been pioneered by the Gorrie family in Levuka in the 1870s, and they now became stalwarts of the Antigua Lawn Tennis Club. He presided over the inaugural meeting of the Antiguan Horticultural Society in 1885, urging members to encourage the cultivation of useful as well as ornamental plants and to beautify the city of St Johns as well as their own gardens. In fact, a Botanic Garden should be set up, he said, to give an impetus to experimentation with new plants and crops, as well as new varieties of cane. He hoped that when the Society began to organize shows they would include cottage gardens, so as to encourage the labouring classes to take an interest in horticulture; members should conduct the Society "in a free and popular spirit, and free from all exclusiveness". Gorrie's sociability, commented on frequently in the local newspapers, was pleasantly suggested by his reply to a toast at a ball at St Kitts Government House when he was its temporary occupant:

> It does so sweeten life to meet with the ladies and gentlemen where we reside . . . When my wife comes [his family was still in Britain] we may hope to have many such gatherings, as my daughters – and I have some daughters, Gentlemen—are bricks for dancing, whilst my wife, I am pleased to say, is never so happy as when she is entertaining the people of a colony where her husband is an official.

Even before his family arrived, we find him organizing a subscription ball at the St Johns Court House in honour of the visit of Prince George of Wales in 1884.[48]

Gorrie often gave public lectures, and these seem to have been well received. He spoke on the topic "Fiji, its customs and people" in aid of the

Building Fund of St Johns parish, to a large audience; and on the theme "Public men whom I have seen or known" for the Young Men's Literary and Recreational Club of St Johns. News of this last lecture prompted a wit in St Kitts to suggest "an alternative lecture subject which would . . . provide a more instructive and infinitely more amusing text for our Judge to discourse from. Suppose, Sir John, instead of nauseating an Antigua audience with anecdotes of 'public men you have met', you treated them to 'Counsel whom I have bullied and Councillors I have vilified'?"[49] With his abundant energy, as well as his organizational skills, he took on quasi-public assignments of one kind or another. He was asked by the governor to investigate the settlement possibilities of a district in Dominica known as the Layou Flats, and undertook an expedition through the woods across the island "so as to judge himself of the value and availability for settlement of the comparatively flat valleys in the interior known as the Layou and Zara Flats". This did not please his old opponent, William Davies of the *Dial*, who pointedly asked in the Dominican Legislative Assembly whether any government funds had been spent on this "triumphant but unsolicited march" over the Layou Flats.[50]

Another assignment was to head the organization of the colony's contribution to the Colonial Exhibition of 1886. He told Chesson:

> The governor has approved a large Committee embracing men of the different Islands, of which I am Chairman, and we are working at the matter heartily . . . We intend not only to show what the Islands have produced or are producing, but what they could produce . . . Of course there are difficulties innumerable and chiefly the want of money in consequence of the breakdown of sugar but we do not intend to be discouraged.

The Committee first met in January 1885, hearing a "lengthy speech" from its chairman, who told its members: "All the Capitalists of the world will be at this Exhibition, who will be keenly alive to their interests, and our contributions will be our best advertisement." Gorrie wrote an elaborate "Address to the People of the Leeward Islands" which was widely circulated, calling for public support for the effort to organize a worthwhile contribution for the Exhibition. The benefits to the 'minor industries' and the small cultivators, as well as to the staples and the planters, were emphasized in the Address.[51]

But persuading colonial legislatures, planters and others to contribute money for a display at the Exhibition, at a time of deepening depression in the sugar industry, proved an uphill struggle. The St Kitts legislature refused to vote any public funds, and that of Antigua granted the derisory sum of £50; both islands were almost wholly dependent on sugar. "Sir J. Gorrie is the life and soul of the undertaking", thought the *Antigua Observer*, "and if he could infuse anything like his own energy into others, we might yet make a creditable performance among other colonies at this World's Fair." While in Dominica for the circuit of September 1885, Gorrie addressed a public meeting in Roseau to appeal for subscriptions for the Dominican exhibit, since the island's legislature had also declined to vote public funds. His lengthy speech emphasized Dominica's potential for developing a diversified export trade, especially in fruit. Though the *Dial* ridiculed this meeting, portraying the speakers as mere sycophants currying favour with Gorrie, it seems that by the time he left the Leewards early in 1886 he had succeeded in generating some interest in the Exhibition as a means of drawing the attention of British capitalists to the islands' potential for development. The Committee which included representatives from all the islands resolved just before he left to record "its sense of the value of the services of Sir John Gorrie . . . and its deep regret that his services are to be lost to the colony" and to pledge "to continue earnestly the work which owes so much to [him] for its progress so far".[52]

In true Victorian fashion, Gorrie made several long expeditions on foot or on horseback in the wilder parts of the islands. Early in 1884, he

> distinguished himself as a pedestrian, having made a tour on foot from Roseau to Rosaly on the windward side [of Dominica], and back, a distance of over 30 miles, and comprising some very stiff uphill work. This vigorous sexagenarian [he was actually 55] completed his walk between Monday morning and Tuesday evening.

When he visited the Virgin Islands, "he walked the length and breadth of Virgin Gorda", one of the less developed of these small islands. Back in

Dominica in 1885, he undertook a longer expedition across the interior of the island; this was the "march" to investigate the potential of the Layou district which the *Dial* had criticized. Gorrie described the trip to Chesson:

> I did the other day what very few ever have done in this generation – I went on foot through the interior of Dominica spending four days in the primeval forest, sleeping at night on the ground under improvised shelter, and at length coming out at the Windward side . . . The forest is simply magnificent but we had to cut our way with the cutters and the woods were terribly encumbered with fallen timber from the hurricane of 1883. One day we made only about four miles with eleven hours of toil. When I say 'we' I include the men as carriers and cutters I had with me as nobody else would venture with me as a companion. My objects were two-fold, to see these lands of which I had heard [the Layou Flats] . . . and to see the remnant of the Caribs.

The latter impressed him, though they were

> fast merging into the creoles. They speak the French patois – those who are of pure breed are olive skinned with intensely black eyes and the women have long straight jet black hair. The men are finely built handsome fellows. They have (amongst the 200 of them) about 1000 acres as a Reserve and they seem satisfied as the only two requests the Chief sent to the Governor through me was to have a school and a plan of the lands of the reservation. They are more like the natives of the Gilbert and Marshall group than any other native race I have seen but a Carrib [*sic*] woman who had married a Chinese assured me he was the same nation as herself. They are more Malay like than Chinese looking . . . After that I took to horse and swept round the Windward side of the Island to Prince Rupert's Bay and thence by boat to Roseau – the scenery on the Windward side especially approaching Prince Rupert's is very fine – you see I have not lost my energy. It was very touching to see that remnant of the once proud Carrib race.[53]

Gorrie's involvement in so many different aspects of social and public life in the islands where he lived for only two and a half years fully justified the comment of the *Antigua Standard*: "He is generally considered a valuable member of the community. He is ever ready to promote any scheme that will tend to improve the position of these Islands. He is fully alive to his duties socially, and helps liberally every good cause he is asked to identify himself with." This was no 'bird of passage' official.[54]

But his stay in the Leewards was darkened by a personal tragedy, the death of his wife Marion in 1884. She had joined her husband, along with their first and third daughters (Minnie and Jeanie) and their son Malcolm, in November 1883. Her health deteriorated, and she was advised to return to Britain in mid 1884 to escape the West Indian 'hot', or rather wet, season. The family left Antigua early in June; Marian suffered a relapse during the voyage and died on June 16, four days after leaving St Thomas, and was buried at sea. Her death was attributed to heart disease.[55] Gorrie sought and obtained an extension of leave in Britain, and returned to Antigua in October 1884.

The return of the bereaved Chief Justice was marked by an outpouring of public affection. "The people gave me a very remarkable reception", he told Chesson; "we arrived just as it was getting dark and found the whole population of St Johns turned out. They cheered my landing most enthusiastically and a dense crowd accompanied me home. Certainly they are touched with very little effort to give them justice and do them good." An address signed by over 600 persons "of all classes of the Inhabitants" was prepared for him, but he declined to receive it on the grounds that, as a judge, not a "political person", he could not be identified with any popular demonstration. Persuaded that it was merely an expression of welcome and condolence devoid of any political significance, he agreed to accept it "as mainly a manifestation of sympathy in his bereavement from all ranks of the community". The address, signed by over 600 "Inhabitants of Antigua", stated that his administration of justice "has been marked by such ability, integrity and courtesy as has won the highest appreciation of all classes . . . In your private life, as a member of Society, you have manifested an earnest desire to render yourself useful, and have striven to identify yourself with the interests of the Colony." Gorrie said he would keep the address "as proof of the kindness of the people of Antigua to one who has been able as yet to do little for them, but who heartily wishes for the prosperity of all classes in the Island".[56] We can only speculate on the effects on Gorrie of the loss of his wife of nearly thirty years, but we have noted the evidence of a deterioration in his temper while on the bench in the period immediately after her death.

Towards the end of 1885, Gorrie was appointed Chief Justice of Trinidad (a promotion), but was asked to remain in the Leewards to make final revisions to the Land Titles Bill; he took up his new post at the end of January 1886. The *Dial* greeted the news of his promotion with a bad-tempered editorial which questioned whether he was a suitable recipient of official patronage, while congratulating the Leewards on his departure. Gorrie presided over the Supreme Court for the last time in January, and was addressed by the Attorney-General on behalf of the Bar; ironically, Gatty, no friend of Gorrie, had also been promoted to the same position in Trinidad. In the Leewards, said Gatty, one hopes with a straight face, "the Bar were impressed with the strong manner in which His Honour had always endeavoured to show purity of justice in his judgments". This little speech earned the scorn of the *Dial*: "It passes comprehension how these gentlemen of the Bar, to every one of whom Sir J. Gorrie has been individually and brutally insulting, should have so far condescended to the sycophancy and insincerity of which they have been guilty." A more balanced farewell was delivered by the *Antigua Standard*:

> Sir JOHN takes with him the good wishes of the entire community. He has been an exceedingly useful man, and to Trinidad he will prove himself invaluable . . . The purity of motive that distinguished his judgements, and his genial manner, must be appreciated and remembered gratefully. Sir JOHN had his rough and wrong side as well as most men, but he has qualities of head and heart that more than counteracted such.[57]

CHAPTER SEVEN

'Ah We Judge': Trinidad, 1886-89

Trinidad in the 1880s

In comparison with the islands of the Leewards, Trinidad enjoyed considerable prosperity even during the years of depression in the cane sugar industry between 1884 and 1897. Though sugar was the island's main export crop, it was fairly well capitalized, and the British firms or individual capitalists who owned most of the estates had succeeded in modernizing the manufacturing side of the business, amalgamating small units, and introducing other innovations to make production reasonably profitable even when prices were low. As a result, the Trinidad sugar industry weathered the crisis of the mid 1880s relatively well; it was never in any danger of going under, bolstered as it was by large-scale indentured Indian immigration and substantial injections of metropolitan capital. Moreover, by the 1880s cocoa was rapidly becoming an export crop of almost equal importance. Cocoa had been grown in the island for centuries, but it was only around 1870 that changes in the market situation, as well as developments within the island, propelled a rapid expansion in production. Large estates were established all over the island, usually through the 'contract' system which was to engage

Gorrie's special attention, and thousands of peasants of all races also engaged in small-scale cultivation. By 1890, cocoa was poised to overtake sugar as the island's most valuable export. In addition to the two major staples, 'minor' crops like coconuts, rice and citrus were becoming important, and food crop cultivation was also expanding. In fact, Trinidad's agricultural economy was fairly robust, certainly in comparison with that of the Leeward Islands.

Trinidad's society in the late nineteenth century was complex and distinctly heterogenous. The island had been a Spanish colony for centuries, but it had first been developed largely by French or French West Indian planters, white and mixed-race, who had emigrated there during the last decades of Spanish rule in the 1780s and 1790s. When it became a British possession in 1797, people from Britain and from the older British colonies in the Eastern Caribbean began to arrive. As a result, the island's white elite consisted of people of French, Spanish and British descent, the former – known as the 'French Creoles' – being the most numerous. They saw themselves as forming the true local aristocracy, rooted in the possession of land and in ancestral memories of pioneering settlement and slave ownership. The whites of British origin dominated both the sugar industry and the commercial sector, while the French Creoles (who had absorbed the long-established families of Spanish descent) controlled most of the cocoa estates. Though Trinidad's white elite was divided along lines of national origin and religion (Catholic versus Protestant), its members were becoming conscious of the need to unite in defence of their entrenched privileges as the century drew to a close; and the campaign against the new Chief Justice which soon developed would be led by men of French, Spanish and British descent.

As he had in Mauritius, in Trinidad Gorrie confronted a local white elite which was mainly French in origin, strongly entrenched socially and economically, self-conscious, and confident of its ability to contain or even to eliminate external threats to its position. There was also a growing black and mixed-race middle class, educated, employed in teaching, the professions and the civil service for the most part, and becoming increasingly politicized and resentful of white domination. Some of these men became strong supporters of Gorrie. The masses of the people belonged to two major racial groups. There were the black Creoles, of African descent, who were the descendants of the island's slave population or of post-emancipation immigrants from the Eastern Caribbean and Africa. Second, there were the 'East Indians', as they were called in the Caribbean to distinguish them from the Amerindians; these were the indentured immigrants from India, arriving each year since 1845, and their locally born offspring. By the time Gorrie arrived, the East Indians constituted over a quarter of the total population. Smaller groups included people of mixed racial origins from Venezuela, Chinese immigrants and Portuguese from Madeira. In general, Trinidad's social and demographic picture strongly resembled that of Mauritius, half a world away.

Like Mauritius, Trinidad was a Crown Colony. Captured by Britain in 1797, it had never had an elected Assembly. Its single-chamber Legislative Council was wholly nominated, consisting of top officials (mostly British) and 'unofficials', private citizens chosen by the governor to represent the island's property interests. The governor presided; and, in constitutional theory, the Colonial Office in London and the governor in Port of Spain could carry through whatever measures they wished. In practice, however, the local elite represented by the unofficials exercised wide influence over policy making. Agitation for constitutional reforms which would introduce an elected element into the Council revived just at the time of Gorrie's arrival; the 'Reform Movement', as it was generally known, was active in 1885-89, led by liberal members of the white elite, especially cocoa planters and merchants who resented the domination of the sugar barons, and by black or mixed-race lawyers. This was also a time when educated blacks in Trinidad were beginning to evolve an ideology of race pride with which to confront the institutionalized racism of the period; the Jubilee of Emancipation in 1888 helped to advance this development, with which Gorrie sympathized.[1]

Gorrie's predecessor, Sir Joseph Needham (1870-85), had been famous for his aversion to work, his lack of interest in the judicial business of the colony, and his tendency to give priority to the concerns of his flourishing cocoa estate. Under his long regime of official neglect, complaints about the administration of justice proliferated. The main burden of these protests was that ordinary people felt they had no access to the higher courts, and that the magistrates' courts (where most minor cases were determined) routinely handed down unfair decisions. "If we are to judge by appearances and practice", stated a correspondent to a local paper in 1873, "we have here two distinct laws and customs, one for the favoured few, and the other for the common herd." Fifteen years later the same point was made by a villager in his own way: "When the laws of Trinidad comes in Trinidad we poor fellows don't get none of it, don't hear none at all. When we hear the laws of any case brought before the court we don't know how to speak for ourselves, because we don't hear no laws, for it is hidden from us . . ."[2]

The magistrates, who were responsible for the day-to-day administration of justice, were said to have forfeited the confidence of the ordinary people by arbitrary and oppressive rulings. Only cases involving a fine of over five pounds could be appealed as of right to the higher courts, and the cost of appeals was high. The editor of the *New Era* pointed out in 1881 that an injustice was an injustice whatever the sum in question and that the poor felt the loss of a few shillings more keenly than the rich might feel the loss of a hundred pounds. If there was a right to appeal in all cases, the editor felt, the existing trend to unfair decisions would be checked; indeed, magistrates were known to fix the fine deliberately at just under five pounds. The black Trinidadian scholar and author J.J. Thomas, in his important book *Froudacity*, wrote a forceful indictment of the misdeeds of Trinidad magistrates in the years before Gorrie came to the island. In his view, these "gentry" had converted their powers "into an engine of systematic oppression" aimed especially at the poor, the blacks and the Indians. Thomas gave chapter and verse, naming names, and detailing several particularly scandalous magisterial decisions. He noted that with a do-nothing Chief Justice like Needham, and with governors who showed little concern for the poor, these magistrates were unchecked in their acts of oppression.[3] It is not surprising that Gorrie's efforts to make the courts more accessible to the poor and to keep magistrates and others under check were received with such widespread enthusiasm by the ordinary people of the island and by those who spoke for them.

In November 1885, Gorrie was offered the Trinidad post at a salary of £1800. It was made clear that he would not have a seat in the Council; the Colonial Office had decided that it was wrong for colonial chief justices to sit in the legislature, and Needham's retirement provided the opportunity to implement the new policy. Gorrie was also told that the colony's Supreme Court would be reduced from three to two judges as soon as a vacancy occurred. He took up his new post at the end of January 1886.[4]

The staff of the Colonial Office were aware that the news of his appointment would not be greeted with enthusiasm by the men of substance in Trinidad, nor by their spokesmen in Britain. The influential *European Mail* of London expressed its foreboding : "Now as to this Chief Justice – what is wanted? Why a man who would *not* be likely to express any extreme views that would favour one class to the detriment of another; who would *not* put socialist notions into the mind of an excitable population." In Trinidad, the *Port of Spain Gazette* reproduced this article for its readers, and for good measure also passed on the hostile opinion of the *Dominica Dial.* Gorrie, the editor summed up, "does not certainly come among us heralded by favourable reports of his career elsewhere". The West India Committee, the powerful organ of British sugar interests in London, would not approve, a clerk in the Colonial Office noted; but Sir Robert Herbert, the Permanent Under-secretary, was firm: "Sir J. Gorrie is a strong judge, and there can be no good ground for any section objecting to him. In the West Indies it is generally a good thing to have a Chief Justice who does not care for popularity."[5]

The New Chief Justice

Gorrie took his seat on the Trinidad Supreme Court for the first time in February 1886, and immediately, according to a local paper, made clear his opposition to unjustified delays and his conviction that the law should be cheaply and expeditiously administered. Within a month of his arrival, observers noted a striking contrast with the leisurely, almost casual despatch of business under Needham. "There is violent agitation in our legal atmosphere", one editor noted; "a strong masterful spirit has begun moving over the waters of some of our local courts, and the disturbance is great amongst those who had hitherto swum in cosy prosperity in the current of postponements, affidavits, and other lucrative accessories of ancient legal routine." Lawyers and others with business in the courts reported that his legal knowledge was formidable – "The old gentleman is rather sharp", according to one Counsel – and that he had impressed the legal men that it was impossible to hoodwink him in the smallest detail of procedure. This was "a plain, straightforward and honest judge".[6]

Gorrie's main objective was to change judicial procedures so that ordinary Trinidadians, especially the poor and uneducated, had greater access to the courts. This necessitated cutting through unnecessary red tape and formalities and reducing the cost involved in bringing suits and appeals. Since so many of the people were illiterate, and often ignorant even of spoken English (many of the rural blacks spoke French Creole, and few Indians were competent in English at this period), Gorrie also thought it necessary at times to give informal advice to would-be suitors of this kind. These simple considerations led him to make two much criticized innovations: seeing would-be suitors in chambers and giving them advice about their cases; and permitting suits *in forma pauperis*.

By 1887 both these practices were regularly commented on in the local press. One paper complained that it was difficult to see the Chief Justice on legitimate business because of the long lines of persons from all over the island waiting to see him in chambers about their cases. Even when counsel had been consulted and had advised that no grounds for action existed, Gorrie would say, "Go on – I see grounds!" The Chief Justice, complained another paper, was advising litigants to bring suits which he would later have to try. They were flocking to him with their tales of grievance, some justified, many mere fabrications; he listened, advised action, assigned counsel, and then tried the cases as one of only two judges in the colony (the point here was that there was effectively no Court of Appeal since the Chief Justice could always overrule his junior colleague on the Bench). Moreover, he provided legal aid to those who convinced him that they were destitute by permitting suits *in forma pauperis*, tantamount to "inciting the lower classes to litigation". Such suits had always been provided for; but in the seven years 1879-85, only 15 were filed, while in the three years 1886-88, there were 195. Of these 195 suits, 135 actions were actually entered, and 67 were decided in favour of the plaintiff.[7]

These practices were defended by the papers which claimed to speak for the people. The *San Fernando Gazette* believed that, in advising would-be suitors in chambers and permitting suits *in forma pauperis*, Gorrie was merely trying to protect the people who previously had enjoyed virtually no access to the courts because of the high costs and bewildering red tape of legal action. The editor recognized that there was a risk of frivolous, ill-founded or malicious suits, and suggested that where a suit was shown to be without merit, the costs of the defence should be a fine on the plaintiff, recoverable by summary jurisdiction. *Truth* considered that Gorrie's actions were motivated by his anxiety to check the "spoliation" practised by several local lawyers on poor suitors. The editor of *New Era* believed that before his arrival, the Supreme Court was confined to a privileged aristocracy and the law was a "mysterious temple"; now anyone with a real grievance could get a remedy in the highest court, and public confidence in the judicial system was at its highest ever.[8]

Many of the suits which Gorrie was supposed to have encouraged, some filed *in forma pauperis*, were cases brought by peasants who had been contracted by landowners to plant a plot of land in cocoa or coconut trees. They complained of unfair treatment by the owners; a few landowners had several such suits filed against them. The 'contract system', which was especially important in the cocoa industry, worked like this: A planter cleared a large block of land and entered into an agreement with contractors who agreed to plant cocoa trees, each usually being allotted around three acres. When the trees were bearing, or after a specified period, the owner took over the land, paying the contractor for each tree according to its age and condition. Until that time, the contractor received no wages for his labour, though he was free to plant and use food crops on the land. Most of the larger Trinidad cocoa estates were built up through this system; the planter incurred low expenses and few risks, while the growing trees were security on which he could raise loans to pay the contractors. At best, the latter received a reasonable sum at the end of the contract which might be used to buy a plot of Crown land; but the agreements were unwritten and informal, and there was plenty of scope for misunderstanding and exploitation, especially when the contractors were poor and usually illiterate labourers and the planters typically members of the local white elite.[9]

The suits heard by Gorrie generally asked for damages when a contractor had been 'turned-off' the land without any payment, or without full payment, for the trees he had planted; this might occur when the planter considered that the trees were in poor condition as a result of neglect. It must be remembered that the contractor was not entitled to any wages for his labour in planting and tending the trees. A typical case was *Caesar Congo* v *Clerk*, decided in August 1888. Clerk, the planter, had 'turned off' Congo from his land without compensation because he had allowed much of the plot to go back to bush, smothering the young trees; Congo claimed the large sum of £61.17.4 in damages. Gorrie rejected this claim but awarded him £16.13.4 in damages and £3.3.0 in costs. He felt that Congo deserved adequate compensation for his work in planting the trees and tending them up to the third year, when he "lost heart" and let the bush grow back, but not the full amount which would normally be due for bearing trees in good condition. The planter's case, however, was that the damage done to the young trees in the third year of the contract was irreparable, they could never become profitable, and therefore the contractor was not entitled to any compensation since the whole of the planter's investment had been lost. The majority of these 'contract cases' involved cocoa, but the system was also used in building up coconut estates. In 1888 he heard a number of cases brought by contractors against Eugene Lange Jr, member of a well-known French Creole family and owner of a large coconut property in Oropouche. In four cases, he awarded the plaintiff the full amount claimed (24 cents per tree), and in three others slightly smaller sums.[10]

The spate of 'contract cases' in 1887-88 alarmed and embittered the planters, accustomed to running the contract system on their own terms. The retiring magistrate and Warden of Mayaro, on the island's eastern coast, who belonged to the landowning Ganteaume family, warned the people of his district to beware of "false Syrens" who would prove to be their worst enemies if they succeeded in sowing dissension between cocoa planter and contractor, a not very subtle allusion to Gorrie. Editors of papers unfriendly to him claimed that he automatically saw a villain whenever a respectable planter or merchant was before him as defendant, and an innocent victim when a "poor Creole peasant" was plaintiff. Yet he knew nothing of the cocoa industry, of contracts, of the Creole peasantry, or of the planting community. "A more menacing and dangerous attitude could scarcely be assumed by a Chief Justice." His judgements in the contract cases, and this was a charge to be endlessly repeated throughout his stay in Trinidad, had seriously damaged capitalist confidence in the agricultural industries of the island and had disrupted the hitherto smooth relations between contractors and planters, and labourers and employers.[11]

By making it clear that he would entertain suits against cocoa and coconut planters, filed *in forma pauperis* if necessary, and by finding for the plaintiffs in many of these cases, Gorrie alienated most members of the planting community. His style and procedures in court also infuriated many of the other important interest groups or professionals in the colony. The medical men were among the first to incur his anger and to organize against him. Early in 1887, he accused two doctors of callous indifference in their treatment of a seriously injured Indian woman, who had died the day after they had ordered her removal from a country estate to the main hospital in Port of Spain. Not content with criticizing the two men, he called the whole medical profession "a very unsatisfactory part of the institutions of this country"; and on several other occasions, he handled medical witnesses roughly or attacked specific actions by local doctors. The Medical Board passed resolutions deploring Gorrie's "uniform attitude of incomprehensible hostility" towards the profession and appealing to the governor for protection. Not at all intimidated by the board's dignified protest, Gorrie read a statement in court attacking the resolutions. He insisted that a judge had an absolute duty to question medical witnesses as freely as any others, especially when the case involved strangers ignorant of British laws, customs and values; instanced cases of gross misconduct by local doctors; and ended by proposing that the Medical Board be dissolved forthwith.[12]

This statement elicited a memorial from the board addressed to the Secretary of State. It complained of his "intemperate and insulting" remarks, couched in "the coarse and offensive language so notoriously adopted by the Chief Justice towards medical witnesses". The Medical Board stated that its relations with the Bench had been excellent until Gorrie's arrival and that only "studied insult" had led it to formally defend its members' honour. The men in the Colonial Office thought that on the whole Gorrie had got the better of the row; but Edward Wingfield noted, in a tone of exasperation, "Sir John Gorrie is a violent man and is apt to abuse his position on the Bench to air his political and social crotchets . . . I have little doubt that his cross-examination of the doctors is occasionally insulting or that he likes to show off before the public as a general redresser of wrongs real or imaginary." The Secretary of State's reply, however, was mild: "I regret that the Chief Justice . . . should have cast aspersions, which I consider to be undeserved, upon the medical service of the Colony." Gorrie was by no means finished with the Medical Board, however. In a lively letter to the governor, Sir William Robinson, he referred to the board's "false and extravagant charges against [him], and the intense bitterness they feel against one who has broken the long spell of the evil influence of the Board". The board was merely "a brawling set of trade unionists" with a clear interest in maintaining abuses and protecting the Government Medical Officers, who all enjoyed lucrative private practices and charged poor patients fees which were sometimes positively cruel. But their attacks were to be expected when an official "in the discharge of public duty has offended one or other of the purse-proud magnates of the Colony".[13]

In these collisions with the medical men, the Colonial Office had showed considerable restraint towards Gorrie. But their patience was tested later in 1887, when the acting Police Surgeon complained that the Chief Justice had publicly attacked both his integrity and his professional skill. Herbert minuted: "We cannot allow an unlimited licence of coarseness and insolence to a Chief Justice in a Crown Colony inhabited by French and coloured people"; and the Secretary of State in his reply expressed "strong disapproval" of his conduct. The governor was advised that all the Secretary of State could do was to express regret when public officers complained of damaging statements by the Chief Justice from the Bench, but if this became "so habitual as distinctly to bring the administration of justice into disrepute, it may be necessary to consider whether steps should be taken for the removal of a judge who so abuses his position". This was a clear warning that he could not expect unlimited support from his superiors in London.[14]

A degree of tension between a crusading Chief Justice and local police officers was, no doubt, inevitable, and in 1887 he annoyed Captain A.W. Baker, the police chief, when he stated in court that the police "would swear that black is white if necessary to defend their own body of men". This remark was apparently greeted with noisy delight by the "vagrants and idlers", the "lower and criminal classes", who were present in the court room. Baker claimed that the colony's criminals regarded Gorrie as their "special guardian and protector" and that the habitual contempt for the police which he expressed from the bench could only have dangerous results; the governor agreed. What followed this episode was an absurd correspondence, duly sent to London, about Baker 'cutting' Gorrie one Sunday afternoon in the Port of Spain Botanic Gardens. One can only sympathize with Sir Henry Holland, who minuted: "The S. of S. has enough to do without having to decide whether AB may 'cut' CD in a Colony." But the *European Mail*, while acknowledging that the Gardens scene and the subsequent correspondence were "rich in comedy", thought that it had its "serious considerations" and that it was one more proof that Gorrie was fast losing the confidence of respectable people in the colony.[15]

When Gorrie stated that the police were capable of any kind of perjury to save one of their own, he casually coupled 'the soldiers' in this blanket accusation; and the remark was duly resented by the local military commander as well as by the police chief. These complaints reached the general commanding in the West Indies, the War Office, and even "His Royal Highness the Field Marshall, Commander in Chief". Gorrie's response (addressed to Robinson) was intemperate and almost vulgar in tone, to a degree unusual even for him, full of gratuitous personal insults and implied threats to jail the local military commander for contempt. No wonder that an exasperated man at the Colonial Office minuted on this correspondence, "Sir John Gorrie must be cracked", and that the Secretary of State expressed, yet again, his "great regret" at the tone and language both of the remarks in court and the offensive letter.[16]

But the professional men who came into contact most often with the Chief Justice, and whose interests were directly threatened by his actions, were the members of the local Bar. He had a well deserved reputation for sharpness, even rudeness, towards lawyers who, he felt, were wasting his time or obstructing justice. Less than four months after he arrived, the local Bar met to develop "a firm but respectful resistance to the pretensions of the bench as recently formulated" and to check "that unjust interference with its time-honoured rights and prerogatives, which is such an unfortunate feature in the character of the latest addition to the judicial staff". One line of action taken by the Bar was to press for the appointment of a third judge, against the Colonial Office decision, when Judge Fitzgerald retired in the middle of 1886. When Gorrie made some harsh remarks in court against Frederick Warner and George Garcia, prominent barristers, members of the Council, and political opponents of the Chief Justice, Garcia complained to the Secretary of State, and 65 'leading citizens' signed an address in sympathy with both men.[17]

Nor did jurors always escape a tongue lashing. In 1888, a juryman was so incensed at the Chief Justice's remarks both to him personally, and to the whole jury, when they failed to bring in a guilty verdict in *Q* v *Mahomet*, that he petitioned the Secretary of State for an enquiry into his conduct and for protection for the community from his maladministration of justice. It seems clear that the remarks complained of were both improper and unjudicial, but Gorrie defended his conduct on the grounds that Trinidadian jurymen could not be trusted to act rightly because of deep divisions of race and class, especially when the case involved Indians. There is considerable evidence to suggest that Trinidad courts of the period were often permeated with prejudice against the Indians in particular, but this hardly justified the offensive remarks. The Secretary of State merely replied expressing his regret at Gorrie's remarks to the jury and declining to authorize an enquiry. But Herbert minuted: "I wish we could say something to Sir J. Gorrie as to his scandalous conduct, which we appear to the Colony, no doubt, to be always condoning if not supporting, while there is now quite ground enough for taking measures for his suspension." Yet this severe rebuke was not, apparently, conveyed to him.[18]

Gorrie's relations with the new Attorney-General, Stephen Gatty, his opponent in the Leewards, were predictably difficult. Their first collision centered on the Attorney-General's right to allocate non-capital criminal cases (which were heard by only one judge) between the Chief Justice and the other judge. This had long been the practice in Trinidad. Gorrie, however, insisted that this responsibility was solely his. He believed that some cases, because of their importance or complexity, should be heard by the Chief Justice rather than by the junior judge, and that the power to distribute cases was "inherent in the office". It seems clear that this claim was at odds both with the established practice and the law in the colony; and Gatty was on solid ground when he suggested that it was safer not to permit one judge to decide which cases he would, or would not, hear: "It is most undesirable in a mixed community like this where there are questions of Colour and Nationalities that such a choice should be left to a single Judge." This view made sense to the Colonial Office. Wingfield thought it "dangerous to entrust such a power to so headstrong a man as Sir John Gorrie who is apt to let his social and political views affect his judicial acts – and who might be tempted to pick and choose for trial before himself cases which would give an opportunity for delivering his political sentiments from the bench". The Secretary of State ruled that it was the collective duty of all the judges to allocate cases; the Attorney-General should prepare a provisional calendar for the judges' approval or revision, and if the judges failed to agree the calendar as prepared by him should stand.[19]

Another issue which caused conflict between the two men related to the Attorney-General's duties as public prosecutor. Gorrie, accustomed to the Scottish and Mauritian system whereby the Lord Advocate and his deputies in Scotland and the Procureur-General in Mauritius performed this function in indictable criminal cases and exercised a general oversight over police prosecutions in the lower courts, thought that the Attorney-General in Trinidad should have a similar responsibility. Accordingly, he made remarks from the Bench implying that it was Gatty's duty to supervise the police in the conduct of prosecutions before the magistrates and criticizing him for failing to do so. Gatty denied that it was his duty to direct the police in prosecutions, and appealed to the governor. Robinson took the view that to claim that the Attorney-General was responsible for police prosecutions (or failures to prosecute) was "an absolutely novel doctrine" which he could not accept. Gorrie replied in a lengthy letter explaining his views ("what appears so simple a matter to those of us who have been accustomed to the work of a Public

Prosecutor seems an incomprehensible mystery to your mere English Barrister"), and giving detailed examples of cases which were carelessly prepared for the Assizes because (as he saw it) the Attorney-General had failed to assume the duty of overseeing the work of the magistrates and police. He also insinuated that Gatty was upset because of a recent ruling in a civil case in which he had served as counsel, and accused him of trying "to have me muzzled, and to lead me about with a string". But the legal men in the Colonial Office agreed with Gatty and Robinson: the functions of the Attorney-General in Trinidad were not the same as those of the Procureur-General in Mauritius. Gatty continued to be a strong opponent of the Chief Justice: Gorrie told Chesson that the governor, in a private conversation, had warned him: "Don't make any mistake about it, Gorrie, he is your determined enemy and will destroy you if he can." Gatty played a leading (if necessarily behind the scenes) role in the campaign for an enquiry into the administration of justice in 1887, as Gorrie was well aware.[20]

Enemies and Admirers

In his actions as Chief Justice since his arrival at the start of 1886, therefore, Gorrie had alienated several important professional and interest groups in the colony. It is clear that his tendency to indulge in intemperate outbursts from the Bench was becoming increasingly counterproductive. Not only did these outbursts needlessly infuriate powerful individuals and groups, they also exasperated the men in the Colonial Office, who had usually supported him in the many skirmishes of his colonial career. His natural irritability and his failure to check his tongue were, in fact, beginning to limit his effectiveness as a judge. At the same time, he had won the admiration of those who recognized the need for judicial reforms and acknowledged his strenuous efforts to give the ordinary person greater access to the courts. But, true to the pattern first laid down in Mauritius, he did not confine himself to his judicial duties. He took an active part in the colony's political and public life; and these interventions further alienated many of the influential men of the island.

In 1886 Robinson named him chairman of a Trade and Taxes Commission, charged with enquiring into the tariff system with a view to reductions in order to facilitate trade and lower the cost of living. As a devoted disciple of Cobden and Bright (and a member of the Cobden Club in London), this was an assignment after Gorrie's heart, though Wingfield doubted the wisdom of putting a man "only too prone to plunge into politics and questions of administration" to chair such a body. From the accounts of its sessions, it was virtually a one-man show. Gorrie examined all the witnesses, delivered a marathon summing-up, and wrote the final report. He told Chesson:

> I send you by this mail the first Report of a Commission based on the free trade principles which has ever been carried on in the West Indies. I rather flatter myself upon it, as when we began there was not a soul on the Board who sympathized with me or wished success to the movement inaugurated by the Governor. In the end I got them all to agree to the Report (making concessions of course) . . . I have recommended: – 1. The abolition of all export taxes. 2. Placing immigration of coolies on the basis of the planters paying for them directly in place of by taxation. 3. Making useful recommendations in connection with Trinidad as an entrepot and especially taking off import taxes on horses and cattle so as to improve inter-West Indian trade. 4. The abolition of import taxes on food and necessities of life.'

These recommendations amounted to a radical change in the whole tax structure of the colony.[21]

Although Robinson praised Gorrie for having conducted the enquiry "with singular acumen and signal ability", the merchants united in their attack on his report. They got up a petition against it, signed by 1,952 persons "representing the unanimous opinion of all classes of the community having a stake in the Colony"; in fact, as C.A. Harris of the Colonial Office correctly noted, it was "really a petition of merchants and planters only; it has no value as an expression of popular opinion". The petitioners argued, among other things, that the lower classes were prosperous and well able to bear indirect taxes in the form of duties on imported food and other necessities. When Robinson asked the deputation presenting the petition why more merchants and planters had not testified before the Commission, they answered that Gorrie as chairman "cross-examined" the witnesses who disagreed with him: "The Chief Justice so very evidently showed that he was an ardent free trader, that he took up one side of the question which it was no use for anyone to combat with." The minutes of the evidence suggest that this accusation was substantially true.[22]

Most of the Commission's recommendations were shelved. The united hostility of the Legislative Council, the planters and the merchants was too much for Robinson to combat. In addition, antagonism between Robinson and Gorrie developing early in 1887 made the governor less than enthusiastic to get the measures implemented. The three officials eventually told to draw up legislation to implement its main recommendations, knowing Robinson's real views, reported that they doubted the expediency of changing the tariff. Robinson asked the Commissioners in 1889 whether, in view of the opposition, they would adhere to the report; in the absence of Gorrie, who was in Britain on leave, they resolved with one dissenting vote that the time was not opportune for carrying out their original recommendations. No doubt Gorrie's strong personality and bullying tactics had got them to sign a report which contained much that they disliked. The only change to result from the Commission was that the duties on imported flour and rice were abolished on the direct instructions of the Secretary of State.[23]

It was probably inevitable that an overwhelming personality like Gorrie should come into conflict with Robinson, himself a strong governor. A Conservative, he certainly found Gorrie's radical brand of Liberalism antipathetic. There can be no doubt that Robinson's life was made more difficult by the constant disputes and controversies in which his Chief Justice became involved. Moreover, he was thought to resent Gorrie's political activities, and his evident popularity with the people. As an editor put it, with some hyperbole, Trinidad presented "an unusual spectacle; that of a competitive arena where two rival administrations contend for supremacy in the persons of two colonial officers; one, the Governor, duly accredited by the Crown for the purpose of administering the Government; the other, the Judge who appointed himself to the position". A year later the same editor wrote: "People are beginning to ask seriously whether Sir J. Gorrie is simply the Chief Justice of the Colony or whether he does not hold besides some secret commission which entitles him in so many things to supersede H.E. the Governor in his functions." Robinson himself complained to the Secretary of State that

> there can be no doubt . . . that the administration of this Government has been rendered extremely difficult by Sir John Gorrie's improper and unwarrantable interference in executive matters and by his criticisms from the Bench not only of Ordinances on the statute book but of Ordinances under the actual consideration of the Legislature.

The *European Mail* knew its readers would see the point of its announcement in the summer of 1889: "Sir William Robinson has gone to the United States, Chief Justice Gorrie has come to the United Kingdom. The Peace of the World is thus assured, Bismarck need not trouble."[24]

Gorrie was active in several political and social enterprises. He was chairman of the committee to organize celebrations for the Queen's Jubilee in 1887. His programme – fireworks, religious services, a breakfast for the poor, treats for city children, a banquet and ball, and a sports meeting – seems innocuous enough. But, like nearly everything he was involved in, it provoked indignation. Some prominent citizens disassociated themselves from the official celebrations, ostensibly because they wanted a more permanent memorial than "mere eating and drinking" and because they claimed to believe that the sports meeting would encourage unruly and indecent behaviour from the city's riff-raff, but more likely because any movement led by Gorrie was by definition objectionable. The following year he took part in another Jubilee, the Jubilee of Emancipation (August 1, 1888). There were two rival groups organizing celebrations. One consisted of young black and mixed-race 'radicals', the other mainly of established merchants and professionals, both white and mixed-race. Each group planned a dinner for the night of August 1, and there was much ill feeling between the two. Gorrie's sympathies were with the young radicals, and he had promised to speak at their dinner, but the governor expected all the top public servants to attend the rival function which was seen as the 'official' banquet. The Chief Justice solved the problem by dining at the 'official' dinner, then slipping out and going to the other banquet. He was said to be one of only two white men present (the other was Philip Rostant, a liberal French Creole journalist who was one of his strongest allies), and he replied at great length to a toast in his honour.[25]

What, he asked, was the object of emancipation? Not to make the ex-slaves saints, nor to revolutionize society. The abolitionists had wanted to turn the slaves into a free and independent peasantry, equal before the law, and having the same chance to better themselves as everyone else. This had been achieved, for West Indian blacks were now a free and, he said pointedly, very independent peasantry. Blacks were in every walk of life; they were farmers, artisans, clergymen, lawyers, clerks, jurors; in Barbados there was a 'coloured' Chief Justice dispensing justice to white and black alike. This speech was greeted enthusiastically by the audience, but, needless to say, among other circles it was considered imprudent. The *Port of Spain Gazette* thought that Gorrie had merely confirmed what everyone knew: that he was first and last an antislavery man, a protégé of Exeter Hall. But was it possible for an Exeter Hall man, who saw a slave in every black man and a persecutor in every white, an oppressor in every rich man and a victim in every poor person, to dispense impartial justice?[26]

This argument – that Gorrie's strong social and political views distorted his administration of justice – was joined to the claim that his actions and statements tended to divide the society. A newspaper correspondent rejected the notion that a judge should be a political reformer or a crusader in non-judicial causes. In fact, Gorrie had raised the spectacle "of division being sown broadcast between the different classes in the Colony". His political principles were "suspect" and his utterances on the bench were unjudicial and divisive. Did the Chief Justice consider it nothing, asked the editor, "to inflame a peaceful community with the fire of angry contention and bitter dangerous division"? [27]

To the ordinary people of the colony, and the black or mixed-race professionals and journalists who tried to speak for them, Gorrie was protector and guardian of their rights. He was the first judge since Chief Justice Scotland in the emancipation period who became clearly identified in their mind with the defence of their interests; and as early as 1887, he had become an authentic popular hero. As an editor friendly to him put it: "The humble individual who feels that an advantage is being taken of him by a wealthy man, tells his powerful antagonist, much to his terror: 'Do as you please but THE JUDGE is there'". When he was under attack in the middle of 1887, his supporters composed a ballad, "The Good and Righteous Judge", and had it printed and sold on the streets. "With some doubt and shame-facedness", Gorrie sent this to the Colonial Office through the governor to indicate the kind of popular support he enjoyed:

> All you who have the ears to hear and brain to understand,
> Come listen to Judge Gorrie's praises the wisest in the land,
> He likes the poor to get their right, the rich he does not fear;
> He is the greatest blessing of this great jubilee year.
>
> Before time law was very bad, and justice very sad,
> But he has changed that sort of thing out here in Trinidad.
> The poor man now can get his rights, as well as can the rich,
> And dollars do not dazzle, their sight does not bewitch.
>
> Judge Gorrie's praises let us sing, long may he flourish here,
> To give the poor their rights law, so strict so right and clear.
> May ill betide his enemies, we wish it from our heart,
> And may they not prevent the Judge from playing his great part.[28]

On many occasions, Gorrie was the centre of demonstrations of popular affection which alarmed and annoyed the propertied classes and their spokesmen: " 'Ah we Judge', as Mr [*sic*] Gorrie is affectionately termed by the riff-raff of the other islands, who have immigrated to Trinidad", was enthusiastically greeted when he moved around the island on judicial or other business. At Diego Martin, he and Justice Lumb received "an ovation from a noisy crowd". At Oropọuche in southern Trinidad, where he heard several contract cases brought against a prominent landowner, he was welcomed with cheers, firing of guns, flag-waving and shouts of "Papa Judge! Mi-li! Mi-li!" (Creole for "Look (at) him!") His sojourn in the village was celebrated by drum dances and popular rejoicings. When he visited the remote southern village of Siparia, people turned out *en masse* to greet him with flags and gun salutes. He gathered the 'old heads' together, his private secretary translating (into Creole, and perhaps Spanish), and advised them on agricultural and other matters: "All listened as children would to a respected father."[29] In his last years in Trinidad, this popular affection and respect were to grow until, by his death in 1892, he had attained the stature of a true folk hero.

The Opposition Organizes

Organized opposition to the Chief Justice first developed only four months after his arrival around the issue of whether the Supreme Court should be reduced from three to two judges. It will be recalled that at the time of his appointment, the Colonial Office had announced its intention not to fill the next vacancy on the grounds that the volume of business did not justify three judges. In May 1886 Justice Fitzgerald retired and the local Bar was faced with the prospect of a Court consisting of Gorrie and one junior colleague. The result was a memorial "from Members of the English Bar" in Trinidad praying for the retention of the third judge. The memorial argued that where there was a Chief Justice and only one other judge, the former would always have the decisive vote, and appeals from decisions of the Chief Justice sitting alone would be worthless; moreover, the possibility of the Chief Justice being overruled by the other two judges had "moral and legal" value. The Colonial Office had no difficulty in recognizing this memorial as a move against Gorrie. "No doubt Sir J. Gorrie's unpopularity with a weak bar whom he does not spare accentuates their objection to a two-Judge Court", wrote Wingfield. At this juncture, the Office saw no reason to reverse its decision not to appoint a third judge.[30]

When the decision to abolish the second puisne judgeship was announced in the Legislative Council, Thomas Finlayson, an unofficial, moved that "the unofficial members . . . being of opinion that three judges are absolutely necessary for the satisfactory administration of justice", should request the Secretary of State to reconsider, on the understanding that the Council would vote the salary of a third judge. It is worth pointing out that this motion came at a time of depression in the sugar industry when the planters and their spokesmen were calling for retrenchment and reductions in the colonial establishment. The Colonial Office, however, was unmoved, and informed the Council that the Secretary of State was unable to reconsider his decision in view of the amount of judicial business and the need for retrenchment.[31]

The opposition's next move was to organize a petition from the Chamber of Commerce. It urged the necessity for a proper Court of Appeal: "The present system practically renders appeal nugatory, as in cases tried before the Chief Justice it leaves supreme power in his hands." It further advised that a Court of Appeal should be constituted by the Trinidad judge who did not hand down the original decision being appealed against, and one or more judges from another colony – "in face of recent decisions in the Supreme Court of the Island seriously affecting commercial interests".

This petition was presented to the Council in May 1887. A lively debate ensued, in which Gatty (who sat *ex officio*) directly attacked recent judicial rulings, or charges to juries, by Gorrie. Finlayson moved that the Council believed that the colony's judicial system was "unsatisfactory" and that "confidence" in the administration of justice had been impaired by the lack of a proper local appeal court. Robinson, presiding in the Council, managed to moderate the tone of the resolution so that it simply asked the Secretary of State to reconsider his decision not to appoint a third judge and expressed the view that no judicial system could be satisfactory without ready, inexpensive and efficient local appeals. In transmitting the resolution to the Colonial Office, Robinson made it clear that he supported the request for a third judge.[32]

Gorrie, not surprisingly, complained bitterly about the debate and especially about Gatty's speech, in which the Attorney-General had given "gross caricatures of the full and careful summings up which I invariably give" in referring to specific cases he had recently heard. "I have a right, Sir, to complain that the Attorney-General should attack me in this manner in Council where I cannot reply, and I especially complain that he should so grossly misrepresent the proceedings which take place in the court where he is public prosecutor." Gorrie believed that the Chamber memorial was motivated by recent cases in which he had ruled against two leading members, Edgar Tripp and Eugene Lange; "if I had decided in their favour they would probably have considered the present arrangements perfect". The men in the Colonial Office were clear that Gatty's remarks in the Council debate were improper, and the Secretary of State delivered a severe rebuke. But, faced with the unanimity of the governor, the Council and the Chamber of Commerce, they reluctantly agreed to appoint a second puisne judge even though they recognized that the desire to 'control' Gorrie was the main motive behind the agitation: "Sir J. Gorrie has some excellent judicial qualities", Herbert minuted, "and some abominable judicial and personal qualities. He will be a valuable C.J. and a valuable member of an Appeal Court of three." Once the third judge had been appointed, the judges were to take over the Petty Debt Court and (following a suggestion by Gorrie) to hold sittings in places other than Port of Spain and San Fernando.[33] Gorrie's opponents had won this round, though there is no evidence to suggest that he was against the appointment of a third judge, and he worked well with his two colleagues on the bench.

Soon after this episode, influential opponents in Trinidad were able to persuade a British MP with West Indian interests to ask a question in the House of Commons about Gorrie. Baden Powell asked:

> whether the Chief Justice gave daily audience in his chambers to from 20 to 40 persons coming to him for advice in regard to grievances and difficulties upon which he might ultimately have to adjudicate in Court; whether a majority of the persons seeking audience were intending litigants; whether [the Secretary of State] was aware of dissatisfaction being manifested in Trinidad at the action of the Chief Justice; and whether such action was customary or had the approval of the Secretary of State.

Holland replied as follows:

> I am informed that some statements to this effect have appeared in a Trinidad newspaper; but I have no official information on the subject. I am not aware of such action on the part of the Chief Justice or of dissatisfaction having been manifested, but I will cause enquiry to be made. Such action on the part of a judge is not customary and would not have the approval of the Secretary of State.

The Colonial Office minutes which went into the preparation of this reply make it clear that the officials were contemplating, not a formal 'enquiry' of any kind, but merely an explanation from the Chief Justice.[34]

Recognizing that the question in the House and the reply amounted to a serious attack on his judicial practices, Gorrie moved to defend himself. He told the governor that he had simply directed ignorant petitioners, who often spoke no English, how to get their claims heard, and had permitted some to sue *in forma pauperis* as the law allowed (indeed, required), but had never 'advised' potential litigants in the corrupt way that his enemies implied: "I feel it keenly that the Secretary of State should not at once have repelled such an insinuation against a Chief Justice of my standing, and whose character for impartiality – acquired in the most difficult colonies it was possible to serve in, is dear to him." He explained his procedures in more detail: he told some of the people who petitioned him

> to go and consult an Attorney, directing some one that his remedy lies in the Magistrates' Court, authorizing another who pleads that he is too poor to fee a counsel, to appear for himself; and so on with the numerous applications which are constantly and rightfully and properly made to the head of the Supreme Court in a community as this . . . absolutely necessary for the ends of justice, and which I intend to continue so long as I am here.

In a private letter to Wingfield, Gorrie explained that he had spent at least two days a week during the court vacation dealing with petitioners who complained that they could not get justice:

> Of course, I need not say there is no advising of possible litigants in the corrupt sense which was basely insinuated in the Question, but the disposal of complaints concerning administration of justice, and the removal of impediments when such exist to cases being brought before the Courts. It is a most useful and necessary work where so many of the people are unlettered rustics, speaking the French and Spanish patois, or the Hindustani, and the reason for there being goodly numbers of such Petitioners is simply that . . . the course of justice in regard to that class of H.M.'s subjects had practically been stayed under [my] predecessor.[35]

These explanations were repeated (and developed) in a much longer 'official' reply which Gorrie had printed and widely circulated in Trinidad. He ended this elaborate production with a passionate declaration:

> I will never drive any suppliant harshly from my doors, and the poorer and the more ignorant they are, and the less they know of the English tongue and English ways the greater will be their claims upon me to be treated with consideration . . . I have seen in another West Indian Colony [Jamaica] what is the bitter fruit of refusing justice to the people, and while I live I will strive in order that no responsibility of the kind shall ever lie at my door.

Gorrie's explanations satisfied the Colonial Office, which thought that he had clearly refuted the accusations of corrupt practices; Herbert was moved to comment that "he is a good and just judge".[36]

Gorrie also tried to mobilize support in Britain. He wrote to Chesson, sending him a copy of his printed defence, which he also intended to send "to all the newspapers in the West Indies and to a good few at home", and asking his friend to write "a well stated paragraph" in his defence for the British press. Chesson was also requested to send copies of his defence (and related papers) to "any of our friends of the Aborigines Protection Society whose esteem one would not like to lose and to show them that I am still fighting the good fight although now somewhat grizzled and grey". Gorrie asked Chesson for advice on further action, namely, whether sympathetic MPs should be requested to ask another question in the House, so that the 'slur' cast on his good name by the episode in Parliament might be removed. Even more influential friends were canvassed for advice, including Lord Derby, a former Secretary of State, who advised that no further parliamentary action was called for since he had been "fully justified" by the Colonial Office.[37]

When the text of the question in the House and the reply was telegraphed out to Trinidad, Gorrie's enemies made the most of it. They interpreted the reply to be a promise of a formal enquiry into his judicial practices, and produced a petition ostensibly from the Chamber of Commerce calling for "a full, perfect, and independent inquiry by some legal Commissioners" appointed by the Secretary of State and charged with a wide-ranging investigation into the whole administration of justice in the colony. This petition was presented to the Council by Frederick Warner, one of the lawyer unofficial members; but Robinson directed the official members to vote against it being allowed to "lie on the table". He did so for two reasons: he had not received word from the Secretary of State that a formal enquiry of any kind was contemplated, and he knew that the petition emanated from a meeting of only eight persons, five of whom had recently had adverse judgements in the Supreme Court, and was therefore "biased, premature, and unworthy of consideration". The five litigants were named in *Public Opinion*, a paper edited by Gorrie's ally Philip Rostant, and details of the judgements against 'The Five' provided.[38] This was a rebuff, but the opposition quickly produced a second Chamber of Commerce petition, this time addressed to the Secretary of State. The new petition repeated the earlier request for a full and independent enquiry into all aspects of the administration of justice in Trinidad. According to *Public Opinion*, both petitions had emanated from "secret conclaves" from which journalists were excluded.[39]

When the second Chamber petition appeared, Gorrie's allies led by Rostant decided to mobilize their support. This is how Rostant described what followed:

> As soon as it became known to the general public that 'THE FIVE' were again conspiring, a general cry of indignation, such as had never before been known in Trinidad, burst forth from every part of the town, from every class of the population of Port of Spain, and from the centre to every part of the island . . . The office of this paper [*Public Opinion*] was invaded by indignant citizens calling on the Editor to take the lead . . . A counter petition to the Secretary of State was at once drafted . . . Then was seen a sight never to be forgotten by those who witnessed it; hundreds of volunteers crowding the office of *Public Opinion*, either to sign the petition or take away the lists to have them signed. Some even volunteered to take them to the country districts, joyfully spending time and money in furtherance of the good work. At every moment messengers came to the office with the lists that they had filled and taking new ones to be signed. Of course it was not to be expected that at such short notice, the country districts could be well represented, but

> wherever the railroad reached, the volunteers managed to get a large number of signatures . . . It was indispensable that the petition should be closed and presented to the governor in time to be sent by the same mail that carried the [Chamber] one . . . This under any other circumstances would have been considered an utter impossibility; but the enthusiasm of the population conquered every difficulty. Lists of signatures were actually handed to the Deputation appointed to present the petition to H.E. the Governor, whilst they were waiting in the Council Room to be introduced into the Governor's office! For several days after that new lists continued to come in so that the number of signatures is really much greater than those attached to the petition [5,061].[40]

The 'No-Inquiry Petition', as it came to be known, was addressed to the Secretary of State from "inhabitants of Port of Spain, San Fernando, and the neighbourhood thereof". The petitioners had "learned with great concern that an attempt is being made, by a very small section of the inhabitants of Port of Spain, to inspire a feeling of distrust in the administration of justice in the island" and felt bound to assure the Secretary of State "that the most unbounded confidence exists throughout the length and breadth of the island in the administration of justice by the Supreme Court presided over by the present Chief Justice". The petitioners affirmed

> that since the arrival of Sir John Gorrie not a single instance can be adduced of miscarriage of justice, whilst the records of the Court abound in cases of rights adjusted, wrongs redressed, and justice, in general, dispensed, with a degree of fairness and impartiality which commands the utmost respect and admiration. Wherefore your petitioners most humbly pray that you will be pleased to take no heed of the clamour that is raised by interested parties against one of the most upright and conscientious Judges that have ever adorned the Bench of any of the Colonies of Great Britain.[41]

This petition, got up in "a remarkably short space of time by a mere handful of gentlemen, some of whom I do not even know", as Gorrie told Chesson, was indeed proof of "the universality of the support which I so cordially receive". He sent Chesson a detailed analysis of the 5,061 signatures, and noted:

> the largest number from any individual class is that of the Cocoa Planters [1,420] who are the backbone of the Island. If the getters up of the Petition had had time to go to the country it would have been signed by ten times this number, but they wished to show at once how angry and disgusted the people were with the attempt to throw doubt on my impartiality.

Predictably, Gorrie's detractors worked hard to discredit the No-Inquiry Petition and its signatories. The *Port of Spain Gazette* claimed (probably with some justice) that the 1,420 "cocoa planters" were not the wealthier and educated proprietors but "ignorant labourers" who had managed to acquire small plots of land; the 90 merchants were not the respectable members of the Chamber of Commerce; the 540 householders did not belong to the educated classes. The *New Era* asked how the signatures were collected, and answered that canvassers misled the people, making them believe that the poor would materially benefit if Gorrie remained in office. Of the 90 'merchants' said to have signed, not a single Englishman could be found to form part of the deputation to the governor; not one lawyer had signed. In sum, the vast majority of the signers were persons "whose names cannot bear the light of day".[42]

As the men in the Colonial Office considered the deluge of petitions, counter-petitions and related papers, Robinson expressed his concern (in a private letter to Wingfield headed by a rather plaintive note saying "please send out the other judge without delay") that

> matters are coming to a head here in regard to the C.J. and we shall have a serious row before long . . . He resembles the metaphorical 'Bull in a China Shop'. He wanted me to lay his case before the Legislative Council but I declined to do so as I did not intend to convert the Council Chamber into an arena for a free fight between himself and his detractors. I fancy he has been sailing pretty near the wind but on the other hand there is no doubt that the work of the Supreme Court has hitherto been disgracefully scamped.

The weight of the evidence seemed to be on Gorrie's side, and Wingfield was certainly correct when he wrote that: "An enormous majority of the inhabitants of Trinidad appreciate Sir John Gorrie's desire to do substantial justice." The Secretary of State replied that:

> Having received an explicit denial from the Chief Justice of the course of action impliedly attributed to him in the question . . . in the Commons, and having received no information supporting either the particular charge implied in that question, or the general allegations made in the . . . petition of the Chamber of Commerce which are contradicted by a counter-petition signed by over 5,000 persons, I see no reason for directing the enquiry desired by the Chamber of Commerce.[43]

This decision, which became known in Trinidad in November 1887, was a significant victory for Gorrie and his supporters and a set-back for the opposition. The episode made his opponents realize that he had influential support in Britain, and they did not resume their campaign for an enquiry into the administration of justice until 1891. But skirmishes between Gorrie and his influential detractors, especially the unofficial members of the Council, continued.

In 1888 the Council debated an ordinance on agricultural contracts which Gorrie strongly disapproved of. While holding court in San Fernando, he was reported in the press as having said: "There are contractors here. I may tell them that the Legislature is trying to pass an Ordinance by which these [contract] cases will be tried by County Magistrates and they will be prevented from coming to the Supreme Court where they can get justice. Let them look to it." These remarks were brought up in the Council by G.T. Fenwick, an unofficial member, who thought that they were "calculated to have a most injurious effect upon the community by creating a serious mistrust in the Magistrates . . . and bringing this Council, this Government into serious contempt". The governor simply expressed disbelief that Gorrie could have uttered such words in court and stated that he expected him to deny the newspaper report. He did no such thing; instead, he admitted that he had made the remarks "incidentally and

Sir John Gorrie as Chief Justice of Trinidad and Tobago in 1889
(From *European Mail*, August13, 1892, p. 23)

conversationally", and insisted that he had the right to make his views known on a piece of legislation which proposed to alter the jurisdiction of his Court. Gorrie rejected Robinson's view that his words reflected contempt for the Legislature: "I have seen, perhaps more closely than Your Excellency, how questions connected with the administration of justice lie at the very foundation of such Colonies as these, and I think I showed my respect for the Legislative Council by endeavoring to prevent the passing of such an Ordinance." Indeed, he had cause to thank Fenwick for the publicity he had given to the remarks.[44]

Robinson took this skirmish more seriously than it perhaps deserved, sending all the documents on the subject to the Colonial Office "as it is possible that a question may be asked in the House of Commons". But the Office declined to take fright. Wingfield noted in a resigned tone: "Only the Chief Justice posing once more as the black man's friend and puffing his own justice shop. I should hope the House of Commons would have something better to do than to take up this little row". The Secretary of State declined to express any opinion on the episode, and no question was asked in the Commons.[45] The substantive issue – the proposed ordinance on agricultural contracts – continued to preoccupy Gorrie in 1889 and subsequently.

After three years in Trinidad, Gorrie's actions had made him both a popular hero and the *bête noire* for most of the influential and affluent persons in the colony. The more educated sectors of the community had become divided between supporters and opponents; the former could mobilize impressive numbers of adherents, while the latter could count on the main organized groups in the colony. Gorrie's opponents had suffered set-backs in 1887-88, but they were well entrenched, and not without considerable support in Britain. He had survived the two Chamber petitions of 1887, memorials from the Bar and the Medical Board, protests from the police and the Army, questions in the House of Commons and the local Legislature. As 1889 began, he became involved in the affairs of Tobago when that island was linked to Trinidad and he became the Chief Justice of the united colony, and Tobago controversies were of great importance to him in 1889-91. He was also preoccupied in these years with issues surrounding agriculture, land and labour. By 1891, the opposition was ready to resume their campaign for an enquiry into his administration of justice in Trinidad and Tobago, and this time they succeeded.

Towards the end of 1888 Gorrie suffered a devastating blow in his private life with the sudden death of his youngest daughter, Jeanie. His children did not join him in Trinidad when he arrived early in 1886, and it was not until late in 1887 that he could tell Chesson: "I have got my family out and feel like a new man again. It far more than counter-balances any discomfort at finding I have sleepless and most bitter foes." His family consisted of his two unmarried daughters, Minnie (Marion) and Jeanie (Isobel – 'Charlie' – was in Fiji with her husband), and his son Malcolm, a law student at the Middle Temple who temporarily abandoned his legal studies to join his father and act as his unofficial private secretary. After only a year in Trinidad, Jeanie died at the age of 22 of one of those sudden infections (probably dysentery of some sort) which were so common in the nineteenth century tropical empire. Her funeral was attended by virtually everyone of importance in the island, headed by the governor, and the streets of Port of Spain were lined with ordinary people as the procession passed by.

Even allowing for some exaggeration in the elaborate report published in Rostant's *Public Opinion,* the attendance at the funeral, and the crowd's presence, must be seen as impressive testimony both of the popular affection for Gorrie, and of his standing as a private man in Trinidad's small educated community. Jeanie was described as a kind and warm-hearted girl, "bright, graceful and accomplished", deeply religious, who had been active in temperance work while living in London in 1886-87, and was involved in religious and charitable work in Trinidad. "Every Sunday evening she used to gather round her at Errol Park [the Gorrie house outside Port of Spain] as many of the children of the neighboring village as she could get together and there she held an impromptu Sunday School class". The "pity and sadness" of her sudden death struck everyone, and even the editor of the *New Era*, no friend of Gorrie, described her funeral as "an impressive display and a striking proof of the high and public appreciation of the merits of the Chief Justice. It was a general assent on the part of the community to mourn with him who has a common sympathy for all sorts and conditions of men." After an impressive service in the Anglican Cathedral, where the family seems to have worshipped despite their Presbyterian roots, Jeanie was buried in a small consecrated ground, reserved for senior public officers and their relatives, in the middle of the Botanic Gardens of Port of Spain. Here a simple granite cross marks her grave, surrounded by tall trees and lush vegetation. Her father expressed his grief in two moving poems on his child's life and death. Jeanie's death, coming only four years after her mother's, must have seemed to him part of the heavy price he had paid for his many years of service in the colonies.[46]

CHAPTER EIGHT

'That cane the Judge will grind it': Tobago, 1889-92

On January 1, 1889, the Order in Council uniting Trinidad and Tobago came into effect. Though union was not generally welcomed by the planters and merchants of the smaller island, the mass of Tobagonians probably hoped for tangible benefits. Soon after, the Chief Justice of Trinidad, now Chief Justice of the united colony, came to hold the first session of the Supreme Court of Trinidad and Tobago in Scarborough, the smaller island's capital. Gorrie's record in Trinidad made it likely that his arrival might alleviate some of the difficulties faced by ordinary Tobagonians in their struggle to survive in an impoverished and declining sugar economy.

Tobago and the Chief Justice

Tobago's sugar industry had been in trouble at least since the 1830s. Its limited, hilly terrain was far from ideally suited to extensive sugar cultivation, and its planters, mostly absentees, faced the classic West Indian problems of soil impoverishment, primitive machinery and chronic indebtedness. These difficulties were aggravated by the emancipation of the labouring population, by the commercial and financial crises of the late 1840s, and by a disastrous hurricane in 1847. Many ex-slaves withdrew from plantation labour; but most remained partly or wholly dependent on the estates, typically combining wage labour with the cultivation of canes on a portion of estate land under a metayer (sharecropping) agreement, with the resulting sugar divided equally between metayer and landowner. This metayage (or metairie) system spread rapidly after the late 1840s and allowed Tobago's planters to keep their estates in production and maintain exports without any substantial decline. The great advantage of metayage was that it allowed estate-based production to continue with only a small outlay for wages, a critical point for Tobago's chronically cash-poor planters.[1]

Relations between plantation management and labour were far from cordial after emancipation, and most labourers/metayers lived in poverty. Wages were low, and often irregular. Metayage itself, though it became entrenched in the island, was a fertile source of conflict between metayers and planters; the former complained of long delays in grinding their canes which caused them to lose money. As early as 1850, a magistrate reported that sometimes these cases were so flagrant that "heart-burning and distrust" made the metayers "unsettled and erratic". High taxes, especially taxes on small land holdings and on farm animals, were another difficulty, as well as very limited access to land for independent cultivation before the 1880s.[2] Labourers and metayers protested these conditions with strikes in 1846-48, with a near-riot against the land tax in Scarborough in 1852, and with riots in Roxborough in 1876 caused mainly by chronic disputes over wages, wage stoppages, and the truck system.[3] The notion that relations between planters and labourers/metayers were idyllic before Gorrie's arrival was a convenient myth, put out by his detractors in 1889-90.

Metayage kept the Tobago sugar estates limping along until the 1880s. But the crisis of 1884-85, caused by the dramatic fall of prices for crude sugar on a British market glutted with subsidized European beet, proved a virtual death-knell for the island's export sugar industry. The collapse of Gillespie Bros., a British firm on which over half of the plantations had depended for credit and supplies, was the signal for a dramatic fall in Tobago land values and a wholesale turnover in estate ownership. Many estates were abandoned; others were sold to British, Barbadian, Trinidadian or Tobagonian speculators for the proverbial song. By the late 1880s, as a result, planter-labour relations were volatile; new owners tried to maximize profits in a depressed industry by altering the traditional customs which had governed the metayage system and by withdrawing 'privileges' long enjoyed by resident labourers, who tried to defend their 'rights' by whatever means were at hand. In 1888, for instance, the *Tobago News* complained that the labourers would not work, helped themselves to the planter's grass and timber without permission, stole his provisions and stock, and frequently "ridiculed and defied" their employers. The paper cited the Goldsborough estate as an example: here, "the result of the strained relationship between the parties is evidenced by the frequent rows, threats, and lawsuits which may, on any day, culminate in a serious rupture of the peace of the district".[4] Gorrie's entry into Tobago affairs, therefore, came at a time of economic depression and social disturbance, when traditional agrarian relationships were under challenge.

Gorrie regarded the union of Tobago with Trinidad as a golden opportunity for the economic and social rehabilitation of the smaller island, and as an extension of his own sphere of action. He insisted on going there in January 1889 to preside over a session of the Supreme Court, brushing aside the objection of L.G. Hay, Commissioner of Tobago, that the island's finances could not bear the expense: "I do not think that its finances will be improved, or its prosperity promoted, if the people of the island were not to be stirred out of their lethargy by seeing from the presence of the new Officers, Executive and Judicial, amongst them that the union is complete." Hay believed that his visit was unnecessary because the acting Chief Justice of St Lucia had held a court sitting in Scarborough in December 1888 (before union, Tobago had been part of the Windward Islands judicial system and had been periodically visited by the chief justices of those islands, of which St Lucia was one). But the island's only newspaper complained that a visit of less than three weeks, following a period of eight months with no court session, was grossly inadequate for the work to be done. Governor Sir William Robinson– now governor of the united colony – took Hay's line, and so, retroactively, did the Colonial Office; but the strong-willed Chief Justice was "rigid in his representations" that he should go in January 1889, and go he did.[5]

At the court sitting in January, several metayers brought actions *in forma pauperis* against their landowners, mostly for damages because their canes had not been ground, or not at the right time, and Gorrie ruled in their favour in most of the cases. As he had done in Trinidad, he interviewed suitors in his chambers to advise them whether they had good grounds for an action, and, if so, how to draw up their suits and apply for a waiver of court and solicitors' fees. According to a hostile source (the Tobago Planters' Club), the Chief Justice's conduct of one such metayer case – giving the defendant very short notice so that he was unable to marshall his evidence, granting permission to sue *in forma pauperis* without the proper formalities, the "clear displeasure" shown against the defendant, and the heavy damages awarded the plaintiff – generated "much expectation" among the people. "In many of these cases", the Planters' Club continued, "the case for the metayer or labourer was well known to be unfounded, and the results with the demeanour of the Judge became a great incitement to the people to bring cases before the same Judge."[6] It would be more correct to conclude that Gorrie's willingness to allow this kind of suit while waiving court fees and costs, his evident determination to listen to the metayers' grievances, and his refusal to be intimidated by the great men of the island, convinced many Tobagonians that they would at last receive justice from a colonial judge. As one metayer of the Goldsborough estate wrote to his employer, asking for his "half of suggar" which he believed was owed him: "Gurry will cool each and every one of us" when he came; "Sir Tobago Court House does draw nice green tea and if you want us to drink some wee will as soon as Judge Gurry come".[7]

The planters' response was predictable. Though their relations with their metayers and labourers had been unsettled since 1884, if not earlier, they pretended that the latter had become disaffected and threatening as if overnight. "Suddenly, and indeed as if by magic", intoned the *Tobago News*, "there has sprung up a class antagonism that seriously imperils the peaceful relationship hitherto existing between employers and employees. Simultaneously with the . . . advent of Sir J. Gorrie . . . the labourers nearly all over the Island have become rude, boisterous and domineering." His advent gave rise to a rumour that he had come to order the planters to pay much higher wages, though the editor had to admit that Gorrie had never actually suggested such a thing; nevertheless, "his name is now commonly employed by the working classes to employers and planters as a threat to enforce their insolent and unreasonable demands".[8]

Robinson was probably aware that much of the disaffection among Tobagonian labourers at the start of 1889 was due to the belief that union meant that Trinidad wage rates would automatically be introduced in the smaller island. This belief had nothing to do with Gorrie's visit. According to the Tobago correspondent for *Public Opinion,* it was fostered by Tobagonians resident in Trinidad, who told their countrymen back home that "annexation means one and the same rate of wages for labourers in both countries and that they must not work for less".[9] In Trinidad male indentured Indians were guaranteed by law a minimum wage of 25 cents (about one shilling) a day; the average daily wage in Tobago was eight pence. Hay, and other officials, were well aware of the popular delusion about wages. Nevertheless, when Robinson visited the island in February 1889, he reported privately to the Colonial Office:

> The people are most unquiet – and Sir John Gorrie has done much harm there – I met 3 or 400 of them and you know what they are – they are clamouring for *Trinidad Wages* which Sir John Gorrie said they ought to get. They also said the 'Planters [are] united to oppress them'. This is a Sir John Gorrie phrase . . . This man has been little less than a curse in this Colony.

At the Scarborough Court House, Robinson addressed a large crowd of "country people . . . whose unblushingly rude and boisterous demeanour were [*sic*] noticed and much commented on".[10]

Such demonstrations of 'rudeness' and 'insolence' from the rural proletariat were alarming to the island's planters, only too well aware of the mounting resentment against their recent policies. An incident at Studley Park estate, where some metayers with grievances against the new owner about charges for grinding their canes apparently behaved badly in a meeting with the owner and the local magistrate, heightened these fears. It afforded a pretext for sending a gun-boat to patrol the island, the "time-honoured panacea for labour troubles", as a Colonial Office clerk cynically noted. Despite the gun-boat, the 'Gorrie Mania' continued throughout February 1889.[11]

The 'agitation' in Tobago in the first two months of 1889 convinced both Hay and Robinson that Gorrie must be stopped from returning to hold the next session of the court due in May; another judge should go instead. Quiet persuasion was first attempted, and Gorrie, rather surprisingly, seems to have agreed; but when he heard of the incident at Studley Park, he changed his mind, and decided that far from waiting until May, he should proceed to Tobago at once:

> In place of pledging myself, according to Your Excellency's unheard of request, not to go to Tobago in May, I now, as Chief Justice of the Colony, advise that the legal question [the metayers' grievances at Studley Park] should be put to rest at once, and by myself, in whom the people have proclaimed their confidence as a Judge.

Gorrie announced that he would embark immediately for Tobago to hold a special court; he continued:

> I have no doubt whatever that this storm in a tea-cup . . . will be allayed in five minutes so soon as my arrival is known. Depend on it, Sir, that legal questions are much better settled by Judges than by men-of-war . . . If, after this offer, Your Excellency should delay, until the feelings of the people get exasperated by seeing their canes spoilt after all their labour, I: at least, will know where to place the responsibility.

Not surprisingly, Robinson responded to this "dictatorial and offensive" letter by refusing to permit the Chief Justice to hold a special court.[12]

By this time, the men in the Colonial Office were close to deciding that Gorrie would have to be stopped from returning to Tobago. Edward Wingfield believed that his

> negrophilism run mad makes him a serious danger and if he goes again to Tobago and lets his tongue run in the usual reckless style there may

> be bloodshed. I think he ought to be told that . . . one of the other Judges should hold the next sitting of the Court in Tobago (if he insists on going it may have to be considered whether steps should be taken for his removal from office).

Other senior officials concurred.[13] Their hand was strengthened by a petition signed by 31 'inhabitants of Tobago' requesting that Gorrie should not hold the next court session in the island. Most of the signers were merchants, planters and estate managers; many had just received adverse judgements in suits brought against them by metayers and others. Hay reported to Robinson that "a feeling of much anxiety prevails among the more respectable and order-loving classes here lest the Chief Justice should return to Tobago before the effects of his last visit have been obliterated from the minds of the people and thus cause much harm to ensue."[14]

Armed with this petition, and with the strongly anti-Gorrie representations of both Hay and Robinson, the Colonial Office took the extraordinary step of authorizing the governor to introduce an ordinance into the Trinidad and Tobago legislature providing that the sittings of the Supreme Court in Tobago should be held by one of the puisne judges, ostensibly on the grounds of economy (the salary of a puisne judge, which would have to be paid from Tobago funds for the period he was in the island, was slightly less than that of the Chief Justice). In a confidential letter, the Secretary of State warned the governor against encouraging any idea that the ordinance had been introduced to keep Gorrie out of Tobago. This, of course, was *pro forma*; there could be no doubt in any quarter that the sole purpose of Ordinance 7 of 1889, which was duly enacted, was precisely that. It immediately became known as the 'Gorrie Exclusion Bill'.[15]

The Chief Justice fought back. He made the obvious point that the ordinance was aimed against him personally and that it was universally so regarded in both islands. To remove the pretext of economy, he offered to forgo the difference between his own salary and that of a puisne judge for his visits to Tobago. Recognizing that the ordinance, if allowed by the Queen, would represent a major setback not only to his own position but also to the people of Tobago, he obtained leave to travel to London and present his case for disallowance in person. Arriving in Britain in May 1889, he saw the

Secretary of State, Lord Knutsford, at the end of that month, and was told that the latter would "take no action" on the ordinance for the time being.[16]

In a long and impassioned letter, Gorrie argued the case against allowing the ordinance. He had, he wrote, always stood for impartial justice for

> all races and conditions of the subjects of the Crown . . . But no one who knows the strong prejudices which have so much vitality, especially in old slave colonies, but must be aware that the man who attempts such a work must necessarily expose himself to attacks proportional in bitterness to the very success of his work. The attacks are not made because they believe the Judge to be unjust, but they are made by persons whose material interests are involved, because they dislike justice, and because they hold the pernicious theory that it is not good that coolies, negroes, natives or whatever the humbler class may be should receive the same measure of justice as they themselves.

He argued that colonial judges deserved, and needed, the support of the crown – in other words, the Colonial Office – as much as any executive officer, and should never be lightly censured. He appealed to the Secretary of State "not to weaken my hands in the discharge of duties which are sufficiently heavy and responsible in themselves".[17]

While in London, Gorrie also wrote an elaborate rebuttal of statements made against him by Commissioner Hay. In his view, Hay was merely the mouthpiece for the local magnates who objected to the great principle he was "teaching the people of these Islands . . . that there is no privileged class before the law". This letter included accounts by Gorrie of his 'conversations' with various groups of Tobago labourers and peasants (Hay had accused him of encouraging disaffection among them). He had advised one group of Roxborough estate workers to "get a bit of land for yourselves and so not be dependent on the estates", advice which derived from observing how the labourers of Antigua and St Kitts were "half-starved" when they had no gardens of their own. Another 'conversation' was with women of the Roxborough district,

> not about wages or strikes, but one much more important to the future of the West Indies, viz, the number of married persons in the village

> compared to those who were living according to the West Indian custom of concubinage. I explained to them how children were prejudicially affected after the death of their parents where there had been no marriage, and urged the duty of marriage upon them all.[18]

The men in the Colonial Office were exasperated by the tone of the several letters from Gorrie on Tobago, letters which, one of them wrote, were "those of a reckless man with a strong bias against the executive government and a readiness, if not a desire, to foment discontent amongst the more ignorant classes". But Knutsford took a balanced view of the issues. He decided to advise disallowance of the ordinance, hoping that the whole episode would put Gorrie "on his guard for the future".[19] It seems likely that Gorrie's letters, as well as the audience with him, helped to change Knutsford's mind. It was a victory for the Chief Justice, and it meant that he would be able to return to Tobago and hold a further session of the Supreme Court there in February 1890.

Accusations and Petitions

During the period January to July 1890, 196 cases were filed in the Tobago Supreme Court; this contrasted with 124 for the six years before January 1889. About 150 cases relating to metayers' grievances were filed in January-February 1890 alone, nearly all after Gorrie had arrived in the island. There were so many cases that he was forced to stop new suits about two weeks before his departure. Most of the metayer cases were claims for damages for failure to grind canes, some dating back a few years but most relating to recent crops. Court fees were waived for most of these actions, though no affidavits of poverty were filed; the Chief Justice simply made a 'general order' that fees were to be suspended in these cases.[20] This outpouring of actions by metayers – what Gorrie's enemies called "the rush to the Court" – reflected the resentment built up over many years, and especially since 1884, against sharp practice by planters against their labourers and sharecroppers, as well as the latter's recognition that at last there was a judge prepared to give them a serious hearing. Gorrie found for the plaintiffs in most of these cases and awarded damages, plus costs, against the defendants. It is noteworthy that most of the metayer cases were filed against a small group of planters who had acquired their estates since 1884.

A Tobago correspondent to the *Agricultural Reporter* of Barbados (probably R.B. Anderson, a proprietor who was defendant in several metayer cases heard in February 1890) described this court session as a "cataclysm", a "tornado of law". He claimed that planter defendants were given no chance to explain why metayers' canes were not ground, if that was the case: "Respectable witnesses were sneered at – jeered at – shouted at – and stamped at by the Judge." In the few cases lost by metayer plaintiffs, the Chief Justice refused to award costs, telling one counsel for the defendant that "he ought to be *ashamed* to ask for costs against a poor old man".[21]

In addition to the actions for damages for failing to grind metayers' canes, Gorrie also addressed the nature of the metayer's tenure, and this was the subject of his most famous Tobago ruling, *Franks* v *Anderson*, delivered in February 1890. Joseph Franks was a 73 year old metayer on Castara estate, recently purchased by R.B. Anderson. Born a slave on the same estate, Franks had been a metayer for 45 years and was also the estate carpenter. Anderson decided to charge rent for his provision ground (hitherto rent-free, one of the 'privileges' enjoyed by resident labourers), to stop his wages as carpenter, and finally to evict him from the estate by a simple notice to quit. Franks, emboldened no doubt by Gorrie's presence, sued Anderson for damages. Gorrie used his ruling in this action to make a general survey of the development of metayage in Tobago, stating: "If there is any soul of goodness in the Metairie [metayage] system it is because the number of metayers who have undertaken to grow sugar for themselves and the estates gives a value to the property, and becomes a source of credit by which sufficient means can be raised to tide over the out-of-crop season". In the key section of his ruling, Gorrie went on:

> If either the proprietor could cut short the arrangement by a notice to quit or the metayer could get rid of his obligations by a similar notice to the proprietor, the whole value of the system would be destroyed . . . If it be good for the proprietor to have his metayers assured to him for the purpose of raising money to work with, it is equally good for the

> metayer to have fixity of tenure, because otherwise there would be no inducement to him to pay out his labour and sweat upon another man's land without wages, and only on the precarious chance of reaping the sugar from a year or two's labour.

Gorrie ruled, therefore, that Anderson had no legal right to evict Franks from the portion of land he cultivated as a metayer by a simple notice to quit. When either party desired to terminate a metayer agreement, he would have to approach the Court for this to be done; neither could do so at will. Moreover, Anderson had no right to suddenly charge rent for Franks' provision ground, for this amounted to an arbitrary change in the metayer agreement, and could be legal only with mutual consent. Gorrie scornfully rejected Anderson's claim that Franks had consented:

> In those cases which frequently occur when consent is alleged on the part of one who is . . . in the power of another, or any very old or weak person, or anyone enfeebled by disease, or a very rustic and ignorant person . . . a Court of Law will take special care to be advised that the consent of such a person was perfectly free and unforced. Here the plaintiff is a man enfeebled by age and hard toil, born a slave and therefore receiving none of those advantages of education which the young people now may enjoy, having lived on the Castara estate all his life and naturally unwilling to leave it, unable to read or write, dominated by the pronounced character of the defendant . . . a man not distinguished for meekness or a desire to avoid lawsuits.

Ruling that Franks could not be evicted as a metayer or charged rent for his ground, and that he was entitled to back wages for his work as carpenter, Gorrie awarded him damages of £20 plus costs. Finally, he challenged the island's planters in these words:

> It is most lamentable to see the want of cultivation of this Island, and I cannot but fear it has occurred from the Courts not knowing their powers, or the various parties to the [metayer] contract being ignorant how to enforce their rights. I shall be prepared while in the Colony to hear applications from the proprietor or metayers of the defendant's estate or of any estate similarly situated.[22]

In thus ruling that the metayer enjoyed "fixity of tenure" with respect to the portion of estate land which he cultivated in canes, Gorrie fundamentally challenged Tobago's new, and far from secure, plantocracy. It was this ruling more than any other which led directly to the determined efforts to nullify his various decisions and pronouncements on metayage through the Tobago Metairie Commission.[23]

Though most of the cases before Gorrie in 1890 dealt with metayers' grievances, he also heard actions in which peasants claimed plots of land on the basis of long established customary occupation. For instance, he upheld Henry Quashie's suit against eviction from a plot in the Charlotteville area which he claimed to have occupied since 1847. These rulings caused almost as much disquiet as *Franks* v *Anderson*. One planter complained that after the Quashie case, the Charlotteville people seemed "to think they have been told they only have to squat on a piece of land anywhere, it did not matter much where, and they were provided for life, and were not to be disturbed ever after". Gorrie was accused of systematically encouraging casual squatters to set up frivolous claims to freehold titles. This charge was investigated by the Judicial Enquiry Commission in 1892. It noted that when persons complained to the Chief Justice that they had been dispossessed of land allegedly theirs, he directed the claim (if he thought it genuine) to be tried by application for certificate of title under the Real Property Ordinance. There was no proof that he advised people to apply for title without being first satisfied that the claim was made in good faith and with some plausible grounds. The Commission – by no means friendly towards Gorrie – accordingly acquitted him of this charge.[24]

The 1890 rulings provoked a spate of petitions from aggrieved litigants against the Chief Justice's doings in Tobago. Petitions for investigation and redress to the Queen in Council (*ie* the Privy Council) were sent by Anderson; by Alexander Davidson, an absentee owner, through his Tobago manager – none other than Anderson; and by 'Inhabitants of Tobago'. A fourth petition, addressed to the Secretary of State, was also from 'Inhabitants of Tobago'. As Wingfield noted, the first three petitions mixed up "matters which are for the Court of Appeal . . . with personal and not very definite charges against the Chief Justice". Gorrie himself dismissed the first two petitions to the Queen by explaining that all the cases involving Anderson had been dealt with in the Appeal Court "according to the ordinary procedures" and were in various stages of determination, and that Davidson had not authorized any petition on his behalf; Anderson had acted alone. The Colonial Office sent the first three petitions to the Council Office for its comments, *pro forma*, knowing that its answer to the request for investigation and redress would be negative.[25]

The fourth petition, addressed to Knutsford from 'Inhabitants of Tobago', asked for an enquiry into the administration of justice in Tobago by a commission of independent judges. This was answered by Gorrie in an immensely detailed reply, dated June 19, 1890; according to Robinson, he had one hundred copies printed and distributed. Of the 32 persons who signed this petition, 28, said Gorrie, were litigants against whom he had delivered judgements; some had appealed, "and are thus attacking a Judge pending the law suits". In a characteristic outburst, Gorrie wrote that if, "allowing myself to be intimidated by what took place last year [1889], and feeling afraid of the effect of these men's Petitions upon the mind of the Secretary of State, I had given judgement in favour of these so-called proprietors of Tobago, there would have been no Petitions". In fact, "it is scarcely possible to convey to an English mind the squalor of everything about the Island, so that the Secretary of State must not be misled by such words as 'proprietor', 'merchant' or 'planter'. I venture to say there are not six of those who sign the Petitions who could pay their passages to England."[26]

The petitioners had set out six major grievances against the Chief Justice. They claimed that his visit to Tobago had caused widespread disorder and disruption of work on the estates; that he interviewed and advised potential suitors in chambers; that he ignored the required procedures in waiving court and solicitors' fees; that he awarded unfairly heavy damages against planter defendants; that he had ignored past judicial opinions and rulings in his decision on *Franks* v *Anderson*; and that his actions had undermined the authority of the magistrates and their courts. Gorrie dealt with each. He acknowledged that his return to Tobago early in 1890 had been "an event" and that the people had shown their joy, but denied that work stopped in the countryside or that Scarborough was disorderly while the court was sitting:

"everything was as quiet as a Sunday". He did not deny that he interviewed potential suitors in chambers, as he had always done in Trinidad; instead, he indicated the nature of those interviews by a few examples taken from the clerk's notes:

> Judge: What is your complaint?
>
> Peasant: (Presents petition, which at a glance is seen to be a complaint that his canes were not manufactured into sugar for 1888)
>
> Judge: You don't say how much you have lost. What was the size of your allotment?
>
> Peasant: Two acres, Your Honour!
>
> (As this would give two hogsheads at least, equal to £16, Judge writes on Petition 'referred to Solicitor'.)
>
> Judge: Take this to Solicitor. He will make enquiries, and if summons necessary will move to shorten time of service, so that case be heard at this Sittings.
>
> [Peasant passes out at exit door while another enters.]
>
> Judge: Well, you are an old man – are you metayer?
>
> Peasant: No, yer Honour – me hab land of me own this fifty year.
>
> Judge: Well, what brings you here?
>
> Peasant: Missi Turpin says the land his, and he agoin to turn me out. Fifty 'ear, massa, me labour 'um. Oh, me massa!
>
> Judge: Have you been served with any written notice to quit?
>
> Peasant: No, but he come and say to we – must go.
>
> Judge: [After some explanation sends peasant to Sub-Registrar that he may make application for Certificate of Title under new Real Property Ordinance, Turpin to have special notice that he may enter caveat.]
>
> Two Women: We are labourers in town. We worked for Mr —— and he has not paid us. He owes us each £1.
>
> Judge: That is a matter for Magistrate's Court.

The Women: The Magistrate asks 5s. from each of us for the summons. We not paid our wages, how can we pay 5s.?

Judge: [Sends Memo to Magistrate, who writes in reply that under new District Court Ordinance the fees are 3s. for summonses and 2s. for hearing fee charged at the same time. Judge replies that matter can surely be taken under Master and Servants Act, and that where claim seems *bona fide* could suspend fee till case heard] The women go and get summons.

Judge [to next applicant]: Well, Madame, what have you to say?

Female Peasant: I got judgement from Judge Lewis October last. No got sugar.

Judge: What was name of case? [Sends for papers] After looking how case stands – You have asked defendant (a Petitioner) for the sugar you got judgement for?

Female Peasant: Often, often, sah; me feet weary going, sah. He say he won't give it for no Judge.

Judge: Give her a summons in Chambers calling upon defendant to show cause why the judgement for the amount of sugar should not be changed into a judgement for a sum of money to be paid forthwith. [This was done and money paid].[27]

Interviews of this kind, Gorrie argued, were essential for illiterate metayers and labourers to obtain justice, and he made the same defence of his practice of waiving court fees for poor suitors. The "absolute want of money in Tobago" meant that to exact five shillings for a summons and court fee "would have been to shut out the people from the Courts of Justice altogether – a result the Petitioners wish". He denied that "speculative actions" were encouraged by this practice; Tobago was so small that everyone knew the business of everyone else, so that frivolous actions were unlikely. Nor did he impose "crushing penalties" as the petitioners claimed, only reasonable damages plus costs. In *Franks* v *Anderson*, he merely ruled that in the case of a metayer contract, six months notice could not be given; it could only be terminated by the Court on complaint by one party. Nor did his ruling force the planters to stay in sugar; he clearly stated that cultivation could be changed by mutual consent.[28]

Finally, Gorrie insisted that the people had no confidence in the magistrates' courts: Tobago's two salaried magistrates were known friends of the planters, let alone the unpaid justices. "The question of Magistrates is by far the most difficult one in the West Indies." If the people had no confidence in the lower courts, the petitioners claimed they had none in the Supreme Court: "They forget that if the 20,000 other inhabitants of Tobago have that confidence, it would be impossible to give 28 men a Supreme Court to themselves." The Appeal Court in Port of Spain provided the only proper forum for reviewing any of his decisions to which the petitioners objected; the judge himself could not be 'reviewed' except by the Judicial Committee of the Privy Council, upon precise charges, "which must be different from the reckless complaints of such litigants as these".[29]

This was an impressive, if occasionally intemperate, letter, and it did impress the Colonial Office. It was agreed that the only possible answer to the petition to Knutsford was that he could not appoint a commission of enquiry; but "if the petitioners have any grievances against the Chief Justice, apart from his decisions which can be brought by appeal before the higher Court, they should present them to the Governor stating their complaints in a definite and precise manner".[30] Of course, Gorrie regarded this last statement, which was incorporated in a despatch to Robinson, as an open invitation to the petitioners to make new charges against him "to the Governor [Robinson] who would enquire into them, the key man who has been working with Mr Hay against me from the beginning! Imagine a Judge subjected to these indignities for doing his duty, his independence assailed and his assailants receiving aid and comfort from a Minister of the Crown". He asked the Aborigines Protection Society to help " in bringing Lord Knutsford to reason. It affects the administration of justice throughout the whole West Indies, and any insult to me is trivial in comparison."[31]

Gorrie felt that he had been betrayed by the Colonial Office. He wrote to several influential acquaintances in Britain asking for their advice and, if necessary, intervention; he thought an appeal to Parliament should be made. Lord Derby was the only one of these notables (who included the Earl of

Rosebery and Lord Selbourne) to offer specific counsel. Derby saw no reason for an appeal to Parliament, and told Gorrie, "I do not read Lord Knutsford's letter in the sense you give to it. He does not seem to me to be inviting complaints against you, but merely telling the complainants that their objections, if they have any to make, must be brought in regular form".[32] Despite this advice, Gorrie's old friend and colleague at the *Morning Star*, Justin McCarthy, now an MP, asked a question in the House of Commons about the Chief Justice and Tobago. The Parliamentary Under-Secretary for the Colonies replied that the petitions to the Queen had been referred to the Council President who did not consider that the Privy Council had any grounds for action. As for the petition to Knutsford calling for an enquiry, he had instructed the governor to inform the petitioners that no commission could be appointed. But the Under-Secretary repeated Knutsford's advice to the complainants – that they should state their complaints to the governor "in a definite and precise manner" – adding ominously "so that if necessary further enquiry might be made by the Governor and Executive Council". This can only have further infuriated Gorrie, and the *European Mail* in London seemed confident that a formal 'complaint' against him had been put before the Governor in Executive Council.[33]

But it seems that this step was not, in fact, taken, and no hearing before the Executive Council took place. The men behind the four anti-Gorrie petitions got up in 1890 failed in their immediate objectives. But the man whom Gorrie identified as "the mainstream of the whole of this Petition movement", R.B. Anderson, had only just begun his campaign against the Chief Justice, a campaign which continued long after the latter's death.

Anderson was an English doctor who had lived in Tobago since the early 1870s; he had served as Colonial Surgeon until the post was abolished in the 1880s; he was in private practice; and, along with his brother, he became the owner of Castara sugar estate and 'attorney' (non-resident manager) for others. There is evidence that he was deeply unpopular with many Tobagonians, though his friends claimed that he always acted "fairly and humanely to the natives upon his estate". W.G. Donovan, the editor of the *Grenada People*, who had informants in both Tobago and Trinidad, claimed that Anderson routinely charged a guinea for his visits to poor Tobagonians and that as a merchant (another of his activities) he was known as the "embodiment of extortion". As owner of Castara, Donovan charged, he drove the metayers off the estate rather than allowing them to share in its profits, reducing it to near abandonment. The record suggests that he was both a mercenary minded doctor and a callous merchant/landlord/employer. Several actions were filed against him in 1889-90, including *Franks* v *Anderson*; others were filed against the Davidson estates for which he served as attorney.[34]

At the 1890 session, Anderson was plaintiff or defendant in seven cases, six of which he lost. He appealed most of them, and petitioned the Queen for redress while the appeals were still pending. When a magistrate fined him for making a disorderly scene in court, Anderson brought an action for £1,000 damages against the magistrate; Gorrie dismissed it with costs (*Anderson* v *Fraser*). The Chief Justice was by no means exaggerating when he told Knutsford that Anderson "lives and revels in litigation, but woe to the Judge or Magistrate who decides against him". Anderson believed that he had been denied justice, that his evidence was "stifled", and that Gorrie "refused to allow me to ask questions which were relevant . . . Owing to the Chief Justice's manner towards me [in court] I was mobbed, and had I not exercised some degree of tact, I dare say I should have been murdered".[35]

At least two actions involving Anderson stemmed from his medical practice. In 1889, he sued John des Vignes for money allegedly owed for medical treatment. Judgment was given for him in Des Vignes' absence. When the latter complained, Gorrie issued an 'interlocutory order' to reopen the case. It was against this order that Anderson petitioned the Queen. What may have especially irked him in this case was that Gorrie, in his order, described the sum claimed for medical care as "on the face of it . . . excessive". In any case, he fired off *two* petitions to the Queen, and two letters to Robinson complaining of delays and injustices, though even the governor was forced to admit that Anderson had failed to make out "a case of wilful delay".[36]

Anderson's barrage of petitions and letters complaining about Gorrie's judicial actions was, to put it mildly, provocative; and he was the last judge on earth to turn the other cheek. When Robinson referred the two petitions to Gorrie for his observations, expecting him to reply in a confidential letter, the

Full Court (the Chief Justice and Justices Lumb and Cook) issued a rule in June 1890 "calling upon Anderson to show cause why he should not be committed for contempt of Court". It seems that the other two judges had "qualms of conscience" about putting into force "the terrible machinery of contempt" against Anderson, but the Chief Justice overruled them. Long after Gorrie's death, the Lord Chief Justice of England gave it as his opinion that "it was quite unjustifiable to issue such a process [of contempt] against a suitor who had merely petitioned the Queen complaining of delay".[37]

A second case involving Anderson's medical practice became even more complicated, and something of a *cause célèbre.* In 1889, he treated a Mrs Marshall; she was dissatisfied with his care, she and her relatives became obstreperous (in Anderson's view) and he ceased to treat her. When she failed to pay his fee, he entered an action in the Petty Debt Court; but Mr and Mrs Marshall sued Anderson for damages for professional neglect. In February 1890, Gorrie upheld their suit and awarded damages and costs, stating that Anderson as a medical man had no right to abandon her case. When he failed to pay the damages and costs, now amounting to about £42, the Marshalls took out a summons against him. The case was tried by Justice Cook. In January 1891, Cook adjourned the case and ordered Anderson to give security in £500 and bail in the same amount to appear at the adjourned hearing. Failing to produce these sums, Anderson was jailed and spent eight days in prison until five prominent Trinidadians (including three members of the legislature) paid the £1000. Anderson appealed against Cook's imposition of £1000 in bail and security, but the Appeal Court (Gorrie, Cook and Lumb) upheld it. This was the basis for an action against Gorrie and the other two judges which Anderson commenced in England in 1891. This action dragged on even after Gorrie's death in 1892, and in 1894 the Lord Chief Justice gave it as his opinion that Cook's action, in fixing security and bail of £1000 for a debt of £42, had been illegal and unjustifiable. Nevertheless, Anderson lost the action on the technical point that "no action could lie against a Judge for an act done in his judicial capacity", a ruling that was confirmed on appeal.[38]

There seems little doubt that both Gorrie and Cook, exasperated by Anderson's constant attacks on the Bench and by his barrage of suits and counter-suits, were provoked into unjustifiable actions as his cases went through the courts. The 1892 Judicial Enquiry Commission concluded that they mounted a "judicial persecution" against him, while conceding that Gorrie "thought he was acting for the public good". Cook's fixing of £1,000 bail and security and Anderson's imprisonment were indefensible, the Commission believed, and when the Chief Justice

> gives the weight of his sanction and even his encouragement to such proceedings as these, we think the due administration of justice in the Colony is in serious danger, because no litigant will feel sure that in the vigorous prosecution of his case he may not expose himself to the displeasure of the Chief Justice and have to incur consequences similar to those which, for no other fault, Dr Anderson incurred.[39]

The provocation was considerable; but this rebuke to Gorrie and Cook seems amply justified.

Anderson was not merely a dissatisfied litigant whose hobby was fighting lawsuits and whose *bête noire* was the Chief Justice. He, and the Tobago planters he spoke for, resented Gorrie's success in cheapening and expediting justice for poor Tobagonians and in protecting metayers and labourers from exploitation. This is why a group of landowners in both islands helped Anderson to begin his action in London against Gorrie and his colleagues. A Civil Rights Defence Fund was established to raise money to send him to England to prosecute his action, and with Barbadian support a West Indian Civil Rights Defence Union was set up with branches in Trinidad, Barbados and London. In the early 1890s, Anderson posed as a liberal reformer ostensibly agitating for representative institutions for the colonies and for redress of colonial grievances. That this pose was a sham was obvious to most liberals whether in England or in the West Indies. Anderson's agitation, originating as it did in "the judicial grievances of a litigious planter", received very little support and faded away by 1894, the year in which he finally lost his action against the Trinidad judges.[40]

The Tobago Metairie Commission

A significant victory was achieved by the anti-Gorrie forces in Tobago when Robinson appointed, in mid 1890, the Tobago Metairie Commission to enquire into metayage. It was clear that Gorrie's rulings in the metayer cases heard earlier in the year had prompted this enquiry. The selection of members ensured that the Commission would be hostile both to him and to the metayers. Its chairman was S.H. Gatty, the Attorney-General of Trinidad and Tobago, long an enemy of the Chief Justice; Commissioner Hay had been an opponent since Gorrie's first visit; and R.S.A. Warner was a Trinidad lawyer and Robinson's son-in-law. All three were white, none was a native of Tobago, and none had shown any interest in, or sympathy for, the metayers and labourers of the island.[41]

The Commission's brief was to investigate how metayage was working and to make recommendations, not to 'review' Gorrie's metayer rulings. As Gatty said, "We are not here as Commissioners to enquire into recent litigation . . . I don't want you to think I am going to enquire into the administration of justice in the island. All we are here for is to find out what this Metairie system is and whether any suggestion can be made to improve it." Nevertheless, the questions put by the Commissioners often revealed their determination to discredit Gorrie's judicial proceedings and to blame them for all difficulties in planter-metayer relations. In examining B.A. Blake, a 'petition-writer' and 'friend of the people', Gatty asked:

> *Q*: Do you think that it is only Sir John Gorrie who gives aid to [the people]? – *A*: Over and over again, and he is the only one who ever looked at the poor. There were terrible cases. – *Q*: That is your opinion? – *A*: Yes, justice for the poor black. – *Q*: Do you say in fact that they think he is the Judge who favours the black? – *A*: No, not favour, but that he does justice in an equal way to all.

On another occasion, Gatty questioned a metayer who said he wanted the planter to pay for the carting and grinding of metayers' canes:

> *Q*: Who told you that was a good thing? – [No reply] Go along, answer. – *A*: Myself. – *Q*: Did you ever talk in the town about it, in

> Scarborough, about it? – *A*: I myself thought of it. *Q*: Did you go before the Judge? – *A*: I went to hear the Judge. – *Q*: Did you go and see Mr Blake? – *A*: No, sir.

Moreover, the Commission refused to allow Edgar Maresse-Smith, a Trinidadian solicitor and Gorrie ally, to appear before it on behalf of the metayers. After a long and hostile examination, Gatty ruled that he could neither appear on behalf of metayers nor put questions; he could only give the Commission written questions on metayage, and written statements on behalf of named clients.[42]

Much of the Commission's examination of witnesses focused on the question of metayer tenure; it wanted to show that the notion of 'fixity of tenure' upheld by Gorrie in *Franks* v *Anderson* was previously unheard of. Several planters testified that fixity of tenure was impossible with metayage. Metayers took off two or three crops from their plot and then insisted on applying for a new piece of land. They not only moved from plot to plot, but often from estate to estate, refusing to bind themselves to any one planter; many had metayer plots on several plantations. Plots were never transmitted from father to son, unless a man died within the three-year period which was the normal length of a metayer agreement. The custom was that the owner could terminate an agreement with six months notice, and up to 1889 this was readily accepted by the metayers. In fact, they were "always migrating from place to place. What they want is not fixity of tenure or anything like it." A lawyer who had represented metayers for many years testified that he "would never, in appearing for people, think of raising such a thing as fixity of tenure, because it seems quite out of the nature of [metayage]".[43]

Planter after planter testified that their relations with their metayers and labourers had been serene until the arrival of the Chief Justice. As one of them put it: "Since then, a spirit has come over the metayer who now looks on the proprietor as inimical to him . . . We have had single cases before, but we never experienced such a general, such a universal feeling as that." This witness was a member of the island's white oligarchy, but the same view was expressed by Paul Tobago, a black ex-metayer and now an estate owner: "[The metayers] are very troublesome, and if you can ask them to do better I shall be glad. It is your Sir John Gorrie; we never felt displeased with each other before he came." Since Gorrie's advent, the planters testified, labourers and metayers were making unheard-of claims. The right to pasture stock on the estate without charge had always been regarded as a privilege, not a 'custom', but since 1889 the metayers said "the Judge has given them the right to go all over the estate and they claim right of pasturage for their stock"; Paul Tobago stated that his metayers "now say Sir John Gorrie said they must not pay pasturage or ground rent". Moreover, metayers were encouraged by the Chief Justice's rulings to insist that their canes must be reaped and ground regardless of weather or other conditions over which the planter had no control, a notion hitherto unknown. Metayers and labourers were refusing to work: "Since Sir John Gorrie came to the colony they won't obey. They won't work; they want more pay; if they don't get a shilling they won't work, Sir John never tell them so". And D.S. Gordon, also an ex-metayer and recent purchaser of an estate, complained, "if you tell [your employee] anything, he tell you to go to old Nick . . . You can't command them. I am one myself and I know he can do and won't do it; he will do what he likes."[44]

Much of the evidence to the Commission dealt with the repercussions of Gorrie's visits to Tobago and his rulings. A characteristic view was that expressed by a veteran planter:

> I have been here 45 years and I never knew the people to be such a pack of impertinent people as they are now. Every day there are threats . . . Philip Thomas, up to this morning, one of my own metayers, threatened me. In fact it amounted to intimidation. Every hour I may say I am told 'I will put Gorrie upon you; I'll file a petition'.

Metayers weie said to be deliberately refusing to help reap each other's crop. "They say 'That cane the Judge will grind it'; and they get the money out of me; the Judge will grant it and what does it signify because they get the money quite easy". Officials as well as planters complained that the people's behaviour had worsened: "Their demeanour since the arrival of Sir John Gorrie has changed. They have become rude and you cannot get law and order maintained." A planter testified: "Their spirit is such that one has to be very careful. I go about the country generally, and the people sing out, 'The Judge will give you a hanging'."[45]

This picture of Tobago on the verge of revolution inspired by the Chief Justice was not supported by the metayer witnesses, or by those who spoke for them. But several did state unequivocally that ordinary Tobagonians saw Gorrie as their only chance for justice. B.A. Blake, who wrote 'petitions' for metayers and others with grievances, told the Commission: "I will let you understand before [Gorrie] sat on the throne the metayers' canes they would be left in the field unground, and the owner would snap his fingers and tell them to grind itself." "Do you say there was no justice administered in Tobago?" asked the Chairman. "Oh, yes!", Blake replied, "Splendid justice! But all on one side. To the poor negro labourer justice was one-sided . . . We find annexation [*ie* union] is good. Trinidad is a free country." Jackson O'Connor, a metayer, said that before 1889 people like him could not go to court. "But lately we find the Judge have to ask to have the cases taken up and he go through them and the people have a chance to go to law. How could they go through the law with empty hands, and it is 3 guineas for a lawyer besides Court expenses?" And a local barrister confirmed O'Connor's point when he said that there would have been no actions by metayers in 1889-90 "had they not been permitted to sue *in forma pauperis*".[46]

In January 1891 the Metairie Commission submitted its report. It rehearsed the complaints about Gorrie's administration of justice in Tobago in some detail, though its brief was supposed to be an investigation of the metayage system, and it accepted uncritically the planter view of his impact on the people. The Commissioners recorded what they alleged to be the belief of everyone of importance in the island, that the metayer would get whatever he wanted from the Chief Justice, whether his claim was sound or not, and concluded that the mutual confidence essential for the working of the metayage system had been destroyed by Gorrie's rulings in 1889-90. In particular, his judgement in *Franks* v. *Anderson* bore no relation to the actual operation of that system. But the Commission believed that metayage should continue in Tobago as long as sugar was grown, because the planters' lack of capital made it necessary, and that it would survive even the "rude shocks" of Gorrie's rulings. Planters and metayers would simply have to "come to terms".[47]

The Chief Justice had always understood that the report would be essentially an attack on his actions in Tobago, and he responded in a long, vituperative letter to the Secretary of State. Gorrie began by attacking the choice of three men notoriously hostile to him and to the metayers, and then provided detailed examples of how the Chairman, in his examination of witnesses, had revealed that hostility. He went on to show that the Commission took evidence well beyond the scope of its mandate, and acted as if its brief was to enquire into the Chief Justice's doings while he was not present to cross-examine or give evidence on his own behalf; and he asked Knutsford to expunge portions of the report and evidence relating to his judicial acts. With considerable force, Gorrie went on to show how one-sided the Commission was: nearly every question had the object of either discrediting him, or showing that metayers had no grounds for complaint. Maresse-Smith was prevented from marshalling the metayers' evidence or cross-examining on their behalf. The Commissioners refused to ask questions which might have elicited the truth: that metayer discontent had begun in 1884 and that the litigation of January 1890 was caused by gross neglect of metayers' crops on several large estates. Turning to the condition of Tobago, Gorrie noted how impoverished the island was after fifty years of metayage, how wretched its infrastructure and social services; and he asked whether a serious Commission would not have enquired how far the system discouraged agriculture and enterprise generally. He recommended that metayage should be abolished and all metayers should be converted into cane farmers, who would grow canes on a six-year lease and be paid at a fixed rate per ton delivered to the mill. He concluded, however, that he did not expect "that prosperity will be brought back to Tobago until the union with Trinidad has been made much more absolute, abandoned estates sold in lots to peasant proprietors, and men with new ideas entrusted with the Government".[48]

The Colonial Office took its time to go through the voluminous papers relating to metayage and Tobago affairs since 1889, and its final conclusions were, by and large, a vindication of Gorrie's views. The Secretary of State announced that he was obliged to disagree with the Commission's endorsement of metayage, that he believed the system's defects outweighed its advantages for both parties, and that the evidence was clear that metayer discontent had begun in 1884. While he felt unable to recommend the abolition of metayage because of the planters' lack of funds, he advised that the metayer should be given the same right as the planter to end the contract with six months notice. Nor did Knutsford approve of the Commissioners' approach to the litigation of 1889-90. Their report implied that metayers filed suits in the belief that they could not lose a case if Gorrie heard it, but no metayer witness had stated this, and Knutsford noted that the actions were for the most part against a handful of large planters and that they mostly succeeded because the cause of the litigation was the failure of these few owners to carry out their side of the metayer agreement. In a measured rebuke, he wrote "I regret that I am unable to approve either of the manner in which the Commission conducted its inquiry as regards the proceedings of the Supreme Court in Tobago or the terms of that portion of the Report which refers to those proceedings." While he was not prepared to expunge the sections to which Gorrie objected, he directed that Gorrie's letter, and his own despatch, should be printed along with the report as a Council Paper. Apart from the now almost customary rebuke to Gorrie for the 'tone' of his letter on the report, the Secretary of State had upheld the Chief Justice's acts in Tobago, and his view of metayage, almost entirely.[49]

By this time Gorrie had only one more year to live, and his enemies, including Anderson, shifted their attention from Tobago affairs to a more general attack on his administration of justice in the united colony. He returned to Tobago for one last visit in May 1892. In the previous year, he had purchased King's Bay estate on Tobago's southern coast for his son Malcolm, an indication perhaps of his genuine interest in the island. It was reported that when he died the following year the estate was fully mortgaged.[50]

When Gorrie went to Tobago in May 1892 to hold court, his arrival, imminent and actual, caused almost as much excitement as in 1890. A Port of Spain newspaper stated:

> The presence of Sir John Gorrie in Tobago being synonymous with disorder among the mob and agricultural labourers, a deputation of four gentlemen . . . [asked] for a squad of police to be sent to Tobago by the Royal Mail steamer, in the event of a disturbance. The reasonable grounds for this request were the utterances of some of the bad characters of Tobago as to something going to happen in case Sir John

> was not allowed to return as Judge to Tobago in consequence of the [Judicial Enquiry] Commission.

When he did arrive, "Scarborough was *en fête*. The Court House was thronged with people of the labouring class who had heard that Sir John Gorrie was to be tried – they did not know for what, but – they supposed for locking up Dr Anderson." Made to understand that there was to be no trial and that the Commission was not coming to Tobago, "before they went home in the evening they had heard that Dr Anderson had locked up Sir John and wanted to know if bail was required".[51]

Gorrie's visits to Tobago in 1889-92, the consequence of the first phase of the unification of Trinidad and Tobago, were important events in the smaller island's history. His unique approach to justice, and his social and political views, gave Tobagonian metayers, peasants and labourers the confidence to assert their rights during a period of depressed sugar prices and rapid changes in land ownership. His actions also confirmed many black Tobagonians' view, contrary to that of most of the island's merchants and planters, that unification was likely to serve their interests.

But Gorrie came to Tobago too late. By the time he handed down his celebrated and much maligned ruling in *Franks* v *Anderson*, Tobago's sugar economy, and hence metayage itself, were in their last phase of existence. The island's impoverished landowners could not cope with the rock-bottom prices for inferior muscovado sugar which prevailed in the 1880s and 1890s. In both decades, planters sold out, the Crown put abandoned estates onto the market; planter control of access to land was finally broken; exports of sugar virtually ceased by the late 1890s; metayage began to disappear with the sugar cultivation that had brought it into being. The former metayers, the descendants of Tobago's slaves, were able to purchase small plots (and, in some cases, whole estates) and establish a diversified agrarian economy based on food crops, cocoa and livestock, with a lively export trade to Trinidad.[52] A sturdy peasant economy had come into being by 1900, precisely the development which Gorrie had wished for the island for whose people he had come to feel so much concern. They kept his memory alive among them, and Gorrie was a popular first name in Tobago well into the twentieth century.[53]

CHAPTER NINE

The Storm Bursts: Trinidad, 1889-92

Politics in Britain

In May 1889, Gorrie went to Britain on leave, his first visit since his brief, sad trip in 1884 after his wife's death. He obtained leave in order to lobby the Colonial Office on two issues: his right to hold court in Tobago as Chief Justice of the united colony of Trinidad and Tobago, and some pending Trinidad legislation about which he held strong views. He may also have wanted to prepare the ground for a re-entry into British public life. Back in 1887, he had told Chesson, "I was 58 three days ago and hope soon also to be home and to take part in Parliament with those who have some experience of the colonies. I have had a fair spell of penal servitude and wish to spend some years in home service before the end." Two years later, visiting the Court of Session in Edinburgh, he saw "several of the men of my own standing, who are now on the bench, two of them belonging to my own year, and one old comrade of the Volunteer movement sitting as the lately appointed Lord Justice-Clerk. If I had remained at home, most probably I would have been where they are . . . " Charles Cooper, his old colleague at the *Morning Star* and now editor of *The Scotsman,* recalled that at this time Gorrie thought he might be given a seat on the Scottish Bench: "I did not think so, and told him what I thought."[1] But whatever his nostalgic regrets at revisiting old haunts in the Scottish capital, his real ambition was for Parliament in London, not the Bench in Edinburgh.

Even before he left Trinidad, the well-informed *European Mail* told its readers: "If Sir John can find a constituency who will be willing to elect him to a seat in the British House of Commons he will undoubtedly give up official life in the Colonies and devote his attention to party politics at home." In August 1889, Gorrie visited Edinburgh and his native county, Fife, and offered himself as the Liberal candidate for the 'St Andrews Burghs' at the next General Elections. The *East Fife Record* introduced the prospective candidate to its readers with a brief biographical sketch and stated: "We understand it is his intention to resign his judicial appointment and then come forward as a candidate for the burghs. He is a supporter of Mr Gladstone on the Home Rule Question and a Liberal on other questions . . . [and] remains faithful to the political creed of his early manhood." After he had returned to Trinidad, the same paper announced that he intended "to resign within a year. He will then have been twenty years in the Colonial service and will be entitled to his full pension." Since he still held a colonial appointment, the announcement could only be tentative, and he told a reporter from the *European Mail* that the newspaper accounts were "quite unauthorized"; but the reporter "judged from the twinkle in his eye" that the information they contained was "not altogether incorrect".[2]

The *Dundee Advertiser* published a lengthy, and very flattering biographical article, which reads as if it had been dictated by Sir John, and was subsequently printed in pamphlet form, no doubt for circulation in the 'burghs'. Of most interest in this production is a letter to the editor, reproduced in the pamphlet, which is worth quoting at length:

> A short time ago Mr Froude published a book giving an account of his travels in the West Indies. It is full of the arrogant domineering spirit which treats the subject peoples as an inferior race . . . Under the title of 'Froudacity', a negro J.J. Thomas of Trinidad has written a telling expo-

> sure of Mr Froude's gross errors of facts. In this volume, written without the slightest knowledge or expectation that Sir John Gorrie's name would ever be mentioned as a candidate for Parliament, occurs an important line . . . 'With a Chief Justice so vigilant, fearless and painstaking as Sir John Gorrie, the entire Magistracy of the Colony must be so beneficially influenced as to preclude the frequency of appeals being made to the higher Courts . . .' Perhaps this unconscious but striking testimony by a negro to the honour and fairness of Chief Justice Gorrie may make it worth the while of the electors of St Andrews to have a look at this Fife man.[3]

But by May 1890 he had made it clear that he would not be available as a candidate. The *Scotsman* told its readers that he had "informed his friends in the constituency that he will not return to this country in time to stand for the burghs at the next election". In Scotland, the *East Fife Record*, which had promoted him the year before, pronounced him "a fickle candidate", and told its readers:

> It was thought that when Sir John arrived in Trinidad he would make all arrangements for coming into this country again and have a tour round the Burghs. Until the other week letters were received from him stating that he would be here in October. But now on the back of this comes another note saying he cannot be here in time for the general election . . . Some dispute has arisen between the Government and Sir John as to monetary matters and there is now no chance of it being settled for some time to come.[4]

The monetary dispute involved payment during the period that Gorrie was on leave in 1889; but it is hardly likely that this was the real reason for his decision not to seek a Parliamentary seat. He was increasingly embattled in Trinidad with the fallout from his Tobago interventions of 1889-90, especially the interminable litigation involving R.B. Anderson, and also deeply engaged in various projects, including the establishment of a 'People's Bank'. He told Charles Cooper that "the people [of Trinidad] wish me to remain with them for some time longer", and in their interest he "gave up hopes of Parliament for the time". But a tragic incident in Britain, which occurred just at the time that he announced his decision not to stand, may also have influenced him. In May 1890 his nephew Daniel Gorrie, eldest son of his younger brother, was convicted of murder in London; he was hanged in June 1890. The trial, which was covered extensively in the London papers, including *The Times*, was also briefly reported in the *East Fife Record*. Neither in the London papers, nor in the *East Fife Record*, was Daniel's relationship to the Chief Justice of Trinidad mentioned. But the possibility of the link becoming public knowledge in Fife may have been a serious deterrent to his going through with his plan of seeking a seat.[5]

In addition to his flirtation with Parliamentary politics in Scotland, Gorrie enjoyed social and political life in the capital. In June 1889, he was presented to the Prince of Wales by the Secretary of State at a levée; in July, he attended the annual conversazione of the Royal Colonial Institute, where "colonists alike from the West Indies and Fiji seemed glad to have a chat with Sir John", and the annual general meeting of the Cobden Club, at which he appeared as one of the Club's 'shining lights'. Gorrie was also hard at work lobbying the Colonial Office on matters related to Tobago and to legislation pending in Trinidad. Clearly, he did not allow himself to be too distracted by a complicated dispute about his salary while on leave, which resulted in his drawing only half pay for several weeks and suffering (he claimed) considerable financial loss "for the public service".[6] A reporter from the *European Mail* who interviewed him just before he left London was impressed by his 'robust' good health, considering he was a man of 60 who had served in the tropical empire for two decades: "Sir John Gorrie is a living wonder . . . as active today as when he set out in 1865 for Jamaica."

Land and Credit Issues

Gorrie had been concerned about the contract system in Trinidad's cocoa and coconut industries since 1886-87, and he had heard many cases in which contractors sued for damages from planters for nonpayment of sums they believed they were entitled to. He was convinced that the contractors needed protection from unscrupulous planters, especially since they received no wages for their work in clearing bush, planting the trees and tending them;

the cash paid for each tree at the end of the contract represented their only monetary recompense for five or six years' labour. But the planters, alarmed at the flood of contract cases, persuaded the governor, Sir William Robinson, that legislation was necessary to put the system on a 'secure' footing. The result was the Agricultural Contracts Ordinance, No. 9 of 1889. It provided that once a contractor had agreed to a contract stating that he would receive no payments for six years, he could not sue for payment within that period; compensation would be strictly dependent on the number of bearing trees after six years. It also stated that disputes arising from agricultural contracts would be heard in the magistrates' courts, not the colony's Supreme Court.

Gorrie fought this Ordinance from the moment that discussion on it began. In October 1888, commenting on an early draft, he told the acting governor that its whole "scope and tendency" made it unacceptable as a government measure. He insisted that the law was simply an attempt by the cocoa planters to "prevent the contractors having access to the Supreme Court . . . and to make them subject in matters which involve the payment of their whole five years' wages to the decision of the Magistrates". Moreover, many of the magistrates in Trinidad were, he believed, "quite unfitted" to exercise jurisdiction in such matters. The Ordinance was "framed upon vicious principles which will lead to great injustice".[7]

This intervention, and his remarks in court attacking the Ordinance, failed to put a stop to the proposed measure, and in January 1889 he wrote an immensely detailed, clause by clause critique. He began by raising a fundamental question about the nature of the system: what were contractors, labourers or tenants? In Trinidad, cocoa contractors seemed to be "a new class of persons in connection with the cultivation of the soil, who are neither labourers, tenants nor owners . . . The contractors are in fact labourers, the payment of whose wages is postponed for six years, a condition of things which the law has never hitherto tolerated." Why then was the system popular; why did people seek to become contractors rather than wage labourers? Gorrie explained that peasants valued the relative independence, the freedom from "the control of overseers and drivers", and that "there are always good and kind employers of contractors in sufficient numbers to make the defects of the system less apparent". But the great problem had always been that dishonest planters tried to cheat the contractors out of their due at the end of the contract. This practice had been remedied "by making the Supreme Court in its Summary Jurisdiction accessible to the contractors and compelling dishonest owners to pay up". Now, the Ordinance sought to deprive the contractors of this protection and to give the magistrates the right to determine contractors' claims of up to £50 and even to order ejectment from the land. "These alterations of the law as it now stands are not made in the interest of both parties, but solely in the interest of the owner. The contractor was making no complaint of the Supreme Court, but some of the owners saw with surprise and vexation that the contractor received the same measure of justice before the Supreme Court as the owner himself." After a detailed review of several key clauses, Gorrie concluded that if enacted, the Ordinance would cause discontent among contractors and "would destroy the chance of honest owners from getting any benefit from this contract system".[8]

The men in the Colonial Office carefully considered Gorrie's criticisms; they also had before them comments supporting the Ordinance from the governor, the Attorney-General and the Solicitor-General. In a thoughtful comment, Edward Wingfield rejected most of Gorrie's criticisms of the Ordinance, pointing out that:

> he entirely ignores what is the most important consideration for the contractor, viz the crops of ground provisions which he grows and partly consumes and partly sells during the period of his possession under the contract. This I believe is much more value to him than the money payment at the end of the term. [Gorrie] however seems to assume that all contractors are oppressed and that there is an enormous crop of litigation. But even the recent outbreak of litigation which is generally attributed to his reckless utterances only amounts in two years to 39 cases out of the many thousand contracts.

He believed that legislation was necessary to overcome the existing uncertainty and dissatisfaction on both sides, and advised that the Ordinance, with a few amendments, should be brought in again and the official members of the Council be required to support it; the Secretary of State concurred.[9]

One of Gorrie's reasons for going to Britain on leave in May 1889 was to lobby against the Ordinance. Probably at his request, Sir R.N. Fowler, an MP who was a leading supporter of Chesson's Aborigines Protection Society, asked in the House of Commons whether the Government was aware of hardships suffered by cocoa contractors in Trinidad and whether the contract system might be said to resemble slavery. The Under-Secretary of State replied: "Complaints have recently been made that this system has in some instances caused hardship to the contractors but it does not appear to be in any sense a form of slavery." The *European Mail* was sure that the Commons question "shows traces of the hand of the distinguished Trinidad judge now on leave in England"; but the paper doubted that the new Ordinance would do much good. The contract system had been "practically killed by the attacks which have been made upon it from the Judicial Bench".[10]

In London, Gorrie appealed to Wingfield to reverse the Colonial Office's position. He cited the series of coconut contract cases he had heard in 1888 against Eugene Lange: Lange had made contracts with two alternative dates of payment, six years after the contract was entered into, or when the trees were bearing. In fact coconuts did not bear at six years, and several contractors brought suit for payment after that period. Gorrie decided that this was a reasonable interpretation and ordered payment, deducting when the trees seemed neglected. Yet Lange continued to resist: he spun out the time for appeal; ultimately appealed and lost; tried and failed to raise a public subscription for a Privy Council appeal; and frightened a young solicitor from putting the judgements in force. "These are the sort of cases you are going to send to Magistrates! the neighbours, friends, and daily associates of the proprietors." He claimed that the Ordinance would reverse Colonial Office policy ever since emancipation, to insist on short contracts and frequent payment of wages to ex-slave labourers; instead, it permitted "semi-slavery length of conracts and nonpayment of wages". In his view, "the dishonest and fraudulent planter is as well known now in the West Indies as in its worst days, and the ignorant negro or free Coolie as much needs protection". To allow an uneducated person to contract out of the right to sue for his wages for six years was "a long stride in a retrograde policy". But the Secretary of State sanctioned the Ordinance, and the flood of contract cases was stemmed.[11]

Another law related to agriculture and land engaged Gorrie's attention in 1889, the Real Property Ordinance, No. 8 of 1889. The purpose of this measure was "to simplify the Title to and the dealing with Estates in land, to provide for the indefeasibility of titles, to register the sale of Mortgaged Properties and to provide a system of Crop Advances to registered proprietors". This Ordinance sought to achieve much the same benefits as the Land Titles Act which Gorrie had written for the Leeward Islands; but the Trinidad law, according to the *European Mail,* was the work of his old friend and superior, Arthur Gordon, when he had served as governor in 1870. It had "remained in abeyance out of deference to legal practitioners of influence in the island" who thought that they would lose financially from the measure, and was based (like the Leewards Act) on the Torrens Act in Australia. Gorrie's influence was responsible for the revival and redrafting of this Ordinance, enacted in 1889. After the new Ordinance and the supporting arrangements had been in operation for a year, the Registrar-General reported that the measure had greatly facilitated the transfer of land titles. As an illustration, he cited a transfer of valuable freehold. It took in all 25 minutes to execute the Memorandum of Transfer, cancel the Certificate of Title, and issue a fresh title to the new owner as proof of his having an indefeasible title guaranteed by the Crown. The vendor and the new owner, both experienced landowners, expressed pleasurable surprise "that a transaction which under the old system would have involved much delay, labour, trouble and expense without any guarantee could have been so inexpensive, simple and complete in so short a time". The Ordinance had, in fact, "amply vindicated" its usefulness.[12]

Gorrie's experience in the Leeward Islands and in Trinidad and Tobago had convinced him that the provision of cheap credit to landowners was urgently needed if the agricultural sector was to be strengthened, and he took this issue up with his usual energy in 1889-92. Most of the smaller landowners in Trinidad were hopelessly in debt to the merchants; even the large proprietors encountered serious difficulties in attracting capital. The only commercial bank, the Colonial Bank, was prohibited by its charter from advancing money on the security of land. In September 1889, he explained his plan for a Land and Mortgage Bank in a lengthy interview in the *European*

Mail.[13] But the scheme for a Land and Mortgage Bank failed to get off the ground, for reasons which are unclear. Perhaps the moneyed men of Trinidad refused to have anything to do with Gorrie's brainchild; or it may be that the large corporations and individual capitalists who controlled the island's sugar industry by the late 1880s felt no need for it.

While the Land and Mortgage Bank had been designed to benefit large landowners, in 1890 Gorrie turned to the idea of an institution to extend cheap credit to smallholders, on the security of their crops. A scheme for a People's Bank was presented to the governor in mid 1890, and Robinson endorsed it. But it was controversial from the start. Many wondered whether it was appropriate for the colony's Chief Justice to take the lead in promoting a private commercial undertaking, however benevolent its aims. Moreover he indiscreetly criticized the Government Savings Banks in a public address, telling his audience of small cultivators that "there is something wrong" with them, and in effect advising them that they should withdraw their deposits and invest the money in the People's Bank when it was established. The Colonial Office had grave forebodings about the Bank; C.A. Harris minuted: "They will make a mess of this Bank altogether if they do not apply more Scotch canniness – Sir J. Gorrie has very little that is Scotch about him but the excitable impetuosity of a sixteenth century clansman." And Wingfield noted: "Sir J. Gorrie talks a good deal of nonsense and I am afraid he may plunge his bank into rash dealings". Hostile questions about his public speeches promoting the Bank were asked in the Legislative Council, but an Ordinance incorporating the People's Bank was enacted in June 1891.[14]

But trouble lay ahead for the Bank and its chief promoter. Though it began operations early in 1892, it failed to attract substantial deposits. According to a resident of Port of Spain, everyone with money steered clear of the Bank, and the only shareholders who could be persuaded to join were poor cocoa peasants and contractors who bought $5 shares. Not surprisingly, the "more important" newspapers in the colony, reflecting the views of the men "with a stake in the country", condemned the Bank as impracticable and predicted its imminent collapse: "Sir John doubtless means well by the masses of the people in Trinidad but the impression seems to be that he does not know sufficient of financial matters to enable him to successfully organise a concern of this kind." After just a few weeks of operation, there was a 'run' on the Bank, and it was forced to close its doors.[15]

Moreover, the Colonial Office began to have serious doubts about the propriety of Gorrie's involvement in the Bank, whether it succeeded or not. At the end of 1891, an unofficial member of the Trinidad legislature gave notice of a motion that the Council believed it "undesirable, as prejudicial to the pure and impartial administration of justice in a small community, that officers holding high legal appointments should be engaged in banking and other commercial pursuits". Though the motion was withdrawn, Robinson's successor as governor, Sir F.N. Broome, asked the Secretary of State to order Gorrie to disengage from the Bank: "It is indeed pernicious in the extreme", he wrote, "in a small community that the Chief Justice should descend from the Bench, and should mix himself up in these matters, and all the more so when, as in the present instance, they are not only commercial but political." The Secretary of State instructed Gorrie to disassociate himself from any commercial undertaking. This provoked an extraordinary response. After attacking his predecessor, notoriously "the leading cocoa lord of the place", and Robinson, a shareholder in at least three local commercial enterprises, Gorrie announced that he would defy the order. So convinced was he of the good to be derived from the Bank, so sure that it was his 'mission' to establish it, he refused to withdraw from its promotion and thus "have a great and good work for Her Majesty's much neglected West Indian subjects prevented or destroyed".[16]

In the event, the Colonial Office insisted that amendments would have to be made to the Ordinance incorporating the Bank before it could be permitted to resume operations. These amendments were unacceptable to Gorrie and the other promoters, and the People's Bank did not reopen. Gorrie then turned to the idea of a Crop Advance and Discount Company which would take over the assets of the People's Bank and carry out some of its functions, and the new institution started to operate at the end of March 1892. The *European Mail* told its readers:

> Sir John Gorrie seems to have got his Crop Advance & Discount Co. into going condition in Trinidad . . . rising from out of the ashes of that miserable financial fiasco, the People's Bank . . . Sir John is a man of

> great courage, who never knows when he is beaten, and he may yet make something of his financial scheme. That his action is philanthropic in intention is not denied.

The company provided cheap credit to its shareholders, who were mainly small farmers, on the security of their crops, bought their produce at 'honest prices', and purchased supplies for them at the lowest possible rate. Gorrie himself purchased 100 shares at $5 each, and just before he left the island in June 1892, he told the company manager that he intended to return – probably no longer as Chief Justice – to devote all his time to its affairs. The company paid dividends in 1893, and it still existed in 1900, when it had 1500 shareholders and assets of about six thousand pounds. And in 1897 the Trinidad Cooperative Bank was established on the model of Gorrie's People's Bank, and this institution, known popularly as the 'Penny Bank' and always associated with the encouragement of thrift and savings among poorer citizens, existed until the early 1990s (when it was merged with two other local banks).[17]

Folk Hero

The enthusiasm and affection which ordinary Trinidadians felt for Gorrie deepened in 1890-92. He was seen by many as their champion and protector. The authorities felt that this had a sinister side and that it encouraged insubordination among the lower orders and the quasi-criminal elements. The police chief complained, in 1890, that his men in the charge room frequently heard

> muttered threats of the Chief Justice . . . the way in which the name of His Honour the Chief Justice is now used by certain classes, with the idea that the mere dread of being brought before that gentleman will cover any amount of insubordination, is a thing which in the interests of discipline and good order must be put down at once.

Thus prompted, the West India Committee told the Secretary of State, "According to the advices that we receive from the island, there exists an insubordinate feeling among the lower classes such as has not been known to have existed before". Yet none of the dire prophesies of disorder materialized during Gorrie's six years' tenure. Indeed, on at least one occasion he solemnly warned the people against violence. A group of men had attacked policemen in Arouca because they had tried to stop a drum dance. Before sentencing them, Gorrie told them that any resistance to lawful authority would be "put down most firmly by the full force of the law; there are plenty of ways for you, probably more now than ever before, of getting rid of anything that you think annoys or oppresses you or deprives you of any of your rights as citizens, but that must be done by special remonstrances and persuasion to those who have got the control over you. Nothing will ever be gained in the British Empire by resorting to force".[18] The point was that by opening the courts to lower class suitors Gorrie hoped to create legitimate and peaceful channels for hostility and resentment, so as to avoid explosions such as that at Morant Bay 25 years before. But the privileged classes refused to see this.

In the last three years of his life, the evidence suggests that Gorrie became a true folk hero to the Creole masses of the island. When he returned from leave in October 1889, he was greeted by an extraordinary demonstration of popular affection. Even allowing for some exaggeration in the lengthy report published in the pro-Gorrie *Public Opinion*, hundreds if not thousands turned out to welcome him, crowding the environs of the wharves and the sections of Port of Spain closest to them. An arch of branches at the jetty bore the inscription "Welcome back Sir John: God preserve the fearless Judge". Nearly a hundred small boats with their crews waited near the jetty, where the 'Creole Amateur Band' prepared a musical welcome.

> On either side of the jetty, half way up, two well dressed negresses, one in a black silk dress and the other in a reddish brown gown with neatly tied yellow and black turbans and exhibiting a great quantity of jewelry stood ready with large bouquets with which to present 'Serjon Gorrie' as they styled His Honour.

The reporter estimated that at least 10,000 persons were present when Gorrie finally stepped onto the jetty; the noise of the cheers was deafening, children strewed flowers in his path and threw them over him, and two bands played suitable airs. After a flattering address signed by 7,297 persons had been read by the Mayor of Port of Spain, Gorrie entered his carriage and

> a hundred hands unharnessed the horses and then dragged the carriage amid the plaudits of the whole city towards the Court. A long procession of public carts decked with ribbons and flags followed the horses and mules all of which had bells attached to their harness making a fitting finale to the procession.

A further demonstration awaited him when he reached his house in the then rural Diego Martin valley to the west of the city. Despite the large numbers of 'lower class' Creoles crowded together in the city, the organizers of the demonstration (Rostant of Public Opinion and several black or mixed-race lawyers and teachers) were gratified that not a single 'incident' took place.[19]

When Gorrie left Trinidad in June 1892, as it turned out for good, another great crowd came out to see him off. There were remarkable displays of devotion from the ordinary citizens of Port of Spain, mostly black Creoles. An admittedly hostile witness reported that "the enthusiasm of the crowd took the form of hurling the vilest epithets at the respectable classes, always concluding in the suggestion to lick them. One man in our hearing went so far as to say that he would be the first to begin killing the white people". Gorrie's retinue, according to this source, consisted of "a howling, half frenzied mob, composed of the chronic law-breaking element known as diametes [jamets]: lewd and lawless women vulgarly gesticulating and dancing; insolent and besotted draymen". The Police Chief claimed to believe that the slightest incident would have sparked off a riot. A more objective witness noted that Gorrie kept saying to his rowdy fans, as they escorted him to the wharf, "Be quiet – behave yourselves", and reported that the whole demonstration took place without a single act requiring the intervention of a policeman, despite the large numbers of excited people. The police estimated that about 1,700 persons escorted Gorrie to the jetty, some half of them women; his buggy was pulled all the way from his Diego Martin house by about 36 'runners'. All the reports of this scene agree that the great majority of the people present were "of the lower classes" and that the women were especially vocal. "Our Caesar will come back and do justice to us" was a popular chant.[20]

As the hero of the Creole masses, Gorrie was celebrated in at least two calypsoes, that authentic expression of the African-Trinidadian. 'Papa Gorrie' was depicted in a Carnival band in 1888, and in 1892 the People's Bank was the theme of a costumed band. After the 1891 Carnival, a false rumour spread that Gorrie had remitted the fines of people charged with 'Carnival offenses' and freed those in jail. These people would have been mostly men and women of Port of Spain's lower class, and especially those belonging to the semi-criminal groups, the 'jamets' or 'diametes' who were most prominent in Carnival at this time. A calypso was composed in French Creole, translated as: "Stollmeyer open the door / What a good man Sir John Gorrie is! / What a good papa / He let us go free." Men and women were reported to have roamed the streets, singing the calypso and shouting, "We are Gorrie men". Another calypso, also in Creole, was about the acquittal of a murder accused, Louis Camille, following Gorrie's summing-up in a 1891 trial which attracted much publicity. Camille's release was greeted with "great rejoicing and high jinks" in the city slums and a calypso sung during the 1892 Carnival celebrated: "Judge Gorrie who put Camille outside / Camille went up, Camille went down / Camille fell in the water. / Judge Gorrie it was Camille who killed Eligon / Camille went up, Camille went down / Camille fell in the water." Moreover, Gorrie contributed an element to the island's rich Carnival tradition. He habitually wore a large red sash or cummerbund around his middle, apparently to "protect his spleen", and this was widely copied in Trinidad. One newspaper reporter referred to "the red sash which he has made so popular since his arrival here in 1886". When the Judicial Enquiry Commission to investigate the administration of justice arrived in the island, a newspaper commented tongue in cheek that "red belly bands are expected to go up in the market (as the defence will adopt them as their badge in honour to their chief)".[21] The scarlet cummerbund or 'belly band' became an important item in the Carnival costume of the jamets, the Port of Spain underworld types who controlled the festival, and remained so, well into the middle of the twentieth century. A cummerbund is still called a 'gorrie' by older Trinidadians.

The Judicial Enquiry Commission

Gorrie's political and social views made him unacceptable to most members of the island's landowning, commercial and professional elite, along with their allies in Britain. Late in 1891, his opponents renewed their campaign to remove him from the Bench. They were helped by the fact that one of the other judges, Cook, apparently drank heavily and may sometimes have appeared in court under the influence. An unofficial member of the Council, A.P. Marryat, moved that there should be a full and independent enquiry into the charges against Cook. Another unofficial, G.T. Fenwick, pointed out that the general dissatisfaction with the administration of justice in the colony was not directed solely at Cook, but also at Gorrie, and called for an enquiry into the whole judicial regime. Two separate resolutions were put to the Council; Broome instructed the official members to abstain. The resolution relating to Cook was carried by all eight unofficial members; the second, relating to justice generally, was supported by six of them. The two dissenting were among Gorrie's relatively few elite allies, Charles Leotaud and Eugene Cipriani, both associated with the People's Bank and the Crop Advance Company.[22]

It was very much in character for Gorrie to reply to this proceeding in open court. He defended Cook as an "assiduous and painstaking judge" and dismissed the charges against him as "an unheard of outrage". As for the attack on himself

> it does not mean that I have not done my duty, but that I have done it too well for the taste of these my accusers. If they say *they* have no confidence in my administration of justice, I thank God and take courage . . . For whom do they speak? Whom do they represent? Let the people speak for themselves, and then the Secretary of State will know better than from the vote of the rump of the council on Monday whether we are drunken imbeciles or whether we are just judges.

His supporters rallied in his defence as they had in 1887. H.P. Ganteaume, the secretary of a pro-Gorrie 'General Committee', informed the local government in January 1892 that petitions protesting against any enquiry were being circulated all over the island and that thousands of signatures were pouring in. A circular signed by Ganteaume called on people to form local committees and to be ready with "cases of hardship and refusal of justice under the former system and also any such cases of the redress of grievances by means of the Courts" if testimony was needed. Supporters were also urged to organize local petitions. One such petition from "the Inhabitants of the Wards of Montserrat, Couva and Chaguanas" – rural districts in the centre of the island – was signed by over 4,000 people; expressing complete confidence in the administration of justice, it rejected the Council vote as reflecting the views of a few dissatisfied litigants and asked the Secretary of State to refuse an enquiry. As Wingfield noted, "No doubt if a plebiscite were taken Sir John Gorrie would be acquitted triumphantly." The *San Fernando Gazette* called the six unofficial members of Council "traitors" to the community, impelled by personal enmity towards Gorrie and distaste for impartial justice; at least 99 percent of the population were opposed to an enquiry, it claimed.[23]

In Britain, pressure was put on the Colonial Office to allow an enquiry. The *European Mail* claimed to believe that if no action was taken, a "serious agitation" would be carried on by the friends of Trinidad in the mother country; "the Colonial Office may be able to ignore colonial feeling, but that policy will not act against public feeling on this side". This paper consistently argued for a full scale enquiry. In this it was joined by the London *Truth,* a journal owned and largely written by Henry Labouchere, a prominent Liberal politician. In a lengthy article, Labouchere gave a detailed account of the events leading up to the Council resolutions, reproduced most of Marryat's speech, and called for an immediate enquiry as well as a full explanation for the previous failure to act on numerous complaints against both Cook and Gorrie. The *St James Gazette*, also of London, echoed the call for an enquiry. A question was asked in the House of Commons at the end of February 1892.[24]

The ball was now in the Colonial Office's court. Gorrie insisted that the six unofficial members were motivated either by recent court rulings against them (E. Lange, G.T. Fenwick, W.G. Gordon) or by a belief that he had disrupted the cocoa industry in which they had interests (A.P. Marryat, L. de Verteuil, A. de Boissiere). If the Crown listened to such prejudiced legislators justice would be endangered. Governor Broome made no specific recommendation, but advised that the situation had become "dangerous" because of the high feeling on both sides. A leading unofficial member had told him that he fully expected to be stoned with his colleagues one day outside the Council chamber, and the editor of an anti-Gorrie paper said he feared that his premises would be wrecked. The Office decided that it must give way. The enquiry into the charges against Cook, the Secretary of State wrote, was clearly necessary in fairness to the judge himself. He agreed to an enquiry into the general administration of justice with "more hesitation". But

> that grave dissatisfaction with the administration of justice in the Supreme Court of Trinidad and Tobago exists, is proved by the fact that the complaints which have been addressed to the Governor of the Colony and to the Secretary of State . . . have been far more numerous than those which have been made in any other colony, and as the general prevalence of such dissatisfaction has now been affirmed by a large majority of the Unofficial Members of Council, I feel that the usefulness of the Court must be so seriously impaired by the continuation of this state of things that an inquiry into the causes of the dissatisfaction is desirable in the interests of the Colony and in justice to the Judges themselves.

A Commission would be sent out from England to enquire into the charges against Cook and the administration of justice generally and to make recommendations.[25]

The Judicial Enquiry Commission consisted of two distinguished British jurists, Sir William Markby, the chairman, and Sir Frederick Pollock. Markby had served for years as a puisne judge in Calcutta, and was a Reader in Indian law at Oxford. Pollock was also at Oxford as Professor of Jurisprudence, and was said to be a barrister of wide experience. The Commission began sessions in Trinidad on April 14, 1892, and issued its final report on June 16. During these weeks, the island press was almost exclusively preoccupied with its proceedings and with the issues which surrounded its enquiry.[26]

As the Commission carried out its work, support for the embattled Chief Justice, and for Cook, was shown in a number of ways. Two of the island newspapers, the *San Fernando Gazette* and the *Trinidad Times*, consistently defended them. Numerous letters were published in these papers expressing admiration for Gorrie, some of them written in a style which suggests that the authors had little formal education, and the editors of both frequently appealed to the public to come forward and make their feelings known. The Loyal Defence Association was set up in San Fernando to mobilize support. Its secretary, E.A. Nunes, stated that the body was formed to combat the "vile aspersions" against Gorrie and to bear witness to the country's satisfaction with his administration of justice. It published a pamphlet by Nunes entitled "Sir John Gorrie, in connection with the Helpless and Downtrodden Race". San Fernando was especially strong in its support for Gorrie. When R.B. Anderson went there to speak in July 1892, he found "the atmosphere so saturated with Gorrieism that it would be impossible for an anti-Gorrieite to breathe".[27] Moreover, some of Gorrie's supporters linked their advocacy of the Chief Justice with their desire to secure constitutional reform. The newly formed Colonial Reform Association held a meeting in May 1892 to agitate for elected members in the Legislative Council and to express "approbation" of the administration of justice under Gorrie. But perhaps the most amusing evidence of popular support for (and fascination with) Gorrie was the experience of an enterprising San Fernando merchant. He ordered a large quantity of cheap handkerchiefs "each bearing a portrait of His Honour", sold "hundreds" in San Fernando, Princes Town and Couva (all in the southern part of the island), and procured 600 more, which he sold in Port of Spain "in a short time, and hundreds more could have been sold". This was not, certainly, likely to impress the Commission; but it was testimony to the popular devotion to the 'martyred' Judge.[28]

The Commission was required to investigate both the specific charges against Cook and "the manner in which justice has been administered in this colony". At the formal opening session, Markby announced that the charges against Cook would be taken first; sittings would be public; and everyone was invited to give evidence. When the first session to hear the charges against Cook began, Gorrie attempted to make a protest against the manner in which the Commission had been established, but Markby refused to hear him on the grounds that the Commissioners were then concerned only with the Cook matter and, therefore, Gorrie had no *locus standi* for such a protest. He agreed to wait until the Commission began the second part of its work, and it proceeded to hear evidence on Cook. The Chief Justice's "Protest" was said to be a bulky document reviewing and justifying his six years' tenure in Trinidad.[29]

By the end of April, the Commission had issued a preliminary report on Cook: the charges against him were well founded, and the interests of justice required that he be removed from the Bench. He was interdicted from performing his duties by the governor, suspended from his post after a 'trial' by the Executive Council, and eventually dismissed by the Crown without pension. The pro-Gorrie papers passionately defended Cook against the charges of intemperance and inappropriate conduct, and the evidence as presented to the Commission does indeed seem ambiguous. But the point was that Cook was an ally of Gorrie (unlike the other judge) and therefore the findings against the former were seen as adverse to him. As a pro-Gorrie paper put it, his enemies intended "to strike at Sir John Gorrie over the shoulders of Mr Justice Cook".[30] At the start of May 1892, the Commission began to hear evidence on the general administration of justice. Gorrie's 'Protest' was sent to the Commissioners, but they decided not to allow him to read it at a public session; a hostile newspaper reported, presumably in jest, that it would have taken five days to read. He stated that in his view no tribunal had the authority to call his judicial acts into question, except for a properly constituted Court of Appeal, or the Privy Council in London. But the Commission proceeded to hear evidence on the Anderson and other Tobago cases; on the administration of infants' funds and suitors' monies; on procedures relating to mortgaged properties; on suits *in forma pauperis*; on advising potential litigants in chambers; and on other alleged violations of proper court procedures. Gorrie, assisted by his son Malcolm and his private secretary Broderick Collins (neither a lawyer), took part in these proceedings by examining witnesses and 'putting in' voluminous documents; the 'Unofficial Committee' – the unofficial members of Council who had called for the enquiry – was represented by three barristers. For most of the sessions Pollock carried on alone, as Markby fell victim to a 'colonial fever'.[31]

Both Commissioners were present on May 19, however, when Gorrie announced that he would have nothing further to do with the Commission.

SHYLOCK : Is that the law?
PORTIA : Thyself shall see the act.
For, as thou urgest justice, be assured,
Thou shalt have justice, more than thou desirest.—*Merchant of Venice, Act IV. Sc. I.*

NURSERY RHYMES.

Thus spake a Chief Justice named John,
Who likes not to be sat upon,
I will duly protest
And my case there I'll rest,
The meanwhile my war-paint I don.

But his friend, Charlie Fred, said I'll change,
And to a milk diet I'll range
And I'll sit until 2
The Practice Court through,
In the hope the horizon may change.

Sir John Gorrie as seen by a Trinidadian cartoonist, 1892

(*Quiz*, May 18, 1892, p. 23)

He interpreted their decision not to go to Tobago to hear witnesses there (as they had planned), and their remark that they did not need to hear further evidence from the counsel for the 'prosecution', as proof that they had made up their minds already, without waiting to hear his evidence or his 'observations' on the testimony given by others. He announced:

> In these circumstances, it would seem to me a waste of time and energy to bring forward my case before this Commission. That case would include the number of abuses corrected since I have filled my present office, the sound administration of justice by the Supreme Court as between man and man, whatever their colour, condition or race, and the general satisfaction of the community in such administration of justice as opposed to the dislike of the prejudiced few, who have called for this enquiry. I shall reserve the presentation of such a case, as well as the evidence in answer to that already given, for the consideration of the only Tribunal which can bring to a legal issue the question involved in these inquiries. I shall, therefore, not trouble Your Honours any further.

The Commissioners, of course, denied that they had come to any foregone conclusion, but Gorrie "thanked them for their statement, and retired".[32]

The Chief Justice was ridiculed by the anti-Gorrie papers for his 'cowardice' in refusing to 'face' the public enquiry, and accused him of deliberately seeking to obstruct its work by his withdrawal. His supporters felt that he was right not to go through the motions when the Commissioners, and especially Pollock who was thought to be 'disrespectful' in his manner towards him, had so clearly made up their minds.[33] No doubt Gorrie had (correctly) concluded that the Commissioners were moving towards an unfavourable verdict. His health, moreover, was beginning to deteriorate, and he may have decided that he should save his energy for the ultimate battle in London, with the Colonial Office and the Privy Council, when he could hope to mobilize his friends in Britain. By the start of June 1892, the Commission had ended its public sessions. The Commissioners handed their final report to the governor on June 15, and left Trinidad the following day.[34]

A Melancholy End

Their report was carefully written and thorough. It began by pointing out that the 'Unofficial Committee' had functioned like a plaintiff, bringing up specific complaints and retaining counsel, while Gorrie, who refused counsel and appeared in person at first, was in effect the defendant. The charge was that, in specified cases, he had disregarded "positive rules of law and practice, and established judicial usage, leading to grave miscarriage of justice". Gorrie, however, had ceased to attend sittings after May 10, first because he was in Tobago holding court, then because of his withdrawal. Through informal correspondence, the Commissioners had tried to persuade him to change his mind, but failed; they decided not to compel him to attend out of respect for his office. In his absence, the Commission tried to rely on the records of the Supreme Court rather than on oral evidence alone, which Gorrie might have countered had he been present.[35]

The report then proceeded to consider the indictment against Gorrie under eight headings. First was the charge that he set aside established modes of looking after and investing private funds placed in the Supreme Court's keeping, especially infants' estates and suitors' monies. The Commission felt that this had indeed happened, though Gorrie believed he was acting for the general good: "He openly assumed a patriarchal authority to deal with parties' money in what might seem the best way not to themselves, but to the Chief Justice or his Registrar." Suitors, or the representatives of minors, were often not even informed that their monies were being lent out. Some people who benefitted as borrowers were personally known to Gorrie, such as Madeleine Joseph, a Creole smallholder with property in Diego Martin where he lived. The Commissioners did not, however, impute any improper motives in this matter. On the charge that he had interfered with the rights of mortgagees, the Commission found several irregularities in twelve specified cases.[36]

One of the major charges against Gorrie was that he permitted suits *in forma pauperis* without the necessary preliminaries set out in the Rules of Court. The Commission was clear that he did, from time to time, permit persons to sue *in forma pauperis* even though he knew that they could not make the necessary declaration of poverty. He stated that he had the power to dispense with the requirement if he judged it necessary, a claim which the Commissioners thought highly dubious. A second complaint was permitting irregular proceedings by summons. A suitor presented a petition to the Chief Justice complaining of grievances and praying for relief; after seeing the person in chambers, he issued (if he saw fit) a summons calling on the party complained of to show cause why relief should not be granted. When the party duly appeared, orders were made on the summons which were in effect final judgements even though no regularly constituted action was before the Court. Sometimes the order was really a compromise or settlement made by the parties in the presence of the Chief Justice, but not always. Usually no court fees or stamps were paid by the suitor. This, it was said, amounted to the introduction of new and unauthorized procedures which no judge of a Court bound by fixed rules could adopt on his own. Though Gorrie claimed that he was carrying out the spirit of the relevant Rules of Court, the Commission felt that he had no grounds for such a significant departure from clearly laid-down procedures. Another charge was that he appointed receivers as a sort of universal remedy for encumbered estates, and kept the receiver on the estate for an indefinite period. This was a practice unknown in English jurisprudence. Gorrie defended it as beneficial under local circumstances, but the Commission believed there had been little check on the receivers' actions, or accounts, and little benefit to the creditors.[37]

Another charge was that Gorrie had been guilty, on many occasions, of "intemperate conduct and language" in court. The Report referred to seven such incidents, noting that on each occasion he had been formally rebuked, either by the Secretary of State, or by the Legislative Council. To make the point that he was far from repentant, the Commissioners quoted a document he had written for them which described the unofficial members of Council who supported the enquiry as

> men subject to every local bias and prejudice, men who have no sympathy with an impartial administration of justice, men who would not and do not hesitate to use their public positions to make charges and demand inquiries with a view of getting control of the judiciary. As a British Judge I refuse to submit to their dictation and challenge their usurped power. The Legislative Council I know and its legal definition

> is well defined but the rump of it which asked for this inquiry has no known status or existence.

On the charge of intemperate language, the report simply stated: "We must leave the language used and the character of the imputations made to speak for themselves."[38]

Finally, the Commission considered the allegations of miscarriages or denials of justice arising out of suits filed in Tobago, many involving R.B. Anderson. It found that serious irregularities had occurred in the Anderson cases, but felt that what might otherwise have amounted to a denial of justice had been mitigated in the course of proceedings either by the Supreme Court itself or by acquiescence of the parties concerned. Noting that Gorrie had asserted that his actions in all the Tobago cases complained of were aimed at giving the poor and illiterate access to the courts, the Commissioners stated that a judge could have no excuse for transgressing the limits set by the law to judicial discretion: "The first duty of judges as of other citizens is to obey the law." The report concluded that the charges of perverse disregard of the facts of the case and of the law were well founded with respect to *Franks* v *Anderson* and to several other cases involving the latter.[39]

In its conclusion, the Commission stated that most of the complaints were "to a considerable extent well founded. That conclusion involves . . . a condemnation of the administration of justice by the highest judicial officer in the Colony." However, the Commissioners wrote, "We do not attribute to the Chief Justice any unworthy motives. We see no reason to doubt that Sir John Gorrie was actuated by a desire to do justice." Nevertheless, the Report concluded:

> The administration of justice in the colony cannot be placed on a satisfactory footing unless measures are taken by which all classes can feel confidence in the Supreme Court and its Chief. We regret to think that such confidence does not now exist, and the evidence brought before us has led us to the conclusion that this want of confidence is well founded.[40]

This opened the way for Gorrie's immediate removal. Governor Broome tried to persuade him to resign, but he refused: "My judicial reputation must be vindicated first, whatever the ultimate consequences." He was then interdicted from any further performance of his duties, pending his 'trial' by the Executive Council under the Colonial Regulations with a view to his suspension from office or reinstatement. Broome told the Legislative Council that the interdiction would remain in force until a final decision about his fate had been made by the 'highest authority', presumably the Privy Council, since it was a foregone conclusion that the Executive Council would, on the basis of the findings of the Commission, order his suspension from office. Gorrie protested against this procedure as a violation of the rules of service for colonial judges and as an act of high-handed disregard of the immunities surrounding judical office.[41]

He immediately applied for leave to go to Britain, in order to put his case personally to the Colonial Office, and the Privy Council if necessary, and also to deal with the Anderson litigation against the Trinidad judges. Broome refused on account of his pending 'trial' by the Executive Council. Gorrie then sent in a medical certificate, and was granted three months' sick leave in Britain. He told his allies that he intended to return to Trinidad, probably no longer as Chief Justice, to live permanently in the island as a private citizen. An anti-Gorrie paper queried whether he was so ill as to require immediate 'home leave', instead of remaining for two more weeks, during which the 'trial' could have taken place. "It is suspected that though too ill to stand his trial before the local Executive, he will be well enough in England to move all possible influences which can prevent the humiliation of that trial, and perhaps even his fall."[42]

This scepticism is understandable, and there is no question that Gorrie did intend to fight hard in Britain. But there is equally no question that by June 1892, his health had seriously deteriorated. His doctor's letter indicated that he was completely run down and that he had "by persistent mental overwork together with deficient and irregular feeding – resulting in faulty digestion – produced an anaemic condition that requires, and should have without delay, a regular course of treatment at some Cure". The detailed accounts of his departure on June 30 make it clear that he was by then in bad shape. "It was clearly visible that the once powerful frame and robust constitution which might safely have been called distinguishing features in our Chief Justice, had received the touch of time's blighting influence and the Sir John of yesterday was but a shadow of his former self." A pro-Gorrie paper declared: "The venerable figure who had always appeared before them as the very impersonation of robust health and untiring energy, was seen to walk with difficulty, his beloved face as pale as death, the paler for the emotions which agitated his frame." In Tobago the month before he had suffered a severe attack of malarial fever, and he seemed to observers, on the day that he left the island, to be near collapse. A hostile source described him as "haggard looking, with a death-like pallor overspreading his face". On the short journey from his house to the ship, he fainted twice, the second time on the boat going out to the steamer, when the people around him thought it might be the end. When his steamer called at St George's, Grenada, a sympathetic observer thought "the grim hand of death" was already upon him.[43]

Extraordinary demonstrations of popular affection took place on the day of his departure. He received addresses from the people of Port of Spain, San Fernando and Couva, and another one from the Loyal Defence Association. Large crowds turned out to see him off and to wish him restored health. The scene in the city was said to be reminiscent of the great welcome he had received when he returned from leave in 1889; but, on this occasion, there was sadness because of the visible deterioration of the 'martyred judge'.[44]

In London, the *European Mail* welcomed the Commission's report, and thought that the duty of the government was plain: Sir John must cease "from troubling the Trinidadians". News of the its findings would be heard with no surprise in each colony in which Gorrie had served. *Truth* reproduced the conclusion of the Report, and commented that the Commissioners had, if anything, let Gorrie down too lightly when they stated that they believed he was actuated only by a desire to do justice. "The simple truth is that for years the liberty and property, if not the very lives, of the citizens of this corner of the empire have been at the mercy of a judicial tyrant." The British press – with the exception of *Truth*, of course – had failed to come to the defence of the Trinidadians by publicizing the scandal: "With what irony must the British subject whose lot has been cast in Trinidad repeat his Civis Romanus sum!" Both the *European Mail* and *Truth* anticipated a stiff fight from the Chief Justice when he arrived in London. "He proposes to himself to upset the whole work of the Commission and those who know what a militant character he is will readily believe that he will fight bitterly to the bitter end."[45]

But Gorrie was close to death by the time he reached England. During the crossing he was very ill, but he rallied on landing at Plymouth; he arrived on a stretcher and remained in a hotel there for a week. It was decided to try to get him to Ayrshire in easy stages, and he and Malcolm were joined by his two daughters who were both in England at the time. But on reaching Exeter, he was so ill that he had to be taken "almost lifeless" by ambulance to the City Hotel. The doctors consulted agreed that there was nothing organically wrong but that he was suffering from "functional troubles". At the hotel, he "wasted away, suffered from nausea, was most irritable, and his mind seemed to give way. Fears were then also entertained that mental derangement would supervene, even if he rallied physically." The hope was still to get him to Scotland, but he then died, rather suddenly, on August 4, 1892, and was buried in St David's Churchyard, Exeter. He was 63 years old, and had enjoyed good health all his life.[46]

The news of his death became known in Trinidad about a week later, and was greeted with shock. For the pro-Gorrie papers, his death was a calamity for the island as well as a private tragedy. In San Fernando, where he was revered, people reacted first with disbelief, then with grief; in Port of Spain, "universal grief" was expressed. People spoke of their dismay that "the fearless and upright Judge, the great and kind-hearted man, the sincere philanthropist" was gone. The reaction of the two anti-Gorrie papers was more restrained, but they both reported the expressions of popular grief. The courts were closed the day after the news was received, along with the Public Library (Gorrie had been active in its management), and the offices of barristers and solicitors closed early, but public offices remained open and the flag on Government House was not lowered, which the pro-Gorrie papers attributed to the mean-spiritedness of Broome and Gatty. A Scottish businessman in Port of Spain told Malcolm that people simply could not believe that Gorrie was dead; it affected them profoundly, and "there is a strong feeling that his death was hastened, if not caused, by his unfair treatment . . . There is an uneasy feeling about, and I have heard many say, whom I would not consider friends of Sir John's, that we will not get as good a man to replace him."[47]

The *San Fernando Gazette* called on those who admired and loved Gorrie to support his work by subscribing to the Crop Advance Company so that it could grow and prosper. Even more important, the paper urged citizens to agitate for the reform of the Legislature so that members elected by the people would replace the nominated unofficial members who had led the campaign against Sir John. A British general election was imminent; a Liberal victory would bring down the ministry, and the Secretary of State, who had connived in the destruction of their Chief Justice. This was a great opportunity for the people of Trinidad. "The death of Sir John Gorrie has been an enormous loss. His presence in Trinidad, untrammelled by the ties of office, would have led us to a prompt victory. But though he is gone from us, his spirit is with us." The people owed it to "the great and good man who has laid down his life" for them to mobilize for constitutional reform. In nearby Grenada, the radical editor of the *Grenada People*, W.G. Donovan, described Gorrie's death as a blow to all West Indians, especially the poor blacks: "His biography is one record of good done for the human family", above all the 'subject races' of the Empire. Donovan published accounts from "our correspondent in Trinidad" – perhaps Rostant, or E.A. Nunes – which depicted the popular reaction to his death, and a letter from J.S. de Bourg, later active in Trinidad labour politics, calling him "the only friend of the poor and oppressed".[48]

In Britain, several newspapers published obituaries. *The Scotsman* of Edinburgh carried a short (and rather inaccurate) account of his career, which ended by describing him as "a man of impulsive disposition, of most generous sympathies and a thorough gentleman. Some of the land legislation which he drew up will doubtless become the model for legislation of a like kind in other colonies." A longer, and more accurate, article appeared in *The Times*. It noted that in the last years of his life, in Trinidad, "his sympathies with the coloured population were becoming more and more pronounced", bringing him into conflict with the governor and the planting interest. This obituary drew a letter from Sir Arthur Gordon, who corrected an inaccuracy about Gorrie's career in Mauritius, and "readily and gratefully" acknowledged the "assistance of the utmost value" which, as governor of Mauritius, he had received from Gorrie in all matters connected with the island's labour laws. Gordon also wrote a moving letter of condolence to Malcolm, saying that he had expected to see Gorrie soon, "as I thought that I was probably one of the friends whom he might wish to consult as to the course to be adopted by him in the very painful circumstances in which he had been placed". He told Malcolm that he could

> never forget the invaluable assistance rendered to me by your father in Mauritius. In saying this I by no means overlook or undervalue his services in Fiji, but it was in Mauritius that I was in the highest degree indebted to him, for without the help he gave me, and the courageous and uncompromising attitude he assumed it would probably have been quite impossible to expose the abuses which at that time prevailed in the colony.

The *European Mail*, which had followed his West Indian career with great interest, and no friendly feelings, noted his death after a troubled career in the colonial service:

> The storm which had begun to gather around Sir John's head in Fiji, and which grew in intensity during his career in the West Indies, burst the other day . . . Sir John Gorrie was essentially an enemy-making man, especially as his lot was cast in those tropical Crown Colonies where white and coloured peoples are found together. Through thick and thin he fervently espoused the cause of the coloured people, and the lengths to which he went in this direction often brought him into serious conflict with the whites.[49]

Gorrie had died under a cloud, unable to vindicate his judicial reputation or clear his name by his own efforts. It was – as his old friend Charles Cooper wrote a few years later – "a melancholy end".

EPILOGUE AND CONCLUSION

At least one supporter in Trinidad urged Malcolm Gorrie and his sisters to "try to get your father's political friends to try to . . . vindicate his character and clear his memory now of the stain cast upon it by such unprincipled and unscrupulous persons". They may have lobbied their father's influential friends privately; but it was his brother, the journalist and writer Daniel Gorrie, who wrote to the new Liberal Secretary of State to express "the strong desire of myself and other relatives . . . to know if things are to remain in this painful condition, with a shadow resting upon the name of one who has done long and distinguished service to the country in different parts of the world". He received a gracious if guarded reply, stating that Gorrie's death had put an end to any further enquiries into the charges against him; but the new Secretary of State, Lord Ripon, "would have been very glad if the further inquiry, which, but for Sir John Gorrie's lamented death, would have taken place, should have had the result of sustaining the high reputation which he had justly acquired in the earlier stages of his Colonial service". The men in the Colonial Office were quite prepared to acknowledge that "the quarrels in which he was frequently involved arose from his rooting out abuses, which but for him might have remained undiscovered for an indefinite time". The family had to remain satisfied with this; Daniel Gorrie had the reply published in *The Times*. It is ironic that the Liberal election victory of August 1892, from which Gorrie's allies, and perhaps he himself, had expected so much, occurred too late to be of any help to his cause.[1]

Gorrie died virtually penniless. He was not prudent in financial matters, and it is likely that he lost money in the People's Bank. The King's Bay estate in Tobago which he purchased in 1891 in Malcolm's name was fully mortgaged. Malcolm told a friend in Trinidad that if his married sister and her husband had not been in Britain when his father died, he and Minnie (his unmarried sister) would have been forced to avail themselves of the charity of friends. It does not seem that Gorrie had any life insurance or other assets when he died; he had not even left a will, so that Malcolm had difficulties in obtaining the small sum (about £120) due to his father in salary at his death.[2] Malcolm, a young man, well educated, who had already begun to read for the Bar and must have absorbed a great deal of legal knowledge from his years of working with his father, could fend for himself. But Minnie was left with nothing.

In 1893, a family friend (Eben Connal of Glasgow) wrote to Ripon, both as Secretary of State, "and as a member of that political party to which the late Sir John Gorrie also belonged", asking for assistance to Malcolm and Minnie, "to which the long and brilliant services of their Father so justly entitles them". Connal told Ripon, "Unfortunately for himself and those dependent on him he was so carried away by his love for and deep interest in official life that he neglected his own private affairs and as a natural consequence at his death these were found in a most unsatisfactory condition and his family left quite unprovided for." Malcolm was unemployed; he had helped his father "in his official duties" for several years but had never held a salaried post although (Connal claimed) "to all intents and purposes a Civil Servant". Connal asked Ripon if he could be found a post. On Minnie's behalf ("Miss Gorrie tho' not in absolute want is wholly without means, and quite dependent on her own exertions for a livelihood"), he asked that the widow's allowance to which Lady Gorrie would have been entitled, if she had not died in 1884, should be granted to her. The men in the Colonial Office were not unsympathetic to Connal's appeal. But Malcolm "did not seem the sort of man for whom it would be at all easy to find suitable employment", and

Ripon replied that he could make no promises. As for Minnie, they knew it was futile to appeal to the Trinidad legislature for a special grant. The only alternative was to request a grant from the Royal Bounty Fund, as Connal urged ("I can confidently say that there can be no more deserving or sadder case"), but the Office felt that granted the many claims on this Fund, there was no prospect of success.[3]

Malcolm did not obtain a government post. He was eventually called to the Bar and migrated to Canada, where he settled in British Columbia. Minnie, an intelligent and observant woman with the family's talent for writing, supported herself as a lady's 'companion' for the rest of her life. At the time of her father's death she was already 35, an age at which "a fresh start in life is a matter of great difficulty", as Connal observed.

It was not until the year after Gorrie's death that the report of the Judicial Enquiry Commission was laid before Parliament. In March 1893, the Earl of Stamford asked in the Lords whether the Secretary of State would lay the report on the table. He implied in his speech that there had been unnecessary delay in dealing with the complaints about the Trinidad judiciary and that follow up action was called for. Ripon denied that his predecessor had been guilty of undue delays – "It was a very serious thing to frame charges against judges" – and went on to tell the House that although the report "showed that the late Chief Justice fell into errors during the later part of his career", he had the "honour of acknowledging his earlier service". He said, further, that "two judges [Gorrie and Cook] had ceased to be judges of [the Trinidad] court"; and that he had "removed another judge [Lumb] to a different colony". He concluded that the court in Trinidad was, therefore, "newly constituted". Lord Knutsford, the Secretary of State between 1887 and 1892, explained that the earlier complaints against Gorrie had been carefully considered, but he had decided not to intervene; "it was in the highest degree undesirable that the Executive should interfere with the judiciary". The report was then formally presented to the Lords, and (in the following month) to the Commons. The *European Mail* commented sardonically "perchance some 'new chum' member may be found asking the government one of these days what action they propose to take in the matter!" But the Colonial Office considered that the removal, by death, dismissal or promotion, of the three judges who had served during the period which the Commission had investigated was all the action required of the British Government.[4]

However, the litigation against the Trinidad judges which had been initiated by R.B. Anderson dragged on for years after Gorrie's death. It was not until 1894 that his action for damages for illegal and malicious prosecution finally came before the Lord Chief Justice. He ruled against Anderson on the technical grounds that no action could lie against a judge for an act done in his judicial capacity. Anderson appealed this ruling, lost the appeal and tried to raise funds for an approach to the Privy Council. It was not until the end of 1895 – three years after Gorrie's death – that the Anderson litigation against the Trinidad judges finally ground to a halt.[5]

Throughout his colonial career, Gorrie attempted to use the law and the courts to protect labourers, peasants and indigenous people from unfair treatment. But the entire structure of the empire worked against his efforts to protect the "humbler subjects of Her Majesty" in Mauritius, Fiji and the Caribbean. The interests of capital, the reality of plantation regimes in nonwhite societies managed by Europeans, the social and racial structures of ex-slave communities, all reduced his effectiveness and severely restricted his impact on the colonies where he served. This was especially the case in the former slave-holding colonies, with their entrenched white oligarchies, of Mauritius and the Caribbean.

In Mauritius, Gorrie played a significant role in securing important reforms in the treatment both of the indentured Indians and of the 'old immigrants' who had completed their indentures. Arthur Gordon, the governor who initiated the process of reform, stated unequivocally that without Gorrie's help, "and the courageous and uncompromising attitude he assumed, it would probably have been quite impossible to expose the abuses which at that time prevailed in the colony".[6] This was a real achievement. He also helped to secure some modest reforms in archaic legal procedures and in laws relating to land. But Mauritian society was too firmly established, and its elite too secure in its control over the island and its people, for a crusading judge (or even governor, for that matter) to make much of an impact apart from these specific reforms.

Fiji was very different. It was on the frontier of white expansion in 1876; the crucial decisions about its development as a colony were yet to be made. There was no entrenched colonial elite and no traditions of slavery. Here Gorrie was able to take part in shaping a new society. Thanks to his close relationship with Gordon, as well as his own ability and energy, he did far more than a colonial chief justice would normally have done. He helped to govern the new colony, to make policy and to prepare legislation. With Gordon, J.B. Thurston, and a few others, he laid the foundations for modern Fiji. Through the Western Pacific High Commission, Gorrie helped to bring British subjects in this part of the world within reach of the law and to control the worse abuses arising out of their contacts with the islanders, especially through the labour traffic. He was both an agent of imperial expansion (advocating annexation in islands like Samoa where the local rulers seemed to be losing control to unscrupulous settlers), and an agent of imperial control over the whites actually in the Pacific. And since he and Gordon were on the spot when the High Commission was established, they helped to shape its mandate and its operations, though they did not always get what they wanted. In Fiji, Gorrie enjoyed greater scope for his talents and his energies, and probably had a greater impact over the long term, than in any of the other colonies where he served.

Gorrie spent the last ten years of his life in the Caribbean, where his colonial 'career' had begun with his visit to Jamaica in 1866 and his involvement in the 'Jamaica case' as one of a small group of men who publicized the Eyre massacres in Britain and sought to prevent a recurrence of such events in the empire. The editor of a newspaper in Barbados (where he never worked) wrote in 1890 that Gorrie had reformed the laws and promoted the colonists' prosperity in the Leeward Islands; he had squashed corruption and jobbery in Trinidad, and had dispensed equal justice to all (according to his own views) in both Trinidad and Tobago. In fact, this editor concluded, "if ever the modern history of the West Indies comes to be written, few men will figure more conspicuously in its pages than Sir John Gorrie".[7]

But these Caribbean islands were long-settled communities composed mainly of the descendants of slaves and slaveowners, with entrenched white elites who cherished racist traditions and had influential allies in Britain. Gorrie's belief in equality before the law and his willingness to defy the opinions and values of the local oligarchs generated strong and persistent opposition which culminated in Trinidad in the last years of his life. These forces also limited his effectiveness as an agent of change.

In the struggling little islands of the Leeward group, Gorrie achieved important reforms in the law, especially laws relating to land and mortgages, and his short but bracing term as Chief Justice probably helped to upgrade the judicial administration generally. In Tobago, also poor and struggling at the time of its union with Trinidad in 1889, his judicial visitations may have bolstered the confidence of the local peasants, metayers and labourers in their confrontations with their landlords and employers. His actions almost certainly made ordinary Tobagonians, unlike most of the island's planters and merchants, optimistic about the effects of union with Trinidad. It is possible that the end of metayage was hastened by his rulings, though the collapse of the sugar industry in Tobago was clearly inevitable by 1889. Gorrie would have welcomed the island's subsequent transformation into a peasant based economy, but it is difficult to see that he did much to bring it about. Yet his defiance of the island's elite and his willingness to open the courts to poor suitors with grievances against the planters made him a folk hero in Tobago.

It was certainly in Trinidad, of all the Caribbean colonies in which he served, that Gorrie had the greatest impact, an impact that was political rather than legal. His enemies were wrong when they argued that his actions seriously undermined capitalist confidence in the island's economy or caused the flow of British investment to dry up. There is no evidence for either assertion. Trinidad's cocoa industry flourished right through the 1890s and until after the First World War; her sugar industry weathered the crisis of the 1890s and enjoyed some prosperity in the early twentieth century; 'minor' crops expanded despite the hostility of the sugar barons.

The procedural innovations so much deplored by Gorrie's enemies did not last in the hands of his successors. By the end of 1892 the judicial regime had been transformed: Gorrie, Cook and Lumb were all gone. In the Legislative Council, Gorrie's old opponents recommended that the office of the second puisne judge be dispensed with, reversing their position in 1886-87; the troublemaker was safely dead and there was no further need to keep a Chief Justice under control. But complaints soon began to resurface about the poor being denied justice. In 1894, it was noted that suits in the Supreme Court *in forma pauperis* were again as rare as they had been before Gorrie. It was hard enough for simple men to approach even the lower courts, when solicitors and court fees had to be paid. In criminal cases, the poor man had to find money to bring a case, say, of assault or verbal abuse, so he simply put up with the wrong against him. Was it right for a man to be at the mercy of violence merely because he lacked means?[8]

But Gorrie did influence the island's political development in the years after his death. The *San Fernando Gazette* (then edited by his old ally Philip Rostant) had called on Trinidadians to mobilize for constitutional reform as a way of paying tribute to the late Chief Justice, and the course of the 'Reform Movement' of 1892-95 was certainly influenced by him. On the one hand, some prominent men who had earlier supported the introduction of elected members in the island's legislature now abandoned the cause, ostensibly because of alarm at Gorrie's radicalism. One of these was Eugene Lange, the defendant in the coconut contract cases of 1888. In a Council debate on constitutional change, he attributed his opposition to reform to the "reign of terror" by a "socialist judge". Edgar Tripp, one of the leaders in the anti-Gorrie campaign since 1887 and the secretary of the 'Unofficial Committee' in 1892, said he had come to understand "how much harm one hot-headed wrong-minded Radical" could do, and had reversed his earlier support for elected members.[9]

Many active in the Reform Movement supported Gorrie because they shared his liberal social views. Among them were Rostant, a French Creole; William Howatson and George Goodwille, Scottish businessmen of Port of Spain and members of the Council; J.S. de Bourg and E.A. Nunes, both black men involved in the 'radical' wing of the movement. Other reformers sympathized with his political and social convictions but opposed his judicial methods. Henry Alcazar, a mixed-race lawyer who was one of the main leaders of the movement, told the Council that he was

> no admirer of Sir John Gorrie but he would do him the justice to say this – that so far as [his] career as a politician, not as a Judge, was

> concerned, he had never noticed any ill effects from his policy . . . for if there was any change the labouring classes had learned that they were entitled to hold up their heads as well as anybody else, entitled to look to the future for a change in their position.[10]

Rostant had been Gorrie's most consistent and active supporter since 1887, mobilizing first *Public Opinion*, and then the *San Fernando Gazette*, to defend him, and helping to organize the various pro-Gorrie petitions and demonstrations of 1887-92. A veteran journalist, he was the main leader of the campaign for reform in 1887-89, and remained active in 1892-95. In 1895 Rostant declared his pride in his consistent support for the "late, great Chief Justice" against the attacks "of those who would revive all the hideousness of slavery whereby the Pierre Congos would be deprived of their rights and liberties".[11]

The campaign for constitutional reform in the early 1890s failed; in 1895 a new Conservative Secretary of State, Joseph Chamberlain, refused to allow elected members in the Legislative Council. But the Reform Movement was important in helping to politicize Trinidadians and in bringing to the fore crucial issues of social, political and economic development. Several men who became key leaders in political and labour movements in the early twentieth century learned leadership skills in the campaigns of 1887-89 and, especially, 1892-95. Some had been strong supporters of Gorrie, such as J.S. de Bourg. It seems fair to argue that Gorrie played a significant role in this development, and in the general politicization of important sectors of the middle and working classes of the island.[12]

For many educated blacks in late nineteenth century Trinidad and Tobago, and to some extent in the Eastern Caribbean generally, Gorrie was one of the few influential supporters and defenders of their people; "the only friend of the poor and the oppressed race", as de Bourg put it; and the enemy of "our hereditary foe, the West Indian oligarch", in W.G. Donovan's words.[13] The spokesmen for the race in the islands had not forgotten Gorrie's work in Jamaica after Morant Bay, and a Dominican editor had reminded his readers that the Chief Justice deserved the gratitude of West Indian blacks for his advocacy of G.W. Gordon and the other martyrs of 1865. In 1888 Gorrie supported the young black and mixed-race teachers and lawyers who called for public celebrations of the Jubilee of Emancipation in Trinidad. He won the admiration and support of their leader, Edgar Maresse-Smith, a solicitor who subsequently worked with him in Tobago. In general, Gorrie developed close and mutually respectful relations with several black or brown professional men in Trinidad, including the Solicitor-General, Michael Maxwell Philip, the Registrar-General, C.H. Phillipps, de Bourg, Nunes and Maresse-Smith. Alcazar admired his views though not all his judicial practices. Donovan of Grenada thought he had sacrificed his life in the defence of the 'negro race' against its – and his – oppressors. Gorrie's social and political views, his defiance of the local island elites, and his willingness to work with black, mixed-race or white men who shared his ideas, must have helped to bolster the confidence of politically active blacks in the rightness of their cause and their aspirations for the progress of their people.

Moreover, Gorrie became an authentic popular hero in Trinidad and in Tobago. The evidence makes it clear that the ordinary people of the islands, especially the Creole blacks, saw him as their champion and protector and publicly demonstrated their respect and gratitude on many occasions. This seems to have been equally true of the working class of Port of Spain and San Fernando as of the rural masses in the remoter villages of Trinidad and Tobago. The organization of the 'No-Inquiry Petition' in 1887 by Gorrie's supporters, moreover, probably marks the first attempt at popular mobilization for a political purpose (outside Carnival) in the history of Trinidad, involving as it did thousands of ordinary urban and rural people, in marked contrast with the Reform Movement of 1892-95, largely an affair of educated, middle-stratum men. Creole women, too, took a prominent part in the public demonstrations of gratitude to 'Papa Gorrie', according to the newspaper accounts. Lacking prominent leaders and heroes from their own ranks or even from the black middle stratum, denied access to political institutions or formal channels for political mobilisation, the Creole masses of Trinidad and Tobago turned 'ah we Judge' into a folk hero, perhaps the first in the history of the two islands. It was a strange apotheosis for a British chief justice serving in a nineteenth century crown colony, but it is striking evidence of the impression made by Gorrie's actions and personality on a people who knew themselves to be oppressed. And it was not until the advent of A.A. Cipriani and T.U.B. Butler in the 1920s and 1930s that these people found leaders and heroes with the popularity and mass support that Gorrie (though in very different ways, of course) had attracted in the 1880s and 1890s.

But the Caribbean elites were skilful and persistent enemies. In Britain they had powerful allies. The West India Committee lobbied for them (Donovan thought that the Committee had named the Judicial Enquiry Commission and had insisted that its findings must be hostile to Gorrie), and they could always find MPs with West Indian connections to lobby or to ask questions in Parliament. They often dominated local legislatures. Even in Trinidad, a crown colony with no elected members in the Council, the unofficial members, representing the propertied interests, usually had things their way. It was a group of unofficial members (the 'Unofficial Committee') which engineered the Judicial Enquiry Commission, functioned like prosecuting counsel during its sessions, and helped to ensure that its findings were adverse to Gorrie. After his death, these same members got the Council to agree to pay all the expenses of the 'Unofficial Committee' and even to reimburse R.B. Anderson for his costs in coming from Britain to testify against the Chief Justice.

Gorrie's career illustrates the power of local elites in the Caribbean colonies, even under crown colony government, to deal with British officials whom they disapproved of. Though the men in the Colonial Office supported Gorrie in a long succession of skirmishes with influential colonial citizens, they yielded in 1891-92. It is true that he often tested their patience by his lack of finesse, his 'bull in a china shop' approach to most issues, and his failures to control his temper and his tongue. But they knew that he was dedicated to reforming abuses and dispensing substantive justice, and they allowed a hostile enquiry into his administration of justice in the full knowledge that the vast majority of Trinidadians and Tobagonians had complete confidence in him. In the final analysis they were unable to withstand the oligarchs. In this, as on so many issues, the Colonial Office was trapped by its long history of serving the interests of the British and colonial capitalists despite the rhetoric of trusteeship which justified crown colony government.

Throughout the nineteenth and twentieth centuries, British imperialism threw up from time to time men like Gorrie, maverick colonial officials who tried to serve the interests of the 'subject peoples' and to make a reality of the doctrine of trusteeship. In Trinidad, Chief Justice Scotland, who served at the time of slave emancipation, had acquired this kind of reputation; and a century later, during the widespread labour protests of 1937, the governor, Sir Murchison Fletcher, and the colonial secretary, Howard Nankivell, risked their careers by acknowledging the hardships and grievances of the labourers and the inevitability of the strikes and riots. Gorrie's contemporary, Chief Justice Joseph Beaumont of British Guiana, was removed from his position because he angered the local oligarchs and the governor.[14] As a case study of a colonial official of this type, Gorrie's career seems to illustrate the limited impact that these mavericks could make on the colonies where they served. His work did have a lasting influence on the course of events in Fiji, because of the special circumstance of his close relationship with Arthur Gordon and his service at the beginning of the islands' history as a British colony. In the other places where he worked, though his short-term impact on political and legal developments was considerable, especially in Trinidad and Tobago, his influence over the longer term was probably quite limited.

Gorrie's crusade to put into practice the trusteeship doctrine of British imperialism was a failure, despite specific reforms here and there which he helped to bring about. The whole structure of the nineteenth century empire ensured that the interests of investors, owners and planters would ultimately prevail over concerns for indigenous or imported labourers or peasants. It is not that the men in the Colonial Office were indifferent to those concerns; and time and time again, they supported Gorrie in his many confrontations with colonial elites. Their correspondence and minutes make it clear that some of them admired his efforts to dispense impartial justice and to open the courts to the poor. But when the magnates of Trinidad and their allies in Britain decided that Gorrie was a threat to their fundamental interests, and moved against him, the Colonial Office capitulated. Gorrie's propensity for intemperate public outbursts, and his 'bending' of judicial procedures, provided cover for their decision to allow an enquiry which was bound to lead to some action against him. Fifty years later, Fletcher was forced to resign, and

Nankivell was demoted and transferred out of Trinidad, because the local capitalists and the Colonial Office felt that their sympathy for labour was subversive. The British empire did not run on moral premises.

Throughout his colonial career – and even earlier, in his political and journalistic work in Edinburgh and London – Gorrie tried to advance the causes he had taken up as a young man. His flaws of personality and temper became increasingly counterproductive, especially in the last years of his life when family tragedies and a sense of grievance embittered him, and these flaws clearly limited his effectiveness in many ways. Yet without his determination, his passionate beliefs, his forceful, even bullying personality, and his indifference to popularity, he would probably never have persisted as a crusading judge. He wanted to serve humanity, and he would have been pleased with the epitaph pronounced by W.G. Donovan, the Grenadian journalist and editor whom he probably never met: "His biography is one record of good done for the human family."[15]

NOTES

Abbreviations used in notes

Names of persons, offices, officials

JG John Gorrie

WDV William Des Voeux

SS Secretary of State (for the Colonies)

FO Foreign Office

CJ Chief Justice

AG Attorney-General

AG Arthur Gordon

WR William Robinson

CO Colonial Office

HMG Her Majesty's Government

OAG Officer administering the Government

PJ Puisne Judge

SC/SR Special Commissioner/Special Reporter (for the *Morning Star*)

(S)PG (Substitute) Procureur-General (Mauritius)

MP Ministère Public (Mauritius)

FC F.W. Chesson

Col Sec Colonial Secretary

Titles of newspapers

Britain:

MS *Morning Star*

EFR East Fife Record

FJ *Fifeshire Journal*

EM *European Mail*

EC *Edinburgh Courant*

WHM *Weekly Herald & Mercury*

Jamaica:

CS *Colonial Standard and Jamaica Despatch*

Mauritius:

CG Commercial Gazette

Fiji:

FT *Fiji Times*

FA *Fiji Argus*

ST *Suva Times*

Leeward Islands:

AO Antigua Observer

AS *Antigua Standard*

DD Dominica Dial

Dom *Dominican*

SCI *St Christopher Independent*

SCG *St Christopher Gazette*

Trinidad and Tobago:

TRG *Trinidad Royal Gazette*

PO *Public Opinion*

POSG Port of Spain Gazette

NE *New Era*

SFG *San Fernando Gazette*

Tel *Telegraph*

TN *Tobago News*

TT *Trinidad Times*

NB Citations of newspapers refer to editorial comment unless otherwise indicated.

Other

Min(s) Minute(s)

Conf Confidential

Encl Enclosed (in)

Tel Telegram

Memo Memorandum

Ev Evidence (of)

BFASS British and Foreign Anti-Slavery Society

illeg illegible

APS Aborigines Protection Society

PP Parliamentary Papers

Leg Co Legislative Council

CP Council Paper

JRC Jamaica Royal Commission (1866)

JC Jamaica Committee

MRC Mauritius Royal Commission (1872-74)

PIC Police Inquiry (or Enquiry) Committee (Mauritius,1871-72)

LC Lands Commission (Fiji)

Sup Ct Supreme Court

WPHC Western Pacific High Commission

HC High Commissioner

JC Judicial Commissioner

LI Leeward Islands

POS Port of Spain

TTC Trade and Taxes Commission (Trinidad, 1886)

JEC Judicial Enquiry Commission (Trinidad, 1892)

TMC Tobago Metairie Commission (1890)

CD Diary of F.W. Chesson (unpublished)

JRL John Rylands Library, University of Manchester

BL British Library, London

ERO Edinburgh Record Office

NB Correspondence between Arthur Gordon (Lord Stanmore) and John Gorrie has been cited in the notes as follows:

1. When printed in Lord Stanmore, *Mauritius, Records of Private and of Public Life, 1871-74*. 2 vols. (Edinburgh 1894, privately printed): as AG to JG with the date of the letter followed by Stanmore, 1 or 2, and page reference.

2. When printed in Lord Stanmore, *Fiji Records of Private and of Public Life, 1875-1880*. 4 vols. (Edinburgh 1897-1912, private and confidential): as AG to JG with the date of the letter followed by S/F, I: II, III, or IV, and page reference.

3. When seen in the Stanmore Papers, British Library: as AG to JG with the date of the letter followed by the British Library Mss. numbers (49203 or 49205).

4. When seen in the private collection of the late Graham Gorrie of Brisbane: as AG to JG with the date of the letter but no further reference. These letters, along with other family correspondence cited without any further references, have been read and cited by permission of the family.

Introduction

1. Exeter Hall was the name of a London meeting place which antislavery groups frequented; the term came to mean the whole British antislavery movement.

2. Lord Coleridge's ruling (April 1894) in *EM* 9/5/94. For the Anderson cases, see chapter 8.

3. C. Bolt, *The Anti-Slavery Movement and Reconstruction* (London 1969), 151; B. Semmell, *Jamaican Blood and Victorian Conscience: the Governor Eyre Controversy* (Boston 1963), 140-41.

4. *Grenada People* 18/8/92.

Chapter 1

1. M.F. Conolly, *Biographical Dictionary of Eminent Men of Fife* (Edinburgh 1866), entry on Daniel Gorrie.

2. H.F. Conolly, *Biographical Dictionary*; R. Small, *History of United Presbyterian Congregations 1733-1900* (Edinburgh 1904); *Fifeshire Herald* 1/4/52 and *Fife Journal*

1/4/52: Obits; Isobel Gorrie to Malcolm Gorrie n.d. *c.*1902.

3. D. Gorrie, "My Grandmother's Portrait" in W.A. Clouston (ed), *The Book of Scottish Story* (Edinburgh 1876).

4. Isobel Gorrie to Malcolm Gorrie n.d. *c.*1902.

5. Isobel Gorrie to Malcolm Gorrie, n.d. *c.*1902; D. Gorrie, "My Grandmother's Portrait" and "Nanny Walsh, the Minister's Maid" in Clouston, *Scottish Story* and *Geordie Purdie in London* (London, n.d. [?1873]), 48-49; ERO, Fife: Register of Inventories, D. Gorrie 24/9/52.

6. J. Thompson, *The Madras College 1833-1983* (Kirkaldy n.d. [?1983]), 1-25; *FJ* 5/8/41: Advt.; 1841 Census: St Andrews.

7. Thompson, 25-36; *FJ* 4/8/42: Madras College Annual Examinations.

8. *FJ* 5/8/41: Madras College Prize List; Letters from J. Currie, University Archives, University of Edinburgh, 5/8/1988 and 18/7/1989; Lord Macmillan, *A Man of Law's Tale* (London 1952), 13.

9. G.E. Davie, *The Democratic Intellect Scotland and her Universities in the Nineteenth Century* (Edinburgh 1961), xii.

10. Davie, xvii, 4-7; D.B. Horn, *A Short History of the University of Edinburgh 1556-1889* (Edinburgh 1967), 117-20, 137-44; Macmillan, 13-14.

11. Davie, 4-7, 12-17, 51; Macmillan, 14-18; Horn, 117-20.

12. Davie, 68-70; Horn, 157-67.

13. *St Andrews Citizen* 13/9/92; 1851 Census: Fifeshire; ERO, Fife: Register of Inventories D. Gorrie 24/9/52.

14. *ST* 11/11/82; *Age* 31/3/60; *St Andrews Citizen* 13/8/92; *Scotsman* 9/8/92; *EFR* 16/8/89, 23/8/89; C.A. Cooper, *An Editor's Retrospect Fifty Years of Newspaper Work* (London 1896), 147.

15. JG to Isabella Gorrie, Cupar, 17/1/51.

16. Letter from Deputy Librarian, Advocates Library, Edinburgh, 4/11/1988; Davie, 53-55; Macmillan, 22-33.

17. Macmillan, 25-33.

18. J. Gorrie, *Memories of Many Lands* (Port of Spain 1888), 1; Macmillan, 37; HMSO, *The Legal System in Scotland* (Edinburgh 1981), 1-7; M.C. Meston et al., *The Scottish Legal Tradition* (Edinburgh 1991).

19. Macmillan, 39-43, 84-87; J.B.Mackie, *The Life and Work of Duncan McLaren* (London 1888: 2 vols.), I: 192; II: 123-24. See also an editorial in the *Morning Star*, almost certainly written by Gorrie, denouncing the Lord Advocate's powers of patronage: *MS* 19/2/67.

20. *Morning Journal* (Jamaica) 13/1/66; HMSO, *The Legal System*, 23-24.

21. Mackie, I: 167-77; II: 215-21.

22. Mackie, I: 225-46; II: 1-19.

23. Mackie, II: 25-58; *Scotsman* 29/12/58.

24. *EC* 14/10/56, 5/11/56, 8/11/56, 24/10/57; *Scotsman* 18/10/56, 22/10/56, 29/10/56, 5/11/56, 24/10/57; *Edinburgh Directory*, 1857/58.

25. *WHM* 17/11/60.

26. Mackie, I: 178-210; *MS* 20/2/67: Annuity Tax Abolition (Edinburgh) Bill.

27. *Scotsman* 16/10/60.

28. *Scotsman* 25/10/60.

29. Mackie, I: 178-210.

30. G.M. Trevelyan, *The Life of John Bright* (London 1913), 276; Mackie, II: 148-49; *EC* 16/12/58, 18/12/58; *Scotsman* 18/12/58, 29/12/58; *Truth* 18/8/92.

31. For this and the preceding paragraph, see E.L. Woodward, *The Age of Reform 1815-1870* (Oxford 1962), 178; G.M. Young (ed.), *Early Victorian England, 1830-1865* (London 1934 2 vols.), II: 483; W. Stephen, *History of the Queen's City of Edinburgh Rifle Volunteer Brigade* (Edinburgh & London 1881), "No. 8 (First Artisan) Company"; *Age* 16/7/59; *WHM* 10/8/60; *Scotsman*, 16/7/59, 22/11/60; *Scots Magazine*, Feb 1987: 518-23; *Dundee Advertiser* 26/8/89.

32. R.Q. Gray, *The Labour Aristocracy in Victorian Edinburgh* (Oxford 1976), 141-43; I. MacDougall (ed), *The Minutes of the Edinburgh Trades Council 1859-1873* (Edinburgh 1968), 30/11/61, 25/3/62; *Edinburgh News* 9/2/61; *Age* 30/1/58 and Advertisement for 1860; ERO, South College St, U.P. Church, Edinburgh: Session Mins 1858-59, Managers' Meetings Mins 1855-60; *Dundee Advertiser* 26/8/89; *EFR* 13/12/89: "Sir John Gorrie on the duty of Christians".

33. C.D. Rice, *The Scots Abolitionists 1833-1861* (Baton Rouge and London 1981), 158-60, 187-94; H. Temperley, *British Anti-Slavery 1833-1870* (Columbia 1972), 213, 244-45; Mackie, I: 320; C. Hall, "The economy of intellectual prestige: Thomas Carlyle, John Stuart Mill, and the case of Governor Eyre", *Cultural Critique* 12 (spring 1989): 188-89.

34. Gorrie, *Memories*, 1-2.

35. *Memories*, 2-5; *Edinburgh News* 9/2/61: Lecture by JG 2/2/61.

36. Marion Graham's certificate of baptism; Will of Michael Graham, 5/2/40; ERO, Sassine (Property) Index Books: several entries re Grahams 1846-59; 1861 Census, Edinburgh; Declaration by JG to Collector of Fund 26/6/56 and Letter from J.C. of the Fund to JG 23/1/63: Records of Advocates' Library, Edinburgh; *CS* 27/2/66, quoting *Fifeshire Courant*, January 1866; Gorrie Family Bible.

37. *ST* 11/11/82.

38. Macmillan, 48-49, 56, 75; Gorrie, *Memories*, 5; *St Andrews Citizen* 13/8/92; *Scotsman* 9/8/92; *Dundee Advertiser* 26/8/89.

39. Woodward, 472-73. Cf an editorial in *Morning Star*, quite possibly written by JG, advocating radical reform in the English legal system: *MS* 25/2/67.

40. J. McCarthy, *Reminiscences* (London 1899), 1: 167-68.

41. Trevelyan, 214; McCarthy, *Reminiscences*, 1: 163-64; John Morley, *Early Life and Letters of John Morley* (London 1927), 1: 155; H.R. Fox -Bourne, *English Newspapers* (London 1887), 2: 238-39, 241; Cooper, 140-47.

42. McCarthy, 1: 167; J. McCarthy, *Portraits of The Sixties* (London 1903), 111-12, 118-19; Cooper, 114.

43. McCarthy, *Reminiscences*, 1: 167-68, 169-71; Fox-Bourne, 2: 271-72; Cooper, 98-100.

44. *ST* 11/11/82.

45. McCarthy, *Reminiscences*, 1: 185-87; Morley, *Early Life*, 1: 154-57; *MS* 6/1/68; Fox-Bourne, 2: 271-72; Cooper, 140-47.

46. CD 1/10/69, 8/10/69.

47. Cooper, 108-09, 147-49.

48. *Dundee Advertiser* 26/8/89.

49. Temperley, 248-58; C. Bolt, *The Anti-Slavery Movement and Reconstruction; a Study in Anglo-American Cooperation, 1833-1877* (London 1969), 26-32; D.A. Lorimer, "The role of anti-slavery sentiment in English reactions to the American Civil War", *Historical Journal* 19 (2), (1976): 405-421.

50. CD 12/1/63, 29/1/63, 6/2/63; *MS* 20/4/63, 7/5/63, 14/5/63, 21/9/63, 22/9/63, 28/9/63, 21/10/63.

51. CD 3/12/64, 15/12/64, 26/8/65; Bolt, 54-65.

52. *Kelso Mail* 29/7/68; *MS* 29/7/68, 30/7/68; *Times* 28/7/68.

53. *Kelso Mail* 1/8/68; *Times* 31/7/68.

54. *MS* 17/3/66: From Our Special Commissioner 22/2/66.

Chapter 2

1. For accounts and interpretations of these events and their background, see: Gad Heuman, *'The Killing Time': The Morant Bay Rebellion in Jamaica* (London 1994) – the main title is taken from one of Gorrie's newspaper articles; D. Hall, *Free Jamaica 1838-1865* (London 1969), chapter 8; P. Curtin, *Two Jamaicas* (New York 1975), chapters 8 and 9; D. Robotham, " 'The Notorious Riot': the socioeconomic and political bases of Paul Bogle's revolt" (Mona, Jamaica: ISER Working Paper 1981); T. Holt, *The Problem of Freedom: Race, Labor and Politics in Jamaica and Britain, 1832-1938* (Baltimore & Kingston 1992), chapter 8; A. Bakan, *Ideology and Class Conflict in Jamaica* (Montreal & Kingston 1990), chapter 3. See also J. Gorrie, *Illustrations of Martial Law in Jamaica* (London 1867).

2. Eyre to Cardwell 20/10/65 with postscript 23/10/65 in *MS* 20/11/65; see *Times* 3/11/65 and 17/11/65 for initial reports.

3. *MS* 20/11/65: Letter from L.A. Chamerovzow 17/11/65 and from unnamed correspondent in Jamaica, 28/10/65; also Chamerovzow to Editors 22/11/85, printed circular, JRL, Box 21 no. 26; *MS* 30/11/65.

4. Bright to McCarthy 13/11/65, 6/12/65, in McCarthy, *Reminiscences*, 1: 91-93; F. Harrison, *Autobiographic Memoirs* (London 1911), 1: 304-05; CD 4/12/65, 15/12/65.

5. McCarthy, *Reminiscences*, 1: 282; printed circular from Chamerovzow 2/12/65 and petition 24/11/65, in JRL Box 21 no. 6; B. Semmell, *Jamaican Blood and Victorian Conscience: the Governor Eyre Controversy* (Boston 1963), 22-28, 62-65; H.L. Malchow, *Agitators and Promoters in the Age of Gladstone and Disraeli* (New York 1983), 243-45 for a complete list of JC's membership.

6. *Morning Journal* 13/1/66; CD 15/12/65, 16/12/65; Gorrie, *Memories*, 5; Bright to JG 16/12/65.

7. *MS* 16/1/66: JC's Case and Lawyers' Opinion, 13/1/66.

8. *MS* 19/1/66: Letter of Instruction from Shaen and Roscoe to JG and J.H. Payne, Jan. 1866; W.F. Finlason, *The History of the Jamaica Case* (London 1869), 368.

9. *CS* 8/1/66, 22/1/66; *MS* 30/1/66: Letter from SC 8/1/66.

10. *MS* 3/3/66: From SC 8/3/66; *CS* 27/1/66, 1/2/66: Proceedings of JRC; JRC, 1866, Part II, 1; all references are to Part II unless stated otherwise.

11. *CS* 26/1/66: Proceedings of RC; JRC, 690, Qs 33829-33840; Gorrie, *Illustrations*, 11-13.

12. JRC 263, Qs 13599-13601; 489, Qs 24865-24867; 188, Qs 9537-9543.

13. *MS* 13/2/66: From SC 24/1/66; Gorrie, *Memories*, 5, *MS* 3/3/66: From SC 8/2/66.

14. Gorrie, *Illustrations*, v-vii; *CS* 17/2/66, 19/2/66, 24/2/66. 'Quashie', a version of an Ashanti man's name, was used in the West Indies to refer to an uneducated black.

15. Gorrie, *Illustrations*, 2-4; *MS* 13/2/66: From SC 24/1/66; *MS* 31/3/66: From SC 26/2/66. For a balanced assessment of the rebellion, based on extensive research, see Heuman, *'Killing Time'*.

16. JRC 188-89, 336-39, 284-88, 359-61; C.S. Roundell, *England and her Subject-Races with special reference to Jamaica* (London 1866), 31.

17. *MS* 3/3/66, 17/3/66, 31/3/66, 12/4/66: All from SC.

18. *MS* 19/6/66: Extracts from RC Report d. 9/4/66 & Laid on Table 18/6/66; and editorial, probably written by JG.

19. Daniel Gorrie to JG 17/4/66; *MS* 12/4/66: From SC 24/3/66.

20. *CS* 24/2/66, 25/2/66, 8/3/66, 10/3/66, 14/3/66, 24/3/66. "Nancy" refers to Anansi, an Ashanti trickster-hero of Jamaican folklore; a "Nancy story" means a tall tale.

21. Daniel Gorrie to JG 17/4/66; *CS* 25/2/66; 8/3/66: Our London Correspondent 16/2/66; 13/3/66; 14/3/66; 24/3/66; 13/4/66.

22. *Morning Journal* 2/3/66, 16/3/66, 2/4/66, 20/4/66.

23. *CS* 24/3/66.

24. *MS* 17/3/66: From SC 21/2/66; 31/3/66: From SC 26/2/66; 19/4/66: From SC 26/3/66.

25. *MS* 31/3/66: From SC 26/2/66; 19/4/66: From SC 26/3/66.

26. The best account of the controversy in Britain over the rebellion is Semmel, *Jamaican Blood.* See also B.A. Knox, "The British Government and the Governor Eyre controversy, 1865-1875", *Historical Journal* 19 (4), (1976): 877-900; C. Hall, "Economy of intellectual prestige", 167-96; Holt, *Problem of Freedom*, 279-85.

27. CD 14/4/66, 9/5/66, 11/5/66, 16/4/66.

28. CD 26/6/66; Semmell, *Jamaican Blood*, 68-80; *MS* 1/8/66: Commons debate 31/7/66; Mill's speech published in JC, *Jamaica Papers*, no. 111 (London 1866), 7-13.

29. CD 3/8/66; *MS* 12/10/66: Address from JC to Friends; 15/11/66: Advt: The JC Ten Thousand Pounds Fund; JC Circular, Oct. 1866: JRL, Box 21, no. 29; *Jamaica Papers*, no. 111: Statement of JC, 27/7/66.

30. Marquis of Lorne, *A Trip to the Tropics and Home Through America* (London 1867), 117-19, 74-75 – Lorne repeated in his 1867 book the statements in the earlier letter to *The*

Telegraph; *MS* 14/9/66: Letter to editor from JG 13/9/66; Lorne to JG, Kilmory, 19/9/66.

31. T. Carlyle, "Shooting Niagara: and after?" in *Essays* (London 1964), 1: 308-309; *MS* 13/9/66; Semmell, *Jamaican Blood* 102-16; C. Hall, 167-96; McCarthy, *Reminiscences*, 2: 320.

32. Semmell, *Jamaican Blood*, 130-132; Harrison, *Autobiographic Memoirs*, 1: 313-314; Roundell, 18-20.

33. *Times* 13/11/65, quoted Bolt, 43; Reply to Address by Custos of Kingston 24/7/66, quoted G. Dutton, *The Hero as Murderer* (London 1967), 321.

34. *MS* 25/5/66: editorial (perhaps written by JG); Semmell, 125-26; *MS* 22/5/68.

35. *MS* 7/2/67, 8/2/67, 9/2/67, 11/2/67, 13/2/67: Bow Street.

36. *MS* 13/2/67, 20/2/67, 25/2/67: Bow Street.

37. *MS* 18/2/67, 6/3/67; *MS* 25/3/67: From Market Drayton.

38. *MS* 26/3/67, 27/3/67, 28/3/57, 29/3/67, 1/4/67: Market Drayton.

39. *MS* 30/3/67, 1/4/67; 4/4/67: Letter from JG 2/4/67.

40. *MS* 1/4/67. Cf L. Stephen, *The Life of Sir James Fitzjames Stephen* (London 1895), 229-30; CD 24/5/67.

41. Stephen, 229; Harrison, 1: 313-14; *MS* 11/4/67: Cockburn's Charge, 10/4/67, and editorial.

42. *MS* 29/5/67: Cockburn's Charge, and editorial.

43. Carlyle, "Shooting Niagara", 308; *MS* 12/4/67: Central Criminal Court; *MS* 13/4/67, 29/7/67: Shaen & Roscoe to AG 10/7/67 and AG to Shaen & Roscoe 13/7/67.

44. *MS* 16/5/68, 20/5/68, 21/5/68: Bow St; W.F. Finlason, *Report of the Case of the Queen* v *Edward John Eyre* (London 1868), 2, 13.

45. *MS* 21/5/68: Bow St, and editorial.

46. *MS* 3/6/68: Court of Queen's Bench 2/6/68; evidence, indictment and charge published in Finlayson, *Report.*

47. *MS* 3/6/68; 4/6/68: Letter from Jurist, Temple, 3/6/68.

48. *MS* 5/6/68: Letters from Eyre to *Times* 2/6/68 and JG to editor 4/6/68.

49. *MS* 23/7/68: Letter from Mill, Taylor, Chesson to Members of JC 15/7/68; *MS* 26/5/68: Commons 25/5/68; *MS* 6/6/68, 18/6/68, 23/6/68; Semmell, 176-77; Knox, 877-900.

50. CD 28/5/66, 7/6/66; Gorrie, *Illustrations.*

51. J.S. Mill, *Autobiography* (New York 1924), 176-77; Taylor quoted in Semmell, 176-77; J. McCarthy, *A History of Our Own Times* (London 1880), 4: 50-51.

52. Goldwin Smith quoted in E. Wallace, *Goldwin Smith Victorian Liberal* (Toronto 1957), 24. The response to a later British massacre, Amritsar in 1919, closely parallels the Morant Bay controversy; see D. Sayer, "British reaction to the Amritsar Massacre, 1919-1920" in D. Segal (ed.) *Crossing Cultures: Essays in the Displacement of Western Culture* (Tucson & London 1992), 142-81.

53. *MS* 15/11/66, 17/9/67, 20/4/69.

54. *MS* 14/4/68.

Chapter 3

1. Storks to JG 22/1/69. Presumably Jamaica is an error for Mauritius: Bright to JG 22/1/69, 21/5/69.

2. CO 167/516 Barkly to Granville 28/5/69 no. 129: Draft Granville to Barkly 10/8/69 no. 201 and Cox to JG 10/8/69; CO 167/523 JG to Sir F.R. Sandford 12/8/69, JG to Granville 18/10/69; CO 167/524: Barkly to Granville 5/1/70 no. 1.

3. CO 167/525 Barkly to Granville 6/4/70 Conf. CO 167/525 Barkly to Granville 8/4/70 no. 92: Draft Kimberley to OAG 4/8/70 no. 15; CO 167/528 OAG Smyth to Kimberley 15/9/70 no. 65.

4. CO 167/528 OAG Smyth to Kimberley 15/9/70 no. 65 Encl JG to OAG Smyth 11/9/70.

5. CO 167/546 Gordon to Kimberley 18/9/72 Conf. Encl. W.E. Frere to Gordon 6/9/72 Conf.

6. For nineteenth century Mauritius, see W.L. Mathieson, *The Sugar Colonies and Governor Eyre, 1849-1866* (London 1936), 32-46, 51-52, 97-99; J.K. Chapman, *The Career of A.H. Gordon, First Lord Stanmore* (Toronto 1964), 102-154; B. Benedict, *Indians in a Plural Society; a Report on Mauritius* (London 1961), 16-31; *MS* 28/1/69.

7. *CG* 1/2/70, 13/6/70; CO 167/516 Barkly to Granville 28/5/69 no. 129.

8. CO 167/528 OAG Smyth to Kimberley 23/9/70 Conf. Encl. Memo as to the office of SPG by JG, 23/9/70.

9. CO 167/567 Phayre to Carnarvon 3/2/76 no. 63; *CG* 1/2/70.

10. *CG* 8/3/71; JG to AG 7/3/73, in Lord Stanmore [A.H. Gordon], *Mauritius, Records of Private and of Public Life, 1871-1874* (Edinburgh 1894; Private and Confidential; 2 vols.), 2: 149-50; hereafter cited as Stanmore, 1 and 2; CO 167/525 Barkly to Granville 8/4/70 no. 92.

11. AG to Lord Richard Cavendish, June 1871, Stanmore, 1: 124-5; JG to AG, 13/10/74, in Lord Stanmore, *Fiji Records of Private and of Public Life 1875-1880* (Edinburgh 1897-1912; Private and Confidential, 4 vols.), 1: 28-29; *CG* 31/3/75.

12. JG to FC 2/6/71, C 135/157 and C 135/159, Papers of the APS, Rhodes House Library, University of Oxford. AG's Journal, 2/6/74; JG to AG 1/6/74; JG to AG 19/8/74: in Stanmore, 2: 611, 682.

13. *CG* 3/6/71: Letter from P. D'Unienville; *CG* 11/3/75: Assizes 11/3/75; *CG* 23/11/75: Assizes 22/11/75; *CG* 20/11/72.

14. *CG* 29/10/72: Sup Ct 25/10/72; *CG* 20/3/73; *CG* 6/5/74; *CG* 12/2/76: Sup Ct 9 & 10/2/76; *CG* 11/9/73: Assizes 11/9/73; *CG* 26/11/73: Assizes 25/11/73.

15. *CG* 30/12/74, 20/2/75, 6/9/75, 6/1/76, 20/3/76.

16. CO 167/560 Gordon to Carnarvon 26/8/74 no. 241, Encl Report as to the Notaries and Attorneys of Mauritius by JG, 22/6/74.

17. *CG* 17/8/70, 22/8/70, 24/8/70: Sup Ct 15/8/70.

18. *CG* 28/9/70: Sup Ct 27/9/70; 4/10/70: Sup Ct 30/9/70; 24/10/70: Sup Ct 25/10/70 and editorial; 19/11/70; 17/6/73: Sup Ct 13/6/73; 29/7/73 & 30/7/73: Sup Ct 13/6/73 and editorial; 2/8/73; 7/8/73.

19. See note 16; Minutes 19/10/74 & 20/10/74 and Carnarvon to Phayre 29/3/75 no. 55.

20. Report on the Land Laws of Mauritius by JG, Jan. 1874, paras 155-68; *CG* 14/6/73, 17/6/73, 24/6/73, 16/7/73.

21. CO 167/568 Phayre to Carnarvon 27/3/76 no. 106, Encl Gorrie to H.E. in Council 6/3/76 and Opinion of PG in Mins of Executive Council 8/3/76; Carnarvon to Phayre 22/5/76 no. 98.

22. *CG* 3/12/73: Assizes 2/12/73; JG to FC 12/11/75, 30/4/75.

23. *CG* 22/11/70: Assizes 21/11/70; 12/3/73: Assizes 12/3/73; 13/3/73; 14/3/73: Letter from Justitia 14/3/73; 18/12/73: Bail Court 11/12/73; 26/3/74; 9/4/74: Assizes 9/4/74; 6/9/75.

24. Report on the Land Laws of Mauritius by JG, Jan. 1874, paras 1-69, 71-104.

25. Ibid, paras 132-53, 155-60, 170-71.

26. CO 167/560 Gordon to Carnarvon 23/6/74 no. 171; Carnarvon to OAG Newton 4/8/74 no. 180; CO 167/562 G.B. Colin to Henry Holland 2/4/74; Carnarvon to Gordon 11/4/74 no. 80.

27. Judges of Sup Ct to Phayre 15/1/75, Minute by Phayre 3/11/77 and Ag PG to Ag Col Sec 9/8/81, printed with JG's Report.

28. For Gordon's career before 1871 see Chapman, chapters 1-3.

29. Stanmore, 1, AG to Lord R. Cavendish, June 1871, 124-25; ibid, 2, Journal 21/6/74, 639; ibid, 2, AG to V. Williamson 30/6/74, 641; JG to FC 26/5/75. For CJ Beaumont of British Guiana, see B. Mangru, "The Hincks-Beaumont imbroglio: partisan politics in British Guiana in the 1860s", *Boletin de Estudios Latinoamericanos y del Caribe* 43 (Dec. 1987): 99-114. Beaumont, a radical chief justice, seems to have had much in common with Gorrie.

30. JG to FC 2/6/71; Stanmore, 2, JG to AG 19/8/74, 682.

31. JG to FC 30/4/75, 22/7/75, 12/11/75, 1/8/76.

32. Stanmore, 2, AG to V. Williamson 30/6/74, 641.

33. JG to FC 22/7/75, 16/9/75, 30/3/76; CO 167/565 Phayre to Carnarvon 3/11/75 no. 227 Encl JG to Phayre 13/9/75 & Colin to Phayre 28/9/75; CO 167/570 Shand to R. Meade 3/1/76 & Carnarvon to Phayre 24/1/76 no. 18.

34. JG to FC 5/2/75.

35. Stanmore, 2, JG to AG 7/3/73, 149-50; ibid, JG to AG 30/3/74, 507; Mins of College Committee of Council of Education, 27/7/70 and 5/8/74; JG, President of Council of Education, to Col Sec, 23/3/75.

36. H. Tinker, *A New System of Slavery* (Oxford 1974), 106-08, 196-201, 188-94; Benedict, 18-28; Chapman, chapter 4.

37. *CG* 22/3/71: Assizes 22/3/71; Stanmore, 1, AG's Journal, 24/4/71 & 1/5/71, 70-72; CO 167/551 OAG Newton to Kimberley 28/3/73 no. 64 Encl Evidence of AG to RC, Q 11336, p. 572; *CG* 30/5/71, 1/8/71, 3/8/71, 20/9/71.

38. CO 167/536 Gordon to Kimberley 17/11/71 no. 197 Encl Petition of Old Immigrants of Mauritius; Tinker, 243-44; Stanmore, 1: 135-36.

39. Petition of Old Immigrants (note 38): Observations by de Plevitz; *CG* 4/10/71, 7/10/71, 20/10/71, 26/10/71.

40. CO 167/536 AG to Kimberley 10/11/71 Conf; Tinker, 244; Stanmore, 1: chapter 8; Chapman, 122-24; *CG* 4/5/72.

41. For the PIC Report see CO 167/543 AG to Kimberley 2/5/72 no. 147 Encls; Stanmore, 1, chapter 8; *CG* 24/4/72: Summary of Conclusions of Report of PIC.

42. See note 41.

43. CO 167/546 AG to Kimberley 20/9/72 no. 290 Encl J. O'Brien to RC, 24/8/72; CO 167/545 AG to Kimberley 23/8/72 no. 269 Encl Col Sec to Hon J. Fraser 23/8/72; Stanmore, 1, chapter 8.

44. Stanmore, 1: 680-86; CO 167/546 AG to Kimberley 20/9/72 no. 290 Encl J. O'Brien to RC 24/8/72 and JG to Col Sec 12/9/72.

45. *CG* 31/10/71, 21/11/71, 28/12/71, 19/1/72, 30/1/72, 16/4/72, 24/4/72, 25/4/72, 27/4/72, 27/4/72, 24/5/72, 28/6/72.

46. Stanmore, 2: 169, 175-76, 188, 191-92; Tinker, 249-51; Chapman, 125-33; MRC Report (5/11/74), C1115 1875 PP XXXIV.

47. JG to FC 10/1/73, 26/6/73, 5/2/75, 30/4/75.

48. MRC Report, paras 4101-160; Chapman, 128-33; Tinker, 249-51.

49. JG to FC 22/7/75, 16/9/75, 30/3/76; JG to AG 24/6/75 BL 49205 ff 33-37.

50. Stanmore, 2: 192; Tinker, 255-58.

51. Stanmore, 2, AG to Williamson 27/5/74, 606; JG to AG 1/6/74, 611.

52. *CG* 23/3/76.

53. JG to AG 24/5/75 BL 49205 ff 25-28 Encl JG to Carnarvon n.d.; JG to FC 26/5/75.

54. CO 167/568 Phayre to Carnarvon 31/3/76 no. 121 and Phayre to Meade 31/3/76; Tel 12/4/76; JG to FC 30/3/76.

55. *CG* 17/3/76, 20/3/76, 23/3/76.

56. *FT* 15/12/77; JG to FC 30/3/76, 1/8/76.

57. JG to FC 16/9/75; *FT* 15/12/77.

58. *CG* 21/3/73: Letter from Amicus Curiae 21/3/73; Stanmore, 1, JG to AG 28/4/72, 548; JG to AG 26/6/72, 613; JG to AG 1/3/72, 459; JG to FC 10/1/73.

59. JG to AG 24/5/75 BL 49205 ff 25-28.

60. Gorrie, *Memories.*

61. JG to FC 12/11/75, 26/6/73.

62. Undated MS of untitled novel by JG, presumably written in Mauritius 1870-76.

Chapter 4

1. For this and the preceding paragraphs, see: A. Burns, *Fiji* (London 1963); J.M.R. Young (ed.), *Australia's Pacific Frontier Economic and Cultural Expansion into the Pacific: 1795-1885* (Melbourne 1967); D. Scarr, *Fiji A Short History* (Sydney & London 1984); J.D. Legge, *Britain in Fiji 1858-1880* (London 1958); W.P. Morrell, *Britain in the Pacific Islands* (Oxford 1960); H. Britton, *Fiji in 1870* (Melbourne 1870).

2. For this and the preceding paras, see note 1; and Chapman, *A.H. Gordon*, chapter 5.

3. CO 167/570 Tel no. 37 Carnarvon to Phayre 22/2/76 and Carnarvon to Phayre 24/2/76 no. 38 Mins by Ommaney, Herbert, Carnarvon.

4. Gorrie, *Memories*, 10-11; CO 83/10 AG to Carnarvon 27/9/76 no.158 Encl JG to AG 26/9/76; CO 83/22 AG to Hicks-Beach 2/2/80 no. 22 Encl JG to AG 2/1/80.

5. For the salary disputes, see voluminous correspondence and minutes in CO 83/10, 83/12, 83/18, 83/20, 83/21, 83/22, 83/24.

6. Diary of Marion 'Minnie' Gorrie, 1876: entries of 19/7/76, 19/8/76, 17/9/76, 7/12/76; Poem by JG, "Homecoming", undated (1877), last verse.

7. C.F. Gordon Cumming, *At Home in Fiji* (Edinburgh 1881), I: 26; A. P. Maudslay, *Life in the Pacific Fifty Years Ago* (London 1930), 152; A.H. Gordon, *Letters and Notes Written during the Disturbances in the Highlands of Vitu Levu, Fiji* (Edinburgh 1879) I: 463-64; Lord Stanmore (A.H. Gordon), *Fiji Records of Private and of Public Life 1875-1880* (Edinburgh 1879-1912; Private and Confidential, 4 vols.), II: 47. These four volumes contain numerous letters between AG and JG (as well as extracts from AG's journals and his vast correspondence while governor of Fiji). Citations hereafter will be to S/F, followed by volume and page numbers.

8. *Daily News* 23/8/76: article by Our Correspondent 5/7/76; Rachael Gordon to M. Shaw-Lefevre October 1876 in S/F, II, 169.

9. S/F, II: 62, 65, 122, 678.

10. S/F, II: 513, 310; 3: 436; 4: 46.

11. S/F, II: 704-705; IV: 203-204, 428; also JG to FC 19/8/78.

12. JG to FC 25/4/85; S/F, III: 442-443, 495, 518, 485-486, 533; D. Scarr, *The Majesty of Colour Life of Sir John Bates Thurston.* Vol. 2. *Viceroy of the Pacific* (Canberra 1980), 98-99.

13. For MacGregor, see R.B. Joyce, *Sir William MacGregor* (Melbourne 1971), especially 22-94; Scarr, *Thurston*, 98-99; S/F, III: 487, 521, 532-33; MacGregor to AG 30/3/79, BL 49203, ff 1-9.

14. S/F, II: 116, 296, 575-76, 577; *FA* 2/2/77.

15. S/F, II: 709; CO 83/16 AG to Hicks Beach 20/6/78 no. 70 and Draft Hicks Beach to OAG 29/9/78 no. 93; *FA* 15/2/78: Leg Co 31/1/78.

16. CO 83/19 WDV to Hicks Beach 4/3/79 no. 35 and CO 83/20 AG to Hicks Beach 13/10/79 no. 119 and enclosures; Draft Hicks Beach to AG 23/1/80 no. 8; CO 83/20 AG to Hicks Beach 13/10/79 no. 118 and enclosure; Draft Hicks Beach to AG 23/1/80 no. 7.

17. CO 83/23 AG to Kimberley 9/11/80 no. 123 Min Wingfield 12/3/81; CO 83/25 WDV to Kimberley 22/2/81 no. 30 Encl CJ to WDV 16/2/81 Min Wingfield 27/6/81; CO 83/25 WDV to Kimberley 18/4/81 no. 63 Min Wingfield 24/11/81.

18. CO 83/25 WDV to Kimberley 22/2/81 Encl CJ to WDV 16/2/81; S/F, IV: 239-40.

19. S/F, II: 577, 696; *FA* 28/6/78: Address by AG 27/6/78 at Nasova.

20. For this and the preceding para, see Chapman, 202-11; Legge, 170-97; Morrell, 378-95; Burns, chapter 7; P. France, *The Charter of the Land Custom and Colonization in Fiji* (Melbourne 1969), 114-23.

21. JG to FC 16 or 26/1/77; S/F, II, 101-02, 116, 194; *FA* 11/8/76, 25/8/76, 1/9/76.

22. JG to FC 16 or 26/1/77; S/F, II: 195-96.

23. *FA* 16/2/77, 23/2/77; *FT* 10/2/77, 24/2/77; S/F, II: 325, 330, 331, 332.

24. S/F, III: 81-82.

25. CO 83/13 AG to Carnarvon 14/3/77 Conf Encl Memo by CJ March 1877.

26. CO 83/14 AG to Carnarvon 9/8/77 no. 124 Bound with despatch: Memo by AG 28/9/78 Encl CJ to AG 17/6/77; PP 1883 XLVI C 3584, 3-9: Speech by CJ in Leg Co on Ordinance 25 of 1879; Legge, 186-87.

27. S/F, IV: 180; *FA* 11/6/80, 2/7/80, 16/7/80; JG to FC 7/10/81.

28. PP 1883 XLVI C 3584, Final Report of Lands Titles Commissioners d. 2/2/82, 28-34, 54-86; and PP 1884-85 L111 C 4433, Report by JG on claims by German subjects in Fiji, Sept. 1884.

29. *FA* 22/12/76; JG to FC 16 or 26/1/77; CO 83/13 AG to Carnarvon 11/1/77 no. 6; S/F, II: 264-73, 117, 194-95, 367, 590.

30. H.S. Cooper, *Our New Colony Fiji* (London 1882), 46-48.

31. CO 83/8 Carnarvon to Gordon 22/3/75 no. 2: Ordinance 14 of 1875.

32. S/F, III, 436; *FT* 1/9/77; S/F, II: 194, 599, 634-35.

33. For this episode, see S/F, IV: 190-96, 200, 204, 223-32; CO 83/26 AG to Kimberley 21/5/81 Fiji no. 10.

34. 'The Vagabond', *Vox Populi British Despotism in the South Sea Islands* (Wellington 1883), 5-6. 'The Vagabond', who wrote for various Australian papers, seems to have had another pseudonym, Julian Thomas; his real name was Stanley James.

35. *FA* 27/7/77: Sup Ct 19/7/77 and editorial; CO 83/16 AG to Carnarvon 1/2/78 no. 24; S/F II: 323, 366-67.

36. *FT* 21/7/77: Sup Ct 19/7/77; CO 83/16 as in note 35.

37. *FT* 21/7/77, 28/7/77: Sup Ct 26/7/77; S/F, II: 528, 530-31. For Griffiths, see *Fiji Times Centennial Supplement* 4/9/1969.

38. *FT* 21/4/77: Sup Ct 16/4/77; *FA* 20/4/77: Criminal Sessions 16/4/77; CO 83/13 AG to Carnarvon 5/5/77 no. 78 and enclosures.

39. JG to FC 2/4/78; CO 83/13 Carnarvon to AG 29/8/77 no. 81; S/F, II: 631-34.

40. CO 83/17 WDV to Hicks Beach 10/9/78 no. 96 Encl CJ to WDV 3/9/78 Hicks Beach to WDV 27/1/79 no. 7; CO 83/21 AG to Undersec. for Cols 13/1/79; S/F, III: 238-39; *FA* 14/5/80, 15/10/80.

41. *FA* 30/7/80: Criminal Sessions 15 & 16/7/80 and editorial.

42. CO 83/23 AG to Kimberley 13/9/80 no. 107; AG to Kimberley 28/12/80 Encl CJ to AG 9/11/80; Scarr, *Thurston*, 83.

43. *FT* 20/10/77: Sup Ct 15/10/77; *FA* 7/11/79: Letter from Mercy.

44. CO 83/17 WDV to Hicks Beach 29/8/78 no. 93; S/F, III: 397, 400, 402, 406; W. Des Voeux, *My Colonial Service* (London 1903),1: 351-53.

45. CO 83/17 WDV to Hicks Beach 29/8/78 no. 93 Min by AG 30/11/78 Thurston to AG 16/9/78; S/F, III: 410-11.

46. W.J.E. Eason, *A Short History of Rotuma* (Suva n.d.), 78-79; AG to JG 12/1/81; CO 83/27 WDV to Kimberley 19/8/81 no. 128.

47. JG to FC 1/8/76; S/F, III: 496-97, 550.

48. *FA* 17/8/77; S/F, II: 117, 337, 528; III: 435-36.

49. S/F, III: 385; IV: 101-02, 436, 500; *FA* 12/11/80, 10/12/80; J. Gorrie, "Fiji as it is", *Proceedings of the Royal Colonial Institute* Vol. XIV (1882-83): 177.

50. Gorrie, *Memories*, 11-12; Gorrie , "Fiji as it is", 181-85; *The Times* 14/8/84: Letter from JG 13/8/84.

51. O.W. Parnaby, "The regulation of indentured labour to Fiji, 1864-1888", *Journal of the Polynesian Society* (March 1956): 55-65; T.P. Lucas, *Cries from Fiji and Sighings from the South Seas* (Melbourne 1885), 64-77; I.M. Cumpston, "Sir Arthur Gordon and the introduction of Indians into the Pacific", *Pacific History Review* (Nov. 1956): 375-76; K. Gravelle, *Fiji's Times: A History of Fiji* (Suva n.d. ?1980), Book 2, 25-26.

52. JG to FC 16 or 26/1/77; *FT* 17/2/77.

53. S/F, IV: 307; Scarr, *Thurston*, 75. For evidence of local attitudes to Fijians, see C. Knapman, *White Women in Fiji 1835-1930* (Sydney 1986), 120-26; and W.F. Parr, *Fiji 1880* (Sydney 1883), 9-13.

54. Scarr, *Thurston*, 98-99; Chapman, 223-24; S/F, III: 434.

55. The voluminous correspondence on this episode is in S/F, III: 442-443, 474, 485-87, 489, 495, 500, 518, 521, 532-33, 540.

56. JG to AG 4/3/79 BL 49205 ff 38-46. See chapter 3, note 29 for Beaumont.

57. S/F, IV: 431, 428; Chapman, 223-24; Des Voeux, II: 65; JG to AG 28/12/81.

58. MacGregor to AG 16/5/81 BL 49203 ff 22-26; CO 83/26 WDV to Kimberley 1/6/81 no. 89 and enclosures.

59. AG to JG Private 19/12/81; JG to AG 21/1/82 Private & Conf BL 49205 ff 65-66; JG to FC 30/1/82.

60. The correspondence on *Everett* v *Crown* is in CO 83/31, despatches no. 152, 162, 168, 177 with enclosures and minutes; CO 83/32, no. 10 with enclosures and minutes and Derby to WDV 13/5/83 no. 44; CO 83/35 JG to Derby 8/2/83 and to Herbert 27/3/83 and minutes; see also *FT* 21/11/82, 1/11/82, 4/11/82, 25/11/82.

61. CO 83/30 WDV to Kimberley 14/6/82 no. 80; WDV to Kimberley 14/6/82 no. 83 and enclosures; WDV to Kimberley 17/8/1882 no. 123 and enclosures and minutes; Des Voeux, II: 46-47; *FA* 26/5/82, 9/6/82; *FT* 31/5/82, 7/6/82, 10/6/82.

62. CO 83/31 WDV to Kimberley 10/11/82 no. 154 and enclosures; Derby to WDV 8/2/83 no. 10, Branston to JG 8/2/83.

63. For this and the preceding two paras, see: H.S. Cooper, *Coral Lands* (London 1880), I: 61-81; Knapman, 54-56, 80, 101; J. Thomas, *Cannibals and Convicts* (London 1887), 14; J.W. Anderson, *Notes of Travel in Fiji and New Caledonia* (London 1880), 7-15; J. Horne, *A Year in Fiji* (London 1881), 141-42, 162; H.C. Thurston (ed), *Brett's Guide to Fiji* (Auckland 1881); Gravelle, Book 2, 76-78; A.J. Schutz, *Suva – A History and Guide* (Sydney 1978), 14-16; Des Voeux, I: 379; II: 82-83, 24-26; JG to AG 28/5/81 BL 49205 ff 69-71.

64. S/F, II: 357-58; Thurston, *Brett's Guide*; Cooper, I: 65-66; *FT* 7/11/77.

65. *FA* 4/2/81; JG to FC 8/11/81; JG to AG Private & Conf 28/11/81; *ST* 18/11/82: advt.

66. S/F, III: 448-49, IV: 153; Cooper, I: 66; *FA* 11/7/79; 28/11/79; 27/12/78; J. Gorrie, "Fiji: notes of a vacation tour", *Contemporary Review* XXXVIII (Sept. 1880): 486-507.

67. *FA* 5/1/77, 31/12/80, 26/5/82, 9/9/81, 16/9/81.

68. *FT* 7/4/77; *FA* 2/11/77, 24/2/82, 2/4/80, 9/7/78, 24/12/80; JG to AG 14/5/81 Private BL 49205 ff 72-79; *ST* 21/10/82, 4/11/82.

69. JG to AG 14/5/81 Private BL 49205 ff 72-79; JG to FC 8/11/81; *FT* 12/4/82; CO List 1892.

70. S/F, IV: 150-51, 154, 223, 448; JG to FC 29/3/80, 8/11/81.

71. JG to FC 29/3/80; JG to AG 26/11/80 BL 49205 ff 61-64.

72. CO 83/21 AG to Herbert 2/6/79 Min by Herbert 3/6/79 and Hicks Beach 4/6/79; S/F, IV: 428; AG to JG 4/3/81 BL 49205 ff 67-68; FC to JG 26/4/81; Letters Patent of JG's Knighthood, May 1881; Tel Kimberley to WDV 21/5/81; *FA* 10/6/81.

73. *ST* 4/11/82; *FT* 25/11/82.

74. *ST* 11/11/82: Farewell dinner to Sir J. Gorrie; *FT* 25/11/82.

75. *ST* 18/11/82: Sup Ct 13/11/82.

Chapter 5

1. W.E. Giles, *A Cruize in a Queensland Labour Vessel to the South Seas*, ed. & intro by D. Scarr (Canberra 1968), 1-28; D. Scarr, "Recruits and recruiters: a portrait of the labour trade" in J.W. Davidson & D. Scarr (eds.), *Pacific Islands Portraits* (Canberra 1973), 225-51; *Brisbane Courier* 13/7/76.

2. For this and the preceding three paras, see D. Scarr, *Fragments of Empire: A History of the Western Pacific High Commission 1877-1914* (Canberra 1967), *passim*; W.D. McIntyre, "Disraeli's colonial policy: the creation of the WPHC, 1874-1877" *Historical Studies, Australia and New Zealand*, IX, XXXV (1960): 279-94; Morrell, *Britain in the Pacific*, chapter VII; J.M. Ward, *British Policy in the South Pacific 1783–1893* (Sydney 1948), 263-71; Chapman, *Gordon*, 265-76.

3. Ward, 267-71, 287; Chapman, 277-89.

4. JG to FC 2/4/78.

5. 'The Vagabond', *Vox Populi*, 12-17; CO 83/16 AG to Hicks Beach 20/5/78 no. 56 and Encls; *FA* 17/5/78.

6. JG to FC 25/4/81.

7. CO 83/16 AG to Hicks Beach 20/5/78 n. 56 Mins by Branston & Herbert; AG to Hicks Beach 22/6/78; CO 225/1 Law Officers to Hicks Beach 28/8/78, Hicks Beach to OAG Fiji 15/10/78 no. 97.

8. *Vox Populi*, 12-17; S/F, IV: 437; Judgment in *Hunt* v *Gordon*, 22/10/80, in S/F, IV: 467-71.

9. AG to JG Private 14/2/82; *Vox Populi*, 23-32. For W.F. Parr and 'The Vagabond', see chapter 4.

10. S/F, III: 208, 435; C.O. 225/1 Hicks Beach to JG 3/12/78 no. 1; Scarr, *Fragments*, 42-43; CO 225/2 JG to Hicks Beach 5/2/79 no. 16 Hicks Beach to JG 16/5/79 no. 7.

11. S/F, III: 304; CO 225/5 AG to Hicks Beach 7/1/80 Encl JG to Hicks Beach 5/1/80

Hicks Beach to AG 23/3/80 no. 10; JG to AG 4/3/79 BL 49205 ff 38-46.

12. Scarr, *Fragments*, 43.

13. JG to FC 2/4/78; S/F, III: 386, 399, 442; CO 225/1 JG to Hicks Beach 19/8/78 no. 1 Min by Herbert 1/11/78.

14. Des Voeux, I: 354; CO 225/1 JG to Hicks Beach 16/9/78 no. 4; S/F, III: 404.

15. CO 225/4 AG to Herbert 21/1/79 Min by Herbert & Hicks Beach to JG 4/2/79 no. 3; CO 225/1 Hicks Beach to JG 3/12/78 no. 1.

16. W. Powell, *Wanderings in a Wild Country* (London 1883), 117-37; *Brisbane Courier* 23/9/78; Scarr, *Thurston*, 36-38; S/F, IV: 125.

17. S/F, III: 431; CO 225/1 JG to Hicks Beach 14/10/78 no. 10.

18. S/F, III: 435; CO 225/1 JG to Hicks Beach 11/11/78 no. 16 & no. 19; Tel Hicks Beach to Governor New South Wales 22/1/79; JG to FC 14/10/78.

19. S/F, III: 247-48; CO 225/1 JG to Hicks Beach 11/11/78 no. 16 Min by Fuller & Tel Hicks Beach to Governor New South Wales 22/1/79; CO 225/4 AG to Herbert 5/2/79; JG to FC 14/9/79; CO 225/5 AG to Hicks Beach 7/1/80 no. 2; S/F, IV: 122.

20. JG to FC 14/9/79; S/F, IV: 120-26; G. Brown, *Pioneer Missionary and Explorer: An Autobiography* (London 1908), 304-11.

21. CO 225/5 AG to Hicks Beach 7/1/80 no. 2 Min by Branston; *Auckland Weekly News* 6/12/79; JG to FC 4/12/79; Brown, 308; S/F, IV: 125-26.

22. *Brisbane Courier* 30/5/79; cf also *Auckland Weekly News* 6/12/79 and *Melbourne Spectator* (date not given) quoted in *FA* 6/2/80; Brown, 311; *FA* 22/11/78, 29/11/78, 9/5/79, 6/2/80.

23. *FA* 31/1/79; S/F, III: 479; CO 225/2 JG to Hicks Beach 5/2/79 no. 12 & Mins; JG to Hicks Beach 5/2/79 no. 16 & Mins; JG to Hicks Beach 1/4/79 no. 23 Hicks Beach to JG 26/6/79 no. 9.

24. CO 225/1 JG to Hicks Beach 19/8/78 no. 2 & Mins; S/F, III: 208; Des Voeux, 1: 355.

25. CO 225/3 AG to Hicks Beach 13/9/79 no. 1 & Encls; Admiralty to Herbert 18/11/79 & Encls & Mins; *FA* 12/9/79; Scarr, *Fragments*, 124.

26. PP 1883 XLVII C 3641, Correspondence Respecting the Natives of the Western Pacific and the Labour Traffic: JG to Hicks Beach 18/8/79 and Hicks Beach to AG 2/12/79, 2-3, 7-8; Ward, 283-85.

27. CO 225/1 JG to Hicks Beach 14/10/78 nos. 8 & 9; JG to Chief of Funafuti 20/9/78.

28. CO 225/3 JG to Hicks Beach 18/8/79 no. 50; JG to FC 14/9/79.

29. CO 225/2 JG to Hicks Beach 28/4/1879 nos. 28 & 29; JG to Hicks Beach 26/5/79 no. 37 Encl JG to Bartlett 17/5/79.

30. JG to Dr Turner 10/6/79; CO 225/2 JG to Hicks Beach 23/6/79 no. 38; CO 225/3 JG to Hicks Beach 8/8/79 no. 46.

31. S/F, III: 401, 405, 435.

32. CO 225/1 JG to Hicks Beach 16/9/78 no. 3 & Mins; JG to Hicks Beach 11/11/78 no. 19; CO 225/4 Law Officers to Hicks Beach 20/3/79 & FO to Herbert 9/5/79; S/F, III: 298-99.

33. AG to JG 28/3/79 BL 49205 ff 47-53; CO 225/2 JG to Hicks Beach 26/5/79 nos. 33 & 35 & Encls.

34. CO 225/3 JG to Hicks Beach 21/7/79 no. 41 & Encl; JG to Hicks Beach 22/7/79 no. 43 & Encl & Mins.

35. CO 225/3 JG to Hicks Beach 18/8/79 no. 51 & Encls & Mins; Ward, 275-78.

36. S/F, III: 244-47; Ward, 274-76; CO 225/3 JG to Hicks Beach 18/8/79 no. 55 & Mins Hicks Beach to JG 14/11/79 no. 32.

37. CO 225/3 AG to Hicks Beach 11/10/79 no. 5 Encl Memo by JG 14/10/79; S/F, IV: 55-59; Scarr, *Fragments*, 48-49; JG to FC 14/9/79.

38. CO 225/5 AG to Kimberley 16/8/80 no. 21 Encl JG to AG 9/8/80; Admiralty to Herbert 22/4/80 & Mins; PP XLVII 1883 C 3641, AG to Kimberley 16/7/81, 40-41; Ward, 278.

39. JG to FC 24/12/80; CO 225/7 AG to Kimberley 11/1/81 no. 5 Encl JG to AG 23/12/80 & Mins.

40. S/F, IV: 202, 256-59; CO 225/5 AG to Hicks Beach 28/4/80 no. 11 Encl CJ's judgement in Aratuga case & Mins; *FA* 2/4/80, 9/4/80, 23/7/80; S/F, IV: 262; Scarr, *Fragments*, 50.

41. S/F, IV: 221-22, 262, 296-97; JG to FC 25/5/80; *FA* 30/4/80; Eason, *Rotuma*, 69; Gorrie, "Fiji as it is", 166.

42. JG to FC 20/3/81, 25/4/81.

43. CO 225/7 WDV to Kimberley 27/8/81 Fiji no. 138 Encl JG to Kimberley 27/8/81; *ST* 11/11/82; *Brisbane Courier* 7/6/79, 27/1/80, 24/3/80, 16/4/80.

44. F.J. Moss, *Through Atolls and Islands in the Great South Seas* (London 1889), 268-70; 'The Vagabond', *Vox Populi*, 19-20.

45. AG to JG 4/3/81 BL 49205 ff 67-68; JG to AG 28/5/81 BL 49205 ff 69-71; JG to FC 20/3/81.

46. PP 1883 XLVII C 3641, Memo by HC for the WP 26/2/81, 29; JG to AG 14/5/81 BL 49205 ff 72-79; CO 225/7 AG to Kimberley 22/4/81 no. 21 Encl JG to AG 18/3/81 & Mins.

47. JG to FC 25/4/81; *FA* 27/1/82; *FT* 25/1/82, 28/1/82, 1/2/82, 11/2/82.

48. CO 225/17 Memo by JG 22/7/84 ff 453-67.

49. CO 225/17 JG to Derby 8/7/84 Min by Herbert 9/7/84.

Chapter 6

1. D.G. Hall, *Five of the Leewards* (Barbados 1971), 169-80; H. Wrong, *Government of the West Indies* (New York 1969), 145-55.

2. B. C. Richardson, *Caribbean Migrants: Environment and Human Survival on St Kitts and Nevis* (Knoxville 1983), chapter 4; B.C. Richardson, "Depression riots and the calling of the 1897 West India Royal Commission", *New West Indian Guide* 66, nos. 3 & 4 (1992): 172-79; R.W. Beachey, *The British West Indies Sugar Industry in the late Nineteenth Century* (Oxford 1957), chapter VIII.

3. Richardson, *Migrants*, chapter 4; H. Fergus, *History of Alliouagana: A Short History of Montserrat* (Montserrat 1975), chapter 9; I. Dookhan, *A History of the British Virgin Islands, 1672-1970* (Epping 1975), chapter 6.

4. M.R. Trouillot, *Peasants and Capital: Dominica in the World Economy* (Baltimore 1988), 55-62, 83-96; L. Honychurch, *The Dominica Story* (Barbados 1975), chapter 14; B. Cracknell, *Dominica* (Newton Abbot 1973), chapter 5; C. Goodridge, "Dominica – the French connexion" in Government of Dominica, *Aspects of Dominican History* (Roseau 1972), 151-62.

5. JG to FC 11/10/83.

6. JG to FC 10/11/83, 25/4/85.

7. *AO* 4/6/83; *SCI* 8/2/83, 16/2/83; *SCI* 22/2/83: Letter from Impartial, 20/2/83; *DD* 23/6/83. The Parr letters are in *DD* 5/1/84, 28/8/84, 18/7/85, 3/10/85.

8. *DD* 8/3/84: Letter from Justin 3/3/84; *DD* 8/11/83.

9. Report of the Royal Commission Appointed in December 1882 to inquire into the Public Revenues, Expenditure, Debts and Liabilities of the Islands of Jamaica, Grenada, St Vincent, Tobago, and St Lucia, and the Leeward Islands . . . PP 1884 C3840 Part III Paras 12-13, 320-26.

10. CO 152/156 Lees to Derby 8/4/84 no. 112 Encl Memo by CJ on administration of justice in LI, n.d.

11. Ibid Encl Min from Col Sec to Lees 22/2/84; C 3840 Part III Para 323.

12. C 3840 Part III Para 320; CO 152/160 Lees to Derby 12/3/85 no. 79 Act 15 of 1884 Encl CJ to Lees 26/2/85 Draft Derby to Lees 11/5/85 no. 119; *AO* 3/12/84: Federal Council 24/11/84; *AS* 16/12/84: Federal Council 27/11/84.

13. CO 152/159 Attached to C 3840: Memo by CJ 4/8/84; CO 152/162 Lees to Stanley 3/9/85 no. 245 Encl CJ to Lees 3/9/85.

14. *AS* 25/2/85; *SCI* 12/2/85: Letter from Querry n.d.; *SCI* 12/3/85; JG to FC 11/10/83; *SCI* 18/10/83.

15. *SCI* 25/10/83, 15/11/83; JG to FC 10/11/83.

16. *AO* 21/5/84: Circuit Court *Q* v *Mary Donaldson*; *AS* 26/5/84: Circuit Court 20/5/84; *AO* 28/5/84.

17. CO 17/12/84: Judgement in *Payne* v *Huggins* 12/12/84.

18. *DD* 8/3/84: Letter from Justin 3/3/84 and editorial.

19. *AO* 7/1/86: Circuit Court 6/1/85; *AS* 6/1/86, 9/1/86, 16/1/86.

20. *DD* 8/3/84: Letter from Justin 3/3/84 and editorial; *DD* 14/6/84: Letter from Justicia n.d.; *DD* 21/6/84.

21. *DD* 7/2/85; cf. ibid: Letter from One of the People 5/2/85.

22. *DD* 14/2/85, 21/2/85, 14/3/85, 21/3/85: Report on Circuit Court 28-30/1/85; for a shorter and more neutral account, *Dom* 12/2/85: Circuit Court; *DD* 7/3/85: "Justices Injustice. A Drama of the Day".

23. *Dom* 26/3/85.

24. *SCI* 19/2/85, 20/2/85: editorials & letters from One who was present, A Witness, & Rusticus; *SCG* 27/2/85: Letter from An Ass.

25. *AS* 25/2/85.

26. *DD* 25/4/85 and 2/5/85, *AO* 15/4/85: Reports of Federal Council 4/4/85, 6/4/85, 8/4/85.

27. *AO* 20/5/85: Circuit Court, Antigua 18/5/85; also *SCI* 28/5/85.

28. *DD* 6/6/85; *SCI* 28/5/85; *AS* 24/6/85.

29. *DD* 12/9/85, 19/9/85: Circuit Court, and edit.

30. *AO* 5/11/85: From article by A Liberal Catholic, *St Kitts Advertiser* 27/11/85.

31. JG to FC 11/10/83.

32. CO 152/157 Lees to Derby 12/5/84 no. 160 Memo by CJ 19/2/84.

33. Ibid; Beachey, 1-39.

34. C.S. Salmon, *The Caribbean Confederation* (London 1888), 37-39; C 3840 Part IV Para 51; Part III Appendix MM Evidence at St Kitts and Nevis, 92-95, 97-99; Memo by CJ 19/2/84, cited in note 32.

35. Memo by CJ 19/2/84, cited in note 32.

36. JG to FC 26/10/84; CO 152/157 Derby to Lees 24/9/84 no. 220.

37. CO 152/160 Lees to Derby 24/3/85 no. 97 Encl Memo on draft Title by Registration Bill, JG, 23/3/85; Minutes by Harris and Wingfield 7/5/85, 3/7/85; Draft Stanley to Gormanston 11/11/85 no. 92.

38. CO 152/163 Gormanston to Stanley 11/12/85 no. 351 Encl JG to Gormanston 9/12/85; Draft Stanley to Gormanston, tel, 5/1/86; Stanley to Gormanston 12/1/86 no. 8.

39. CO 152/164 Gormanston to Stanley 5/2/1886 no. 31; CO 507/4 Stanley to Gormanston, tel, 12/11/85 no. 93; JG to FC 22/1/86.

40. The Council debate was reported in detail in *AS* 13/1/86, 16/1/86, 20/1/86, 23/1/86, 27/1/86 and *AO* 14/1/86, 21/1/86, 4/2/86; *AS* 6/2/86: Official Notice.

41. CO 152/160 Lees to Derby 26/1/85 no. 24; CO 152/161 Lees to Derby 11/4/85 no. 119 Encl Resolution of Council 6/4/85 Attached JG to Wingfield (private) 26/4/85; *Dom* 23/4/85: Federal Council 6/4/85; CO 152/163: Order in Council disallowing Act 17 of 1884; Draft Derby to Lees 16/3/85 no. 68.

42. CO 152/163 Encumbered Estates Commissioner to Wingfield 3/12/85 Draft Wingfield to Sec, WI Encumbered Estates Commission 8/12/85; *AS* 16/9/85.

43. *AO* 12/11/84: Encumbered Estates Court: Estate York and Pearns Point; *SCI* 18/12/84: *Agricultural Reporter* 2/12/84; *AS* 16/9/85.

44. CO 152/164 Gormanston to Stanley 5/2/86 no. 31 Draft Granville to Gormanston 20/3/86 no. 26.

45. CO 152/163 Berkley to Harris 21/5/85 Mins by Harris and Wingfield 18/6/85, 3/7/85.

46. CO 152/162 Lees to Stanley 1/10/85 no. 278 Encl JG to Lees 29/9/85 Draft Stanley to Gormanston 16/12/85 no. 121; CO 152/164 Gormanston to Stanley 27/1/86 no. 16.

47. *AO* 30/1/84; *SCI* 31/1/84; *AO* 28/1/85, 2/7/83, 29/4/85.

48. *AO* 9/7/83; *AS* 11/11/85, 26/10/83; *AO* 2/1/84.

49. *AO* 5/3/84, 26/3/84, 13/7/85; *AS* 12/8/85; *Dom* 20/8/85; *SCI* 6/8/85: Notes and Notions.

50. *Dom* 2/4/85; *DD* 30/5/85: Legislative Assembly 28/5/85; *DD* 2/1/86: Review of 1885.

51. JG to FC 25/4/85; *AO* 28/1/85; *AS* 18/3/85: Address . . . ; *AO* 11/3/85; *DD* 4/4/85: Letter from Momus 1/4/85.

52. *AO* 25/6/85; *SCG* 10/7/85; *Dom* 17/9/85: Indian and Colonial Exhibition; *DD* 12/9/85: Public Meeting; *EM* 8/10/85; AS 16/1/86: Colonial Exhibition.

53. *DD* 9/2/84; *AS* 11/4/85: Review; JG to FC 25/4/85.

54. *AS* 25/2/85.

55. *AO* 11/6/84, 16/7/84; *SCI* 12/6/84, 17/7/84.

56. JG to FC 26/10/84; *AO* 15/11/84; *SCI* 6/11/84; *SCI* 18/12/84: Correspondence.

57. *DD* 28/11/85; *AS* 20/1/86: Sup Ct; *DD* 11/2/86; *AS* 23/1/86.

Chapter 7

1. For Trinidad in the late 19th century, see Bridget Brereton, *Race Relations in Colonial Trinidad, 1870-1900* (Cambridge 1979).

2. Tel 16/4/73: Letter from Diogenes; Royal Franchise Commission (Trinidad), 1888: Evidence of Henry Richardson, Fifth Company Village, 33.

3. NE 9/6/73, 3/10/81; J.J. Thomas, *Froudacity* (London 1889, 1969), 95-107.

4. CO 152/162 Various telegrams, November 1885; Stanley to Gormanston 16/11/85 no. 98; Stanley to WR 16/11/85 Trinidad no. 122.

5. *EM* 19/11/85; *POSG* 12/12/85; CO 295/307 Havelock to Derby 25/6/85 no. 166 Mins by R. Antrobus & R. Herbert 2/11/85.

6. *NE* 8/2/86, 22/2/86.

7. *POSG* 6/7/87; *NE* 15/7/87; *TRG* 22/5/89: CP no. 46.

8. *SFG* 17/9/87; *Truth* 16/6/88: Sir John Gorrie; *NE* 19/10/88.

9. For the contract system see C.Y. Shepherd, *The Cacao Industry in Trinidad* (Port Of Spain 1932), Part 3.

10. *POSG* 24/8/88: *Congo* v *Clerk*; 11/9/88: Letter from A Cocoa Planter; 19/12/88: *Pierre Congo* v *E. Lange*; 17/11/88.

11. *NE* 21/6/86: Cartoon "A Country Court of Justice"; 14/6/86; *POSG* 13/8/87, 11/7/88; *EM* 24/1/89: The West Indian in London.

12. *POSG* 16/4/87: Legal Intelligence; 20/4/87; 23/4/87: Medical Board; 28/4/87: The Chief Justice and the Medical Board; CO 295/313 WR to Holland 29/4/7 no. 108 and encls.

13. CO 295/313 WR to Holland 29/4/87 no. 108 Mins by Wedgewood & Wingfield 16 & 17/5/87; CO 295/314 WR to Holland 6/5/87 no. 122 & encls; Holland to WR 15/6/87 no. 109; WR to Holland 27/5/87 no. 139 Encl Memo by JG 27/5/87.

14. CO 295/315 WR to Holland 28/10/87 no. 299; Holland to WR 8/12/87 no. 256; *POSG* 15/10/87.

15. CO 295/315 WR to Holland 28/10/87 nos. 297 & 298 and encls; *POSG* 15/10/87; *EM* 17/11/87.

16. CO 295/315 WR to Holland 28/10/87 no. 300 & encls; CO 295/316 WR to Holland 8/12/87 & encls; Holland to WR 6/12/87.

17. *NE* 31/5/86; *POSG* 26/11/87; CO 295/315 WR to Holland 26/11/87 Conf.

18. CO 295/319 WR to Knutsford 19/11/88 no. 300 & encls & mins; Knutsford to WR 20/12/88 no. 228; W. Look Lai, *Indentured Labor, Caribbean Sugar Chinese and Indian Migrants to the British West Indies, 1838-1918* (Baltimore 1993), 133-35.

19. CO 295/312 WR to Stanhope 6/12/86 no. 287 & encls & mins; Stanhope to WR 8/1/87.

20. CO 295/312 WR to Stanhope 7/12/86 no. 288 & encls & mins; Stanhope to WR 8/1/87; JG to FC 16/9/87.

21. *TRG* 11/8/86:Commission of TTC; CO 295/311 WR to Stanhope 7/8/86 no. 185 & min; JG to FC 21/12/86; *TRG* 12/1/87: Report of TTC, 25/11/86.

22. CO 295/313 WR to Holland 4/6/87 no. 150 & encls & mins; *POSG* 26/2/87: Deputation to Governor.

23. CO 295/324 OAG Fowler to Knutsford 19/9/89 no. 332 & encls & mins.

24. *NE* 23/12/87; *POSG* 11/5/87, 5/9/88; CO 295/329 WR to Knutsford 29/7/90 Conf; *EM* 13/6/89: The West Indian in London.

25. *NE* 10/6/87: Packet Summary; Bridget Brereton, "'The Birthday of Our Race': a social history of Emancipation Day in Trinidad, 1838-1888", in B.W. Higman (ed.), *Trade, Government and Society in Caribbean History* (Kingston 1983), 77-79.

26. *NE* 3/8/88; *Truth* 4/8/88. The Barbados CJ was Sir Conrad Reeves. *POSG* 8/8/88.

27. *POSG* 11/5/87: Letters from *Truth* and E. Tripp; 9/11/87.

28. *Truth* 20/9/88; CO 295/314 WR to Holland 13/5/87 no. 127 encl in JG to WR May 1887; three verses omitted.

29. *NE* 10/6/87: Packet Summary; *EM* 3/5/88; *POSG* 17/11/88; *SFG* 1/12/88: Communicated. 'Ah we' is Creole for 'our own'.

30. CO 295/310 WR to Granville 29/5/86 no. 137 & encls & mins; *NE* 31/5/86.

31. *TRG* 3/11/86: Leg Co 11/10/86; 9/2/87: Leg Co 1/2/87.

32. *TRG* 4/5/87: Leg Co 2/5/87 & CP no. 48; *POSG* 4/5/87: Leg Co 2/5/87; CO 295/314 WR to Holland 13/5/87 no. 128 & encl.

33. CO 295/314 WR to Holland 13/5/87 no. 127 & encl; Holland to WR 9/6/87 no. 98; 295/314 WR to Holland 13/5/87 no. 128 & encls & mins; Holland to WR 11/6/87 no. 99; *TRG* 6/7/87: CP no. 62.

34. CO 295/316 Trinidad 16679 House of Commons 19/8/87; *The Times* 23/8/87: House of Commons 22/8/87; *EM* 25/8/87.

35. CO 295/314 WR to Holland 27/8/87 no. 234 Encl JG to WR 25/8/87 & JG to Wingfield 3/9/87 Private.

36. CO 295/315 WR to Holland 17/9/87 no. 254 Encl JG to WR 16/9/87.

37. JG to FC 16/9/87; Derby to JG 29/11/87.

38. *EM* 22/9/87; CO 295/315 WR to Holland 12/9/87 Conf; *PO* 2/9/87: Leg Co 1/9/87; 6/9/87: The Five; *POSG* 3/9/87: Leg Co 1/9/87; *TRG* 7/9/87: Leg Co 1/9/87.

39. *EM* 6/10/87; CO 295/315 WR to Holland 14/9/87 no. 249 & encl; *PO* 29/11/87:

Sir John Gorrie.

40. *PO* 29/11/87: Sir John Gorrie. 5,061 signatures were attached.

41. Text in *EM* 6/10/87 & *PO* 29/11/87.

42. JG to FC 1/10/87; *POSG* 28/9/87, 19/11/87; *NE* 23/9/87; *EM* 6/10/87.

43. CO 295/315 WR to Holland 17/9/87 no. 255 & mins; WR to Wingfield 16/9/87 Private & Conf; Holland to WR 19/10/87 no. 201.

44. CO 295/321 WR to Knutsford 17/1/89 Conf Encl JG to WR 31/12/88; *POSG* 19/12/88: Leg Co 17/12/88.

45. Ibid: min by Wingfield 4/2/89; Knutsford to WR 4/2/89.

46. JG to FC 1/10/87; *PO* 11/9/88: Death of Miss Jeanie Gorrie; *NE* 14/9/88: Obit; *NE* 28/9/88; poems by JG, "In Memoriam" and "In Memory of Miss Jeanie Gorrie", n.d. (1888).

Chapter 8

1. See W.K. Marshall, "Social and economic problems in the Windward Islands, 1838-65" in F. Andic & T. Mathews (eds.). *The Caribbean in Transition* (Puerto Rico 1965), 234-35, and "Metayage in the sugar industry of the British West Indies, 1838-65", *Jamaican Historical Review* V (May 1965): 28-55.

2. D. Niddrie, "Kaye Dowland's book – a record of mid-19th century Tobago", *Caribbean Quarterly* 9 (December 1963): 51; Marshall, "Metayage", 38. See also S.E. Craig, "The popular struggle to possess land in Tobago, 1838-55", paper presented to 22nd Conference of Caribbean Historians, Trinidad, 1990.

3. W.K. Marshall, "The social and economic development of the Windward Islands, 1838-65", PhD thesis, University of Cambridge, 1963, 358 n.3; B. Brereton, "Post-emancipation protest in the Caribbean: the 'Belmanna Riots' in Tobago, 1876" *Caribbean Quarterly* 30 (3 & 4): 110-23; Craig, 44-45.

4. E.E. Williams, *A History of the People of Trinidad and Tobago* (London 1964), chapter 10; *TN* 7/7/88.

5. CO 295/321 WR to Knutsford 11/1/89 no. 17 Encl JG to WR 31/12/88; Mins by Wingfield and Herbert 5/2/89; Draft Reply Knutsford to WR 6/2/89; *TN* 29/12/88.

6. CO 295/321 WR to Knutsford 1/4/89 no. 109 Encl Hay to WR 30/3/89. TMC Appendix VIII Report by Tobago Planters' Club, n.d. (1890),190.

7. *POSG* 30/1/89: Letter from James Smith to William Tucker, Goldsborough, 26/11/88; original spelling retained.

8. *TN* 16/2/89, in *POSG* 20/3/89. Cf *TN* 7/7/88.

9. *PO* 4/6/89: Tobago 10/5/89: From a Correspondent.

10. CO 295/321 WR to Knutsford 28/2/89 Attached WR to C.A. Harris, n.d. [Feb.1889], Private.

11. CO 295/321 WR to Knutsford 28/2/89 Min by Wingfield 16/3/89 and Encl no. 4: JG to WR 8/3/89; WR to Knutsford 1/4/89 no. 109 Encl Hay to WR 30/3/89. See also *EM*

4/4/89: Advices from Tobago.

12. CO 295/321 WR to Knutsford 16/3/89 Encl JG to WR 8/3/89, WR to JG 11/3/89, JG to WR 11/3/89.

13. CO 295/321 WR to Knutsford 28/2/89 Mins by Wingfield and ? [illeg.] 16/3/89 and by Knutsford 22/3/89.

14. CO 295/321 WR to Knutsford 12/4/89 no. 133 Encl Petition from Inhabitants of Tobago, n.d. [March 1889] and Hay to WR 9/4/89. *PO* 4/6/89.

15. CO 295/321 Knutsford to WR 3/4/89 no. 74. CO 295/326 WR to Knutsford 8/5/89 no. 178 Encl Ordinance 7 of 1889; Min by Wingfield 30/5/89.

16. CO 295/326 WR to Knutsford 8/5/89 no. 179 Encl JG to WR 24/4/89, 25/4/89; and Draft Wingfield to JG 8/6/89; JG to Knutsford 25/5/89.

17. CO 295/326 JG to Knutsford 24/6/89.

18. CO 295/326 JG to Knutsford 24/6/89 (printed letter).

19. Ibid Mins by Wingfield, by ? [illeg.] and by Herbert, 4/7/89, and by Knutsford 6/7/89. Wingfield to JG 10/7/89; JG to Knutsford 12/7/89.

20. TMC Appendix IX Return of Cases in Supreme Court, Tobago, 202; and Ev Mr Sealy, 59-61.

21. *Agricultural Reporter* 15/4/90: Letter from A Lover of Justice, n.d.

22. The ruling, delivered 10/2/90, is in TMC, Appendix IX, 193-204; see also Williams, 124-27, for comment and quotations.

23. Fixity of tenure for metayers had been guaranteed in St Lucia, a Crown Colony, by an 1850 ordinance, but no such law had been enacted in Tobago, which had an elected legislature up to 1875-76. See Marshall, "Metayage".

24. TMC Ev E.D. Ewen, 115-117. *TRG* 27/6/92: Report of JEC, 15/6/92, Part 7. For more on the JEC, see chapter 9.

25. CO 295/328 WR to Knutsford 21/6/90 Encl Petitions respecting the administration of Justice in Tobago; and JG to WR 20/6/90; Min by Wingfield 5/8/90.

26. CO 295/328 WR to Knutsford 21/6/90 Encl JG to WR 19/6/90, Paras 1-6, 34. This attack on the petitioners was criticized by the *EM* 3/9/90: The West Indian in London.

27. Ibid, JG to WR 19/6/90, paras 35-42.

28. Ibid, paras 47-61, 62-70.

29. Ibid, paras 71-78, 87.

30. CO 295/238 WR to Knutsford 21/6/90 Min by Wingfield 5/8/90, initialled by Knutsford 6/8/90.

31. JG to H.Fox-Bourne 23/10/90 APS Papers C.151/65.

32. Derby to JG 23/11/90. See also Selbourne to JG 22/11/90 and Rosebery to JG 11/6/91.

33. *EM* 10/12/90: House of Commons 1/12/90 and The West Indian in London; 24/12/90: The West Indian in London.

34. Brereton, "Post-emancipation protest", 116; H. Bellot, "A judicial scandal – are judges above the law?" *Westminster Review* March 1896 Part 1, 238; *Grenada People* 14/9/92.

35. See note 26, para 24; TMC Ev R. Anderson, 142-43.

36. CO 295/327 WR to Knutsford 24/4/90 Encl Petition of Anderson to Queen in

Council, n.d.; Report by CJ on Petition, 21/1/90; Anderson to Hay 8/2/90. CO 295/328 WR to Knutsford 19/6/90 and enclosures.

37. CO 295/328 WR to Knutsford 19/6/90; Bellot, Part 1, 238, 244.

38. Bellot, Part 1, 238-44; Obituary of Anderson in *The Lancet*, 24/11/1900, 1525-26; JEC, Report, Part 8, para f.

39. JEC, Report, Part 1.

40. H.A. Will, *Constitutional Change in the British West Indies, 1880-1903* (Oxford 1970), 190-91, 194-200. For a radical Grenadian editor's assessment of Anderson and his agitation, see *Grenada People*, May-July 1892, for several anti-Anderson editorials.

41. Cf JG to Knutsford 6/5/91, Part 1 in *TRG* 23/9/91: CP no. 113. 'Metairie' is an alternative rendering of 'metayage'.

42. TMC Chairman's remarks, 64; Ev B.A. Blake, 144; Ev two metayers on P. Tobago's estate, 161-62; Examination of E. Maresse-Smith, 3-6.

43. TMC Ev Mr McKillop, 7-20; T. Blakely, 20-29; Mr Sladden, 34-42; C.L. Abbot, 96-97.

44. TMC Ev McKillop, 7-20; P.Tobago, 158-62; Sladden, 34-42; Blakely, 20-29; Tobago Planters' Club, Appendix VIII, 190; C. Castellar, 31; D.S.Gordon, 153.

45. TMC Ev Sladden, 36, 42; Castellar, 33; N. Browne, 95; J.H. Thomas, 139-40; Tobago, 160.

46. TMC Ev Blake, 144, 147-48; O'Connor, 158; Abbot, 97.

47. *TRG* 23/9/91: CP no. 113: Report of TMC 16/1/91.

48. Ibid, JG to Knutsford 6/5/91.

49. Ibid, Knutsford to OAG 18/8/91 no. 186.

50. Certificate of Title and Plan, King's Bay estate, Tobago, 26/11/91; *PO* 1/9/92.

51. *POSG* 13/5/92; *PO* 25/5/92: Tobago Letter from our Correspondent.

52. Cf R. Pemberton, "The quest for citizenship in Tobago: the peasant's struggle, 1838-1900", paper presented to UNESCO/UWI conference on slavery, Trinidad 1988, 16-21.

53. S.E. Craig, personal communication, June 1992.

Chapter 9

1. JG to FC 2/4/87; CO 295/326 Trinidad 13171 JG to Knutsford 24/6/89; Cooper, *An Editor's Retrospect*, 148.

2. *EFR* 16/8/89, 23/8/89, 30/8/89, 18/10/89; *EM* 4/4/89, 19/9/89. His potential candidature was also noted in the *Fife Free Press* 24/8/89 and *The Scotsman* 21/8/89.

3. Letter from East Neuk, n.d., *Dundee Advertiser* 26/8/89; see Thomas, *Froudacity*.

4. *Scotsman* 26/5/90; *EM* 29/5/90; *EFR* 30/5/90.

5. Cooper, 149. For Daniel Gorrie's trial, see *Times* 23/5, 24/5, 26/5, 11/6/90; *Lambeth Post & East London Review* 19/4, 26/4, 3/5, 24/5/90; *Brixton Free Press* 19/4/90; *EFR* 25/4, 30/5/90; *Book of Old Bailey Trials*, 8th Session, 1889-90, 748-71; *Illustrated Police News*

26/4/90, 31/5/90. The issue of 26/4/90 includes a sketch of the murder, captioned "Shocking Murder at Herne Hill".

6. *EM* 11/7/89, 11/7/89, 25/7/89: The West Indian in London; 19/9/89: Interview with Sir John Gorrie. The voluminous correspondence on the money dispute is in CO 295/322 WR to Knutsford 9/5/89 no. 181 & encls & mins; 295/326 JG to Wingfield 5/9/89 & mins.

7. CO 295/321 WR to Knutsford 14/1/89 Encl JG to Administrator 17/10/88.

8. Ibid Encl JG to WR 10/1/89.

9. CO 295/326 Agricultural Contracts Ordinance Encls & Min by Wingfield 12/3/89.

10. *EM* 25/7/89: House of Commons 18/7/89 & editorial.

11. CO 295/323 OAG Fowler to Knutsford 20/7/89 no. 262 Encl JG to Wingfield (Private) 22/7/89 & 26/7/89 Knutsford to Fowler 10/8/89 no. 197.

12. Trinidad Blue Book for 1889; *EM* 20/9/88, 4/10/88, 21/3/89; CO 295/324 WR to Knutsford 14/8/89 & Encls Knutsford to WR 31/8/89; 295/326 WR to Knutsford 22/8/89 Encl JG to Knutsford 22/8/89 & mins; *TRG* 3/12/90 CP no. 99.

13. *EM* 19/9/89: Interview with Sir John Gorrie.

14. CO 295/332 WR to Knutsford 11/2/91 no. 46 & 12/2/91 no. 56 & mins; WR to Knutsford 24/3/91 no. 92 Encl Mins Leg Co 16/3/91; *TRG* 17/6/91: Ordinance 15 of 1891.

15. L.O. Innis, *Trinidad and Trinidadians* (POS 1910), 97; *EM* 25/11/91, 2/3/92.

16. *TRG* 30/12/91: Leg Co 23/12/91; CO 295/336 Broome to Knutsford 27/1/92 Conf & Knutsford to Broome 10/2/92 Conf; 295/337 Broome to Knutsford 9/3/92 Conf Encl JG to Broome 5/3/92 Conf.

17. *EM* 30/3/92, 11/5/92; *POSG* 25/3/92, 28/8/93; *TRG* 4/5/92; *SFG* 1/7/92: Meeting at Crop Advance Co.; Share Certificate, Trinidad Crop Advance & Discount Co., 3/6/92; *Trinidad Reviewer*, 1900, 169-70.

18. CO 295/328 WR to Knutsford 23/4/90 Conf & Encls; *NE* 17/6/91.

19. *PO* 4/10/89; *SFG* 12/10/89.

20. CO 295/339 Broome to Knutsford 9/7/92 no. 200 Encl Report by Inspector-Commandant of Police, 4/7/92; *POSG* 1/7/92; *PO* 1/7/92, 4/7/92. 'Jamet/jamette' is a Creole word meaning a disreputable, disorderly, low-life man/woman.

21. *POSG* 13/2/91. Stollmeyer was the Keeper of the Royal Gaol. A. de Verteuil, *Trinidad's French Verse 1850-1900* (POS 1978), 94-95, 152-53. For Carnival in the late 19th century, see J. Cowley, *Carnival, Canboulay and Calypso* (Cambridge 1996), chapter 3, especially110,121, 125-26. Cowley states (193) that a calypso titled "Papa Gorrie", perhaps the 1891 song, was recorded in Trinidad in 1914, but not issued, by the Victor Talking Machine Company. *PO* 4/10/89, 12/4/92.

22. *TRG* 4/11/91: Leg Co 2/11/91; *POSG* 3/11/91: Leg Co 2/11/91.

23. *PO* 6/11/91: Court of Summary Jurisdiction 6/11/91; CO 295/336 Broome to Knutsford 14/1/92 no. 8 & encl & min; Broome to Knutsford 28/1/92 no. 37 & encl; *POSG* 22/1/92; *SFG* 28/1/92.

24. *EM* 25/11/91, 6/1/92, 16/3/92, 2/3/92; *Truth* 24/12/91: Justice in a Crown Colony; *St James Gazette* 14/3/92.

25. CO 295/334 Broome to Knutsford 16/11/91 no. 302 Knutsford to Broome 16/12/91 no. 256.

26. *EM* 16/3/92. A collection of clippings about the JEC from Trinidad and British papers in the old Royal Commonwealth Society Library (now in the University of Cambridge Library) consists of 112 large folio pages, each with three columns.

27. *Eg SFG* 14/4/92: Letters from An East Indian, C.L.D.A., Trumpeter; *SFG* 21/4/92, 5/5/92; *POSG* 12/4/92; *SFG* 1/7/92, 5/8/92; *Grenada People* 11/8/92: Our Trinidad Correspondent. San Fernando, in southern Trinidad, is the island's second town.

28. Advertisement for meeting 24/5/92; *PO* 2/6/92; *TT* 25/5/92, 27/5/92, 2/6/92; *SFG* 2/8/92.

29. *POSG* 15/4/92; *PO* 22/4/92; *POSG* 29/4/92.

30. *PO* 6/5/92; *POSG* 6/5/92; *TT* 18 & 19/5/92, 4/6/92; *SFG* 5/5/92; cf *Grenada People* 19/5/92.

31. *PO* 6/5/92, 13/5/92; *TT* 3/5/92, 5/5/92.

32. *TT* 20/5/92, *PO* 20/5/92.

33. *Eg PO* 20/5/92; *SFG* 21/5/92; *POSG* 20/5/92, 24/5/92.

34. *POSG* 3/6/92, 18/6/92; *SFG* 4/6/92; *PO* 8/6/92.

35. *TRG* 27/6/92: Report of JEC on the Administration of Justice in the Colony, 15/6/92, Preliminary.

36. Ibid Parts 2 & 3.

37. Ibid Parts 4, 5 & 6.

38. Ibid Part 8.

39. Ibid Parts 7, 9. See chapter 8 for Anderson and the Tobago cases.

40. Ibid Conclusion.

41. *TRG* 22/6/92: Leg Co 20/6/92; *POSG* 21/6/92: Leg Co 20/6/92; CO 295/338 Broome to Knutsford 27/6/92 no. 181 Encl Correspondence between Governor and CJ, June 1892.

42. Broome to JG 23/6/92; *POSG* 24/6/92, 28/6/92; *SFG* 28/6/92.

43. *PO* 1/7/92, 2/7/92; *SFG* 8/7/92; *POSG* 1/7/92; *Grenada People* 18/8/92.

44. Ibid.

45. *EM* 20/7/92, 3/8/92; *Truth* 4/8/92, 18/8/92.

46. *PO* 1/9/92; *POSG* 2/9/92.

47. *SFG* 16/8/92; *PO* 12/8/92, 13/8/92; W. Howatson to M. Gorrie 25/8/92.

48. *SFG* 16/8/92,19/8/92, 30/8/92; *Grenada People* 18/8/92, 25/8/92, 15/9/92, 22/9/92.

49. *Scotsman* 9/8/92; *Times* 11/8/92, 13/8/92: Letter from AG 11/8/92; *EM* 13/8/92; see also *St Andrews Citizen* 13/8/92, 20/8/92; AG to M. Gorrie, 10/8/92. In this letter, Gordon asked to be allowed to see his letters to Gorrie during the "ten years we were in constant correspondence" *ie* 1871-82. Malcolm must have complied, as many of his letters to Gorrie are printed in Gordon's volumes about his career in Mauritius and Fiji; see chapters 3, 4 and 5.

Epilogue

1. W. Howatson to M. Gorrie 25/8/92; *Times* 10/9/92: Correspondence on the Late Sir John Gorrie; CO 295/342 D. Gorrie to Ripon 24/8/92 Mins & E. Wingfield to D. Gorrie 7/9/92.

2. CO 295/342 M. Gorrie to Under-Secretary 20/10/92, 9/11/92, minutes and replies.

3. CO 295/349 E. Connal to Ripon 11/7/93, 31/7/93, 31/8/93, minutes and replies.

4. *Times* 21/3/93: House of Lords 20/3/93; *EM* 26/4/93.

5. The Anderson litigation in Britain was extensively covered in the *European Mail*; see *EM* 16/9/91, 9/12/91, 17/2/92, 16/3/92, 28/3/94, 9/5/94, 6/6/94, 1/8/94, 15/8/94, 19/12/94, 6/11/95. See also Will, *Constitutional Change*, 194-200. The litigation originated in rulings on Tobago cases; see chapter 8.

6. AG to Malcolm Gorrie 10/8/92.

7. *Agricultural Reporter* 25/4/90.

8. *Daily News* 6/1/93; *TRG* 1/2/93: Leg Co 5/1/93; *PO* 13/10/94.

9. *POSG* 6/2/95: Leg Co 4/2/95; *POSG* 28/12/94: Letter from E.Tripp, n.d.

10. *POSG* 14/2/95: Leg Co 12/2/95.

11. *SFG* 9/2/95. Pierre Congo was the plaintiff in one of the more celebrated contract cases heard by JG.

12. For the Reform Movement of the late 19th century, see Will, *Constitutional Change*, especially chapters 6 & 7; and A. Magid, *Urban Nationalism: a Study of Political Development in Trinidad* (Gainesville 1988), for early twentieth century developments.

13. *Grenada People* 22/9/92: Letter from J.S. de Bourg, Gran Couva, 15/9/92; 26/5/92.

14. For Fletcher and Nankivell, see Kelvin Singh, *Race and Class Struggles in a Colonial State: Trinidad, 1917-1945* (Kingston 1994). A biography of Nankivell by Brinsley Samaroo, entitled *Anti-Colonial Secretary*, is in preparation. For Beaumont, see Mangru, "The Hincks-Beaumont imbroglio".

15. *Grenada People* 18/8/92.

BIBLIOGRAPHY

A. Primary Sources

1. Manuscript Sources

PUBLIC RECORD OFFICE, LONDON:

CO 167, vols 516-570 (Mauritius)

CO 83, vols 8-31 (Fiji)

CO 225, vols 1-17 (Western Pacific High Commission)

CO 152, vols 150-164 (Leeward Islands)

CO 295, vols 307-349 (Trinidad & Tobago)

BRITISH LIBRARY, LONDON:

Stanmore Papers MSS Nos 49203, 49205: Correspondence of Sir A. Gordon, later Lord Stanmore

RHODES HOUSE LIBRARY, UNIVERSITY OF OXFORD:

Papers of the Aborigines Protection Society: Letters of John Gorrie to F.W. Chesson and H. Fox-Bourne, C135/157, C135/159, C151/65

JOHN RYLANDS LIBRARY, UNIVERSITY OF MANCHESTER:

Diary of F.W. Chesson

EDINBURGH RECORD OFFICE:

Register of Inventories, Fifeshire, 1852

Minutes of South College Street United Presbyterian Church, 1855-60

Sassine (Property) Index Books, 1846-59

ADVOCATES' LIBRARY, EDINBURGH:

Correspondence with John Gorrie re Advocates' Widows and Orphans Fund, 1856-63

SOMERSET HOUSE, LONDON:

British Censuses, 1841, 1851, 1861

PRIVATELY HELD:

(seen and cited by permission of the family of the late Graham Gorrie):

Correspondence of John Gorrie and family members

MS of novel by John Gorrie, untitled, written 1870-76

Poems by John Gorrie, various titles and dates

Diary of Marion (Minnie) Gorrie, 1876

Family papers, baptism and death certificates, wills, John Gorrie's patent of knighthood, genealogies, photographs, etc.

2. Printed Sources

PARLIAMENTARY PAPERS:

1866 C 3683 Report of Jamaica Royal Commission Part 1, Report; Part II, Minutes of Evidence and Appendix

1875 XXXIV C 1115 Royal Commission on Immigrants in Mauritius

1883 XLVI C 3584 Final Report of Land Titles Commissioners (Fiji)

1883 XLVII C 3641 Papers on Western Pacific High Commission

1884-85 LIII C 4433 Report by John Gorrie on Claims by German Subjects in Fiji, September 1884

1884 C 3840 Report of Royal Commission appointed in December 1882 to Inquire into the Public Revenues, Expenditure, Debts and Liabilities of the Islands of Jamaica, Grenada, St Vincent, Tobago, and St Lucia, and the Leeward Islands . . . Part III: The Leeward Islands

LOCAL COMMISSIONS:

1872 Police Inquiry Committee, Mauritius

1886 Trade and Taxes Commission, Trinidad (in *Trinidad Royal Gazette* 12/1/87)

1888 Royal Franchise Commission, Trinidad: Report and Evidence (Port of Spain 1889)

1890-91 Tobago Metairie Commission: Report and Evidence (Port of Spain 1891)

1892 Judicial Enquiry Commission (in *Trinidad Royal Gazette* 27/6/92)

GOVERNMENT GAZETTE:

Trinidad Royal Gazette, 1886-93

NEWSPAPERS:

Scotland

The Scotsman, The Age, Edinburgh Courant, Weekly Herald & Mercury, Edinburgh News, Kelso Mail, Dundee Advertiser, St Andrew's Citizen, East Fife Record, Fifeshire Journal

England

Morning Star, The Times, European Mail (West Indian edition), *Daily News, The Echo, Truth, St James Gazette, Punch, Illustrated Police News*

Jamaica

Colonial Standard & Jamaica Despatch, Morning Journal

Mauritius

Commercial Gazette

Fiji

Fiji Times, Fiji Argus, Suva Times

Australia

Brisbane Courier

New Zealand

Auckland Weekly News

Antigua

Antigua Observer, Antigua Standard

Dominica

Dominica Dial, The Dominican

St Kitts (St Christopher)

St Christopher Independent, St Christopher Gazette & Charibbean Courier

Grenada

The Grenada People

Barbados

Agricultural Reporter

Trinidad & Tobago

Port of Spain Gazette, New Era, Telegraph, Public Opinion, San Fernando Gazette, Truth, Quiz, Trinidad Times, Daily News, Tobago News, Trinidad Reviewer

PRINTED CORRESPONDENCE AND JOURNALS OF SIR ARTHUR GORDON (LORD STANMORE):

Sir A. Gordon, *Letters and Notes Written During the Disturbances in the Highlands of Viti Levu, Fiji 1876.* 2 vols. Privately Printed, Edinburgh 1879

Lord Stanmore, *Mauritius. Records of Private and of Public Life, 1871-74.* 2 vols. Privately Printed, Edinburgh 1894

Lord Stanmore, *Fiji. Records of Private and of Public Life, 1875-1880.* 4 vols. Private and Confidential. Edinburgh 1897-1912

MISCELLANEOUS:

Misc. Printed Papers of Jamaica Committee 1865-67: Box 21

Misc. Printed Papers of Anti-Slavery and Aborigines Protection Societies: Box 20; both in John Rylands Library, University of Manchester

Edinburgh Directory, 1857/58

I. MacDougall (ed.), *The Minutes of the Edinburgh Trades Council, 1859-1873* (Edinburgh 1968)

CONTEMPORARY BOOKS AND ARTICLES

Anderson, J.W. *Notes of Travel in Fiji and New Caledonia.* London 1880.

Bellot, H. "A judicial scandal – are judges above the Law?" *Westminster Review* 145 (3) March 1896. Parts I & II.

Brewster A. B. *King of the Cannibal Isles.* London 1937.

Bright, John. *The Public Letters of the Rt Hon John Bright.* (edited by H. J. Leech). London 1895.

Britton, H. *Fiji in 1870: Being the letters of The Argus Special Correspondent.* Melbourne 1870.

Brown, George. *Pioneer Missionary and Explorer: an Autobiography.* London 1908.

Carlyle, Thomas. "Discourse on the nigger question" (1849) and "Shooting Niagara: and after?" (1867), in *Essays.* 2 vols. (Everyman's Library 1964).

Chesson, F. W. "The Past and Present of Fiji". Paper read to Royal Colonial Institute, 16 February 1875.

A Colonist. *Fiji Remarks on the Address delivered by Sir Arthur Gordon, GCMG, at the Colonial Institute, March 18 1879.* Levuka 1879.

Conolly, M. F. *Biographical Dictionary of Eminent Men of Fife.* Edinburgh 1866.

Cooper, Charles. *An Editor's Retrospect. Fifty years of Newspaper Work.* London 1896.

Cooper, H. S. *Coral Lands.* 2 vols. London 1880.

_____. *Our New Colony Fiji.* London 1882.

Cumming, C. F. Gordon. *At Home in Fiji.* 2 vols. Edinburgh 1881.

Cyclopedia Co. of Fiji. *The Cyclopedia of Fiji.* Sydney 1907.

De Ricci, J. H. *Fiji Our New Province in the South Seas.* London 1875.

Des Voeux, Sir William. *My Colonial Service, in British Guiana, St Lucia, Trinidad, Fiji, Australia, Newfoundland and Hong Kong.* 2 vols. London 1903.

Finlason, W. F. *Commentaries Upon Martial Law.* London 1867.

_____. *Report of the Case of the Queen v Edward John Eyre.* London 1868.

_____. *The History of the Jamaica Case.* London 1869.

Forbes, L. *Two Years in Fiji.* London 1875.

Fox-Bourne, H. R. *English Newspapers,* Vol 2. London 1887.

Giles, W. E. *A Cruize in a Queensland Labour Vessel to the South Seas* (edited & introduced by D. Scarr). Canberra 1968.

Gordon, Sir A. "Paper on the system of taxation in force in Fiji", Royal Colonial Institute, 18 March 1879.

_____. "Native councils in Fiji", *Contemporary Review* XLIII (1883).

Gorrie, Daniel. *Summers and Winters in the Orkneys.* Edinburgh & London, n.d. (*c.*1870)

_____. *Geordie Purdie in London Or the Adventures of a Fifeshireman in the Metropolis.* London 1873.

_____. "My grandmother's portrait", "The probationer's first sermon", "Nanny Walsh, the minister's maid", "The villagers of Auchincraig" in W. A. Clouston (ed.), *The Book of Scottish Story.* Edinburgh 1876.

Gorrie, John. *Illustrations of Martial Law in Jamaica* (Jamaica Papers No.VI). London 1867.

_____. *The Jamaica Disturbances: The Case of Mr Philipps.* London 1867.

_____. "Fiji: notes of a vacation tour", *Contemporary Review* XXXVIII (September 1880).

_____. "Fiji as it is", *Proceedings of Royal Colonial Institute* XIV (1882-83). (Speech and Discussion, 13/3/83).

_____. *Memories of Many Lands.* Port of Spain 1888.

Harrison, Frederick. *Autobiographic Memoirs.* 2 vols. London 1911.

Horne, J. *A Year in Fiji.* London 1881.

Hume, H. *The Life of Edward John Eyre Late Governor of Jamaica.* London 1867.

Innis, L. O. *Trinidad and Trinidadians.* Port of Spain 1910.

Ivimey, A. J. "Fiji", *Victorian Review* (August 1882).

Jamaica Committee. *Jamaica Papers,* nos. I, II, III, IV, V (1866-67).

Lorne, Marquis of. *A Trip to the Tropics and Home Through America.* London 1867.

Mackelvie, W. *Annals and Statistics of the United Presbyterian Church.* Edinburgh 1873.

Mackie, J. B. *The Life and Work of Duncan McLaren.* 2 vols. London 1888.

McCarthy, Justin. *A History of Our Own Times.* Vols 3 & 4. London 1880.

_____. *Reminiscences.* 2 vols. London 1899.

_____. *Portraits of the Sixties.* London 1903.

M.A.T.E. *Fiji Today.* Sydney 1886.

Maudslay, A. P. *Life in the Pacific Fifty Years Ago.* London 1930.

Mill, J. S. *Autobiography.* New York 1924.

Morley, John. *Recollections.* Vol 1. London 1917.

_____. *Early Life and Letters of John Morley* (ed. F.W. Hirst). Vol 1. London 1927.

Moss, F. J. *Through Atolls and Islands in the Great South Seas.* London 1889.

[Parr, W. F.] *Fiji in 1877.* n.p., n.d. [Levuka 1877].

_____. *Fiji 1880.* Sydney 1883.

Powell, W. *Wanderings in a Wild Country; or, Three Years among the Cannibals of New Britain.* London 1883.

Public Opinion (Trinidad). *Brief Notices of the Administrative and Judicial Careers of Sir William Robinson KCMG, Governor, and Sir John Gorrie, Kt, Chief Justice, of Trinidad.* Port of Spain 1888.

Romilly, H. H. *Letters from the Western Pacific and Mashonaland.* (ed. S.H. Romilly). London 1893.

Roundell, C. S. *England and her Subject-Races with Special Reference to Jamaica.* London 1866.

Salmon, C. S. *The Caribbean Confederation.* London n.d. [1888].

Stanley, E. L. *Treatment of Indian Immigrants in Mauritius.* London 1876.

Stephen, Leslie. *The Life of Sir James Fitzjames Stephen.* London 1895.

Stephen, William. *History of the Queen's City of Edinburgh Rifle Volunteer Brigade.* Edinburgh 1881.

Thomas, Julian [The Vagabond]. *Cannibals and Convicts: Notes of Personal Experiences in the Western Pacific.* London 1887.

_____. *Vox Populi: British Despotism in the South Sea Islands, and the Persecution of Mr W.J. Hunt by Sir Arthur Gordon.* Wellington 1883.

Thomas, J. J. *Froudacity.* London 1969. [1889]

Thurston, H. C. (ed.). *Brett's Guide to Fiji.* Auckland 1881.

Williams, B. T. *The Case of George William Gordon.* London 1866.

B. Secondary Sources

Bakan, A. B. *Ideology and Class Conflict in Jamaica.* Montreal & Kingston, Ont. 1990.

Beachey, R. W. *The British West Indian Sugar Industry in the Late Nineteenth Century.* Oxford 1957.

Benedict, B. *Indians in a Plural Society. A Report on Mauritius.* London 1961.

Bolt, C. *The Anti-Slavery Movement and Reconstruction.* London 1969.

Brereton, Bridget. *Race Relations in Colonial Trinidad, 1870-1900.* Cambridge 1979.

_____. *A History of Modern Trinidad, 1783-1962.* London, Kingston, Port of Spain 1981.

_____. "Post-emancipation protest in the Caribbean: the 'Belmanna Riots' in Tobago, 1876", *Caribbean Quarterly* 30: 3 & 4 (1984).

_____. "The Birthday of our race: the celebration of Emancipation Day in Trinidad, 1838-1888" in B.W. Higman (ed.), *Trade, Government and Society in the Caribbean, 1700-1900.* Kingston 1983.

Burns, A. *Fiji.* London 1963.

Chapman, J. K. *The Career of A.H. Gordon, First Lord Stanmore.* Toronto 1964.

Cowley, J. *Carnival, Canboulay and Calypso.* Cambridge 1996.

Cracknell, B. *Dominica.* Newton Abbot 1973.

Craig, S. E. "The popular struggle to possess the land in Tobago, 1838-55". Paper presented to 22nd Conference of Caribbean Historians, Trinidad 1990.

Cumpston, I. M. "Sir Arthur Gordon and the introduction of Indians into the Pacific: the West Indian System in Fiji", *Pacific Historical Review* (November 1956).

Curtin, P. D. *Two Jamaicas.* New York 1975.

Davidson, J. W., & D. Scarr (eds.). *Pacific Islands Portraits.* Canberra [?] 1973.

Davie, G. E. *The Democratic Intellect Scotland and her Universities in the Nineteenth Century.* Edinburgh 1961.

De Verteuil, A. *Sir Louis de Verteuil his Life and Times.* Port of Spain 1973.

_____. *Trinidad's French Verse 1850-1900.* Port of Spain 1978.

Dookhan, I. *A History of the British Virgin Islands, 1672-1970.* Epping 1975.

Dutton, G. *The Hero as Murderer.* London 1967.

Eason, W. J. E. *A Short History of Rotuma.* Suva n.d.

Fergus, H. *History of Alliouagana: a Short History of Montserrat.* Montserrat 1975.

France, P. *The Charter of the Land Custom and Colonisation in Fiji.* Melbourne 1969.

Gillion, K. L. *Fiji's Indian Migrants: a History to the End of Indenture in 1920.* Melbourne 1962.

Goodridge, C. "Dominica – the French connexion" in Government of Dominica, *Aspects of Dominican History.* Roseau 1972.

Grattan, H. C. *The Southwest Pacific to 1900: a Modern History.* Ann Arbor 1963.

Gravelle, K. *Fiji's Times A History of Fiji.* Vol 2. Suva n.d. [1980?]

Gray, R. Q. *The Labour Aristocracy in Victorian Edinburgh.* Oxford 1976.

Hall, C. "The economy of intellectual prestige: Thomas Carlyle, John Stuart Mill, and the case of Governor Eyre", *Cultural Critique* 12 spring (1989).

Hall, D. *Free Jamaica.* London 1969.

_____. *Five of the Leewards 1834-1870.* Barbados 1971.

Heuman, G. '*The Killing Time*': *The Morant Bay Rebellion in Jamaica.* London 1994.

HMSO. *The Legal System in Scotland.* Edinburgh 1981.

Holt, T. C. *The Problem of Freedom Race, Labor, and Politics in Jamaica and Britain, 1832-1938.* Baltimore & Kingston 1992.

Honychurch, L. *The Dominica Story.* Barbados 1975.

Horn, D. B. *A Short History of the University of Edinburgh 1550-1889.* Edinburgh 1967.

Houghton, W. E. *The Victorian Frame of Mind, 1830-1870.* New Haven 1957.

Johnson, H. "Crown colony government in Trinidad, 1870-1897". Unpub. DPhil thesis, University of Oxford 1969.

_____. "Merchant credit and the dispossession of the cocoa peasantry in Trinidad in the late 19th century", *Peasant Studies* 15, no. 1 (fall 1987).

Joyce, R. B. *Sir William MacGregor.* Melbourne 1971.

Knapman, C. *White Women in Fiji, 1835-1930.* Sydney 1986.

Knox, B. A. "The British Government and the Governor Eyre controversy, 1865-1875", *Historical Journal* 19, no. 4 (1976).

Legge, J. D. *Britain in Fiji, 1858-1880.* London 1958.

Look Lai, W. *Indentured Labor, Caribbean Sugar: Chinese and Indian Migrants to the British West Indies, 1838-1918.* Baltimore 1993.

Lorimer, D. A. "The role of anti-slavery sentiment in English reactions to the American Civil War", *Historical Journal* 19, no. 2 (1976).

Macmillan, Lord. *A Man of Law's Tale.* London 1952.

McIntyre, W. D. "Disraeli's colonial policy: the creation of the Western Pacific High Commission, 1874-1877", *Historical Studies, Australia & New Zealand,* IX, XXXV (1960).

Magid, A. *Urban Nationalism: a Study of Political Development in Trinidad.* Gainesville 1988.

Malchow, H. L. *Agitators and Promoters in the Age of Gladstone and Disraeli.* New York 1983.

Mangru, B. "The Hincks-Beaumont imbroglio. Partisan politics in British Guiana in the 1860s", *Boletin de Estudios Latinoamericanos y del Caribe* 43 (December 1987).

Marshall, W. K. "Social and economic problems in the Windward Islands 1838-65", in F. Andic & T. Mathews (eds.), *The Caribbean in Transition.* Puerto Rico 1965.

_____. "Metayage in the sugar industry of the British West Indies, 1838-65", *Jamaican Historical Review* V (May 1965).

_____. "The social and economic development of the Windward Islands, 1838-65". Unpub. PhD thesis, Cambridge University 1963.

Mathieson, W. L. *The Sugar Colonies and Governor Eyre, 1849-66.* London 1936.

Meston, M. C., W. Sellar, & Lord Cooper. *The Scottish Legal Tradition.* Edinburgh 1991.

Morrell, W. P. *Britain in the Pacific Islands.* Oxford 1960.

Niddrie, D. "Kaye Dowland's book – a record of mid-19th century Tobago", *Caribbean Quarterly* 9 (December 1963).

Olivier, Lord. *The Myth of Governor Eyre 1849-1866.* London 1933.

Parnaby, O. W. "The regulation of indentured labour to Fiji, 1864-88", *Journal of the Polynesian Society* (March 1956).

Pemberton, R. "The quest for citizenship in Tobago: the peasant's struggle, 1838-1900". Paper presented to UNESCO/UWI conference on Slavery, Emancipation and the Shaping of Caribbean Society, Trinidad 1988.

Pope-Hennessy, J. *Verandah: Some Episodes in the Crown Colonies 1867-1889.* London 1964.

Rice, C. D. *The Scots Abolitionists 1833-1861.* Baton Rouge 1981.

Richardson, B. C. *Caribbean Migrants.* Knoxville 1983.

_____. "Depression riots and the calling of the 1897 West India Royal Commission", *New West Indian Guide* 66, nos. 3 & 4 (1992).

Robbins, K. *John Bright.* London 1979.

Robotham, D. " 'The notorious riot': the socioeconomic and political bases of Paul Bogle's revolt" (ISER Working Paper no. 28). Mona, Jamaica 1981.

Sayer, D. "British reaction to the Amritsar Massacre, 1919-1920", in D.Segal (ed.), *Crossing Cultures.* Tucson & London 1992.

Scarr, D. *Fragments of Empire: a History of the Western Pacific High Commission 1877-1914.* Canberra 1967.

_____. *The Majesty of Colour Life of Sir John Bates Thurston.* Vol 2, *Viceroy of the Pacific.* Canberra 1980.

_____. *Fiji: a Short History.* Sydney & London 1984.

_____. *The History of the Pacific Islands: Kingdom of the Reefs.* Melbourne 1990.

Schutz, A. J. *Suva – A History and Guide.* Sydney 1978.

Semmel, B. *Jamaican Blood and Victorian Conscience: the Governor Eyre Controversy.* Boston 1963.

_____. *The Rise of Free Trade Imperialism.* Cambridge 1970.

Shepherd, C. Y. *The Cacao Industry in Trinidad.* Port of Spain 1932.

Singh, Kelvin. *Race and Class Struggles in a Colonial State: Trinidad, 1917-1945.* Barbados/Jamaica/Trinidad-Tobago 1994.

Small, R. (ed.). *History of United Presbyterian Congregations 1733-1900.* 2 vols. Edinburgh 1904.

Temperley, H. *British Anti-Slavery 1833-1870.* Columbia, S.C. 1972.

Thompson, J. *The Madras College 1833-1983.* Kirkaldy n.d. [1983?].

Tinker, H. *A New System of Slavery.* Oxford 1974.

Trouillot, M.R. *Peasants and Capital: Dominica in the World Economy.* Baltimore 1988.

Underhill, E. B. *The Tragedy of Morant Bay.* London 1895; New York 1971.

Wallace, E. *Goldwin Smith Victorian Liberal.* Toronto 1957.

Ward, J. M. *British Policy in the South Pacific, 1783-1893.* Sydney 1948.

Will, H. A. *Constitutional Change in the British West Indies, 1880-1903.* Oxford 1970.

Williams, E. E. *History of the People of Trinidad and Tobago.* London 1964.

Woodward, E. L. *The Age of Reform 1815-1870.* Oxford 1962.

Wright, C. *Mauritius.* Newton Abbot 1974.

Wrong, H. *Government of the West Indies.* Oxford 1923.

Young, G. M. (ed.). *Early Victorian England, 1830-1865.* 2 vols. London 1934.

Young, J. M. R. (ed.). *Australia's Pacific Frontier Economic and Cultural Expansion into the Pacific: 1795-1885.* Melbourne 1967.

INDEX